International Investment Law and the Global Financial Architecture

FRANKFURT INVESTMENT AND ECONOMIC LAW SERIES

Series Editors: Rainer Hofmann, *University of Frankfurt, Germany,* Stephan W. Schill, *University of Amsterdam, the Netherlands* and Christian J. Tams, *University of Glasgow, UK*

The Frankfurt Investment and Economic Law Series addresses a core field of international law whose importance is likely to increase further as globalization progresses: international economic law. Serving as a forum for dialogue and cutting-edge debate, its scope takes in the legal regime governing international economic relations at large with a particular focus on international investment law.

Seeking to look beyond practical concerns raised in this field, the series addresses conceptual and foundational issues relating to the theory of international investment law – including questions of legitimacy and policy, the interaction with other fields of international and domestic law (both public and private), and interdisciplinary approaches to investment law and policy. Its intellectual foundations link to the workshops held in Frankfurt in connection with the annual Frankfurt Investment Arbitration Moot Court.

Titles in the series include:

International Investment Law and Development
Bridging the Gap
Edited by Stephan W. Schill, Christian J. Tams and Rainer Hofmann

International Investment Law and the Global Financial Architecture
Edited by Christian J. Tams, Stephan W. Schill and Rainer Hofmann

International Investment Law and the Global Financial Architecture

Edited by

Christian J. Tams

Professor of International Law, University of Glasgow, UK

Stephan W. Schill

Professor of International and Economic Law and Governance, University of Amsterdam, the Netherlands

Rainer Hofmann

Professor of Public Law, Public International Law and European Law, University of Frankfurt, Germany

with

Alessandra Asteriti

FRANKFURT INVESTMENT AND ECONOMIC LAW SERIES

Edward Elgar
PUBLISHING

Cheltenham, UK • Northampton, MA, USA

Published by
Edward Elgar Publishing Limited
The Lypiatts
15 Lansdown Road
Cheltenham
Glos GL50 2JA
UK

Edward Elgar Publishing, Inc.
William Pratt House
9 Dewey Court
Northampton
Massachusetts 01060
USA

A catalogue record for this book
is available from the British Library

Library of Congress Control Number: 2016953877

This book is available electronically in the **Elgar**online
Law subject collection
DOI 10.4337/9781785368882

ISBN 978 1 78536 887 5 (cased)
ISBN 978 1 78536 888 2 (eBook)

Typeset by Columns Design XML Ltd, Reading

Printed on FSC approved paper

Printed and bound in Great Britain by Marston Book Services Ltd, Oxfordshire

Contents

PART III BANK RESCUE MEASURES

PART IV ALTERNATIVE CLAIMS AND DEFENCES: NEW ACTORS

Contributors

Alessandra Asteriti, Ph.D. (University of Glasgow), LL.M. (University of Glasgow), MA (University of Essex), MA (University of Rome) is Junior Professor of International Economic Law at Leuphana University in Lüneburg. She has written in the areas of investment law, international law and legal theory.

Phoebus Athanassiou, Ph.D. (King's College), LL.M. (King's College), LL.B. (Queen Mary) is Principal Legal Counsel with the Legal Services of the European Central Bank. He is the author of *Hedge Fund Regulation in the EU* (2009), the editor of *Research Handbook on Hedge Funds, Private Equity and Alternative Investments* (Edward Elgar Publishing, 2011), and the author of several refereed journal papers of relevance to financial services, capital markets regulation, public and private international law. He sits on the Editorial Board of the ECB Legal Working Papers Series and the International In-house Counsel Journal, and is a qualified Greek Lawyer and Member of the Athens Bar.

Charles N. Brower is a former Judge at the Iran-United States Claims Tribunal, The Hague, and a Judge *ad hoc* at the International Court of Justice, The Hague. He is a member of 20 Essex Street Chambers, London and regularly sits as an arbitrator in investment disputes.

Anna De Luca holds a Ph.D. in international law (University of Milan) and is an international law scholar and practitioner specialising in international investment law and arbitration, European external economic relations and trade law. She regularly lectures on these topics at Università commerciale Luigi Bocconi, Milan. She has been practicing in the field of investment arbitration since 2007 and is a Member of the ICSID List of Conciliators.

Alexandra Goetz-Charlier is a Barrister and Solicitor of New Zealand, *Avocate à la Cour*. She was formerly International Arbitration Law Clerk to Judge Charles N. Brower and an Associate at St James's Place (J Rothschild).

Matthias Goldmann is Junior Professor of International Public Law and Financial Law at Goethe University in Frankfurt. After studying Law in Würzburg and Fribourg, he obtained an LL.M. from NYU and a Ph.D. from the University of Heidelberg. Prior to joining Goethe University, he was a Senior Research Fellow at the Max Planck Institute of Comparative Public Law and International Law in Heidelberg.

Anastasios Gourgourinis is Lecturer in Public International Law at the National and Kapodistrian University of Athens, Faculty of Law. He is also a Research Fellow at the Academy of Athens and an advocate with the Athens Bar in Greece.

Rainer Hofmann is Professor of Public Law, International Law, and European Law, and Co-Director of the Wilhelm Merton Centre for European Integration and International Economic Order at the University of Frankfurt/Main. He is Member of the Advisory Board on International Law of the German Ministry for Foreign Affairs and President of the German Branch of the International Law Association (ILA). He sits on the Executive and the Management Board of the EU Fundamental Rights Agency, representing the Council of Europe.

Hayk Kupelyants is the Clifford Chance Lecturer in the Conflict of Laws at the University of Cambridge. His main areas of research are conflict of laws, international arbitration, and international finance. Hayk conducted his Ph.D. research at the University of Cambridge on the topic of sovereign debt litigation. He also practiced international dispute resolution with a major US firm.

Yanying Li is an associate with Clifford Chance, London. She mainly works in the field of banking and finance and is a member of the firm's Sovereign Debt Restructuring Group. Prior to joining Clifford Chance, Yanying was an assistant legal counsel at the Permanent Court of Arbitration in The Hague. She has published extensively on inter-creditor equity in sovereign debt restructuring.

Maurice Mendelson QC is a Barrister at Blackstone Chambers, London, and Emeritus Professor of International Law in the University of London (University College London). He practises in all aspects of international law, but specialises in, among other things, international investment law. He also sits as an arbitrator.

Michael Wolfgang Müller, LL.M. (Cambridge), is a law clerk (Rechtsreferendar) at the Munich Higher Regional Court and a lecturer at LMU Munich.

Christoph Ohler holds the chair for Public Law, European Law, Public International Law and International Economic Law at the Friedrich-Schiller-University of Jena, Germany.

Martins Paparinskis is a Reader in Public International Law at UCL Faculty of Laws. He is a generalist international lawyer with a specialist interest in international investment law. He is a Member of the Panel of Arbitrators of the International Centre for Settlement of Investment Disputes.

Prabhash Ranjan is an Assistant Professor of Law, South Asian University, New Delhi. Prabhash holds a Ph.D. from King's College London. As a British Chevening scholar, he read for an LL.M. at SOAS and UCL. He has been a visiting fellow at the Lauterpacht Centre for International Law, University of Cambridge. Prabhash teaches and publishes in the area of international investment law and world trade law.

Stephan W. Schill, Dr. iur. (Frankfurt), LL.M. (NYU), LL.M. (Augsburg) is Professor of International and Economic Law and Governance at the University of Amsterdam and Principal Investigator in the ERC-project on 'Transnational Public-Private Arbitration as Global Regulatory Governance'. He is admitted to the Bar in Germany and New York and is a Member of the ICSID List of Conciliators. He is also the Editor-in-Chief of the Journal of World Investment and Trade and author/editor of several books and articles on international investment law.

Marie Sudreau is a sovereign debt expert who worked for the United Nations Conference on Trade and Developmemt from 2010 to 2016. She contributed to the launch of the UN Principles on Responsible Sovereign Lending and Borrowing as well as other initiatives aimed at enhancing international regulation in the field of sovereign debt and financing for development. Before joining the UN, she worked with the *Organization for Economic Cooperation* and *Development* and the World Trade Organisation on matters related to international trade. She holds an MPA (Sciences-Po) and is also a Ph.D. candidate in international law (University of Geneva).

Christian J. Tams is Professor of International Law at the University of Glasgow, where he directs the Law School's LL.M. in international law. He is a German lawyer (qualified in 2005) and holds an LL.M. and Ph.D. from the University of Cambridge. He is a member of Matrix Chambers, of the Scientific Advisory Board of the *European Journal of International Law* and of the Young Academy of Scotland.

Preface and acknowledgements

The early years of the 21st century have tested the regulatory architecture of international finance. In response to financial and debt crises, governments and international institutions have agreed on a range of (traditional and novel) regulatory measures. The preservation of financial stability has emerged as a major policy goal; and we have become used to discussing 'sovereign defaults', 'bail-outs' and, more recently, 'bail-ins'. These developments have implicated international investment law. Investment arbitration in particular has become a site of contestation in the struggle pitting crisis responses against investor protection. But should investment law protect against defaults, bail-outs or bail-ins, including where these have the support of multilateral institutions? Where is the line to be drawn between legitimate regulation and undue interference with investor rights? And who draws it? The contributions to this book – the second volume in the *Frankfurt Investment and Economic Law Series* – engage with these questions. They identify key challenges facing decision-makers, analyse arbitral decisions and treaty practice, and evaluate ways towards a balanced system of investment protection in the financial sector. In doing so, they offer a detailed analysis of the interaction between investment protection and financial regulation in fields such as sovereign debt restructuring and bank rescue measures. As editors, we hope that they will contribute, at least in small measure, to a better understanding of one of the major challenges facing the contemporary regime of investment protection.

***

In the preparation of this book we have incurred many debts. As editors, we have been fortunate to count on a group of dedicated authors willing to put up with deadlines and editorial comments of variable degrees of firmness. In Frankfurt, Dr. Philipp B. Donath and Dr. Jakob Kadelbach, (then) both at Goethe University, provided vital assistance towards the organization of the 2014 Frankfurt Investment Law Workshop, which inspired the publication of this book. Dr. Alessandra Asteriti (initially at Glasgow, then in her role as a Junior Professor at Leuphana University in Lüneburg) was in charge of much of the editorial process.

We have also benefited from generous support by our host institutions, which we gratefully acknowledge. Stephan W. Schill would particularly like to acknowledge support in the preparation of this book and the research leading up to it by a European Research Council Starting Grant on 'Transnational Private-Public Arbitration as Global Regulatory Governance: Charting and Codifying the Lex Mercatoria Publica' (LexMercPub, Grant agreement no: 313355).

Finally, our thanks are due to Edward Elgar Publishing whose continued cooperation we value. Ben Booth, David Fairclough, Sue Sharp and Amber Watts have helped see this book through to completion, and have done so patiently. Sally Philip has been a diligent copyeditor. We are grateful to all of them.

PART I

Overarching perspectives

1. International investment law and the global financial architecture: Identifying linkages, mapping interactions

Christian J. Tams, Stephan W. Schill and Rainer Hofmann

I. INTRODUCTION

Linkages between international investment law and other areas of international law and regulation are frequently explored. Investment law's relationships with human rights, environmental protection and the law of sustainable development have been studied in detail;[1] interactions with other areas of international economic law (such as international trade

[1] For a general account see the contributions to Rainer Hofmann and Christian J Tams (eds), *Investment Law and Its Others* (Nomos 2012). On the relationship of investment law and human rights, see, e.g., Ursula Kriebaum, *Eigentumsschutz im Völkerrecht: Eine vergleichende Untersuchung zum internationalen Investitionsrecht sowie zum Menschenrechtsschutz* (Duncker & Humblot 2008); Pierre-Marie Dupuy, Ernst-Ulrich Petersmann and Francesco Francioni (eds), *Human Rights in International Investment Law and Arbitration* (OUP 2009); Diana Desierto, *Public Policy in International Economic Law: The ICESCR in Trade, Finance, and Investment* (OUP 2015); Lone Wandahl Mouyal, *International Investment Law and the Right to Regulate: A Human Rights Perspective* (Routledge 2016). On linkages between investment law and environmental law, see, e.g., Jorge E Viñuales, *Foreign Investment and the Environment in International Law* (CUP 2012); Pierre-Marie Dupuy and Jorge E Viñuales (eds), *Harnessing Foreign Investment to Promote Environmental Protection: Incentives and Safeguards* (CUP 2013). The relationship between investment law and development is addressed in Stephan W Schill, Christian J Tams and Rainer Hofmann (eds), *International Investment Law and Development; Bridging the Gap* (Edward Elgar Publishing 2015).

disciplines) also attract much attention.[2] This notwithstanding, scholarship so far remains rather unbalanced as many white spots remain on the academic map. The relationship between international investment law and the relatively fuzzy regime of rules regulating global financial markets is one such white spot. This regime, which is referred to here as the 'global financial architecture', consists of binding and non-binding rules of national, regional, supranational, and international law that are dispersed across different regimes, including European Union (EU) law, world trade law, the international law governing capital controls, banking and financial market regulation. It is influenced by institutions as diverse as the World Trade Organization (WTO), the International Monetary Fund (IMF), or the International Organization of Securities Commissions (IOSCO). The global financial architecture is clearly related to international investment law, but quite how the two regimes affect each other still remains uncertain and insufficiently conceptualized. The contributions to the present book seek to dispel some of that uncertainty and map out linkages.

The book proceeds from the assumption that the interactions between international investment law and the global financial architecture are increasingly important, and that they should be studied in more detail. They are not entirely novel, to be sure. As parts of the international legal infrastructure governing the global market economy, international investment law and the global financial architecture have never been sealed off from one another. The most visible aspect of international investment law – viz. its most relevant procedural arm, the dispute settlement mechanism established under the Convention on the Settlement of Investment Disputes Between States and Nationals of Other States (ICSID Convention)[3] – was established under the auspices of a leading financial institution, the World Bank, and continues to benefit from this patronage.[4]

---

[2] See, e.g., Rainer Hofmann, Stephan W Schill and Christian J Tams (eds), *Preferential Trade and Investment Agreements: From Recalibration to Reintegration* (Nomos 2013); Jürgen Kurtz, *The WTO and International Investment Law: Converging Systems* (CUP 2016).

[3] Adopted 18 March 1965, entered into force 14 October 1966, 575 UNTS 159.

[4] See ICSID Convention, fifth preambular paragraph ('*Desiring* to establish such facilities [for international conciliation or arbitration] under the auspices of the International Bank for Reconstruction and Development'); and further Christoph Schreuer, Loretta Malintoppi, August Reinisch and Anthony Sinclair, *The ICSID Convention. A Commentary* (2nd edn, OUP 2009) 8 (mentioning ICSID's 'close administrative ties to the World Bank', which 'have proven to be

Likewise, at least since the *Fedax* case,[5] financial instruments of one sort or another, have been objects of investment arbitration,[6] just as tribunals, since investment treaty arbitration's early times, have addressed disputes relating to a government's treatment of banks.[7]

And still, interactions have recently increased, quantitatively as much as qualitatively. They have done so mainly, albeit not exclusively. in the

---

extremely useful'). For a more cautious account see Julien Fouret, 'The World Bank and ICSID: Family or Incestuous Ties?' (2007) 4 Int'l Org LRev 121.

[5] *Fedax NV v Republic of Venezuela*, ICSID Case No ARB/96/3, Decision of the Tribunal on Objections to Jurisdiction (11 July 1997) paras 20–40.

[6] See, e.g., *Fireman's Fund Insurance Co v The United Mexican States*, ICSID Case No ARB(AF)/02/1, Award (17 July 2006) (debentures); *Continental Casualty Company v Argentine Republic*, ICSID Case No ARB/03/9, Award (5 September 2008) (certificates of deposit); *Abaclat and others v Argentine Republic (formerly Giovanna A Beccara and others v Argentine Republic)*, ICSID Case No ARB/07/5, Decision on Jurisdiction and Admissibility (4 August 2011) (sovereign bonds). For further examples see Charles N Brower and Alexandra Goetz-Charlier, 'International Investment Arbitration and the Global Financial System: Are They "Yin" and "Yang" or like Oil and Water?' (in this volume) 23, 27 ff.

[7] See, e.g., *Alex Genin, Eastern Credit Ltd, Inc and AS Baltoil v The Republic of Estonia*, ICSID Case No ARB/99/2, Award (25 June 2001); *Ceskoslovenska Obchodni Banka, AS v The Slovak Republic*, ICSID Case No ARB/97/4, Award (29 December 2004); *Saluka Investments BV v The Czech Republic*, UNCITRAL, Partial Award (17 March 2006). More recent examples include *Valeri Belokon v Kyrgyz Republic*, UNCITRAL, Award (24 October 2014) and *Hesham T M Al Warraq v Republic of Indonesia*, UNCITRAL, Final Award (15 December 2014). Virtually all of these cases concern the observance of host State regulators of general rule of law standards in administering existing domestic financial markets and banking regulation. To our knowledge, there are, by contrast, no cases where investment treaty cases were brought against the very regulation of financial markets or the banking sector. This may be explained by the fact that financial market participants operate in highly regulated markets in the first place, where regulation as such is not considered an interference with the right to property or the freedom of enterprise as long as the regulatory framework is applied in a non-discriminatory manner and administered according to accepted, transparent and fair rules of procedure. For rare exceptions – both dismissed on jurisdictional grounds – where the regulatory approach as such, or rather the alleged lack thereof, was at stake, see *Alasdair Ross Anderson et al v Republic of Costa Rica*, ICSID Case No ARB(AF)/07/3, Award (19 May 2010) and *Ping An Life Insurance Company of China and Other v Belgium*, ICSID Case No ARB/12/29, Award (30 April 2015).

wake of crises:[8] the early twenty-first century disruptions of financial markets – most prominently the Argentinean debt crisis of 2001, the global financial crisis of 2008, and the ongoing sovereign debt crisis – have tested the regulatory architecture of international finance and highlighted its weaknesses. On the institutional level, these crises have prompted calls for strengthened transnational cooperation (culminating in calls for the establishment of an international financial organisation[9]) and led to increased powers of monitoring bodies at the international, regional and national levels. The global financial architecture has thickened institutionally as a result.[10]

The global financial architecture has also shown its teeth, at least at times. Recent years have seen governments around the world re-regulate (or consider re-regulating) markets in response to financial, banking, and sovereign debt crises. Re-regulation is most clearly felt in the banking sector, but has also affected capital markets, rating agencies, and cross-border finance. It has in some cases led to intrusive measures, from unilateral debt restructurings, to compulsory bail-ins and (in exceptional cases) the nationalisation of banks. These measures have typically been taken to stabilise financial markets and to reduce the exposure of governments and central banks, but also of supranational and international institutions (such as the IMF, the European Central Bank, or the European Stability Mechanism) as lenders of last resort. Their overarching rationale has been to preserve macroeconomic stability: the

---

[8] The relationship between international investment law and the global financial architecture is not just one of crisis, of course. However, crises and crisis-management measures have thrown interactions and linkages into sharp relief.

[9] See for an analysis of debates Rosa M Lastra, 'Do We Need a World Financial Organization?' (2014) 17 JIEL 787.

[10] The United Nations Conference on Trade and Development (UNCTAD) provides an overview; see UNCTAD, *Trade and Development Report, 2015: Making the International Financial Architecture Work for Development* (United Nations 2015) Chapter IV: Financial Regulatory Reform after the Crisis <http://unctad.org/en/PublicationsLibrary/tdr2015_en.pdf> accessed 4 July 2016. For excellent accounts see Robert B Thompson, 'Financial Regulation's Architecture Within International Economic Law' (2014) 17 JIEL 807; Christian Tietje, 'The International Financial Architecture as a Legal Order' (2011) 54 GYIL 1; Matthias Goldmann, 'International Investment Law and Financial Regulation: Towards a Deliberative Approach ' (in this volume) 57, 67 ff.

'prevention of systemic failure' has emerged as a 'unifying principle' of international financial regulation.[11]

Re-regulation, in turn, has implicated international investment law, which is based on a different rationale. International investment agreements (IIAs) define and delimit rights of investors, which are to be protected from State interference, including potentially interferences pursued in the name of macroeconomic stability. The question is how far these rights reach, and to what extent they constrain the freedom of regulators even during economic crises. This question has so far primarily been addressed by 'arbitral tribunals [which] have been confronted with more and more disputes related to financial disruptions'.[12] Investment arbitration has become a site of contestation in the struggle pitting crisis responses against investment protection. While these disputes are to be addressed by employing the usual techniques of treaty interpretation and application, the stakes are unusually high: hence dire warnings that by admitting sovereign debt litigation, ICSID tribunals would open 'Pandora's box'[13] or enter 'a vast new field, with incalculable economic and political ramifications' (as noted by Arbitrator Abi-Saab in the controversial *Abaclat* award).[14] The interactions and linkages between international investment law and the global financial architecture are to be assessed against this background: it is no ordinary relationship, but one of high drama.

Assessing the relationship between international investment law and the global financial architecture is not a straightforward task, as there is no overarching, guiding principle that clarifies how the two fields relate to each other, and how their different rationales are to be reconciled (if at all). No master plan defines their interaction. Similarly, no obvious forum or coordinating institution exists in which answers to questions of

---

[11] See R Michael Gadbaw, 'The Prevention of Systemic Failure as a Unifying Principle of International Economic Law' (2014) 17 JIEL 823: 'The financial crisis and its lingering aftermath have focused international economic law on systemic failure.'

[12] Brower and Goetz-Charlier (n 6) 29. See ibid., 23: 'it is now widely accepted that claims made in investment arbitration proceedings may affect the global financial system'.

[13] Michael Waibel, 'Opening Pandora's Box: Sovereign Bonds in International Arbitration' (2007) 101 AJIL 711.

[14] Dissenting Opinion of Arbitrator Abi-Saab, in *Abaclat and Others v Argentina*, ICSID Case No ARB/07/5, Decision on Jurisdiction and Admissibility (8 October 2011) para. 35.

integration or separation could be debated authoritatively.[15] There is no equivalent in international financial law to, say, the (admittedly short-lived) Singapore/Doha discussion about bringing investment disciplines under the umbrella of WTO law.[16] The WTO and its provisions on financial services in the General Agreement on Trade in Services[17] provide a multilateral framework of sorts, but it is not properly integrated with the investment treaty regime and covers only one aspect of global financial market regulation. The same holds true for the IMF, IOSCO, the

---

[15] The dearth of multilateral fora is a widely acknowledged feature of international investment law. In the words of Joost Pauwelyn, 'Rational Design or Accidental Evolution? The Emergence of International Investment Law' in Zachary Douglas, Joost Pauwelyn and Jorge Viñuales (eds), *The Foundations of International Investment Law: Bringing Theory into Practice* (OUP 2014) 11, 14 investment law

> unlike, for example, UN, WTO or EU law … is not organized around a multilateral treaty or central international organization. Instead, [it] is heavily decentralized and composed of a multitude of bilateral, regional and multilateral treaties (BITs, NAFTA, FTAs, the ECT etc.), customary international law, domestic laws, contracts and insurance schemes, and a diversity of arbitral institutions (ICSID, UNCITRAL, PCA, ICC, SCC etc.) and domestic courts and investment agencies, *without* central authority.

As regards financial regulation, the situation is not much different. As Thompson (n 10) 822 observes: 'there is no treaty at its core and there are no hard law rules such as the WTO's dispute resolution system'.

[16] The WTO first Ministerial Meeting in Singapore 1996 decided to establish a working group to assess the relationship between trade and investment; the 2001 Doha Ministerial Declaration expressly '[r]ecogniz[ed] the case for a multilateral framework to secure transparent, stable and predictable conditions for long-term cross-border investment, particularly foreign direct investment' (Doha Ministerial Declaration, WTO Doc. WT/MIN(01)/DEC/1, 20 November 2001 <https://www.wto.org/english/thewto_e/minist_e/min01_e/mindecl_e.htm> accessed 15 June 2016). However, as Andreas Ziegler notes, this attempt at conscious regime expansion was soon given up:

> 'Trade and Investment' became one of the so-called Singapore issues that were envisaged for future negotiations within the WTO. As a matter of fact, when the next round of trade negotiations of the WTO was launched in 2001 in Doha (Qatar) this area still figured prominently in the mandate given by Ministers. However, as early as 1 August 2004, this topic was dropped officially … during the consultations among members in Geneva.

See Andreas Ziegler, 'Preferential Trade and Investment Agreements (PTIAs) and the Bilateralism/Multilateralism Divide' in Hofmann, Schill and Tams (n 2) 189, 208.

[17] Adopted 15 April 1994, 1869 UNTS 183, Annex on Financial Services.

Organisation for Economic Co-Operation and Development (OECD), or other inter-governmental organisations or platforms.

In the absence of an obvious forum or coordinating institution, linkages between investment law and the global financial architecture have so far mainly been explored in arbitral proceedings, at a granular level, in a process of claim and contestation opposing investors and respondent States in the framework of a particular dispute, rather than by conscious regime design. And while some of the more recent IIAs – notably comprehensive free trade agreements (FTAs) – now contain separate chapters on financial services,[18] their detailed rules cannot lightly be read into the majority of older treaties. For the most part, linkages and interactions between international investment law and the global financial architecture are therefore being worked out in the practice of investment dispute settlement and in treaty drafting.

All this is only natural. Both investment law and global financial law have emerged in functionally separate spheres. Each has followed its own ('sector specific'[19]) logic, rather than an overarching, integrated regulatory agenda for international economic relations. And of course, neither field is static; both keep evolving. The dynamic development of investment law is widely appreciated:[20] it has primarily been achieved through a process of 'normative outreach', as a limited set of treaty standards has come to be applied to an increasingly wide range of host State measures, at the instigation of an increasing range of eligible claimant investors. Seen in this light, financial regulation is just one further area of host State activity that (perhaps to the surprise of host States) is being brought before arbitral tribunals, which scrutinise it from an investment law perspective.

Global financial law's trajectory has perhaps not been as clear. Different aspects – monetary policy, banking regulation, fiscal policy,

---

[18] For recent examples see, e.g., Chapter 11 of the Trans-Pacific Partnership (TPP) (5 October 2015) <https://ustr.gov/trade-agreements/free-trade-agreements/trans-pacific-partnership/tpp-full-text> accessed 30 June 2016 and Chapter 15 of the Canada-EU Comprehensive Economic and Trade Agreement (CETA) (29 February 2016) <http://trade.ec.europa.eu/doclib/docs/2016/february/tradoc_154329.pdf> accessed 30 June 2016.

[19] Goldmann (n 10) 62.

[20] See, e.g., Stephan W Schill, 'W(h)ither Fragmentation? On the Literature and Sociology of International Investment Law' (2011) 22 EJIL 875: an 'unprecedented increase in practical importance of this area of international law and dispute settlement'.

etc. – have been addressed separately, in different fora and by different actors. As has been observed perceptively, the structure of the international financial regime 'has something of an *ad hoc* character'.[21] It certainly is more '*bric-à-brac*' than 'coherent system'.[22] This notwithstanding, the global financial architecture as a whole has gained contours following the recent crises, and visibility. No wonder it should attract attention, including from international investment law. And given the absence of specific judicial or arbitral dispute settlement mechanisms in the international financial regime, it is perhaps no wonder either that controversies about the more intrusive financial measures are brought before investment tribunals. With this increasing interaction at the dispute settlement front, treaty makers, in turn, feel the need to define the position of investment agreements vis-à-vis financial regulation with greater precision, resulting in manifold and complex linkages and interactions.

II. A RICH AND COMPLEX RELATIONSHIP

The contributions in this book illustrate the rich and complex relationship between international investment law and the global financial architecture. In line with the broader developments sketched out in the preceding paragraphs, they do so mainly from the perspective of international investment law, inquiring how financial regulation, financial market-related conduct of States in various forms, and considerations that have purchase in the financial field more generally, could influence the making, interpretation and application of IIAs. The potential for such influence is certainly there; this is not a one-way street. And while contributors adopt different, at times competing, approaches, the subsequent chapters illustrate the diversity of linkages that exist between international investment law and the global financial architecture.

Readers will find, in the detailed analyses that follow, considerations concerning the scope of investment protection rules (which may or may not cover financial instruments, and different types of creditors), as well as an in-depth engagement with particular regulatory measures (bail-ins, sovereign defaults, etc.), which may or may not fall foul of investment treaty standards (e.g., the protection against uncompensated expropriation, against unfair and inequitable treatment, and against restrictions on

---

[21] Thompson (n 10) 813.

[22] Cf. Jean Combacau, 'Le droit international: *Bric-à-brac* ou système' (1986) 31 Archives de Philosophie du Droit 85.

capital transfer). And as many regulatory measures are adopted under exceptional circumstances, and often with the prompting of international actors, there is ample consideration of justifications and excuses that could legitimise interference with investor protection (necessity, *force majeure*, contributory fault, etc.) and of the proper addressee of claims.

More specifically, the subsequent chapters are grouped in four parts, based on the type of linkage that is being addressed and the form of engagement with the relationship between international investment law and the global financial architecture.

A. Overarching Perspectives

The two chapters by *Charles N. Brower* and *Alexandra Goetz-Charlier* and by *Matthias Goldmann*, together with this Introduction, comprise the 'General Part' of the inquiry. They contain overarching perspectives on the relationship between international investment law and international financial law. Mapping out diverse linkages between investment law and the global financial architecture, *Brower* and *Goetz-Charlier* query whether the relationship resembles that of oil and water – which are 'immiscible' and 'should be kept apart' – or 'yin and yang' – i.e., 'complement[ing] each other to form a consistent and virtuous whole'.[23] Reviewing recent case-law and treaty-making practice, they find evidence of both: while 'arbitration … has proved its complementing role for the global financial system over the course of major financial disruptions,' States increasingly seem intent to 'shield prudential regulation in the financial sector from investment claims.'[24]

Faced with these diverging trends, *Matthias Goldmann* robustly argues for an approach that sees investment law as part of a broader (and presumably 'virtuous') whole. In his assessment, the 2008 global financial crisis, for all its problems, has raised awareness for the 'systemic interrelations among the various segments of economic policy',[25] that is, monetary and fiscal policy, banking regulation, development finance and investment law. In his view, 'narrow regulatory responses in line with the theory of functional separation'[26] (between different sectors of economic governance) are insufficient (and their insufficiency is increasingly recognised).

---

23 Brower and Goetz-Charlier (n 6) 27.
24 Ibid., 53 and 46.
25 Goldmann (n 10) 67.
26 Ibid., 65.

Goldmann's reform proposals are two-fold: institutional and interpretative. '[I]nstitutional design needs to allow for a coherent, concerted response';[27] yet despite some movement, this remains difficult to implement, especially on the international plane. In the meantime, a 'deliberative approach' focusing on the interpretation and application of the existing law could facilitate solutions that, in *Brower's* and *Goetz-Charlier's* terminology might qualify as 'yin and yang', i.e., result in a consistent and virtuous whole. For *Goldmann*, such a deliberative approach requires openness towards 'different rationalities of various segments of financial regulation'.[28] Investment tribunals more specifically would be required to look beyond the immediate investment treaty context and 'accommodate other perspectives',[29] including by giving some weight to broader macroeconomic goals of financial stability and organised debt restructuring. All this, as *Goldmann* argues, can be achieved by relying on interpretative devices such as the principle of 'systemic integration' laid down in Article 31(3)(c) of the Vienna Convention on the Law of Treaties (VCLT) and by reliance on supplementary means of treaty interpretation (Article 32 VCLT).[30]

But where does (desirable) deliberative openness turn into the (undesirable) watering down of investment treaty standards; at what point does the accommodation of a competing rationality result in a sell-out of investment law's own rationality? The remaining ten contributions can be seen as reflections on how the line – between accommodation and sell-out – has been, or should be, drawn. They are grouped into three further parts, which reflect the most prominent sites of the interaction between investment law and financial regulation.

B. Sovereign Debt Restructurings

Sovereign debt restructuring, which is the focus of contributions in Part II of the book, is one of these sites. Insistence on investment protection here seems to meet with firm opposition. Individual hold-out creditors, so a prominent argument runs, ought not to be able to undermine legitimate restructuring initiatives; investor rights would have to yield to 'the

27 Ibid., 68.
28 Ibid., 69.
29 Ibid., 84.
30 Adopted 23 May 1969, entered into force 27 January 1980, 1155 UNTS 331.

international public interest in financial stability'.[31] In line with this popular view, and despite considerable opposition, UN organs and agencies are pushing a legislative agenda designed to result in the clarification of 'Basic Principles on Sovereign Debt Restructuring Processes', which emphasises the right of States to restructure sovereign debt and the principle of '[m]ajority restructuring [which] implies that … agreements approved by a qualified majority of creditors … are not to be affected, jeopardized or otherwise impeded by … a minority of creditors who must respect the decisions adopted by the majority of the creditors'.[32] Four contributions address the complex legal questions raised by sovereign debt restructuring; together they make up the second part of the present volume.

The first of these, by *Hayk Kupelyants*, approaches the topic from the perspective of the police powers doctrine, inquiring whether reliance on that doctrine could serve to shield debt restructuring from investment treaty claims. Drawing in a comparative law perspective on national case law in order to concretise the meaning of vague investment treaty standards,[33] *Kupelyants* sees only a limited role for the police powers doctrine in relation to sovereign (or 'public', as opposed to private-to-private) debt. In his assessment, national jurisprudence from the United States, Russia and England suggests that 'sovereign debts are subject to the common regime of private contracts; and … the State cannot rely on the police powers doctrine to alter the obligations it has entered into in a unilateral manner'.[34] Only 'in exceptional circumstances, [would] States – facing a genuine financial crisis and ensuring an adequate protection for bondholders – … be able to engage in more or less innocuous modifications of domestic-law bonds'.[35] Where States seek to do more

---

[31] See Christoph Ohler, 'Restructuring Sovereign Debt on the Basis of Collective Action Clauses' (in this volume) 120, 122. For more on the need to ensure orderly restructuring see, e.g., the considerations in UNCTAD, Sovereign Debt Restructuring and International Investment Agreements (IIA Issues Note 2/2011) <http://unctad.org/en/Docs/webdiaepcb2011d3_en.pdf> accessed 30 June 2016.

[32] United Nations General Assembly (UNGA) Res 319 (10 September 2015), 'Basic Principles on Sovereign Debt Restructuring Processes', UN Doc No A/RES/69/319, paras 1 and 9.

[33] For a detailed assessment of the role of comparative law in the interpretation of investment treaty standards see the contributions in Stephan W Schill (ed.), *International Investment Law and Comparative Public Law* (OUP 2010).

[34] Hayk Kupelyants, 'Police Powers of the State in Sovereign Debt Restructurings' (in this volume) 89, 111.

[35] Ibid., 118–119.

than that, they need to look beyond the police powers doctrine. There is, for *Kupelyants*, therefore only limited room to derogate from investment law by unilateral 'police power' action.

In their respective contributions, *Christoph Ohler*, *Yanying Li* and *Marie Sudreau* explore the legal principles governing sovereign debt restructurings not based on police powers. Noting the absence of a coherent 'international practice on sovereign insolvencies,' *Ohler* inquires to what extent collective action clauses (CACs), which allow qualified majorities of creditors to agree to a restructuring that is legally binding on all creditors, could facilitate the search for solutions to sovereign debt crises. In his view, CACs 'promise to offer viable solutions for a complex and burdensome economic situation'.[36] If preceded by *bona fide* negotiations between the State and its creditors, which in turn have been conducted in an inclusive and transparent manner, *Ohler* argues, 'there is no room to assume that a debt restructuring violates international investment law'.[37] In *Ohler's* view, problems of sovereign debt restructuring would thus be addressed preferably through contractual arrangements. This would indeed seem to be an elegant way of avoiding outright clashes between investment protection and the need to ensure orderly debt restructuring.

Yanying Li's chapter continues the discussion of CACs. It contains a detailed analysis of the different types of clauses (notably the single-limb procedure enabling the modification of contract terms on the basis of a single vote across all affected instruments) and the conditions of their operation. Single-limb voting clauses are particularly intrusive from the perspective of minority bondholders and come closest to bankruptcy proceedings for States. To gauge their interactions with international investment law, it thus seems useful to draw an analogy with national bankruptcy laws. According to *Li*, while international jurisprudence on CACs is still in its early stages, national experience with cram-down procedure in domestic bankruptcy law, such as the one found in the United States, could offer guidance, especially in concretising the requirement to treat all creditors in a non-discriminatory manner. By contrast, domestic analogies are unlikely to provide much specific guidance on the level of recovery: while it should 'put in place a mechanism that ensures procedural fairness,' the international community

---

36 Ohler (n 31) 134.

37 Ibid.

would need to 'leav[e] it to the parties to a restructuring to agree on the appropriate amount of debt relief'.[38]

Marie Sudreau's contribution completes the analysis of sovereign debt restructurings. Unlike *Ohler* and *Li*, she looks not to contractual arrangements, but assesses attempts at clarifying the proper interpretation of treaty and customary law rules. More specifically, *Sudreau's* focus is on the most prominent recent normative proposal, namely the 2012 Principles on Responsible Sovereign Lending and Borrowing, elaborated within the framework of the United Nations Conference on Trade and Development (UNCTAD). Intended as a general code balancing creditor and State interests (and operationalised through emphasis on transparency, due diligence, and proportionality), these 15 Principles are formally non-binding – but according to *Sudreau* could help overcome the (at times fractious) debates of the present. For this to be the case, the UNCTAD Principles would need to be taken into account in the interpretation and application of IIAs. This in turn would require some openness towards considerations that are external to investor protection, but could be part of a 'more comprehensive integration of public international law into the interpretation of BITs [i.e. bilateral investment treaties]'.[39]

Just like reliance on CACs addressed by *Ohler* and *Li*, so too, recourse to the UNCTAD Principles is no panacea, and certainly no substitute for the establishment of an 'institutional structure … capable of coordinating the interests and functions of international actors (creditor committees, IMF, Paris Club, etc.)' during debt restructurings. However, openness towards the UNCTAD Principles, according to *Sudreau*, could make investment dispute resolution better equipped to address sovereign lending and borrowing issues.[40] The recipe she prescribes comes perhaps closest to the 'deliberative approach' outlined by *Goldmann*, as investment law would be construed in a manner that is open to a 'different rationalit[y]',[41] namely that of accepting the need for financial stability of indebted States.

---

[38] Yanying Li, 'Sovereign Bond Disputes Before Investment Treaty Tribunals: Safeguarding the Exercise of Collective Action Clauses with a Single-Limb Voting Mechanism' (in this volume) 135, 159.

[39] Marie Sudreau, 'Bilateral Investment Treaties and the Principles on Responsible Sovereign Lending and Borrowing: Working Together Towards the Provision of an International Legal Framework Addressing Sovereign Debt Issues?' (in this volume) 160, 189.

[40] Ibid., 189–190.

[41] See Goldmann (n 10) 69.

C. Bank Rescue Measures

While sovereign debt litigation has a long history, investment arbitration over bank rescue measures, the focus of Part III, is of more recent vintage. Alongside the (partial) nationalisations of financial institutions (such as Northern Rock and Fortis),[42] 'bail-ins' have risen to prominence in the wake of the 2013 Cyprus banking crisis, which was addressed (among other things) through the compulsory conversion of depositor claims into equity. While permitting for the recapitalisation of failing banks without the use of public money, bail-ins were adopted against the wishes of creditors and/or depositors – who, perhaps predictably, have begun to seek recourse before national and international courts and tribunals.[43] As with respect to sovereign debt litigation, these proceedings pit investment protection against measures designed to ensure macro-economic stability and ask how a balance between the two competing interests can be struck. The three contributions comprising the third part of the present volume engage with this question, each offering a detailed analysis of the legal issues raised by on-going disputes on bank rescue measures.

Maurice Mendelson and *Martins Paparinskis* identify the main issues facing investors who seek to rely on BITs to challenge bank rescue measures. Their analysis highlights the uncertain state of the law, which is only beginning to appreciate the legality of bail-ins. As regards the merits of claims, the expropriation standard is of particular relevance. Are bail-ins expropriatory in nature, and if so, would a putative expropriation be lawful or unlawful? *Mendelson* and *Paparinskis* highlight how these standards have been shaped in recent investment jurisprudence and emphasise the importance of 'non-arbitrariness and due process' in the implementation of rescue measures.[44] They also comment on threshold questions of jurisdiction and admissibility, among them the impact of external pressure on States like Cyprus ('apparently nudged in the direction of applying bail-ins to a broad category of depositors by the so-called Troika')[45] and the scope of coverage of BITs (which may or

---

[42] With respect to the latter, see *Ping An v Belgium* (n 7).

[43] See notably the award in *Poštová banka, as and Istrokapital SE v The Hellenic Republic*, ICSID Case No ARB/13/8, Award (9 April 2015) and the judgment of the *Supreme Court of Cyprus, Christodoulou and others v Central Bank of Cyprus and others*, Case 551/2013, 7 June 2013.

[44] Maurice Mendelson and Martins Paparinskis, 'Bail-Ins and International Investment Law: In and Beyond Cyprus' (in this volume) 193, 206.

[45] Ibid., 200.

may not cover deposits). Still, notwithstanding remaining uncertainties, the authors are clear that 'investment protection law … has to be … accounted for as an important element in the complex web of legal rules and procedures framing the responses by States to financial crises … and will form an important part of the background to any resolution'.[46] Put simplistically, one might perhaps say that macroeconomic considerations matter, but do not eclipse investment protection.

Anna De Luca proceeds from the same assumption (viz. that international investment law is relevant), but is perhaps more cautious about the potential for investors to obtain damages awards. Her analysis centres on a particular problem faced by depositors and shareholders affected by bank rescue measures, namely issues of causation. Under general international law, claimants are required to establish that the impugned measure (such as a bail-in) was the proximate cause of economic loss. *De Luca's* analysis of earlier case law on causation suggests that, where claimants have already been in dire financial straits, or even near-insolvent, damages are typically not awarded because the government intervention did not leave them worse off. As *De Luca* summarises, 'tribunals have accorded great weight to the imprudent conduct of investors and the critical financial situation of an investment … these factors were sufficient to break the chain of causation, even where the host State's conduct had been found to be deficient'.[47] As a consequence, 'it may be difficult for shareholders of a rescued bank to establish a sufficient causal link between the rescue measures and the losses suffered … [if] the bank was insolvent or in a precarious financial situation before the measures were enacted'.[48]

Phoebus Athanassiou is also cautious, but his caution, expressed in the final contribution on bail-ins, is of a different nature. He warns that not too much emphasis should be placed on investment law, which is but 'one piece of the puzzle' of bank rescue measures, and typically is overshadowed by considerations of human rights and equal treatment. This premise leads him to challenge views set out in the two earlier contributions. While problems of causation (as addressed by *De Luca*) no doubt exist, the real problems facing investor claims, according to *Athanassiou*, concern the scope of substantive rights: 'the probative demands that human rights law and the [no creditor worse off] principle place on applicants are so high that … the probability of success of the

[46] Ibid., 210.

[47] Anna De Luca, 'Bank Rescue Measures Under International Investment Law: What Role for the Principle of Causation?' (in this volume) 211, 236.

[48] Ibid.

legal challenge brought against them would appear remote'.[49] As regards the threshold issues (addressed by *Mendelson* and *Paparinskis*), *Athanassiou* is not convinced that bank deposits qualify as investment and thus are protected under BITs. In his assessment, '[m]uch will … depend on the type of deposits at stake (an overnight deposit is unlikely to qualify as an investment, and the same is probably true of a deposit that is remunerated at a negative rate; conversely, a high-yielding deposit or a fixed-term deposit are closer to an investment) and on their *amount*'.[50] In his view, then, investment law – if properly interpreted – presents no real obstacle to bank rescue measures undertaken to ensure macroeconomic stability: it can be (and should be) construed so as to accommodate the broader interest in macroeconomic stability. And so, taken together, the three contributions by *Mendelson* and *Paparinskis*, by *De Luca* and by *Athanassiou* highlight the complex legal issues raised by bank rescue measures, and at the same time reflect competing visions of the role of investment law in the search for equitable solutions.

D. Alternative Claims and Defences, New Actors

Disputes relating to sovereign debt and bank rescue measures have thrown the relationship between international investment law and financial regulation into stark relief. They are not the only sites of the interaction between the two fields though. The three contributions comprising Part IV explore other linkages at which the different rationales of investment protection and financial regulation clash.

Prabhash Ranjan's contribution focuses on monetary transfer provisions of IIAs, which seek to restrict host State interference with capital flows. Though not a new element of treaties, monetary transfer provisions are often treated *en passant* and have prompted relatively little jurisprudence so far. However, as noted by Kern, 'it can … be expected that in the years to come, these clauses will be increasingly put to the test'.[51] *Ranjan's* contribution identifies the main categories of transfer clauses and assesses their relationship with the Articles of Agreement of the International Monetary Fund (IMF Articles),[52] which do not *per se*

---

49 Phoebus Athanassiou, 'BITs and Pieces: Reflections on the Relevance of BITs in Resolution-Related Litigation' (in this volume) 240, 253.

50 Ibid., 248–249 (emphasis in the original).

51 Carsten Kern, 'Transfer of Funds' in Marc Bungenberg, Jörn Griebel, Stephan Hobe and August Reinisch (eds), *International Investment Law. A Handbook* (Beck/Hart/Nomos 2015) 870, 886.

52 Adopted 2 July 1944, entered into force 27 December 1945, 2 UNTS 39.

preclude restrictions on capital account transactions.[53] As *Ranjan* notes, straightforward transfer provisions that do not refer to the IMF Articles should be taken at face value – which means they impose real restraints, including during financial emergencies; they should not simply be 'construed away' by reference to some competing interest in financial stability. As a consequence, host States willing to impose capital flow restrictions would be required to rely on non-precluded-measures (NPM) clauses or the necessity defence. As both of these defences do not offer much room for financial manoeuvring, *Ranjan* suggests a move to more carefully drafted transfer clauses, which 'expressly preserve the host country's rights under the IMF Articles.'[54] Treaty drafters can thus help avoid conflicts for the future by limiting the scope of investment protection available during times of disruption. But where they have not done so, *Ranjan* suggests that investment protection does not yield, even during financial crises.

Whereas *Ranjan* addresses an often-overlooked treatment standard, *Anastasios Gourgourinis* sheds light on a widely ignored defence potentially available to States when intervening in financial markets to react to macroeconomic risks. Drawing on a detailed examination of litigation concerning Iceland's bank rescue measures before the European Free Trade Association (EFTA) Court,[55] *Gourgourinis* inquires whether States could rely on *force majeure* to justify a temporary payment default. In his view, there is certainly room for a plausible argument: 'Iceland's assertion in the *Icesave* case – that the 2008 global financial crisis and the wholesale collapse of its banking system qualified as *force majeure* – would appear, at least *prima facie*, tenable.'[56] Just as other defences, *force majeure* is no panacea.[57] However, given 'the rather limited success'[58] of attempts by States relying on necessity and/or NPM clauses, reliance on it may present an attractive alternative argument, one that

---

[53] See notably Art. VI.3 of the IMF Articles, which accepts that member countries may impose controls if necessary to regulate international capital movement. For comment see Prabhash Ranjan, 'Capital-Flow Management Measures and International Investment Law: Never the Twain Shall Meet?' (in this volume) 257, 264–265.

[54] Ibid., 279.

[55] See Case E-16/11, *EFTA Surveillance Authority v Iceland (Icesave)* [2013] EFTA Ct Rep 4.

[56] Anastasios Gourgourinis, 'Financial Crisis as *Force Majeure* Under International Law and EU Law: Defending Emergency Measures, *à l'Européenne*, in Investment Arbitration Under Intra-EU BITs' (in this volume) 281, 304.

[57] Ibid., 315.

[58] Ibid., 289.

suggests that States seeking to preserve macroeconomic stability during times of crisis are entitled to derogate, at least temporarily, from treaty standards established for the benefit of foreign investors.

In the final contribution to the volume, *Michael Wolfgang Müller* 'steps back' from the debates on particular claims and defences to assess the position of international financial institutions within international investment law and arbitration. In so doing, he picks up themes touched upon by many other contributors, among them *Mendelson* and *Paparinskis* (who address the possibility of suing States over measures adopted under international pressure) and *Goldmann* (who highlights the turn to more robust institutional supervision following the 2008 financial crisis). *Müller* of course accepts that '[t]he current legal framework of investment protection is based on investor-State relations.'[59] However, the conduct of international institutions can affect the legal regime governing investor-State relations in manifold ways, notably through the application of rules on attribution, through 'without prejudice'-clauses demarcating the proper scope of investment protection *vis-à-vis* decision-making within international organisations, and as a consideration guiding the interpretation of investment standards. While conduct of international institutions will hardly ever 'exonerate States from international liability tout court', it may help distinguish between justified and illegal forms of interference with investor rights and suggest when investment protection has to give way to a broader interest in macroeconomic stability.

III. OUTLOOK: BALANCING INVESTMENT PROTECTION AND MACROECONOMIC STABILITY

This brief summary highlights the manifold linkages – some convergent, some conflictual – between international investment law and the global financial architecture and points towards modalities of co-existence. There are, in the terminology used by *Brower* and *Goetz-Charlier*, aspects of 'yin and yang' as well as examples of 'oil and water'. And there are, too, instances in which it may be too early to tell which understanding wins the day, viz. whether investment law should be 'kept

[59] Wolfgang Michael Müller, 'International Financial Institutions in Investment Law and Arbitration' (in this volume) 316, 346.

apart' from the regulation of global financial markets or whether the two could 'complemen[t] each other to form a consistent and virtuous whole'.[60]

Notwithstanding these caveats, one trend that does seem to emerge from the more recent interactions is that investment lawyers are aware – perhaps increasingly aware – of the risks of interfering all too lightly with regulatory decisions taken by States in respect of financial markets, including sovereign debt restructurings, especially where these have the backing of one or several multilateral institutions, such as the IMF or the EU. Judging from the discussion in many of the contributions to this volume, international investment law is a factor that affects the global financial architecture. But it can be interpreted and applied in a manner that is mindful of the need for financial stability; broader macroeconomic considerations can typically be advanced in investment arbitrations, whether as part of the construction of treaty standards or under clauses containing defences. In fact, at times investment lawyers might be tempted to avoid any scrutiny. In arbitral awards, such as *Ping An*[61] or *Poštová banka*,[62] tribunals dismissed claims for lack of jurisdiction; perhaps this outcome (while justified on different grounds) was in fact quite convenient as it meant arbitrators would not need to scrutinise decisions taken during times of financial crises? Whatever one makes of those specific decisions and their reasoning, some arbitral restraint may indeed be warranted, not only because of the systemic implications that the decision about a single dispute could have on global financial markets, but also in light of the limited expertise of investment arbitrators, like that of any domestic court, in questions of macroeconomic regulation. Recent arbitral practice, while not uniform, seems to reflect this.

When looking beyond individual disputes, a similar trend characterises the more recent practice of law-making. As noted above, treaty drafters (e.g., when including special 'financial services' chapters in FTAs or negotiating monetary transfer provisions) seem gradually to accept the need for more detailed provisions that deal with the interaction between international investment law and competing areas of financial market regulation and, at least to some extent, exempt the latter from scrutiny by investment treaty tribunals. Relevant developments in treaty-making include, inter alia, provisions that are sensitive to the need for prudential financial regulation or provisions limiting investment treaty claims arising in the context of sovereign debt restructurings. Similarly, while

---

[60] Cf. Brower and Goetz-Charlier (n 6) 27.
[61] *Ping An v Belgium* (n 7).
[62] *Poštová banka v Greece* (n 43).

developments are at an early stage, current debates about sovereign debt restructuring also emphasise respect for a State's right to 'design its macroeconomic policy, including [by] restructuring its sovereign debt'.[63] Just as arbitral practice, so too the recent instances of law-making seem to recognise that international investment law needs to accommodate broader macroeconomic concerns.

Do these trends suggest that international investment law and financial regulation are like 'oil and water'? Probably not, or at least: only rarely. Both fields do interact, after all, and they share basic assumptions, most importantly that global markets will only work efficiently if market participants enjoy freedom from undue government interference, while also benefiting from effective regulation that ensures the functioning of such markets. Instead, what we are witnessing – and what the contributions to the present volume illustrate – is a debate about the *proper balance* to be struck between the competing interests of regulating global financial markets and ensuring investment protection, or between the 'yin' and the 'yang'. In this debate, much depends on how law-makers, adjudicators, and different market participants view the relationship between international investment law and financial market regulation. As just noted, arbitrators and treaty drafters seem prepared in principle to accept market regulation during times of crisis. But at the same time, they condition such acceptance by emphasising the need for good faith conduct of regulators, transparent regulation and non-discrimination of market participants, and by underlining a preference for multilateral solutions for the regulation of global financial markets.

Just quite how the balance should be struck is open to debate, and given the fragmentation of international investment law and the global financial architecture, this debate really is in the form of a series of discussions that take place in different fora and between different stakeholders. These discussions will need to be informed by a level of open-mindedness and awareness for the logic of the 'other' field, that is, in short, by a 'deliberative approach' in *Matthias Goldmann's* phrase. The contributions to the volume – so the editors would hope – are examples of such a deliberative engagement. They highlight its promise and its limits and set the stage for further refinement and fine-tuning as the interlinkages between international investment law and the global financial architecture become more sophisticated.

---

[63] GA Res 69/319 (n 32) para. 1.

2. International investment arbitration and the global financial system: Are they 'yin' and 'yang' or like oil and water?

Charles N. Brower and Alexandra Goetz-Charlier

I. INTRODUCTION

The present chapter follows an inaugural speech given at the 2014 Frankfurt Investment Law Workshop which questioned the interaction between international investment law and the global financial architecture. To frame the issue, it deliberately focused on investment dispute arbitration as the ultimate test of international investment law. In order to elucidate the nature of this relationship, the title of this chapter sets out the terms of the debate with a thought-provoking metaphor, asking the audience whether international investment arbitration and the global financial system are 'yin' and 'yang' or like oil and water. The idea behind this choice of title was to highlight that, for a long time, the link between arbitration and global financial issues remained largely underestimated, leading investment law practitioners to treat them as separate and unrelated matters. While abundant literature has been published on the issue over the last few years, it is now widely accepted that claims made in investment arbitration proceedings may affect the global financial system. Against this background, the question therefore arises as to the extent to which investment arbitration may interfere with mechanisms put in place by States to leverage funds, through either equity or debt financing, and, in particular, through the ever-increasing recourse by States to sovereign bonds.

In addressing this question, certain definitions must be established. First, is there any such thing as a 'global financial system'? The term presupposes both the objective analysis of existing structures and the concept of intentional design. For the sake of the analysis, it is important to establish that we are, in fact, considering two dimensions with this concept, each of which is in a constant state of flux. Global financial structures are extant, but can we say that, collectively, as a whole, they are the product of an integrated design and that they constitute a real system?

Some aspects of the financial markets are of a systemic nature, given that the sector is regulated, at the domestic level, by central banks and independent financial authorities in charge of setting out rules of conduct and maintaining the integrity of the markets. Nevertheless, until recently, the provision of financial services remained largely deregulated in furtherance of neo-liberal orthodoxy. Historically, the end of the Bretton Woods era and the gold-US dollar parity saw the globalisation of the trading of currencies and capital.[1] The liberalisation of financial services was progressively made possible with the General Agreement on Trade in Services (GATS), a multilateral agreement concluded under the auspices of the World Trade Organization (WTO), and its Annex on Financial Services.[2] The de-regulation of the financial sector and the free floating of currencies, however, not only triggered growth in global finance, but also resulted in major financial shocks and shifts affecting the world economy.[3] As a result, States became crucially aware that their economies were tightly interrelated, and thus that financial shocks and volatile capital flows potentially might infect other economies.[4] This led them to reinforce their cooperation at the international level and to re-regulate in an attempt to increase both financial stability and market efficiency.[5] As such, the institutional response to the financial integration of the world economy resulted in the creation of international financial institutions or in the reinforcement of existing institutions, the leading ones being the International Monetary Fund's (IMF), the World Bank, the Bank for International Settlements, and of a plethora of law reform and research organisations.[6] Organisations such as the Financial Stability Board

---

[1] Adrian Buckley, *Multinational Finance* (Pearson 2004) 21.

[2] World Trade Organization 'The WTO's Financial Services Commitments Will Enter into Force as Scheduled' *WTO News* (Geneva, 19 February 1999).

[3] Ralph C Bryant, *Crisis Prevention and Prosperity Management for the World Economy* (Brookings Institution Press 2004) 136–7; Fabrizio Saccomanni, *Managing International Financial Instability: National Tamers versus Global Tigers* (Edward Elgar Publishing Ltd 2008) 36–7.

[4] Ibid.

[5] Ibid.

[6] Buckley (n 1); Saccomanni (n 3); Joseph E Stiglitz, *Globalization and its Discontents* (W W Norton and Company 2003) 12–13.

(FSB), the Basel Committee on Banking Supervision (BCBS) and the International Organization of Securities Commissions (IOSCO) have played an important role in adopting principles aimed at building globally coherent regulation in the finance area. Ultimately, the need for global financial stability culminated in the extension of the IMF's initial mandate of reconstructing the international payment system to a global surveillance role, allowing it to oversee its member countries' public finances and economic policies.[7] Similarly, the European sovereign debt crisis which started in 2008 compelled the European Union (EU) to undertake a vast reform project to make up for the lack of fiscal integration and political convergence, to enforce structural policies more efficiently and to achieve the re-capitalisation of European banks needed to guarantee the stability of the Eurozone.[8] Since then, the EU consistently has reinforced its institutional structures and legislation by expanding the powers of the European Central Bank (ECB).[9] The EU then also established a new operational framework under the auspices of the European Stability Mechanism (ESM) potentially to provide direct bank recapitalisation to distressed banks from an EU reserve fund, if the circumstances so require.[10]

Taken together, these various organisations and initiatives are dominated by the need to achieve global financial stability, and thus have been referred to as the global financial architecture.[11] The reality, however, is that this architecture is not always viewed as being sufficiently solid to achieve these goals. In this respect, some have advocated that the global financial architecture is barely organised as a system.[12] They argue that, paradoxically, this combination of agreements, institutions and practices is crucially deprived of some fundamental systemic features, such as a global political or governance authority responsible for the integrity and the efficiency of the markets[13] and, in particular, a systematic mechanism for debt restructuring which, in the EU case, is still in the making.[14]

---

7 Stiglitz (n 6).

8 Robert M Dunn and John H Mutti, *International Economics* (6th edn Routledge 2004) 486–8.

9 Ibid., 473–4.

10 Martin Kusák and others, 'Legal Aspects of the Treaty on Stability, Coordination and Governance in the Economic and Monetary Union' (2013) 3 The Lawyer Q 102, 103–4.

11 Saccomanni (n 3) xviii.

12 Stiglitz (n 6) 10–13.

13 Ibid.

14 Kusák and others (n 10) 103–4.

More importantly, the global financial system lacks an international judicial forum for the resolution of financial disputes that may arise during financial or currency crises between private international creditors and State debtors.[15] This is particularly true in the area of sovereign debt, where no specific international judicial forum exists in the event that a State would default on its obligations, other than domestic courts.[16] In this context, sovereign bondholders increasingly have had recourse to international investment arbitration by raising breaches of international investment agreements (IIAs) as an indirect means of recovering their interests in sovereign bonds. This has resulted in arbitral tribunals being confronted with issues of major importance in the global financial system involving, inter alia, matters of financial, monetary or fiscal policy. As a consequence, these decisions have opened the door to States being potentially held liable for their actions during episodes of financial turbulence.

The question therefore arises as to the extent to which investor-State arbitration is either supplementing or interfering with the global financial system. The various decisions rendered by arbitral tribunals in the area demonstrate that the relationship between international investment law and the global financial system has been either complementary or conflictual. As such, international investment arbitration has, on occasion, been regarded as providing an efficient and credible forum for the resolution of disputes involving State-held financial obligations, absent any legal remedy or jurisdictional forum to do so within the global financial system. Nonetheless, it has also been criticised for its disruptive effect on States' economies and the global financial order as a whole.

Eventually, the way international investment dispute settlement and the global financial architecture are inter-connected and interrelate with each other may be described by reference to two metaphors: it may be regarded either as 'yin' and 'yang' or as oil and water. The former refers to a commonly known concept of Chinese philosophy that conveys an

---

[15] See Henrik Enderlein and others, 'Debt Disputes: Measuring Government Coerciveness in Sovereign Debt Crises' (2012) 31 J Intl Money Fin 250, 252; Jeromin Zettelmeyer and others, 'The Greek Debt Restructuring: An Autopsy' (2013) Peterson Institute for International Economics Working Paper 13-8, 3 <http://scholarship.law.duke.edu/cgi/viewcontent.cgi?article=5343&context=faculty_scholarship> accessed 15 May 2016.

[16] It should be noted that private international creditors have also initiated claims in front of international courts or tribunals, including the European Court of Human Rights, the Iran-United States Claims Tribunal and various mixed claims commissions; Michael Waibel, *Sovereign Defaults Before International Courts and Tribunals* (CUP 2011) 171–201.

ultimate sense of symbiotic harmony and balance, while, however, being the result of two opposite or contrary forces of nature. It shows that two dynamics may thus be able to reconcile and complement each other to form a consistent and virtuous whole.

The latter, to the contrary, exemplifies irreconcilable conflict. About the inability of oil and water to mix, there is no ambiguity: they are, in a word, immiscible; that is to say, the force of attraction between the molecules within each substance is greater than the force of attraction between the two. From a scientific perspective, they are incapable of being mixed to form a homogeneous substance. Therefore, they are not meant to be put together and should be kept apart.

We shall elaborate further on these comparisons and explain, respectively, the complementary role and the disruptive effect that international investment law may have on the global financial system within two successive sections. For this purpose, we shall refer to empirical research drawn from the disciplines of both international investment law and international finance. Before attempting this analysis, however, we shall explain, in a preliminary part, how the various categories of financial instruments used in the cross-border trade of capital and currencies may fall within the subject matter of IIAs, and thus give private international creditors access to investor-State dispute settlement (ISDS). Although financial instruments are often covered by the definition of protected investments provided in IIAs, recent arbitral practice has, however, revealed great divergences between arbitral tribunals in their assessment of the factual circumstances that may arise in comparable cases.

II. FINANCIAL INSTRUMENTS MAY BE ENCOMPASSED WITHIN THE SUBJECT MATTER OF IIAS AND MAY ALLOW PRIVATE INTERNATIONAL CREDITORS TO ACCESS ISDS

Provided that they satisfy the specific conditions of a given treaty, financial instruments, including debt instruments, may qualify as 'investment(s)' under IIAs (or under a domestic investment law where applicable), and thus give jurisdiction to a privately-appointed arbitral tribunal to rule over alleged breaches of treaty protection. Although they are usually not expressly referred to as protected investments under IIAs, these instruments are generally captured by the open-ended definition of investment typically contained in such agreements. In particular, many Bilateral Investment Treaties (BITs) contain broad asset-based definitions which refer to 'every kind of asset invested as an investor' as protected investments, and are then followed by a non-exhaustive list of examples.[17] Depending on their specific terms, as a general rule, such broad asset-based definitions may include financial instruments within their scope. Therefore, a great variety of financial instruments used by a state treasury have fallen within such wide asset-based definitions, for instance, sovereign bonds,[18] certificates of deposit,[19] commercial loans,[20] debentures,[21] hedging agreements,[22] personal loans,[23] promissory notes,[24] public loans,[25] and treasury bills.[26] Nonetheless, treaty practice may vary and IIAs may impose additional requirements. For instance, in *Rizvi v Indonesia*, the Tribunal refused to consider the shareholding in an Indonesian bank as an investment as the UK-Indonesia BIT contained a requirement that the investment should be made in accordance with

---

[17] Daniella Strik, 'Investment Protection of Sovereign Debt and its Implications on the Future of Investment Law in the EU' (2012) 29 J Intl Arbitration 183, 186–8; Katia Yannaca-Small (ed.), *Arbitration under International Investment Agreements, a Guide to Key Issues* (OUP 2010) 245–7. It should, however, be noted that a few IIAs expressly protect some types of financial instruments, such as 'futures, options, and other derivatives' e.g., the US-Peru Trade Promotion Agreement, CAFTA-DR and the Australia-Chile Free Trade Agreement.

[18] *Abaclat and others v Argentine Republic (formerly Giovanna A Beccara and others v Argentine Republic)*, ICSID Case No ARB/07/5, Decision on Jurisdiction and Admissibility (4 August 2011).

[19] *Continental Casualty Company v Argentine Republic*, ICSID Case No ARB/03/9, Award (5 September 2008).

[20] *Oko Pankki Oyj*, VTB *Bank (Deutschland)* AG *and Sampo Bank Plc v Republic of Estonia* (formerly OKO *Osuuspankkien Keskuspankki Oyj and Others v Republic of Estonia*), ICSID Case No ARB/04/6, Award (19 November 2007); *Ceskoslovenska Obchodni Banka, AS v The Slovak Republic*, ICSID Case No ARB/97/4, Decision of the Tribunal on Objections to Jurisdiction (24 May 1999).

[21] *Fireman's Fund Insurance Company v The United Mexican States*, ICSID Case No ARB(AF)/02/1, Award (17 July 2006).

[22] *Deutsche Bank AG v Democratic Socialist Republic of Sri Lanka*, ICSID Case No ARB/09/2, Award (31 October 2012).

[23] *Alasdair Ross Anderson et al v Republic of Costa Rica*, ICSID Case No ARB(AF)/07/3, Award (19 May 2010).

[24] *Fedax NV v Republic of Venezuela*, ICSID Case No ARB/96/3, Decision of the Tribunal on Objections to Jurisdiction (11 July 1997).

[25] *Continental v Argentina* (n 19).

[26] Ibid.

Indonesian law and be granted admission, which had not been satisfied on the facts.[27]

As a result, major events affecting the functioning of the financial markets have come before arbitral tribunals. In *Saluka v the Czech Republic*, the Tribunal decided that a majority shareholding by an investor in a formerly State-owned commercial bank constituted an investment within the meaning of the Netherlands-Czechoslovakia BIT.[28] Therefore, it declared itself competent to rule over a dispute in connection with the reorganisation and privatisation of the Czech banking sector, a crucial step marking the end of the Communist period and the liberalisation of financial services. The State was ultimately held liable for breaching the fair and equitable treatment standard due to the government's decision to sell the bank for a symbolic price of one crown, in disregard of the private shareholders' interests, including the claimant's major stake in the bank. Another example is provided by the recent case of *Ping An v Belgium* in which Ping An, the second-biggest Chinese insurance company, challenged the rescue measures taken by Belgium after the 2008 financial crisis. The claim was brought under the Belgian-Chinese BIT in relation to an investment in the now defunct Fortis financial services company but did not lead to a ruling on the merits as the Tribunal ultimately declined jurisdiction.[29] Finally, in *Marfin v Cyprus*,[30] a notice of dispute was filed in 2013 by a Greek shareholder in Cyprus Popular Bank (also known as the 'Laiki Bank') on the ground that the bank's bailout and its take-over by State decree eviscerated the investment. The case is currently pending and its outcome is expected to have major repercussions on the financial markets.

With the upsurge of investment claims relating to States' financial obligations, arbitral tribunals have been confronted with more and more disputes relating to financial disruptions. Nonetheless, arbitral practice has not evolved uniformly. Although financial instruments are often covered by the definition of protected investments, crucial differences may be found from one tribunal to another in respect of key issues,

---

27 *Rafat Ali Rizvi v Republic of Indonesia*, ICSID Case No ARB/11/13, Award on Jurisdiction (16 July 2013) paras 198 and 223.

28 *Saluka Investments BV v The Czech Republic*, UNCITRAL, Partial Award (17 March 2006) paras 202–205.

29 *Ping An Life Insurance Company, Limited and Ping An Insurance (Group) Co Ltd v The Government of Belgium*, ICSID Case No ARB/12/29, Award (30 April 2015) para. 240.

30 *Marfin Investment Group v Republic of Cyprus*, ICSID Case No ARB/13/27, Notice of Dispute (23 January 2013).

namely the definition of investment under IIAs, the definition of the same notion under Article 25 of the ICSID Convention and, to a lesser extent, the concept of 'investor'.

A. The Fragmentation of Arbitral Practice as to Whether Financial Instruments May Constitute Protected Investments Under IIAs

The area of financial instruments in general has been the stage for significant disagreements among arbitral tribunals as to what constitutes an investment. As stated above, the express terms of an IIA are determinative as to whether an investment has been made in a given case. From a doctrinal point of view, arbitral tribunals have, however, greatly differed in their findings. The most striking example of diverging decisions may be found in *Abaclat v Argentina*[31] and *Poštová banka v Greece*,[32] two recent decisions involving sovereign bonds. In both cases, the relevant BITs contained an open-ended, asset-based definition of investment. While the *Abaclat* Tribunal recognised security entitlements in Argentinean sovereign bonds to be an investment,[33] the Tribunal in *Poštová banka v Greece* refused to do so for similar interests.[34]

In the former instance, the Argentina-Italy BIT provided, in its Article 1(1), that the term investment was to include, 'without limitation … (c): obligations, private or public titles or any other right to performances or services having economic value, including capitalized revenues'.[35] The Tribunal ruled that the word 'obligation' used in Article 1(1) of the Argentina-Italy BIT could be understood as referring to an economic value incorporated into a credit title representing a loan, although it would be commonly called 'bond' in the English language rather than 'obligation'.[36] Similarly, the term 'title' would more accurately translate into the English term of 'security', meaning 'nothing more than a fungible, negotiable instrument representing financial value'.[37]

The Tribunal rejected the defence argument according to which the connection between the security entitlements and the bonds could be seen as too remote to justify a finding that the dispute was not directly related

---

31 *Abaclat v Argentina* (n 18).

32 *Poštová banka, as and ISTROKAPITAL SE v Hellenic Republic*, ICSID Case No ARB/13/8, Award (9 April 2015).

33 *Abaclat v Argentina* (n 18) para. 707.

34 *Poštová banka v Greece* (n 32) para. 379.

35 *Abaclat v Argentina* (n 18) para. 352.

36 Ibid., para. 355.

37 Ibid.

to an investment.[38] In this respect, the Tribunal noted that the bonds at stake, which had been issued (on the primary markets), were always meant to be divided into smaller negotiable economic values (to be sold on the secondary markets) i.e., securities.[39] It also considered that the claimants as underwriters would not have subscribed to any of the bonds without having previously ensured that the bonds were re-sellable to intermediaries and their end customers.[40] Finally, the security entitlements were the result of the distribution process of the bonds through their division into a multitude of smaller securities representing each a part of the value of the relevant bond. The security entitlements would, however, have no value *per se* independently of the bond. For these reasons, the Tribunal concluded that an investment had been made which deserved the jurisdictional protection envisaged by the BIT.

The *Poštová banka* Tribunal, however, came to an entirely contrary conclusion. The proceedings had been brought by two claimants, Poštová banka, a Slovak bank holding interests in Greek Government Bonds (GGBs), and Istrokapital, a company holding shares in Poštová banka. The GGBs were dematerialised securities issued by syndication and auction in 1994 by the Bank of Greece.[41] The bonds had been freely offered to eligible participants (the participants) in charge of delivering the bonds to financial institutions selected by the State so that these would act as primary dealers (the primary dealers) and would provide funds for the acquisition of the GGBs by the participants. Accordingly, the primary dealers would then be able to sell the GGBs on the secondary market.[42] The initial distribution process was completed once the primary dealers had distributed the interests in the GGBs on the secondary market.[43]

Under the express terms of the Cyprus-Greece BIT and the Slovakia-Greece BIT, an investment was defined as 'every kind of asset and in particular, though not exclusively … c) loans, claims to money or to any performance under contract having a financial value'.[44]

In its decision, the Tribunal stated:

> In Article 1(1)(c) of the Slovakia-Greece BIT, the State parties to the treaty included 'loans' as an example of an investment and Claimants consider that

---

[38] Ibid., para. 358.
[39] Ibid.
[40] Ibid.
[41] *Poštová banka v Greece* (n 32) para. 52.
[42] Ibid., paras 52, 54–55.
[43] Ibid., para. 55.
[44] Ibid., para. 278.

> such term includes the GGBs. The wide interpretation of the text of Article 1(1)(c) proposed by Claimants considers that the GGBs, which are securities, bonds, clearly fit into the category of investments described in the words 'loans, claims to money or to any performance under contract having a financial value.' The Tribunal disagrees.[45]

Although the BIT contained a non-exhaustive list of examples of investments comprising a reference to 'loans, claims to money or to any performance under contract having a financial value', the Tribunal drew a clear distinction between loans and bonds as distinct financial products.[46] It emphasised that the lender generally is a bank or group of banks, normally identified in the relevant contractual agreement.[47] According to the Tribunal, bonds, on the other hand, are generally held by a large group of creditors which are often anonymous. The Tribunal further noted that, unlike loan creditors, the holders of bonds may change several times in a matter of days or even hours, as bonds are traded.[48] Because the tradability of loans or syndicated loans is generally limited, hence, loans generally are not tradable; they are not subject to the restrictions or regulations that apply to securities. Finally, the Tribunal noted that loans involve contractual privity between the lender and the debtor while bonds do not.[49] As such, the lender has a direct relationship with the debtor in a loan agreement, while in the issuance of bonds the contractual relationship of the State is with the intermediaries, i.e., the participants and the primary dealers. Thus, the Tribunal concluded that the State had a contractual relationship only with the intermediary or the clearing house through which the bonds were acquired.[50]

Moreover, the Tribunal also rejected the argument that 'claims to money' as referred to under Article 1(1) of the Slovakia-Greece BIT included bonds or other securities issued by a State, there being no indication that the contracting parties intended such a result.[51] More specifically, it rejected the arguments that the sales in the secondary market constituted a single economic operation, and that such a unified operation should result in Poštová banka having a claim to money under contract against Greece.[52] The Tribunal thus concluded that, absent a

45 Ibid., para. 336.
46 Ibid., para. 337.
47 Ibid.
48 Ibid.
49 Ibid., para. 338.
50 Ibid.
51 Ibid., para. 342.
52 Ibid., para. 346.

direct contractual relationship between Poštová banka and the State of Greece, Poštová banka did not hold a 'claim to money or to any performance under contract having a financial value' as stated in Article 1(1)(c) of the BIT.[53] Rather, it held that Poštová banka held a right in a title, understood as a right *in rem*, against the participants and would have rights against Greece arising from that title but not from a contract with Greece.[54]

The contrast is indeed stark between *Poštová banka v Greece*,[55] in which the express reference to loans was deemed irrelevant and insufficient for sovereign bonds' entitlements to qualify as investments, and *Abaclat v Argentina*,[56] in which the reference in the BIT to the terms 'obligation', 'title' and 'capitalized revenue' ultimately served as the basis for the Tribunal to rule that an investment had been made. In the former, the Tribunal made a very restricted reading of the BIT, whereas in the latter the Tribunal focused on the purpose and the practical significance of the sovereign bonds' entitlements. Similar differences also exist among arbitral decisions as to the definition of investment under the ICSID Convention.

B. Divergences Among Arbitral Tribunals as to the Definition of 'Investment' Under the ICSID Convention in the Specific Area of Financial Instruments

When an investment claim is brought to ICSID, arbitral tribunals usually require that the dispute relates to an investment within the meaning of both the BIT and Article 25(1) of the ICSID Convention. This latter provision restricts the jurisdiction *ratione materiae* of the ICSID Centre to 'any legal dispute arising directly out of an investment' for which the parties to the dispute 'consent in writing to submit to the [ICSID] Centre' while, however, not defining the term investment.[57] The rationale behind this 'double-barrelled' test, as is commonly called, is to delimit, respectively, the State's consent under the BIT, as well as the scope of ICSID jurisdiction and the arbitral tribunal's competence.[58]

[53] Ibid., para. 343.
[54] Ibid., para. 348.
[55] Ibid.
[56] *Abaclat v Argentina* (n 18).
[57] Ibid., para. 344.
[58] Ibid.; *Salini Constructori SpA v Kingdom of Morocco*, ICSID Case No ARB/00/4, Decision on Jurisdiction (23 July 2001) paras 43–58; *Fedax v Venezuela* (n 24) para. 25; *CSOB v Slovakia* (n 20) para. 68.

Absent any definition, two approaches have been elaborated in jurisprudence and by arbitral tribunals to guide them in interpreting Article 25(1) of the ICSID Convention.[59] The former is essentially subjective and traditional, as it concentrates on the intention of the contracting parties to the BIT as to whether they would have viewed the economic operation at stake as an investment.[60] The latter requires an objective approach and has been built progressively through a number of recent arbitral awards since the *Salini v Morocco* award was issued in 2011.[61] Pursuant to this approach, the notion of investment in Article 25(1) contains an additional and autonomous requirement of the ICSID Convention.[62] The leading example of the 'objective requirements' approach is the case of *Salini v Morocco*,[63] in which the reference in the Preamble of the ICSID Convention to economic development was seen as an important factor in defining the nature of an investment for the purposes of ICSID jurisdiction. Accordingly, the doctrine elaborated on the basis of this case, i.e., the *Salini* test, considers that several factors may indicate to the tribunal that an investment was made, namely a contribution made by the investor, the fact that the contract was performed during a certain duration, and the participation by the investor in the risks of the transaction.[64] Arbitral tribunals have also mentioned, on occasion, the economic development of the host State of the investment as an additional condition.[65] As such, these criteria are cumulative and should be assessed globally.[66] These factors may, however, only be regarded as providing guidance to an arbitral tribunal and are, in no event, strict prerequisites to the existence of an investment under the ICSID Convention.[67]

---

[59] Strik (n 17) 191–2.

[60] Ibid.

[61] *Salini v Morocco* (n 58) paras 43–58.

[62] Farouk Yala, 'The Notion of "Investment" in ICSID Case Law: a Drifting Jurisdictional Requirement' (2005) 22 J Intl Arb 105, 107.

[63] *Salini v Morocco* (n 58) paras 43–58.

[64] Emmanuel Gaillard, 'Identify or Define? Reflections on the Evolution of the Concept of Investment in ICSID Practice' in Christina Binder and others (eds), *International Investment Law for the 21st Century: Essays in Honour of Christoph Schreuer* (OUP 2009) 403–4.

[65] Ibid.

[66] Ibid., 404.

[67] Christoph Schreuer, 'Commentary on the ICSID Convention' (1996) 11 ICSID Rev Foreign Investment L J 318, 372; Ibrahim Fadlallah, 'La notion d'investissement: vers une restriction à la compétence du CIRDI?' in Gerald Aksen and others (eds), *Liber Amicorum in Honour of Robert Briner, Global*

While the subjective or traditional approach still dominates arbitral practice, the interpretation of Article 25(1) of the ICSID Convention remains a matter of sharp debate and is highly controversial in the area of financial instruments. In *Abaclat v Argentina*,[68] the majority of the arbitral Tribunal decided that the purchase of security entitlements in Argentina's bonds constituted a contribution which qualified as an investment under both the Argentina-Italy BIT and the ICSID Convention. In this case, the Tribunal rejected the *Salini* test in favour of the subjective approach. The Tribunal considered that, if these contributions made by the claimants that had been deemed an investment under the BIT were to fail the *Salini* test, they would thus not qualify as investments under Article 25 of the ICSID Convention. This would mean that the foreign investor's contributions would not have been afforded the procedural protection of the ICSID Convention, and thus lead to a result in contradiction with its aims.[69] Therefore, pursuant to the subjective approach, the Tribunal ruled that the double-barrelled test had been satisfied.

Nevertheless, in his dissenting opinion to the jurisdictional award,[70] a member of the arbitral Tribunal objected that the Tribunal's ruling with regards to the second step of the test amounted to 'discarding formally and totally the requirements by the ICSID Convention in this regard'.[71] In particular, he emphasised the legal remoteness between the parties to the transaction, i.e., the present interest holders, as opposed to the original bondholders and the Argentinean State.[72] On the basis of this analysis, he decided that the award failed to distinguish between purchases on the primary market, involving the issuer, Argentina, and the initial buyers of the issue, the underwriters, and the secondary market where previously issued securities are traded without any involvement of the sovereign debtor.[73] In addition, he stated that the security entitlements did not satisfy the territorial nexus with the sovereign.[74] As such, an argument has been elaborated in jurisprudence pursuant to which the issuance of sovereign bonds is ultimately purely a commercial act that

Reflections on International Law, Commerce and Dispute Resolution (International Chamber of Commerce 2005) 259, 259 and 267.

68 *Abaclat v Argentina* (n 18) para. 707.

69 Ibid., para. 364.

70 *Abaclat v Argentina* (n 18) Dissenting Opinion (4 August 2011).

71 Ibid., para. 66.

72 Ibid., para. 67.

73 Ibid., para. 70.

74 Ibid., para. 119.

may consequently not be encompassed within the investment protection viewed by the ICSID Convention.[75]

In this respect, the contribution requirement of the objective approach is often understood as a contribution to an economic operation creating value.[76] This has led some arbitral tribunals to distinguish between awards in which financial instruments were linked to an economic transaction with cases involving only financial instruments. In *Joy Mining v Egypt*,[77] the Tribunal decided that a bank guarantee was not to be regarded as an investment in its own right, to the extent that it was not linked to a contract that qualified as an investment. In this respect, the Tribunal disregarded the ruling in *Fedax v Venezuela*,[78] according to which promissory notes qualified as an investment. The Tribunal noted that the promissory notes, in the latter case, had been issued by Venezuela in connection with a contract for the provision of services, i.e., an economic operation creating value. Therefore, the *Joy Mining* Tribunal held that, absent any such operation, the bank guarantee could not be an investment in its own right. The Tribunal also regarded the ruling in *CSOB v Slovakia*[79] as inapposite. It noted that, although the award had recognised a loan to be an investment in that case, the loan was, in fact, part of an overall economic operation of the restructuring of a commercial bank, CSOB, in order to foster its development.

Other tribunals clearly reject the objective approach and point to the fact that the contracting parties to the ICSID Convention deliberately decided not to include a definition of the term investment[80] nor to expressly exclude bonds, loans and capital flow.[81] It follows that, absent any notification made by a State under Article 25(5) of the ICSID Convention to exclude financial instruments as protected investments, or of any evidence of the State's intention to that effect in the *travaux préparatoires*, no additional requirement should be subsequently imposed

---

[75] Michael Waibel, 'Opening Pandora's Box: Sovereign Bonds in International Arbitration' (2007) 101 AJIL 711, 720–21.

[76] *Poštová banka v Greece* (n 32) para. 361.

[77] *Joy Mining Machinery Ltd v Arab Republic of Egypt*, ICSID Case No ARB/03/11, Award on Jurisdiction (6 August 2004) paras 53–63.

[78] Ibid., paras 51 and 60; *Fedax v Venezuela* (n 24).

[79] *Joy Mining v Egypt* (n 77) para. 52; *CSOB v Slovakia* (n 20).

[80] Convention on the Settlement of Investment Disputes between States and Nationals of Other States: Documents concerning the Origin and the Formulation of the Convention (ICSID 1968) para. 59.

[81] Ibid., paras 261, 474 and 709.

through the so-called objective approach.[82] The *Ambiente Ufficio v Argentina* case[83] strongly supports this interpretation. In that instance the Tribunal was asked whether 90 claims brought by Italian nationals over security entitlements to Argentinean sovereign bonds, which the Tribunal had already ruled to be investments under the Argentina-Italy BIT, were also to be regarded as protected investments under the ICSID Convention. To this end, the Tribunal undertook a detailed analysis of the history of the drafting of the ICSID Convention and the economic operation at stake in order to make its determination.

The Tribunal's analysis with regard to the ICSID Convention is particularly instructive. The *Ambiente* Tribunal noted that 'attempts were made in the drafting process of the ICSID Convention to eliminate its application to bonds, loans and capital flow, but all of these were [ultimately] rejected'.[84] It then decided that the omission of any express reference to this form of investment did not mean *per se* that this type of asset was ineligible for ICSID protection. As to the economic operation at stake, the Tribunal followed a holistic approach and looked at the operation as a whole. The Tribunal then found that the very purpose of the bonds was to make funds 'available to finance the Respondent's budgetary needs, with each Claimant holding a proportionate share of that investment'.[85] Therefore, The Tribunal mainly examined what the nature and the purpose of the operation substantially entailed, i.e., to allow additional funds to be allocated to the State's budget.[86] Thus, the Tribunal adopted a similar reasoning as in *Abaclat v Argentina*[87] and adopted the subjective approach.

C. The Definition of Investor Understood Pragmatically

The concept of investor has been less problematic in practice. Arbitral tribunals have found not only entrepreneurs of Foreign Direct Investment (FDI) projects to qualify for investment treaty protection, but also

---

82 Strik (n 17) 193.

83 *Ambiente Ufficio SpA and others v Argentine Republic*, ICSID Case No ARB/08/9 *(formerly Giordano Alpi and others v Argentine Republic)*, Decision on Jurisdiction and Admissibility (8 February 2013).

84 Ibid., para. 469.

85 Ibid., para. 425.

86 Ibid., para. 500.

87 *Abaclat v Argentina* (n 18) para. 707.

shareholders, and, under certain circumstances, financiers, of FDI projects, as well as indirect shareholders.[88]

Nonetheless, investment treaties may impose more stringent requirements limiting the recourse by financial institutions to ISDS. In *Alps Finance and Trade AG v Slovakia*,[89] the claimant attempted in vain to claim under the Switzerland-Slovakia BIT on the basis of an agreement with a Slovak company in which the claimant had purchased credit owed by a bankrupt debtor and for which enforcement had been refused by a Slovakian court. The Tribunal ruled that the claimant was 'far from meeting the standard imposed under the BIT' requiring a Swiss claimant to have its 'seat' and show 'real economic activity' in Switzerland which the claimant was unable to satisfy.[90]

III. THE COMPLEMENTARITY OF INTERNATIONAL INVESTMENT ARBITRATION WITH THE GLOBAL FINANCIAL SYSTEM, ABSENT ANY JUDICIAL FORUM FOR THE RESOLUTION OF FINANCIAL DISPUTES WITH A SOVEREIGN STATE (A 'YIN' AND 'YANG' RELATIONSHIP)

It follows that when a financial instrument falls within the scope of an IIA, it deserves to be protected under the standards contained in the treaty and entitles the investor to have the dispute adjudicated through ISDS. To this extent, international investment arbitration may be viewed as complementing the global financial system by providing private international creditors with a judicial forum for the resolution of disputes occurring over the course of currency and sovereign debt crises.

A. The Possibility for Private International Creditors to Gain Access to an International Judicial Remedy to Challenge a State's Unlawful or Unfair Behaviour During Financial Crises

The financial literature tells us that it would be simplistic, if not erroneous, to view financial crises through a dichotomy between paying

88 *Hesham T M Al Warraq v Republic of Indonesia*, UNCITRAL, Final Award (15 December 2014) paras 169 and 683.

89 *Alps Finance and Trade AG v The Slovak Republic*, UNCITRAL, Award (5 March 2011) paras 213, 219–224.

90 Ibid., para. 224.

States and defaulting States or through the measure of default versus non-default.[91] Empirical studies evidence that, over the course of a crisis, States may not be cooperative with creditors, or even with the institutions of the global financial system, at the risk of jeopardising global stability.[92] States may engage in coercive behaviours culminating in expropriative practices and unwillingness to pay their financial liabilities, even when they may actually have the capabilities to do so.[93] The same studies have questioned the extent to which the global financial architecture, i.e., its institutions, agreements and practices, is able to influence a government's behaviour towards private international creditors during crises.[94] In this respect, the IMF adopted very early on a policy of financial assistance for States in financial distress, conditioning their access to international lending upon an obligation to collaborate with their creditors and negotiate any debt agreement in good faith.[95] This policy requires States to use their best efforts to achieve broad creditor participation, and transparent debt workout process, as well as an early and continuous dialogue and negotiations with creditors.[96]

This, however, is far from being standard practice. States have not always been transparent with their creditors, leading to delays or even to unfair breakdowns in debt negotiations. On occasion, they have been uncooperative with international financial institutions. In fact, such behaviours may harm not only the State's own economy, e.g., by impeding capital flows, international trade, and access to credit, but also the global economy.[97] Finance specialists report that governments have often employed coercive measures in disputes with private international creditors, in particular during sovereign debt crises.[98] Such behaviours may range from mild measures, e.g., declarations of default, suspension of negotiations with private international creditors, to highly coercive measures, including freezing foreign assets for non-residents or enacting discriminatory laws blocking payments made to foreign creditors. Another controversial behaviour may be the State's failure to make a

---

[91] Enderlein and others (n 15) 250–51.

[92] Ibid.

[93] Ibid.

[94] Ibid.

[95] IMF, 'IMF Policy on Lending into Arrears to Private Creditors' (IMF 1999); IMF, 'Fund Policy on Lending into Arrears to Private Creditors, Further Consideration of the Good Faith Criterion' (IMF 2002).

[96] Ibid.

[97] Enderlein and others (n 15) 250–51.

[98] Ibid.

payment to a foreign creditor on political grounds rather than for genuine financial reasons.[99]

By holding States liable for such behaviours, international investment arbitration has clearly contributed to supporting the global financial system. In *Saluka v the Czech Republic*,[100] for instance, the Tribunal ruled that a State which decided to put a bank into forced administration had, in fact, breached the standard of fair and equitable treatment by allowing that bank 'differential treatment without a reasonable justification' in comparison to local banks which were all bailed out'.[101] In particular, the State was held liable for unreasonably frustrating the claimant's good faith efforts to resolve the difficulties faced by the bank.[102] The arbitrary and excessive use of power of a State against a private international creditor during an episode of economic downturn was also held to constitute a breach of international law in *Deutsche Bank v Sri Lanka*.[103] In that case, the investment consisted of hedge contracts entered into with a State-owned company. The German-Sri Lanka BIT was applicable. The decisions by the State to suspend payments due under the contracts when oil prices would decrease below a certain level were held to be breaches of fair and equitable treatment and to amount to unlawful expropriation.[104]

In addition, in *Abaclat v Argentina*,[105] the Tribunal, in accepting jurisdiction, strongly emphasised that the dispute did 'not derive from the mere fact that Argentina failed to perform its payment obligations under the bonds but from the fact that it intervened as a sovereign by virtue of its state power to modify its payment obligations towards its creditors'.[106] Similarly, in *Burimi v Albania*, a private loan agreement between two private companies was not held to be an investment if not affected by a government measure.[107]

---

99 Ibid.

100 *Saluka v the Czech Republic* (n 28).

101 Ibid., paras 76, 407, 498–499.

102 Ibid., para. 499.

103 *Deutsche Bank v Sri Lanka* (n 22).

104 Ibid., para. 591.

105 *Abaclat v Argentina* (n 18).

106 Ibid., para. 324.

107 *Burimi Srl and Eagle Games Sh A v Republic of Albania*, ICSID Case No ARB/11/18, Award (29 May 2013) paras 144–146.

Finally, the decisions rendered in the jurisdictional awards in *Abaclat v Argentina*,[108] *Ambiente Ufficio v Argentina*[109] and *Alemanni v Argentina*[110] encapsulate the idea that, under international investment law, the use by a State of its sovereign power arbitrarily to modify the terms of its financial obligations constitutes *prima facie* a treaty violation.

Consequently, international arbitration tends to limit potentially opportunistic default by States that have used sovereign power in breach of their international obligations towards creditors or refused payment to them on political grounds.[111] As such, international arbitration has allowed private international creditors to gain access to a fair judicial remedy against the misuse of power by States. In this respect, not only is the lack of judicial recourse, in the area, detrimental to the administration of justice in itself, but it also does not prompt States to act responsibly and to fulfil their obligations in light of the overwhelming need for global stability. To this extent, international investment law has greatly contributed to the global financial system by recognising States' responsibility for misbehaving during episodes of crises and by preventing them from escaping their financial obligations without legitimate reasons. It serves both justice and the overarching objective of financial stability. In this respect, international investment arbitration contributes to the rule of law, as a fundamental and much-needed requirement of the global financial system. In the absence of adequate legal recourse, norms of conduct set by governments, international financial institutions and research organisations, States may lack sufficient incentive to meet their financial obligations. Therefore, full access to redress and legal recourse through arbitration allows investors to protect their rights and makes States more accountable with regard to their financial obligations. In the end, the monitoring and enforcement of financial regulation is enhanced and the interests of foreign investors are better protected.

By the same token, international investment law has also highlighted the crucial role of State regulators and their responsibility to ensure that financial markets are safe, fair and efficient. In *Victims of the Stanford*

---

108 *Abaclat v Argentina* (n 18) paras 323–324.

109 *Ambiente v Argentina* (n 83) paras 546, 551.

110 *Giovanni Alemanni and others v Argentine Republic*, ICSID Case No ARB/07/8, Decisions on Jurisdiction and Admissibility (17 November 2014) paras 293, 296–297.

111 Jill E Fisch and Caroline M Gentile, 'Vultures or Vanguards? The Role of Litigation in Sovereign Debt Restructuring' (2004) 53 Emory L J 1047, 1051 and 1053.

Ponzi Scheme v the USA, a claim initiated by the victims of a multi-billion Ponzi scheme managed by Allen Stanford, a US financier, was directly targeted against regulators themselves due to their alleged failure sufficiently to guarantee the application of financial regulation.[112] These claims primarily rest on a violation of the full protection and security standard contained in several IIAs. The claimants alleged that the losses they incurred as a result of the illegal and fraudulent activities of the fund in issue could have been avoided, had the financial regulators acted diligently in performing their mission.[113] As a consequence, these claims clearly reinforce the idea that regulators, too, are accountable for their actions and that they should diligently accomplish their missions so as to achieve global stability.

B. ISDS as an Impetus for the Creation of a Dispute Settlement Mechanism for Sovereign Debt Claims

Other advantages are attributed to international investment law in the specific area of sovereign bonds. In this respect, the way private international creditors may use arbitration is twofold: indirectly to claim payment of their entitlements and/or to challenge the terms of restructuring plans, i.e., through holdout arbitration as an alternative to holdout litigation.[114] This is particularly valuable for minority creditors as debt-restructuring plans may often discriminate against them, or impose unreasonable conditions upon them, 'because a restructuring plan need not adhere to legislative standards or secure judicial review'.[115] Coupled with that, an argument has been advanced that holdout arbitration might actually have positive effects[116] by increasing the liquidity of the financial markets as well as capital flows.[117]

In fact, the lack of effective judicial redress for sovereign debt claims has been problematic for years in the global financial system. Other than in national courts, foreign bondholders have had no legal recourse to sue a State for defaulted payments, unless they attempt to do so indirectly through ISDS. This is also due, in part, to the fact that, irrespective of

[112] *Victims of the Stanford Ponzi Scheme v The Government of the United States of America*, Notices of Intent (8 and 29 December 2012).

[113] Ibid.

[114] Felipe Suescun de Roa, 'Investor-State Arbitration in Sovereign Debt Restructuring: The Role of Holdouts' (2013) 30 J Intl Arb 131, 131, 148–9.

[115] Fisch and Gentile (n 111) 1048.

[116] Suescun de Roa (n 114) 148–9.

[117] Ibid.

their governing law, sovereign bonds may contain a *pari passu* clause. Accordingly, the creditors' respective unsecured entitlements rank equally in proportion to their interests. As a result, any creditor is entitled to start a court action whenever it becomes aware that a payment is to be made to another creditor in a given jurisdiction and to claim an equal entitlement of the amount paid. This can generate a flurry of parallel legal actions by creditors in front of domestic courts in different jurisdictions. So-called 'vulture funds' specialising in obligations of distressed firms and countries often seek to recover their entitlement by making a 'smart' choice of jurisdiction, which is said to achieve mixed results.[118] In practice, sovereign bonds frequently contain a choice-of-jurisdiction clause under which the debtor agrees to a creditor-friendly jurisdiction. One of the most common choices for private international creditors has been New York law. This choice is mainly explained because the Foreign Sovereign Immunities Act[119] limits the ability of a State to raise sovereign immunity or the Act of State doctrine as a defence.[120] In any event, this dispersion of legal actions may lead to unfair results, as some creditors may randomly be able to recover all or part of their entitlement while some other creditors may only be compensated in part, and others may not be compensated at all.

The current arch-example of this is the suit brought in US federal courts by the hedge fund NML Capital against Argentina for payment of bonds. United States District Judge Griesa ruled that 'holdout' NML was entitled to collect from Argentina in tandem *pari passu* with the 93 per cent of bondholders who had accepted 30 per cent or less on the dollar in two rounds of restructuring. Furthermore, Judge Griesa ordered Argentina to place $1.33 billion in an escrow account in order to assure ultimate 100 per cent payment on NML's bond holdings, including interest.[121] Perhaps not surprisingly, not only Argentina, but also the New York Federal Reserve Bank, and the Clearing House, backed by the likes

---

[118] William W Bratton, 'Pari Passu and a Distressed Sovereign's Rational Choices' (2004) 53 Emory L J 823, 823–4.

[119] Foreign Sovereignty Immunities Act, 28 USC, ss 1602-1611.

[120] Karen Halverson Cross, 'Arbitration as a Means of Resolving Sovereign Debt Disputes' (2006) 17 Am Rev Intl Arb 335, 335.

[121] Order, *NML Capital Ltd v Republic of Argentina*, Case No 08-civ-6978 (TPG) (SDNY 23 February 2012) ECF No 371; Opinion, *NML Capital Ltd v Republic of Argentina*, Case No 08-civ-6978 (TPG) (SDNY 21 November 2012) ECF Nos 423-25; Order Concerning the 5 March 2012 Order, *NML Capital Ltd v Republic of Argentina*, Case No 08-civ-6978 (TPG) (SDNY 26 November 2012) ECF No 429.

of JP Morgan Chase, Citigroup, Bank of America and Wells Fargo, voiced organised objections. Nonetheless, the United States Court of Appeals for the Second Circuit affirmed and the Supreme Court declined to consider the case.[122] In a subsequent action, Argentina lost its claim before the Supreme Court that its assets were immune from post-judgment discovery of information concerning its extraterritorial assets.[123]

In the meantime, of course, lenders and borrowers alike have sought to resolve this problem by agreeing on so-called 'collective action clauses'. Such clauses, more colourfully labelled 'cram down provisions,' require bondholders to sue in unison, if at all, or empower a super-majority of bondholders to compel minority acceptance of the terms accepted by the former.[124] This mechanism may appear to be a 'quick fix' rather than a real solution to the spreading of legal actions available to creditors. Moreover, creditors who are not willing to accept a reduced share of their entitlement proposed by the debtor-State as partial satisfaction may still attempt to engage in parallel legal actions and seek to increase that pot separately from the majority of creditors. As a result, collective action clauses do not completely resolve the issue.

In any event, the dispersion of these legal actions is not ideal. In light of the above, the IMF is currently considering a number of initiatives to streamline the resolution of sovereign bond disputes, for instance, the inclusion of arbitration clauses providing for disputes to be submitted to a Sovereign Debt Tribunal (SDT) (also called the 'Paulus' proposal), and a proposal by non-governmental organisations to create a Fair and Transparent Arbitration Process (FTAP) (also called the 'Raffer' proposal).[125] Nevertheless, the IMF is painfully conscious of the fact that

[122] Order Denying Petition for a Writ of Certiorari, *Republic of Argentina v NML Capital Ltd*, 134 S Ct 2250 (2014); *NML Capital Ltd v Republic of Argentina*, 727 F3d 230 (2d Cir 2013); *NML Capital Ltd v Republic of Argentina*, 699 F3d 246 (2d Cir 2012).

[123] Order, *Republic of Argentina v NML Capital Ltd*, 134 S Ct 2250 (2014).

[124] Other remedies to prevent the disruption of the sovereign debt restructuring process may, however, be available, e.g., exchange offers with exit consent (an offer by the state to exchange old debt against new debt), or the Sovereign Debt Restructuring Mechanism (SDRM), a proposal of an international bankruptcy procedure purporting to allow majority creditors to negotiate a restructuring that would be binding on all creditors while discouraging holdouts; see Suescun de Roa (n 114) 148, 151.

[125] Sean Hagan and others, 'Sovereign Debt Restructuring: Recent Developments and Implications for the Fund's Legal and Policy Framework' (2013) IMF Policy Paper, para. 56 <https://www.imf.org/external/np/pp/eng/2013/042613.pdf> accessed 15 May 2016. Accordingly, the:

'because of the higher expected recovery (in dollars, taking into account the likelihood of repayment), bondholders will be more inclined to hold out'[126] and seek payment indirectly, by relying on treaty breaches before arbitral tribunals.

While none of these proposals has yet been implemented, Michael Waibel noted eight years ago, that international investment arbitration may, in fact, adversely affect sovereign debt crises. Parallel proceedings, including holdout arbitration, focus too heavily on the protection of creditors.[127] As a consequence, they potentially 'threaten [the] resolution of ... sovereign debt crises' and go 'against the interests of the creditor majority and ... the international community as a whole'.[128] Therefore, although international investment arbitration may appear as a most welcome foundational component of the global financial system, is it an adequate response to the needs of this system?

IV. THE INTERFERENCE OF INTERNATIONAL INVESTMENT LAW WITH THE GLOBAL FINANCIAL SYSTEM (LIKE OIL AND WATER)

The interference of international investment arbitration in the global financial system is twofold. First, in the case of sovereign debt claims, parallel arbitration proceedings may delay, and even obstruct, the entire debt restructuring process of a State in dire financial distress. In such

---

> SDT envisages a tribunal of arbitrators that could be activated through special clauses in future sovereign debt contracts. Once established, its procedures may eventually create 'spillover effects on the legal treatment of other state obligations,' even if some do not contain arbitration clauses. The FTAP is similar to the SDT, but less institutionalised. It proposes an ad hoc arbitration mechanism that would rule on a case-by-case basis. Debtors and creditors would propose two arbitrators each, who would jointly choose a fifth arbiter to head a panel.

Further procedural mechanisms have also been considered by the IMF.

[126] See Waibel (n 75) 758; Owen C Pell, 'Memorandum to Global Committee of Argentina Bondholders: Re: Recent Argentine Legislation and Bondholder Remedies' (*PRNewswire* 15 February 2005) <http://www.prnewswire.com/news-releases/gcab-releases-legal-memorandum-summarizing-recent-argentine-legislation-and-bondholder-remedies-54081267.html>, accessed 15 May 2016; Halverson Cross (n 120); Suescun de Roa (n 114) 132.

[127] Waibel (n 75) 759.

[128] Ibid.

circumstances, holdout arbitration proceedings may not only hinder the economic salvation of that State but also cause consequential damage to the global economy. Secondly, while it is in the area of sovereign debt claims that the interference of international investment arbitration is most felt, States are increasingly keen to protect their right to regulate financial services in the public interest. In this respect, ISDS is often said to create 'regulatory chill' which may discourage a State from freely exercising its right, as a sovereign, to regulate for fear it may later be found to have breached one of its IIAs. Put differently, ISDS may hamper policy development as policy-makers may consider potential disputes with foreign investors before even starting to draft a policy.[129] States' priority then becomes the avoidance of disputes in preference to the development of efficient regulation in the public interest.[130] In the aftermath of the 2008 financial crisis, there is a growing consensus among governments that they should shield prudential regulation in the financial sector from investment claims.

A. The Disruptive Effect of Holdout Arbitration on Sovereign Debt Restructuring

The growing trend to submit sovereign debt claims to arbitral tribunals raises the question of the significance of arbitral awards on defaulted sovereign bonds for the global financial system. It is one of considerable practical importance, given the central role of government bonds in the development of the financial markets.[131] Thus, the IMF has inquired whether this trend 'could have pervasive implications for future sovereign debt restructurings by increasing leverage of holdout creditors'.[132]

From a State's perspective, the initiation of arbitration proceedings by a foreign creditor for breaches of treaty protections might lead to a potentially long and burdensome process. In addition, any arbitral award holding a State liable for breaching an IIA may increase a State's total liability well above the amount agreed with the bulk of its creditors

---

[129] Kyla Tienhaara, 'Regulatory Chill and the Threat of Arbitration: A View from Political Science' in Chester Brown and Kate Miles (eds), *Evolution in Investment Treaty Law and Arbitration* (CUP 2011) 606, 606–7.

[130] Ibid.

[131] Masamichi Kono and Ludger Schnuknecht, 'How Does Financial Services Trade Affect Capital Flows and Financial Stability?' in Stijn Claessens and Marion Jansen (eds), *The Internationalization of Financial Services, Issues and Lessons for Developing Countries* (Kluwer Law International 2000) 139.

[132] Hagan and others (n 125) 1.

through a negotiated debt restructuring agreement. For these reasons, arbitration may have negative implications for the global financial system as well, especially where the sovereign debt restructuring process involves the input of international financial organisations or other organisations of the global financial architecture.

This is precisely the issue which arose in *Poštová banka v Greece*.[133] The circumstances of that case included a negotiated sovereign debt restructuring between the majority of Greece's private international creditors and the Greek government. The agreement which resulted from these negotiation proceedings was then enshrined in the adoption of a legislative act, Law 4050/2012 (the Bondholders Act), approved by the Greek Parliament on 23 February 2012. Essentially, this law provided for the reduction of Greece's sovereign debt with the consent of the majority of bondholders by way of a 'haircut' amounting to an estimated 59–65 per cent of the total interest.[134] In exchange, the Bondholders Act provided for the introduction of a retroactive collective action clause pursuant to which all debts would be recovered by all creditors through a collective action.[135] As might have been expected, certain non-agreeing bondholders initiated arbitration proceedings against Greece on the basis of two intra-EU treaties, the Cyprus-Greece BIT and the Slovakia-Greece BIT. The minority bondholders claimed that such *ex post facto* legislation breached the standards of protection to which they were entitled under these BITs.[136] At the time, this case raised major concerns as to the consequences which an adverse decision might have had on Greece's debt restructuring. Although the Tribunal declined jurisdiction, this minority has now initiated annulment proceedings. In addition, further proceedings are ongoing against the Greek State in *Cyprus Popular Bank v Greece*,[137] in which the claimant alleged it has been discriminated against by being denied access to the Greek bailout funds.

---

[133] *Poštová banka v Greece* (n 32).

[134] This figure is based on Zettelmeyer and others (n 15) 2 and 11. The authors believe that the haircut was much lower than the 75 per cent haircut which was widely reported in the press. The majority of bondholders was based on a quorum of votes representing 50 per cent of face value and a consent threshold of two-thirds of the total face value taking part in the vote.

[135] Ibid.

[136] Greek Bondholder Act, Law No 4050/12.

[137] *Cyprus Popular Bank Public Co Ltd v Hellenic Republic*, ICSID Case No ARB/14/16, Memorial on the Merits (30 September 2015).

These cases arose in an unprecedented economic and political context.[138] The Greek debt crisis is said to have set a 'world record in terms of restructured debt volume and aggregate creditor losses' greatly surpassing the default and restructuring of Argentina in 2001–05.[139] The magnitude of the Greek debt caused it momentarily to lose access to the capital markets and to be granted a debt-exchange and a major bailout by the international financial community at the expense ultimately of taxpayers. The rescue plan resulted from complex and intense negotiations between Greece and the 'Troika', a tripartite committee led by the European Commission and including the ECB and the IMF.[140] In addition, the austerity measures agreed to by Greece in accordance with the debt-restructuring process involved great human cost, having huge consequences on people's lives.[141] In this respect, it should be noted that the Greek debt restructuring was also designed to limit the propagation of risks to other economies and to rehabilitate trust in the financial markets. In essence, this is what made the Greek negotiated debt restructuring so crucial for the world economy. The restructuring of the Greek debt was not only urgently required by the whole global economy, but also was the outcome of an extremely fragile deal achieved at the cost of high concessions. This in itself questions the adequacy of parallel arbitration proceedings by minority bondholders against a State in dire financial distress. It calls into question whether the protection of the interests of a small group of investors through holdout arbitration may be justified in light of the needs of the global financial system. In this context, international arbitration and the global financial system may well be compared to oil and water: they should be kept apart; immiscibility utterly forecloses their mixing.

---

[138] Zettelmeyer and others (n 15) 2.

[139] Ibid.

[140] Ibid.

[141] Joseph E Stiglitz, 'Interview Joseph Stiglitz' *Public Broadcasting Service* (13 April 2014) <http://www.pbs.org/wgbh/pages/frontline/shows/crash/interviews/stiglitz.html> accessed 15 May 2016. As Stiglitz noted: 'There is a growing consensus that something is wrong with the system, a system that can impose such high costs on so many people, many of whom were not speculating in international markets, were not gambling by borrowing abroad in foreign-denominated currencies.'

B. The 'Regulatory Chill' of International Investment Arbitration on Financial Regulation

The high number of claims that have been initiated by financial service providers in general and the huge impact of these disputes has led some States to reclaim their right to regulate in the area of financial services. This encompasses both the right of the State to regulate the finance industry in ordinary circumstances, and the right to take emergency measures in extraordinary circumstances of financial turmoil. Although the essential right of States to regulate their financial industry has been recognised on numerous occasions by arbitral tribunals, States are concerned with the 'regulatory chill' that investment claims may have on financial regulation.

The right to regulate has, indeed, consistently been taken into account in several arbitral awards. In *Saluka v the Czech Republic*, the Tribunal stated that:

> No investor may reasonably expect that the circumstances prevailing at the time the investment is made remain totally unchanged. In order to determine whether frustration of the foreign investor's expectations was justified and reasonable, the host State's legitimate right subsequently to regulate domestic matters in the public interest must be taken into consideration as well.[142]

As such, when assessing an investment claim, tribunals sometimes engage in a balancing act between the investor's entitlement and the State's legitimate right to regulate the sector. For example, in *National Grid v Argentina*, the Tribunal took into account the principle of 'investment risks,' i.e., the risk of loss inherent in any form of investment when assessing whether the standard of fair and equitable treatment had been breached. The Tribunal held that the legitimate expectations protected by the fair and equitable treatment guarantee in the UK-Argentina BIT must have been reasonable and legitimate in light of the particular context in which the investment was made:

> The protection of investor expectations has been made subject to two significant qualifications: first, that the investor should not be shielded from the ordinary business risk of the investment and, second, that the investor's expectations must have been reasonable and legitimate in the context in which the investment was made.[143]

---

[142] *Saluka v Czech Republic* (n 28) para. 305.

[143] *National Grid Plc v Argentine Republic*, UNCITRAL, Award (3 November 2008) para. 175; see also José E Alvarez and Tegan Brink, 'Revisiting the

Likewise, the condition of the relevant financial market in which the investment was made and the existence of systemic risks also have been consistently taken into account by arbitral tribunals. In *Al Warraq v Indonesia*, the State had bailed out a bank in which the claimant held shares, due to the mismanagement of the bank and liquidity issues.[144] The Tribunal rejected the claimant's claim of expropriation, as the bailout was 'within the discretion and authority of the government and was completely justified, particularly since [the bank] could have caused a systemic risk to the entire Indonesian financial system'.[145] In *Levy de Levi v Peru*,[146] the Tribunal reached a similar decision in the context of the take-over and liquidation of a bank due to liquidity problems and breaches of banking regulations. The Tribunal excluded a violation of fair and equitable treatment and unlawful expropriation. In this context, the Tribunal referred to the right to regulate as nothing less than exercising 'police powers' on the financial markets. In this case, the Tribunal stated:

> [T]he dissolution and liquidation of the bank ... were legitimate acts of 'police power' characteristic of bank officials because, according to Article 2 of the Banking Law, the main purpose of the Law is '... to provide for the competitive, solid and reliable operation of the financial and insurance systems, so as to contribute to national development'.[147]

As several [a]rbitral Tribunals have repeatedly pointed out, no investment treaty is an insurance or guarantee of investment success, especially when the investor makes bad business decisions.[148]

As further stated in *National Grid*, '[w]hat is fair and equitable is not an absolute parameter. What would be unfair and inequitable in normal circumstances may not be so in a situation of an economic and social crisis. The investor may not be totally insulated from [such] situations'.[149]

Similarly, the right to regulate has also been analysed by arbitral tribunals through crisis-related defences. Such a defence may be available to a State dealing with an economic crisis, e.g., a state of necessity defence under either a treaty or customary international law. Generally

---

Necessity Defense: *Continental Casualty v Argentina*' (2012) 9 Transnatl Disp Mgmt 319, 354.

[144] *Al Warraq v Indonesia* (n 88) para. 526.

[145] Ibid.

[146] *Renée Rose Levy de Levi v Republic of Peru*, ICSID Case No ARB/10/17, Award (26 February 2014) paras 2, 34, 166, 476–478.

[147] Ibid., para. 476.

[148] Ibid., para. 478.

[149] *National Grid v Argentina* (n 143) para. 180.

speaking, however, this latter defence may only be invoked provided that cumulative conditions are met, i.e., if the 'emergency' measure was 'the only means for the State to safeguard an essential interest against a grave and imminent peril' and if the State had not contributed to the situation of necessity.[150] In practice, these defences, however, have had varying fates. In *Continental Casualty v Argentina*, the Tribunal rejected the defence as to one of the several investment vehicles involved in that case, and accepted it as to the others.[151] Overall, of the seven other cases against Argentina decided to date that have considered the necessity defence,[152] only one other has accepted it.[153] The other six all have rejected it.

---

150 International Law Commission, 'Draft Articles on Responsibility of States for Internationally Wrongful Acts' YBILC (2001) Vol II Pt Two, art. 25.

151 *Continental v Argentina* (n 19) paras 265–266. The necessity defence was not successfully claimed in relation to the restructuring of the LETEs (Treasury Bills), neither under art. XI of the Treaty nor under customary international law (para. 265, paras 220–222). The necessity defence was allowed for all the other claims of breaches of the fair and equitable standard, i.e., the claims relating to a) the Corralito (the imposition of the bank freeze in December 2001); b) the devaluation of the peso; c) the pesification of the US dollar-denominated contracts and deposits; and d) the suspension of payments (default) and rescheduling of the governmental financial instruments held by CAN (para. 266).

152 The necessity defence based on the severe, economic and social crisis in Argentina in the years 2000 was rejected in the following cases: *CMS Gas Transmission Company v Republic of Argentina*, ICSID Case No ARB/01/8, Award (12 May 2005); *AWG Group Ltd v The Argentine Republic*, UNCITRAL, Decision on Liability (30 July 2010); *BG Group plc v Republic of Argentina*, UNCITRAL, Final Award (24 December 2007); *EDF International SA, SAUR International SA and León Participaciones Argentinas SA v Argentine Republic*, ICSID Case No ARB/03/23, Award (11 July 2012); *Impregilo SpA v Argentine Republic*, ICSID Case No ARB/07/17, Award (21 July 2011); *Suez, Sociedad General de Aguas de Barcelona SA and InterAguas Servicios Integrales del Agua SA v The Argentine Republic*, ICSID Case No ARB/03/17 (formerly *Aguas Provinciales de Santa Fe SA, Suez, Sociedad General de Aguas de Barcelona SA, and InterAguas Servicios Integrales del Agua SA*), Decision on Liability (30 July 2010); *Suez, Sociedad General de Aguas de Barcelona SA and Vivendi Universal SA v Argentine Republic*, ICSID Case No ARB/03/19 (formerly *Aguas Argentinas SA, Suez, Sociedad General de Aguas de Barcelona SA and Vivendi Universal, SA v Argentine Republic*), Decision on Liability (30 July 2010).

153 *LG and E Energy Corp, LG and E Capital Corp, and LG and E International Inc v Argentine Republic*, ICSID Case No ARB/02/1, Award (25 July 2007).

In any event, the cases of *Saluka v the Czech Republic*[154] and *Ping An v Belgium*[155] illustrate well the chilling effect of international investment law on the ability of sovereign States to enact financial regulation. In these two instances, the claims were based on the host State's decision to bailout a number of financial institutions but to exclude others from the rescue plan, including the respective claimants as foreign incorporated entities. Although the measures were motivated, at least in part, by genuine attempts to respond to the crisis and to stabilise the markets, the *Saluka* Tribunal ruled that the State had breached fair and equitable treatment.[156] While the Tribunal declined jurisdiction in *Ping An v Belgium,*[157] it is likely that the State would have been held liable for adopting such measures, absent any provision allowing otherwise in the BIT, had the Tribunal upheld jurisdiction.[158]

As a result, these arbitral awards generated great concern on the part of governments as to the impact of international investment law on the right to regulate in key domains. This is particularly true in relation to financial bailout measures. Very often, a State's spontaneous reaction to a financial crisis may consist of adopting 'too big to fail' measures, i.e., rescuing the largest financial institutions given their importance for the national economy.[159] In practical terms, these institutions are so important to the economy of a country that the State must take measures to prevent them from ceasing to trade or going bankrupt. Due to historical reasons, in most cases, they are likely to be domestic corporations and to be more advantaged by bailout measures than foreign entities. Therefore, such measures may well breach fundamental standards guaranteed under relevant IIAs (e.g., by denying the right to fair and equitable treatment and/or a minimum standard of treatment to a foreign investor or committing an unlawful expropriation).[160]

Another major area of contention relates to future preventive measures. For instance, much has been said about the reform of the bankingindustry through 'ring-fencing', i.e., the segregation of trading activities from

---

154 *Saluka v the Czech Republic* (n 28).

155 *Ping An v Belgium* (n 29).

156 *Saluka v the Czech Republic* (n 28) paras 407, 498–500.

157 *Ping An v Belgium* (n 29) para. 240.

158 Jeannine Birr, 'CETA: A Threat to Financial Stability? A Case for Regulatory Co-operation' (2016) 13 Transnational Dispute Management 1, 8–9.

159 Kevin P Gallagher, 'United States BITs and Financial Stability' (2010) 19 Columbia FDI Perspectives 1, 2.

160 Ibid.

more traditional retail lending and deposit-taking activities.[161] Similarly, such legislative measures could be challenged on the ground that they may potentially violate international investment law.

V. CONCLUSION

In light of the above, answering the question as to how international investment law and the global financial system interact is not a simple task. The evident clash between investment dispute arbitration and the current global financial architecture may appear, at times, and in specific cases, just like oil and water, as an unexpected and momentary isolated phenomenon. On the other hand, arbitration also has proved its complementing role for the global financial system over the course of major financial disruptions. As a result, international investment law and the global financial architecture may both be compelled to adapt to each other so as to achieve the same harmony as in 'yin' and 'yang'.

In fact, States seem to face the same dilemma. While investment protection is still viewed as essential, reform proposals have been formulated so as to integrate safeguard provisions for financial services, in particular, during the negotiations of mega-regional IIAs. These proposals concern both the issue of debt restructuring and balance-of-payment crises, as well as the protection of the right to regulate financial services.

One of the proposed reforms consists of excluding recourse by investors to ISDS during balance-of-payment crises.[162] Accordingly, this means that governments may freely impose capital controls in order to prevent or mitigate a crisis under defined circumstances.[163] A second aspect of the proposal aims also at excluding 'sovereign debt' from the definition of 'investment', or, at a minimum, when 75 per cent of the aggregate principal amount of the outstanding debt under such debt instrument have consented to such debt exchange or other process.[164] Some of these reform proposals have already been implemented. The Peru-Korea FTA, the CAFTA-DR and the US-Uruguay BIT expressly bar

---

[161] Sam Fleming, 'Banks Under Pressure on UK Ring-fencing Plans' *Financial Times* (London, 6 October 2014) 2.

[162] Gallagher (n 159).

[163] Ibid.

[164] Ibid.

investment claims related to debt restructuring.[165] In addition, Article 1139 of NAFTA excludes debts whose maturity is less than three years from the definition of investment.

In contemporary treaty practice, more and more IIAs include specific chapters for financial services, e.g., Chapter 14 of the North American Free Trade Agreement (NAFTA), Chapter 12 of the US-Peru Trade Promotion Agreement, Chapter 12 of the Dominican Republic-Central America FTA (CAFTA-DR), Chapter 11 of the TPP and Chapter 15 of CETA. Under these IIAs, the standards of protection apply widely to financial institutions, investors and their investments in financial institutions and cross-border trade in financial services.[166]

There is a growing trend, however, to define the notion of investment widely but to limit the investment standards (usually national treatment or the most-favoured nation treatment) in substance or in scope.[167] With the recent negotiations of mega-regional IIAs, a clear pattern can be seen in recent IIAs to streamline the protection of financial services. Attempts are made to recalibrate the standards of protection in order to reinforce the right to regulate the finance industry. Therefore, these agreements typically provide for a prudential carve-out, allowing the host State to retain its right to regulate financial services, including taking emergency measures during episodes of crises.[168] The Trans-Pacific Partnership (TPP) contains a specific chapter on financial services which is, however, limited by reservations aimed at guaranteeing the application of financial

[165] See, e.g., US-Peru Trade Promotion Agreement, Annex 9D; CAFTA-DR, Annex 10-A; US-Uruguay BIT, Annex G.

[166] NAFTA, art. 1401; US-Peru Trade Promotion Agreement, art. 12.1; CAFTA-DR, art. 12.1; see also TPP, art. 11.2; CETA, Ch. 15, art. 1.

[167] NAFTA, art. 1404 (Cross-Border Trade), art. 1404 (National Treatment), art. 1406 (Most-Favoured Nation Treatment) and art. 1407 (New Financial Services and Data Processing); US-Peru Trade Promotion Agreement, art. 12.2 (National Treatment), art. 12.3 (Most-Favoured-Nation Treatment), art. 12.5 (Cross-Border Trade) and art. 12.6 (New Financial Services); CAFTA-DR, art. 12.2 (National Treatment), art. 12.3 (Most-Favoured-Nation Treatment), art. 12.5 (Cross-Border Trade) and art. 12.6 (New Financial Services); TPP, art. 11.3 (National Treatment), art. 11.4 (Most-Favoured-Nation Treatment), art. 11.6 (Cross-Border Trade) and art. 11.7 (New Financial Services); CETA, ch. 15, art. 3 (National Treatment), art. 4 (Most Favoured Nation Treatment), art. 7 (Cross-Border Supply of Financial Services) and art. 13 (New Financial Services).

[168] NAFTA, art. 1410; US-Peru Trade Promotion Agreement, art. 12.10; CAFTA-DR, art. 12.10; TPP, art. 11.11(1) and art. 11.12; CETA, ch. 15, arts 5 and 15.

legislation, including the reform adopted under the Dodd-Frank Act in the aftermath of the 2008 financial crisis.[169] This chapter also contains a prudential carve-out[170] and a monetary carve-out for non-discriminatory measures in pursuit of monetary and related credit policy.[171] Similar provisions may be found in CETA and in the latest draft of the Transatlantic Trade and Investment Partnership (TTIP) released by the European Commission in November 2015.[172]

Further procedural mechanisms may also be provided when a State relies on the prudential exception. For instance, some IIAs allow a State to request a committee of financial services experts to issue a binding determination for the arbitral tribunal on whether the State has used the prudential exception as a valid defence to an investment claim.[173] Some IIAs also allow a party to a dispute to request consultations with the other side, with the possible participation of regulatory authorities.[174]

As a result, there is a clear policy in contemporary IIAs aimed at limiting the interference of international investment arbitration with financial regulation and re-regulating financial services in contemplation of global stability. Finally, it should be mentioned that another initiative was proposed by the European Commission in April 2015 to create a framework for regulatory cooperation between the US and the EU for the TTIP.[175] This proposal, however, seems to be a bone of contention between the negotiating parties and has not yet been agreed.[176] Thus,

---

[169] TPP, ch. 11 and Annex III (US Reservations to Chapter 11).

[170] TPP, art. 11.11(1) and 11.12.

[171] TPP, art. 11.11(2).

[172] CETA, ch. 15, art. 5 (Recognition of Prudential Measures), art. 15 (Prudential Carve-Out) and art. 16(1) (Specific Exceptions); draft TTIP, ch. II, s. II, art. 6(3) (this article provides for a prudential exception and states *in fine* that: '[a]dditional provisions, e.g. on restrictions in case of balance of payments and external financial difficulties or for the operation of the economic and monetary union, in the case of the European Union will be inserted in the general/horizontal part of the Agreement and will apply to this article'.

[173] NAFTA, art. 1415; US-Peru Trade Promotion Agreement, art. 12.19; CAFTA-DR, art. 12.19; TPP, art. 11.22; CETA, ch. 15, art. 20.

[174] NAFTA, art. 1413; US-Peru Trade Promotion Agreement, art. 12.17; CAFTA-DR, art. 12.17; TPP, art. 11.20; CETA, ch. 15, art. 18.

[175] Erik Jones and Huw Macartney, 'TTIP and the "Finance Exception": Venue-Shopping and the Breakdown of Financial Regulatory Coordination' (2016) 17 J Banking Regulation 4, 4–5.

[176] Ibid.

this, too, is a testament to the complex relationship between international investment law and the global financial system.

3. International investment law and financial regulation: Towards a deliberative approach

Matthias Goldmann

I. INTRODUCTION

This chapter deals with what one might consider a watershed development in macroeconomic theory. The financial crisis has profoundly modified the way in which economists understand the relationship between the different segments of financial regulation. During the decades preceding the crisis, financial regulation, i.e., the governmental steering of different segments of financial policy (here understood as comprising monetary and fiscal policy, banking regulation, development financing and investment law), followed a theory of functional separation in many domestic jurisdictions as well as on the international plane. Accordingly, there is no single, hierarchically superior actor with overall, systemic responsibility for financial regulation. Rather, different segments of financial regulation, as well as of international economic law, are assigned to different actors. Each actor is strictly confined to the purposes of its segment and may only give marginal consideration to other purposes. The most common example of this regulatory approach is the idea of independent central banks with the principal task of achieving price stability, while giving no, or only limited, consideration to fiscal policy or banking regulation. The idea behind this approach is that each actor only has limited knowledge, making it impossible to pursue several objectives, such as fiscal and monetary policy, at the same time, which have a potential to cancel each other out. In addition, functional separation should reduce conflicts of interest that might arise from the pursuit of competing objectives (e.g., between short-term fiscal interests and long-term concerns for price stability). The current international investment law regime also reflects the theory of functional separation. It is based on the recognition that investment protection might come at the expense of other public policies, including financial regulation. To avoid conflicts of interest, investment arbitration has been laid in the hands of independent tribunals outside the host State's judiciary.

The recent financial crisis has put the theory of functional separation under stress. Systemic risks spread across the various segments of financial regulation and required a more coordinated response. In this chapter, I will argue that a deliberative approach to international economic law might bridge gaps between the various segments of financial regulation and provide for more coordinated, integrative solutions. This has consequences for financial regulation, both *de lege ferenda* for the way in which new rules and policies are designed, and *de lege lata* for the way in which the existing legal rules, including those of international investment law, are interpreted and applied.

In the following part, I will reiterate how the financial crisis has influenced our understanding of the interdependence of various sectors of financial regulation and the need for coordinated crisis responses (II.). Thereafter, I will set out what I understand as a deliberative approach to legal interpretation that reacts to these challenges. This approach to legal interpretation might facilitate the management of interdependencies that exist among the various segments of financial regulation. I will show that this approach can be implemented in international economic law by taking recourse to systemic integration, in conformity with the applicable rules on interpretation (III.). Subsequently, I will elaborate on some of the implications of the deliberative approach for international investment law. Three case studies dealing with sovereign default, banking resolution and monetary policy will illustrate the thesis that the current legal regulation of international investment, and in particular the fair and equitable treatment (FET) standard, is thoroughly amenable to a more integrative understanding of international economic law (IV.).

II. THE THEORY OF FUNCTIONAL SEPARATION AND THE CHALLENGE OF THE FINANCIAL CRISIS

Prior to the crisis, financial regulation in many jurisdictions, including in international law, was to an important extent structured in accordance with the theory of functional separation. This was a result of the post-war evolution of the international economic order (A.). The financial crisis revealed the inadequacy of this setting for dealing with systemic crises (B.). Possible remedies to functional separation might not only come from new, comprehensive institutions, but also from a more integrative approach to legal interpretation within each regime (C.).

A. From Keynes to Tinbergen: The Theory of Functional Separation

The international economic order as we know it today took its shape after the Second World War. As such, it reflects in certain respects the economic theories that dominated the thinking of decision-makers at different times during the post-war period. An influential voice for the design of economic relations immediately after the war was that of John Maynard Keynes. In his theoretical oeuvre, he argued that the level of employment in a given economy resulted not only from the price of labour, as the classical theory of economics had held since the end of the eighteenth century,[1] and not only from the decisions of producers and consumers, as neoclassical equilibrium theories had argued.[2] Rather, he considered the state of the economy as representing an equilibrium resulting from both private and public decisions, including monetary and fiscal policy decisions.[3] In Keynes' eyes, governments should therefore use their capacity for macroeconomic steering. Society and the economy were complex machinery, full of uncertainties due to their organic development. Governments should seek to establish a reliable framework for the decisions of individuals.[4] They should use both demand and supply-oriented policy instruments in order to influence macroeconomic conditions in a way that would be favourable to growth – yet without pre-empting the microeconomic decisions of individuals. Thus, while Keynes rejected the laissez-faire of early capitalism, he meticulously avoided following the anti-liberal agenda of socialist or fascists planning economies.[5]

Keynes' idea of macroeconomic steering exercised great influence on the way in which governments conducted their economic policy in the post-war period. In the 1960s, Germany adopted a law that stipulated the

---

[1] E.g, Adam Smith, *An Inquiry into the Nature and Causes of the Wealth of Nations* (RH Campbell and AS Skinner, ed., first published 1776, OUP 1976) 10.

[2] E.g., Léon Walras, *Théorie mathematique de la richesse sociale* (Corbaz 1883) 40.

[3] John Maynard Keynes, *General Theory of Employment, Interest, and Money* (Palgrave Macmillan 1936) 23 ff.

[4] With respect to financial markets: Keynes (n 3) 147 ff; Sheila C Dow, 'Keynes on Knowledge, Expectations and Rationality' (Center on Capitalism and Society Conference on Microfoundations for Modern Macroeconomics, New York, 19-20 November 2010) 9 <http://capitalism.columbia.edu/files/ccs/DOW%20session%201%202010-11-15.pdf> accessed 16 February 2015.

[5] E.g., John Maynard Keynes, *The End of Laissez-faire: The Economic Consequences of the Peace* (Prometheus Books 1926).

Keynesian equilibrium as the goal of macroeconomic policy.[6] The holistic view of macroeconomic policy-making also informed Keynes' proposals for a worldwide economic order after the war in response to the traumatising experience of the Great Depression. In his view, that order should have encompassed a coherent institutional framework for trade, money, and investments. A new international currency called 'bancor' was to replace the gold standard.[7] An International Clearing Union was to take care of the settlement of current account deficits, requiring States with current account surplus to transfer funds to States with current account deficits.[8] However, due to the reluctance of the US congress to bear the financial burden of the envisaged clearing union, Keynes' plan never came to be realised.

The author of the plan that was realised instead, Harry White,[9] adhered only to a mild form of Keynesianism.[10] Accordingly, only the International Monetary Fund (IMF) and the International Bank for Reconstruction and Development (IBRD) as part of the World Bank Group saw the light of the day.[11] The dollar standard reintroduced the gold standard through the backdoor, countries short of currency were entitled to borrow from the IMF, instead of receiving funds from surplus countries, and the envisaged International Trade Organisation did not come into existence.[12] Still, the newly created institutions featured many institutional and legal links relating them to other sectors of macroeconomic policy-making, such as the provision against restrictions on current account transactions

---

[6] Gesetz zur Förderung der Stabilität und des Wachstums der Wirtschaft, 8 June 1967, BGBl I [1967] 582.

[7] John Maynard Keynes, 'Shaping the Post-War World: The Clearing Union', in John Maynard Keynes, *Collected Writings* XXV (Donald Moggridge ed., CUP 1980) 1, 121. On the Bancor see also Ernst Friedrich Schumacher, 'Multilateral Clearing' (1943) 10 *Economia* 150.

[8] John Maynard Keynes, 'Proposals for an International Clearing Union (1943)' in J Keith Horsefield (ed.), *The International Monetary Fund 1945–1965. Twenty Years of International Monetary Cooperation* (International Monetary Fund 1969) 19 ff <http://www.imsreform.org/reserve/pdf/keynesplan.pdf> accessed 27 August 2014.

[9] Cf. Keynes (n 8).

[10] James M Boughton, 'Why White, Not Keynes? Inventing the Postwar International Monetary System' (2002) IMF Working Paper WP/02/52, 5–6 <www.imf.org/external/pubs/ft/wp/2002/wp0252.pdf> accessed 20 February 2015.

[11] Rosa Maria Lastra, 'The International Monetary Fund in Historical Perspective' (2000) 3 JIEL 507, 511–12.

[12] Michael Trebilcock, Robert Howse and Antonia Eliason, *The Regulation of International Trade* (4th edn, Routledge 2013) 23 ff.

in the Articles of Agreement of the IMF,[13] or Article XV(2) of GATT 1947, the interface between trade liberalisation and exchange arrangements. These links evidence a more systemic, holistic approach in the post-war period.

In the decades that followed, it was not only realpolitik, but also theoretical contestations that changed the tide against Keynes. Friedrich Hayek presented a powerful renewal of the liberal view that relied on decentralised private action rather than governmental macroeconomic steering. He agreed with Keynes that human knowledge was highly imperfect, but he drew the opposite conclusion from this observation. In Hayek's view, society is most successful when it organises in a spontaneous fashion, leaving space for better solutions to emerge. Government interference in macroeconomic regulation should therefore be reduced to a minimum, including the provision of sound rules for competition.[14] In line with this mistrust in the capacity of governments to steer the economy, Dutch economist Jan Tinbergen argued that the different segments of the economy, in particular monetary policy, fiscal policy, and the maintenance of financial stability, should be assigned to different regulators who should then have only one primary task. In this way, macroeconomic regulation would benefit from the advantages of spontaneous organisation.[15] In the field of monetary policy, this approach resonated with the monetary theory of Milton Friedman. He thought that the quantity of money should develop in accordance with strict rules, irrespective of other macroeconomic concerns.[16] In addition, in order to reduce the risk that monetary policy would be abused for short-term governmental interests, or fall prey to the influence of interest groups, Friedman argued that central banks should be independent.[17] This paved the way for an even more fragmented regulation of macroeconomic issues.

---

[13] Art. VIII(2). For further references see Annamaria Viterbo, *International Economic Law and Monetary Measures* (Edward Elgar Publishing 2012) 62–3.

[14] Friedrich August von Hayek, *Law, Legislation and Liberty*, vol 1(U of Chicago Press 1973) 11, 38.

[15] Jan Tinbergen, *Economic Policy: Principles and Design* (North Holland Publishing Co 1956) 186 ff; Jan Tinbergen, *Centralization and Decentralization in Economic Policy* (North Holland Publishing Co 1954) 75.

[16] Milton Friedman, *The Optimum Quantity of Money and Other Essays* (Aldine Transaction 1969).

[17] Milton Friedman, *Capitalism and Freedom* (U of Chicago Press 2002) 51 ff.

After the collapse of the Bretton Woods system of dollar pegging in 1973,[18] functional separation in macroeconomic regulation became the state of the art. Apart from some exceptions and asynchronicities, the legal and institutional framework for the regulation of various macroeconomic issues developed in accordance with Tinbergen's theory of functional separation rather than with the Keynesian theory of interdependence, both on the domestic and on the international levels. Holistic elements that would overcome functional separation and provide a perspective on the entire spectrum of macroeconomic policy, as a consequence, have been relatively rare. Multilateral surveillance of domestic macroeconomic policy by the IMF has remained a relatively toothless tiger. It only gains significance in the exceptional case when a member actually draws on the fund.[19] Only what is now the G8 has provided a cross-sectoral forum for a more integrative discussion of macroeconomic issues since the end of the 1970s. By contrast, effective macroeconomic regulation tends to be sector-specific and is assigned to actors with competences that are usually limited to one particular task:

- In matters of monetary policy, the political momentum promoting the free movement of capital *de facto* overrode the provisions of the IMF Articles of Agreement, which to this day enable the control of capital transfers.[20] More and more States established independent central banks, especially since 1990. The European Monetary Union even made central bank independence an accession requirement.[21]
- In matters of bank regulation, the Basel Committee has developed an informal mode of coordination only since the end of the 1980s. However, it does not cover a number of significant aspects of financial market regulation. They fall under the responsibility of specialised organisations, such as the International Organization

[18] This was due to massive current account deficits of the US which the dollar-based Bretton Woods system did not allow to result in corresponding, necessary devaluations of the dollar.

[19] Armin Schäfer, 'Resolving Deadlock: Why International Organizations Introduce Soft Law' (2006) 12 Eur L J 194.

[20] Art. VI (3) IMF Articles of Agreement. On the development towards the free movement of capital beyond the European Union, see Claus D Zimmermann, *A Contemporary Concept of Monetary Sovereignty* (OUP 2013) 45 ff.

[21] Art. 130 TFEU.

of Securities Commissions (IOSCO), or private and hybrid organisations like the International Swaps and Derivatives Association (ISDA) and the International Accounting Standards Board (IASB).[22]

- In trade matters, the WTO emerged in 1994 on the basis of the substantive provisions of GATT 1947, including those on the relationship with the IMF. However, in practice, the organisation drew a clear line between trade and finance, paying full deference to the IMF for issues within the competence of the latter.[23]
- Other macroeconomic issues, such as fiscal policy (government expenditure), did not experience even the slightest form of international coordination, at least outside the European Union.[24]
- Finally, the law relating to investment protection developed rather independently from other segments of financial regulation.[25] More than that, it is dispersed over a great number of BITs and also has an internally fragmented structure, although it has been complemented with a fairly centralised and standardised system for the settlement of disputes that might induce the incremental development of common rules.[26] But most attempts to achieve its international, multilateral regulation have been in vain.[27]

The theory of functional separation might constitute the underlying deeper reason why international investment law is so highly fragmented, both with respect to other policy areas, and in its internal structure. In fact, both the internal structure of international investment law, and its relation to other policy areas, follows the Hayekian idea of spontaneous

---

[22] Christian Tietje, 'The International Financial Architecture as a Legal Order' (2011) 54 German YB Intl L 11, 20 ff; Maurizia De Bellis, 'Public law and Private Regulators in the Global Legal Space' (2011) 9 Intl J Constl L 425.

[23] Trebilcock and others (n 12) 236–9.

[24] Matthias Goldmann, 'On the Comparative Foundations of Principles in International Law: The Move Towards Rules and Transparency in Fiscal Policy as Examples' in Carlos Espósito, Yuefen Li and Juan Pablo Bohoslavsky (eds), *Sovereign Financing and International Law* (OUP 2013) 113.

[25] On the interaction of international investment law and other fields of international law see, e.g., Rainer Hofmann and Christian J Tams (eds), *International Investment Law and Its Others* (Nomos 2012).

[26] Stephan W Schill, *The Multilateralization of International Investment Law* (CUP 2009).

[27] Andreas F Lowenfeld, *International Economic Law* (2nd edn, OUP 2008) 494.

orders, rather than the Keynesian idea of holistic steering. States negotiate their BITs bilaterally; investors make their investment decisions accordingly; in case of conflicts, dispersed tribunals apply dispersed rules. This all amounts to a philosophy that seeks the supposedly best solution in a situation-specific way, while it mistrusts hierarchical institutional design, believing that chances for incremental development outweigh the risks of systemic failure.

B. The Financial Crisis: Recognising and Fighting Systemic Risks

The past financial crisis has to some extent called into question the theory of functional separation that also seems to underpin international investment law. Two related developments account for this in particular: the recognition of the role played by systemic risk, and the need for coordinated, more integrative responses. The latter became especially apparent in relation to unorthodox measures taken by central banks.

Soon after the collapse of Lehman Brothers, 'systemic risk' became the buzzword of the ensuing sub-prime crisis. In this context, systemic risk referred to a problem intrinsic to banking regulation. The focus of financial regulation on the micro-perspective, i.e., on the financial soundness of a single firm rather than of the entire financial industry, came to be recognised as a crucial factor that facilitated the spread of trouble from one financial institution to others that held similar assets, faced counter-party risks, or were exposed to generally deteriorating market conditions.[28] What is more, the sub-prime crisis soon created trouble for other parts of the financial sector. The deterioration of the financial industry required a monetary policy response that needed to confront a dried-up credit market. Further, it pushed some States into a sovereign debt crisis, due to public sector bailouts of private firms or lack of trust in sovereign debt sustainability because of the protracted nature of the recession, sinking tax revenue, and credit shortage, with a general lack of competitiveness in the background.[29] Systemic risks eventually led to a situation where the crisis affected almost all segments of the financial sector and of the economy.[30] However, hardly anyone had

---

[28] See e.g., Steven L Schwarcz, 'Systemic Risk' (2008) 97 Georgetown LJ 193; Christoph Ohler, 'International Regulation and Supervision of Financial Markets After the Crisis' (2010) 1 EurYB Intl Econ L 3, 19.

[29] See e.g., Gerhard Illing, Sebastian Jauch and Michael Zabel, 'Die Diskussion um den Euro. Endogene Risiken und multiple Gleichgewichte' (2012) 40 Leviathan 156.

[30] For an overview, see Ohler (n 28) 4–5.

expected such a systemic effect since each segment of the financial sector was in the hands of different actors at various levels of government.

Foreign direct investment is no exception in this respect. Exchange rates determine capital flows and consequently investment. Emerging economies like Brazil and Turkey, which benefitted from capital inflows due to low interest rates in developed economies after the crisis, now experience the reverse effects of this mechanism, as interest rates in the US have begun to rise again.[31] Banking crises raise the question of capital transaction controls which might affect those who have invested in the country concerned.[32] Foreign direct investment might also affect the domestic savings rate and hence impact upon financial stability and even monetary policy.[33]

The systemic dimension of the crisis raised doubts about the adequacy of narrow regulatory responses in line with the theory of functional separation. A principal example is the legal dispute arising in relation to certain unorthodox monetary policy measures. Since the beginning of the crisis, central banks have adopted several unprecedented measures that aimed at flooding the market with liquidity. The Federal Reserve and the European Central Bank (ECB) lowered their interest rates and expanded their balance sheets considerably, in order to mitigate the consequences of the banking crisis for the economy as a whole, arguably focusing not only on price stability. They accepted certain categories of troubled assets as collateral, albeit at huge discounts.[34] Moreover, at the height of the sovereign debt crisis, the ECB began purchasing sovereign bonds of troubled States under its controversial Securities Markets Programme (SMP). Whereas this programme had been limited in volume, the same did not apply to its successor, the Outright Monetary Transactions Programme (OMT) announced in July 2012.[35] The latter programme

---

[31] See <www.treasury.gov/resource-center/data-chart-center/interest-rates/Pages/Historic-LongTerm-Rate-Data-Visualization.aspx> accessed 27 August 2014.

[32] Cf. Art. VI(3) IMF Articles of Agreement; Zimmermann (n 20) 42.

[33] Luiz Bresser Pereira, *Development and Crisis in Brazil, 1930–83* (Westview Press 1984).

[34] On central bank balance sheets, see for the Fed <www.federalreserve.gov/monetarypolicy/quarterly-balance-sheet-developments-report.htm>, <www.federalreserve.gov/monetarypolicy/bst_recenttrends.htm>; for the ECB <www.ecb.europa.eu/stats/money/aggregates/bsheets/html/index.en.html> accessed 27 August 2014; on collateral see, e.g., Guideline of the European Central Bank on Additional Temporary Measures Relating to Eurosystem Refinancing Operations and Eligibility of Collateral and Amending Guideline ECB/2007/9 [2014] OJ L240/28.

[35] Decision of the European Central Bank of 14 May 2010 establishing a securities markets programme [2010] OJ L124/8; ECB, Press Release: Technical

never needed to be implemented since the prospect of its implementation, i.e., of massive purchases of sovereign bonds of troubled Eurozone countries by the ECB, calmed down the markets.

The OMT programme led to a dispute about its legality played out before the German Federal Constitutional Court and the Court of Justice of the European Union (CJEU) that calls the adequacy of the theory of functional separation directly into question. Indeed, the dispute reflects the disagreement between the theory of functional separation, on the one hand, and more integrative approaches to macroeconomic regulation, on the other.[36] The ECB considers OMT (as well as SMP) as coherent with its mandate to ensure price stability.[37] Accordingly, OMT and SMP target liquidity problems caused by the lack of market confidence in heavily indebted Eurozone countries. The fact that these policies have fiscal implications does not change their character as monetary policies. Thus, monetary policy may also look at, and affect, other sectors of financial regulation. By contrast, the German Federal Constitutional Court held that programme features of OMT, such as the requirement for States benefitting from sovereign bond purchases to implement an adjustment programme under the auspices of the European Stability Mechanism, revealed that it had a fiscal policy purpose.[38] It thus construed the scope of possible ECB measures much more narrowly, granting the ECB a small margin of discretion while exercising strict review. However, the CJEU followed the ECB's line of argument. It granted the ECB a wide margin of discretion for its monetary policy. In particular, the CJEU considered that the ECB may also tackle fiscal policy as long as it had an overall monetary policy goal and used monetary policy instruments in a proportionate manner.[39] The legal dispute resonates with a scholarly

---

Features of Outright Monetary Transactions, 6 September 2012 <www.ecb.europa.eu/press/pr/date/2012/html/pr120906_1.en.html> accessed 27 August 2014.

[36] Matthias Goldmann, 'Adjudicating Economics? Central Bank Independence and the Appropriate Standard of Judicial Review' (2014) 15(2) German LJ 265.

[37] Art. 127(1) TFEU.

[38] Federal Constitutional Court, 2 BvR 2728/13 of 14 January 2014, English version available at <www.bundesverfassungsgericht.de/entscheidungen/rs20140114_2bvr272813en.html> accessed 27 August 2014.

[39] Case C-62/14 *Gauweiler et al v Deutscher Bundestag*, ECLI:EU:C:2015:400, Judgment of 16 June 2015.

debate about whether and to what extent the concern for medium-term price stability justifies measures targeting financial stability.[40]

Both the experience of overlooked systemic risks, and the debate about more integrative responses, such as OMT, calls into question the theory of functional separation. So was Keynes right? Should economic policy follow a more holistic approach and give up the doctrine of functional separation in order to better recognise and fight systemic crises? Some insights of Hayek and the liberals can certainly not be rejected. Government institutions are subject to political pressures and special interests which decentralised, spontaneous organisation might avoid. One cannot simply return to square one in post-war economic thinking. However, it appears equally illusory to turn a blind eye to the systemic interrelations among the various segments of economic policy, as a crude version of the theory of functional separation would have it.[41] The debate is ongoing, with no identifiable outcome as yet. While having presented the developments in economic thinking in a highly simplified matter, leaving out many nuances, the broad consensus that seemingly existed with regard to the theory of functional separation for the past two decades or so has given way to essential contestations. This also concerns international investment law. How to prevent its detachment from other segments of financial regulation from exacerbating systemic crises then becomes the important question. Sovereign debt litigation before international investment tribunals, to name just one example, is definitely a case in point.[42]

C. Possible Responses: Institutional and Interpretative

There are two ways to give greater recognition to systemic interdependencies and facilitate systemic responses: on the one hand through policy-making and institutional design, on the other hand through the

---

[40] In favour of greater leeway for monetary policy: Committee on International Economic Policy and Reform, 'Rethinking Central Banking'(Brookings Institution 2011) 30 ff; Olivier Blanchard, Giovanni Dell'Ariccia and Paolo Mauro, 'Rethinking Macroeconomic Policy' (2010) IMF Staff Position Note SPN/10/03; with respect to the OMT Programme: Marcel Fratzscher and others, 'A Call for Support for the European Central Bank's OMT Programme' (19 July 2013) <https://berlinoeconomicus.diw.de/monetarypolicy/a-call-for-support-for-the-european-central-banks-omt-programme/> accessed 27 August 2014. For a survey of the respective views cf. Kai A Konrad and others, 'Bundesverfassungsgericht und Krisenpolitik der EZB – Stellungnahmen der Ökonomen' (2013) 93 Wirtschaftsdienst 431.

[41] See, however, the more nuanced view of Tinbergen (n 15) 186.

[42] See below, part IV.A.

interpretation and application of the applicable law. Regarding the former, institutional design needs to allow for a coherent, concerted response. This has led to the creation of new institutions. On the domestic level, bodies like the US Financial Stability Oversight Council (FSOC) and the European Systemic Risk Board (ESRB) now engage in macro-prudential oversight. They have strong institutional links with micro-prudential regulators, as is the case with the ESRB through the European Supervisory Authorities (ESAs) in the frame of the European System of Financial Supervision (ESFS),[43] or are directly involved in micro-prudential regulation, like the FSOC.[44] On the international level, the G20 and the Financial Stability Board (FSB) have become the leading international fora for the coordination of the regulatory response to the crisis. The FSB, which unites the regulatory agencies and central banks of the most important economies, operates under the supervision of the G20. Thus, for the first time, the interdependence of the various segments of economic policy has received recognition in the structure of global institutions. In theory, this might ensure coherence among various segments of economic policy, including trade and investment. Nevertheless, the G20 and the FSB not only lack compulsory decision-making powers, but their agendas have remained limited for a long time. Until far into the sovereign debt crisis, issues of fiscal policy or international investment law did not figure prominently.[45] In fact, it is unclear whether there is an institutional response that might mitigate risks deriving from the functional separation of international investment law from other segments of financial regulation.

Not least for these institutional and political shortcomings, one should take a look at the second set of possible responses, those relating to the interpretation and application of the *lex lata*. As the example of unorthodox monetary policies demonstrates, important parts of financial regulation broadly understood were drafted in accordance with the theory

---

[43] EU Regulation 1092/2010 of the European Parliament and of the Council of 24 November 2010 on European Union macro-prudential oversight of the financial system and establishing a European Systemic Risk Board [2010] OJ L331/1, 1 ff.

[44] Dodd Frank Act, Section 113(a)(1). The FSOC unites the Secretary of the Treasury and the chairpersons or directors of the Federal Reserve and the agencies involved in financial supervision. It monitors the emergence of systemic risks and issues recommendations and warnings.

[45] Christian Tietje, *Architektur der Weltfinanzordnung* (Institut für Wirtschaftsrecht Halle 2011) 27. Note, however, that the 2014 agenda of the G20 includes fiscal and monetary policy and considers their impact on economic growth, cf. <www.g20.org> accessed 27 August 2014.

of functional separation. However, they might be amenable to interpretations that take into account the insights about systemic interdependence gained from the crisis. The following sections first set out a theory of legal interpretation for that purpose, called the deliberative approach (III.), and then illustrate its operation in the field of international investment law (IV.).

III. TOWARDS A DELIBERATIVE APPROACH TO FINANCIAL REGULATION

This part argues that the insights into the systemic interdependence of the various segments of financial regulation gained through the financial crisis should give rise to an approach to legal interpretation in financial regulation that is commensurate to the challenge posed by the need to recognise and fight systemic risks. I call this a *deliberative approach.* It requires aligning the rationalities of different segments of financial regulation. I first develop the deliberative approach on a theoretical level (A.). In principle, the deliberative approach can be applied to financial regulation on the domestic, supranational and international levels. However, as each of these levels has specific rules relating to legal interpretation, I will focus in the subsequent sections on international economic law. I will show that the deliberative approach is in conformity with the rules governing the interpretation of international economic law. They allow taking into account rules relating to other segments of international economic law (B.). Further, systemic integration as an interpretative principle allows aligning the rationalities of the affected segments of international economic law (C.).

A. The Deliberative Approach

The deliberative approach to financial regulation understands law as a discursive framework for the resolution of problems of systemic interdependence, as a toolbox for figuring out situation-specific solutions that take the different rationalities of various segments of financial regulation into account. By contrast, it rejects an understanding of law as an instrument for the demarcation and enforcement of 'red lines' or 'Chinese walls' between those segments.

This approach to interpretation is based on an insight that is as trite as it is important, namely that law is indeterminate. Law, including international economic law, as a language-based normative system is confronted with the paradox that the meaning of language is always contextual,[46] whereas the whole point of legal rules, of their abstract and general character, is to provide more or less de-contextualised rules of behaviour. Indeterminacy is both the vice and virtue of the law. On the one hand, indeterminacy challenges the authority of the law and the whole idea of the rule of law. American Realism and Critical Legal Scholarship therefore tend to dismiss law as a means for steering society. In their view, it is not the law, but the political preferences of the law-applier that decide the outcome of a specific dispute.[47] On the other hand, indeterminacy may also be seen as a virtue of the law. It transforms law into a 'living instrument'[48] that offers some behavioural orientation to its addressees without imposing rigid, inflexible straightjackets.[49]

Indeterminacy therefore makes law an excellent tool for accommodating the diverging rationalities of the various functionally separated segments of financial regulation. The deliberative approach thus calls for a more integrative view of financial regulation, one that aims at aligning the rationality of one segment with the rationality of the rules of another.[50] This requires that one adopts a broader understanding of the rationality, or purpose, of each segment of financial regulation. A specific

---

[46] Ludwig Wittgenstein, *Philosophische Untersuchungen* (16th edn, Suhrkamp 2004) para. 43.

[47] Roberto Mangabeira Unger, *The Critical Legal Studies Movement* (Harvard UP 1986); David Kennedy, 'Theses About International Law Discourse' (1980) 23 German YBIL 353, 367; Martti Koskenniemi, *From Apology to Utopia* (2nd edn, CUP 2005) 590.

[48] *Tyrer v the United Kingdom*, App no 5856/78 (ECtHR, 25 April 1978) para. 31.

[49] Jürgen Habermas, *Faktizität und Geltung* (Suhrkamp 1992) 516 ff.

[50] Methodologically, the deliberative approach is based on the method of rational reconstruction as it has been developed by Jürgen Habermas. This is a general method that helps to construct coherent, understandable structures in an initially disordered environment with the help of guiding normative ideas. Comprehensively: Markus Patberg, 'Supranational Constitutional Politics and the Method of Rational Reconstruction' (2014) 40 *Philosophy & Social Criticism* 501. Habermas initially developed this method in order to reconstruct the practice of language guided by the idea of communicative reason and later applied it to the reconstruction of the practices of rule of law and democracy guided by discourse ethics. This chapter expands it to the reconstruction of the fragmented practice of international economic law guided by the idea of economic interdependence. For a more general approach that explores the potential of Habermas' method of rational reconstruction for legal doctrine ('*Dogmatik*') see Matthias Goldmann, 'Principles in International Law as Rational Reconstructions. A Taxonomy' (2013) <http://papers.ssrn.com/sol3/papers.cfm?abstract_id=2442027> accessed 16 February 2015.

regulatory regime (e.g., international investment law or monetary policy) should not be understood as being limited solely to the purposes of its own segment narrowly understood (to protect foreign direct investment or achieve price stability). Rather, each of these segmental regimes should be understood as implying a concern for the purposes of other segments, too. This is based on the following consideration: if one segment of financial regulation aims at an overall stable economic and financial order, it needs to take into account the multiple interdependencies among the various segments of financial regulation and the ensuing need to recognise and fight systemic risks. To give an example: the protection of foreign direct investment may not be achieved at the expense of severe effects to other segments such as sovereign debt sustainability; investment protection must find its limit where it would destabilise debt sustainability.

Granted, this is a very general, theoretical description of the deliberative approach. The precise extent to which rationalities of other segments should be taken into account defies any abstract definition. Rather, it depends on the circumstances of each specific case. The advantage of the deliberative approach does not lie in its specificity, but in providing a broad, general guideline; an understanding of law that encourages those applying it to look beyond the borders of the segment or regime in which they are operating. Implementing the deliberative approach in a particular legal order requires respecting the specific rules of legal interpretation applicable in that legal order. The following sections carve out the situation for international economic law.

B. Conformity with the Rules of Interpretation of International Economic Law

As far as international economic law is concerned, the deliberative approach is in conformity with the rules of legal interpretation stipulated in Articles 31 and 32 of the Vienna Convention on the Law of Treaties (VCLT). These provisions offer many avenues for taking other international agreements and their rationality into consideration when applying a particular rule of international law. Thus, under Article 31 VCLT, other international agreements can be taken into account in the interpretation of a particular rule of international law, whether they precede the creation of the rule in question (Art. 31(3)(c) VCLT), whether they were concluded in the same context as the rule in question (Art. 31(2) VCLT), or whether they followed at a later point in time (Art. 31(3)(a) and (b) VCLT). This applies to binding and non-binding agreements, although this is controversial with respect of some of the mentioned subsections of

Article 31 VCLT. For example, some would doubt that the term 'agreement' in Article 31(2)(a) VCLT covers non-binding instruments.[51] But these controversies are not central to the question at stake here. My main point is that interpreters will often find a way to take other rules of international economic law into account, if only as supplementary means of interpretation (Art. 32 VCLT) in order to confirm or further clarify the meaning established in accordance with Article 31 VCLT.

C. Systemic Integration in International Economic Law

The question is not only *whether* interpreters should or may take other rules into account, but also *how* they should understand the relationship between these rules. This is crucial for the deliberative approach, which suggests an interlinkage of the rationalities of diverging segments of financial regulation. Explicitly, Articles 31 and 32 VCLT only stipulate the circumstances under which other agreements, rules and practice should or may be taken into account, but not how to fathom out the relationship between the various rules. Two options come to mind in this respect.

A first option would be to apply rules of priority such as *lex specialis* or *lex posterior* that would establish a clear hierarchy among rules from different segments of international economic law. This is the approach pursued by the WTO in matters relating to exchange agreements, an issue which the WTO leaves entirely to the IMF to decide.[52] However, this approach merely reproduces the theory of functional separation. It does not take into account that the various segments of international economic law are interrelated. For example, IMF decisions on exchange arrangements, of course, have effects on trade. Indeed, their effects might be equivalent to that of tariffs.[53] Rules establishing hierarchies among different regimes of international economic law are therefore not helpful for the implementation of the deliberative approach.

---

[51] In favour: Anthony Aust, *Modern Treaty Law and Practice* (2nd edn, CUP 2007) 236; Rudolf Bernhardt, 'Interpretation and Implied (Tacit) Modification of Treaties' (1967) 27 ZaöRV 491, 499; against: Matthias Herdegen, 'Interpretation in International Law' in Rüdiger Wolfrum (ed.), *Max Planck Encyclopedia of Public International Law* (OUP 2010) para. 34. On the role of soft law for treaty interpretation under the VCLT, see Matthias Goldmann, *Internationale öffentliche Gewalt* (Springer 2015) 192 ff.

[52] Cf. supra n 23 and associated text.

[53] Vera Thorstensen, Daniel Ramos and Carolina Muller, 'The "Missing Link" Between the WTO and the IMF' (2013) 16 JIEL.

This brings me to the second option, to the concept of systemic integration. Systemic integration resembles what we know as 'systematic interpretation' in domestic law, although it should be distinguished. Systematic interpretation denotes the interpretation of a provision in the context of the treaty or legislative act of which it is part.[54] It does not refer to the interpretation of a provision in the context of general international law. This is what systemic integration is about. It aims at bringing the fragmented regimes of international law into a coherent order without attributing hierarchical superiority to one particular regime.[55] Systemic integration has often been associated with, and based on, Article 31(3)(c) VCLT. However, courts do not refer to this provision very often when they try to solve conflicts between different regimes in a non-hierarchical fashion.[56] Indeed, they use a host of interpretative techniques to solve conflicts between diverging international legal regimes, including context, purpose and subsequent practice.[57] One could therefore say that systemic integration is an interpretative concept applicable in any situation where Articles 31 and 32 VCLT allow or require the consideration of other agreements.

In principle, the idea of systemic integration appeals to the concern of the deliberative approach, which is to combine diverging rationalities. Nevertheless, there is one risk associated with systemic integration: it might lead the interpreter to take the coherence of international economic law too seriously and understand it monolithically as a fixed order that only requires an omniscient, herculean interpreter to extract its contradiction-free master plan.[58] Such an idea of international economic law would suffer from flaws similar to those of Keynes's holistic idea of macroeconomic steering. Where Keynes overestimated the capacity of

---

[54] Herdegen (n 51) para. 12-3.

[55] International Law Commission, 'Fragmentation of International Law: Difficulties Arising from the Diversification and Expansion of International Law', Report of the Study Group, finalized by Martti Koskenniemi, (2006) YBILC vol II pt 2, paras 410–480; Campbell McLachlan, 'The Principle of Systemic Integration and Article 31(3)(c) of the Vienna Convention' (2008) 54 Intl & Comp LQ 279.

[56] Erika de Wet and Jure Vidmar, 'Conflicts Between International Paradigms: Hierarchy versus Systemic Integration' (2013) 2 Global Constitutionalism 196, 210.

[57] Michael Waibel, 'Demystifying the Art of Interpretation' (2011) 22(2) EJIL 571, 581.

[58] For an elaboration of this approach cf. Ronald Dworkin, *Taking Rights Seriously* (Harvard UP 1977).

governments to implement policies, such an idea of international economic law would overestimate the capacity of courts and others applying international economic law to interpret the law in a holistic manner resulting in an optimal outcome for all of its segments. I believe that this would overburden any interpreter who watches the relevant provisions only from his or her concrete position as an agent of a particular segment of financial regulation, and not from 'above', from a neutral, overarching viewpoint. Even more: in a fragmented field like international economic law, such an overarching viewpoint remains unavailable.[59]

Therefore, a more pluralistic understanding of systemic integration seems apposite for the deliberative approach. It needs to dispense with the idea of a fully coherent international economic order and accept that each segment of international economic law follows its own rationality. In this pluralistic setting, systemic integration as an interpretative principle requires actors in each segment to recognise interdependence among the various segments and to factor the concerns of other segments of international economic law into its own rationality to the extent possible.[60]

The pluralistic variant of systemic integration does not end up in mere casuistry.[61] Rather, the deliberative approach provides methodological, though not substantive, orientation for the establishment of coherence. Again, it requires taking into account other segments of international economic law in the interpretation of a specific provision to the extent that they can be aligned with the purpose of the segment to which that provision belongs. This implies that there might be more than one 'right' solution to a given case, that one and the same case might look different from one segment as opposed to another. But the task of recognising and fighting systemic risks might precisely require different perspectives on one and the same case, provided that they are not blind to each other.

---

59 Rainer Hofmann and Christian J Tams, 'International Investment Law: Situating an Exotic Special Regime within the Framework of General International Law' in Rainer Hofmann and Christian J Tams, (eds), *International Investment Law and General International Law* (Nomos 2011) 9, 11–12. For a thorough theoretical critique of holistic approaches, cf. Habermas (n 49) 272 ff; Ralph Christensen and Andreas Fischer-Lescano, 'Die Einheit der Rechtsordnung. Zur Funktionsweise der holitischen Semantik' (2006) 4 Zeitschrift für Rechtsphilosophie 8. See also Ingo Venzke, *How Interpretation Makes International Law* (OUP 2013) 63 (on the subjective character of semantic authority).

60 This resembles the judicial dialogue model, which has been proposed as a model for systemic integration by Armin von Bogdandy and Ingo Venzke, *In Whose Name?* (OUP 2014) 189 ff.

61 But see International Law Commission (n 55) para. 474.

In principle, any provision of international economic law is susceptible to systemic integration thus understood. Nevertheless, some types of rules might be particularly amenable to it. I think of (1) broadly phrased general clauses that are by definition open to a wide range of possible interpretations, such as the proportionality principle; and (2) rules granting discretion to the decision-maker to choose among different legal consequences. Systemic integration might further (3) inspire courts to apply a specific standard of review: accordingly, a decision is justified if it cherishes the idea of systemic integration, i.e., if it takes the rationality of other segments of international economic law into account, although one might rationally disagree with the result.[62] By contrast, I do not think that specific, technical rules constitute a primary field of application for systemic integration, unless they can be weighed against a rule of the type (1) or (2) mentioned above. An example would be the necessity defence, whether under Articles XX, XXI GATT or the customary law defence codified in Article 25 of the Draft Articles on State Responsibility. Such exceptions compel the interpreter to balance the rationality of the legal regime in question (e.g., trade law) with the rationality pursued by the exception (e.g., human rights, environmental concerns).[63]

IV. IMPLICATIONS FOR INVESTMENT LAW

The methodological approach proposed in the preceding part has implications for international economic law generally, but also for international investment law and the interpretative approaches that should be chosen by investment treaty tribunals. This part presents only a small selection of three case studies that show how investment tribunals might put the deliberative approach into practice. They deal with sovereign debt workouts and their relationship with investment treaty tribunals and their application of the FET standard (A.), with bank rescue operations and the

---

62 Cf. Goldmann (n 36).

63 In the context of investment law, see James Crawford, 'International Protection of Foreign Direct Investments: Between Clinical Isolation and Systematic Integration' in Hofmann and Tams (n 59) 17; Lars Markert, 'International Investment Law and Treaty Interpretation – Problems, Particularities and Possible Trends' in ibid 53, 65–9; in the WTO context: Gabrielle Marceau, 'A Call for Coherence in International Law. Praises for the Prohibition Against "Clinical Isolation" in WTO Dispute Settlement' (1999) 33 J World Trade 87; in relation to human rights, see de Wet and Vidmar (n 56).

national treatment standard (B.), and with unorthodox monetary policy measures and their interaction with the FET standard (C.).

A. Investment Law and Sovereign Debt Workout Measures

The first case study takes the interaction of international investment law with sovereign debt workouts as an example. Today, there are many international efforts to facilitate the resolution of sovereign debt crises, even though a Sovereign Debt Resolution Mechanism did not come into existence when it was proposed by the IMF in 2003.[64] Still, since about the end of the 1980s, international institutions and States have made enormous efforts to facilitate exit from the debt trap. The Paris Club, the venue of bilateral creditors (i.e., States), changed its terms in order to facilitate debt relief.[65] Together with the IMF and the World Bank, it set up the Heavily Indebted Poor Countries Initiative, which has successfully brought over three dozen developing countries out of the debt trap.[66] The IMF has repeatedly changed its access terms with a view to enabling debtor States to receive support in time before their situation gets worse.[67]

These remarkable, although far from perfect, efforts are jeopardised by holdout litigation before domestic courts and international investment tribunals.[68] Since the 1990s, sovereign debt has been increasingly issued in the form of sovereign bonds, and prior syndicated loans were

64 Background: Randal Quarles, 'Herding Cats: Collective-Action Clauses in Sovereign Debt –The Genesis of the Project to Change the Market Practice in 2001 through 2003' (2010) 73 L & Contemp Probs 29.

65 Debt relief began with the adoption of the Toronto Terms of the Paris Club in 1988. See <http://www.clubdeparis.org/en/communications/page/toronto-terms> accessed 23 March 2016.

66 For a current list see <https://www.imf.org/external/np/hipc/eng/pdf/hipccountries.pdf> accessed 23 March 2016.

67 Udaibir S Das, Michael G Papaioannou and Christoph Trebesch, 'Sovereign Debt Restructurings 1950-2010: Literature Survey, Data, and Stylized Facts' (2012) IMF Working Paper 203, <www.imf.org/external/pubs/ft/wp/2012/wp12203.pdf> accessed 16 February 2015; Armin von Bogdandy and Matthias Goldmann, 'Sovereign Debt Restructurings as Exercises of International Public Authority: Towards a Decentralized Sovereign Insolvency Law' in Espósito and others (n 24) 39.

68 For an overview see Michael Waibel, *Sovereign Defaults Before International Courts and Tribunals* (CUP 2011). On domestic litigation Lee C Buchheit and Jeremiah S Pam, 'The Pari Passu Clause in Sovereign Debt Instruments' (2004) 53 Emory LJ 869; Ugo Panizza, Federico Sturzenegger and Jeromin Zettelmeyer, 'The Economics and Law of Sovereign Debt and Default'

transformed into such bonds.[69] They were purchased by private retail investors. In case of a debt crisis, many of them exchange their old bonds for new ones with reduced principal and interest payments. However, some bondholders do not participate in the bond exchanges and instead sue the debtor State for the nominal amount of the old bonds. Some of them do not sue themselves, but sell their bonds at huge discounts to institutional investors, also known as 'vulture funds' who then sue the debtor State in order to make a profit from the difference between the nominal value and the market prices of such bonds.[70] Such suits are known as holdout litigation. Most holdout litigation takes place before domestic courts, but some claims have been lodged before arbitral tribunals. In the recent *Abaclat* case, the ICSID Tribunal held such litigation to be admissible under the applicable investment law agreements.[71] More cases might follow, since sovereign debt instruments might be covered by many BITs.[72] Collective Action Clauses facilitate bond exchanges by majority vote. But they are not included in all bonds, especially old ones. Whether legislative measures to introduce such clauses retroactively will survive judicial scrutiny remains untested.[73]

(2009) 47 J Econ Lit 651; as well as the contributions by Ohler, Li, Kupelyants and Sudreau in this volume.

[69] Lowenfeld (n 27) 681 ff; Manuel Monteagudo, 'The Debt Problem: The Baker Plan (1985) and the Brady Initiative (1989) – History, Experience, Practice and Prospects' in Dominique Carreau and Malcom Shaw (eds), *The External Debt/La dette extérieure* (Brill 1995) 139.

[70] Jill E Fisch and Caroline M Gentile, 'Vultures or Vanguards?: The Role of Litigation in Sovereign Debt Restructuring' (2004) 53 Emory LJ 1043; Kevin P Gallagher, 'The New Vulture Culture: Sovereign Debt Restructuring and Trade and Investment Treaties' (2011) The IDEAs Working Paper Series 2, <http://www.ase.tufts.edu/gdae/publications/GallagherSovereignDebt.pdf> accessed 16 February 2015.

[71] *Abaclat v Argentine Republic*, ICSID Case No ARB/07/5, Decision on Jurisdiction and Admissibility (4 August 2011). But see *Poštová banka, as and Istrokapital SE v Greece*, ICSID Case No ARB/13/8, Award (9 April 2015), where the Tribunal declined to view a bond as an investment under the governing BIT.

[72] Kevin P Gallagher, 'Financial Crises and International Investment Agreements: The Case of Sovereign Debt Restructuring' (2012) 3 *Global Policy* 362; see Charles N Brower and Alexandra Goetz-Charlier, 'International Investment Arbitration and the Global Financial System: Are They "Yin" and "Yang" or like Oil and Water?' (in this volume) 23, 27 ff for further comment.

[73] On the risks of such legislation: Lee C Buchheit and Mitu Gulati, 'How to Restructure Greek Debt' (2010) SSRN Working Paper <http://ssrn.com/abstract=

Where they are applicable, holdout creditors might still manage to acquire a blocking minority so that the bond exchange can be prevented.[74]

On substance, one might therefore consider whether and to what extent the FET standard should afford protection to investors choosing to hold out and litigate under an investment treaty. FET, inter alia, requires respecting the legitimate expectations of investors at the time of the investment.[75] This does not exclude legislative changes as long as they can be considered as part of the normal evolution of regulation.[76] Problems might arise, however, if an investor has received specific assurances from the host State that his or her claim will be respected. Such assurances might derive from a contract, in this case from the sovereign bond. Also, breaking contractual obligations by means of sovereign powers usually violates the FET standard.[77] This results in potential conflicts between investment protection and international efforts at debt relief.

General international law offers a number of potential solutions to this dilemma. Invoking necessity as a defence might be one, but it has not always worked properly for the debtor State.[78] Another, largely untested possibility is to invoke good faith as a general principle of law.[79] One

---

1603304> accessed 27 August 2014, 10 ff. These risks almost materialised in *Poštová banka v Greece* (n 71).

74 Mitu Gulati and Anna Gelpern, 'Sovereign Snake Oil' (2011) 73 Law & Contemp Probs i; Fisch and Gentile (n 70) 1094–5.

75 Rudolf Dolzer and Christoph Schreuer, *Principles of International Investment Law* (2nd edn, OUP 2012) 146.

76 Ibid., 149.

77 Ibid., 152; *Bayindir Insaat Turizm Ticaret Ve Sanayi AS v Islamic Republic of Pakistan*, ICSID Case No ARB/03/29, Award (27 August 2009) para. 377; *Consortium RFCC v Royaume du Maroc* ICSID Case No ARB/00/6, Award (22 December 2003) paras 33 ff.

78 Stephan W Schill, 'International Investment Law and the Host State's Power to Handle Economic Crises. Comment on the ICSID Decision in LG&E v Argentina' 24 (2007) J Intl Arb 265; Christina Binder, 'Changed Circumstances in Investment Law: Interfaces between the Law of Treaties and the Law of State Responsibility with a Special Focus on the Argentine Crisis' in Christina Binder and others (eds), *International Investment Law for the 21st Century* (OUP 2009) 608; Christina Binder, 'Stability and Change in Times of Fragmentation: The Limits of *Pacta Sunt Servanda* Revisited' (2012) 25 Leiden J Intl L 909, 916 ff (emphasising at 933 that regime-specific emergency clauses might work better in economic crises; however, they do not facilitate debt workouts).

79 See UNCTAD, Sovereign Debt Workouts: Going Forward. Roadmap and Guide (2015) <http://unctad.org/en/PublicationsLibrary/gdsddf2015misc1_

might also consider holdout creditors as abusing their rights because they create disproportionate harm to the debtor State, as well as to other creditors.[80]

In addition to these solutions offered by general international law, the systemic integration of the FET standard with efforts to restructure unsustainable sovereign debt might offer another solution in line with the deliberative approach. This requires interpreting the concept of legitimate expectations in a more pluralistic fashion and to accommodate the needs of the regime governing sovereign debt workouts to the extent that they can be aligned with the rationality of international investment law. Accordingly, investment law should ensure fair conditions for investors. It is not among the purposes of investment law to facilitate the unfair treatment of some investors (those who accept bond exchange offers) to the benefit of other investors in the same situations (those who chose to litigate). Hence, the FET standard should only protect investors against unfair sovereign debt workout procedures, for example against non-transparent and inaccessible negotiations, or against unilateral debt repudiation without any negotiations at all. In that respect, investment tribunals' exercise of jurisdiction would be welcome – both from an investment law and a sovereign debt law perspective. Investment tribunals would offer a great opportunity to enforce the procedural rights of creditors and debtors, and ensure the good faith character of negotiations, as long as they do not pose a serious risk to necessary sovereign debt restructurings. In this respect, it is deplorable that the tribunal in *Poštová banka* declined jurisdiction entirely – with reasons related to the special character of sovereign debt that might have better justified a rejection of the claims on the merits.[81]

---

en.pdf>, accessed 23 March 2016, 22–3, 29–31; Matthias Goldmann, 'Necessity and Feasibility of a Standstill Rule for Sovereign Debt Workouts' (2013) Paper prepared for the UNCTAD Working Group on a Debt Workout Mechanism, <http://www.unctad.info/upload/Debt%20Portal/DWM%20Goldmann%20Standstill%20Study%2020140123.pdf> accessed 27 August 2014. For the opposite view, see the judgment of the German Federal Court of Justice, case XI YR 193/14 (24 February 2015); Matthias J Müller, 'Zum Verhältnis von Staaten und ihren privaten Anleihegläubigern. Zugleich Besprechung von BGH, RIW 2015, 294' (2015) 61 Recht der Internationalen Wirtschaft 717.

[80] Cf. UNCTAD Principles on Promoting Responsible Sovereign Lending and Borrowing (2012), Principle 7 <http://unctad.org/en/PublicationsLibrary/gdsddf2012misc1_en.pdf> accessed 7 December 2016.

[81] *Poštová banka v Greece* (n 71) paras 317 ff, especially 320.

B. Investment Law and Rescue Measures in the Banking Sector

The second situation concerns rescue measures for banks which discriminate against foreign creditors. What I have in mind is not the issue of bail-ins and the trouble they might cause for international investment law.[82] Rather, I would like to address the simultaneous default of three Icelandic banks in 2008.

Iceland transferred claims of domestic depositors against these banks to new, publicly guaranteed banks on the basis of an emergency law.[83] By contrast, the claims of numerous foreign depositors remained with the failed institutions.[84] Although the deposit guarantee schemes of the host countries of the failed Icelandic bank's foreign subsidiaries applied to these funds and afforded at least partial compensation to the depositors, some of these claims may also enjoy the protection of international investment law provided that they fall under the definition of investment stipulated in applicable BITs. The financial crisis seems to have increased the definitional mayhem surrounding the term 'investment'. Applying the *Salini* criteria,[85] at least long-term deposits with maturities of two years or more might count as investment under Article 25 of the ICSID Convention.[86] A number of BITs, as well as the 2012 US Model BIT, clearly cover such claims as 'investments' since they cover all debt without qualification as part of their substantive scope of application.[87] For the sake of the argument, I assume in the following that the claims are protected by investment law. Iceland's safeguarding of domestic depositors, as opposed to foreign ones, might therefore violate applicable clauses on national treatment. Had Iceland refrained from compensating

---

[82] See Maurice Mendelson and Martins Paparinskis, 'Bail-Ins and International Investment Law: In and Beyond Cyprus' (in this volume) 193; as well as Maximilian Hocke, 'Have Measures Adopted by States to Cope with the Global Financial Crisis Been in Accordance with Their Obligations under International Investment Law?' (2012) 4 Goettingen J Intl L 177, 192 ff.

[83] Act No 125/2008 on the Authority for Treasury Disbursements due to Unusual Financial Market Circumstances etc, <http://eng.forsaetisraduneyti.is/media/English/unusual_financial_market_circumstances.pdf> accessed 27 August 2014.

[84] For the full story, see Michael Waibel, 'Iceland's Financial Crisis – *Quo Vadis* International Law' (2010) 14 ASIL Insight No 5.

[85] *Salini Costruttori SpA and Italstrade SpA v Kingdom of Morocco*, ICSID Case No ARB/00/4, Decision on Jurisdiction (31 July 2001) para. 53 (English translation at 42 ILM 609 (2003); (2004) 6 ICSID Rep 400).

[86] Disagreeing: Hocke (n 82) 188.

[87] Cf. Herdegen (n 51) 388.

its domestic creditors, the economic and social consequences for its population would have been severe. However, had Iceland extended such compensation to all depositors, the volume would have overburdened Iceland's financial capacity, given that the balance sheets of the three failed banks exceeded the country's gross domestic product by more than 11 times.[88]

The question of national treatment guarantees was examined by the European Free Trade Association (EFTA) Court.[89] Article 4 of the Agreement on the European Economic Area (EEA) prohibits discrimination on the basis of nationality. The EFTA Court found a solution which is specific to the applicable law in this case. The prohibition of discrimination under Article 4 of the EEA Agreement is only applicable to acts falling within the scope of the EEA Agreement, such as the Deposit Guarantee Directive.[90] Technically speaking, Iceland did not make payments to domestic depositors under its deposit guarantee scheme established in accordance with the Directive, but compensated them by transferring their deposits to government-backed banks. Hence, the Court found no discrimination on the part of Iceland.[91] However, under international investment law, such a technical solution that is based on a narrow reading of the scope of Article 4 of the EEA Agreement would be unavailable. Iceland would be faced with a direct discrimination in violation of the national treatment standard.

The approach relying on the deliberative rationality of international investment law might devise a better solution. Old-style BITs contain no exemptions for prudential measures. Accordingly, it would be necessary to explore possible *intrinsic* limits to the national treatment standard. Investment law as a legal regime has the purpose of furthering economic development. It cannot be the point of the investment law regime to force a country into IMF loans and bilateral lending. Investment arbitration should therefore not severely compromise the stability of the economic

---

[88] Willem H Buiter and Anne C Siebert, 'The Icelandic Banking Crisis and What to Do about it: The Lender of Last Resort Theory of Optimal Currency Areas', in Robert Aliber and Gylfi Zoega (eds) *Preludes to the Icelandic Financial Crisis* (Palgrave Macmillan 2011) 241.

[89] A precedent in the field of investment law is *Saluka Investments BV (The Netherlands) v Czech Republic*, Permanent Court of Arbitration, Partial Award (17 March 2006).

[90] Directive 94/19/EC of the European Parliament and of the Council of 30 May 1994 on deposit-guarantee schemes [1994] OJ L135/5.

[91] Case E-16/11, *EFTA Surveillance Authority v Iceland* [2013] EFTA Court Report 4.

and financial system of a whole country. Investment arbitration has rightly held that the full protection and security standard entitles investors to a stable legal system.[92] *Mutatis mutandis*, this should also apply to economic and financial stability concerns. It would be a perverse consequence of international investment law if it gave rise to economic or financial instability. In such circumstances, the overriding interest in the stability of the domestic economy justifies violations of the national treatment standard, or leads to a teleological reduction of its scope of application.[93] Where modern BITs and free trade agreements (FTAs) contain exemptions for prudential measures, tribunals might nevertheless have recourse to these considerations for purposes of interpretation. The scope of such exemptions can be disputed. Thus, Article 1410 NAFTA, which the US government believed to exempt prudential measures entirely from scrutiny by investment tribunals,[94] was interpreted more narrowly by a tribunal which saw itself obliged to examine the reasonableness of prudential measures.[95] This reference to the reasonableness of prudential measures opens the gate for the deliberative approach. An investment tribunal may align the purposes of investment protection and prudential regulation in accordance with what has been said with reference to old-style BITs.

In the example of Iceland, following the deliberative approach, one might consider the measures of the government as justified from that angle. In a situation where all three major banks of a country break down, asymmetric bailouts of domestic creditors can – at least to a certain extent – be justified as measures for the protection of the domestic economy as a whole. The fact that Iceland also imposed restrictions on capital transactions fits into the picture. It therefore seems likely that the asymmetric bailouts would be considered necessary for the protection of economic and financial stability. In case of an old-style BIT, this reasoning would bring asymmetric bailouts in line with the purposes of the treaty. Under a modern FTA or BIT, the bailouts would pass the test of reasonableness.

---

[92] *Siemens AG v The Argentine Republic*, ICSID Case No ARB/02/8, Award (17 January 2007) para. 303.

[93] Cf. also Dolzer and Schreuer (n 75) 203.

[94] US House of Representatives, Hearing before the Committee on Banking, Finance and Urban Affairs, 103rd Congress, First Session, 28 September 1993, Statement of Allene D Evans, 99 <http://www.archive.org/stream/financialservice00unit/financialservice00unit_djvu.txt> accessed 23 March 2016.

[95] *Fireman's Fund Investment Company v Mexico*, ICSID Case No ARB(AF)/02/01, Award (17 July 2006) paras 156 ff.

C. Investment Law and Unorthodox Monetary Policy Measures

The last case study relates to unorthodox policy measures of central banks. I do not want to delve here into the question of capital controls or exchange agreements.[96] Rather, I would like to look at the increase in liquidity resulting from post-crisis central bank policies from an investment perspective. This might put investors' interests at risk, especially if they hold financial assets that are subject to inflationary risks. Economically speaking, the devaluation of debt or other financial assets might amount to partial expropriation. In an investment law perspective, however, expropriation presupposes that the investor does not retain control over the asset in question.[97] Instead, one might ask if and when such monetary policy violates investors' legitimate expectations protected by the FET standard, in particular in jurisdictions where the central bank is legally bound to guard price stability (e.g., under Art. 127 TFEU). If such measures are found to breach the FET standard, investment law might interfere with monetary policy.

Again, the answer the deliberative approach would suggest to resolve this conflict is to analyse to what extent unorthodox monetary policy measures might be considered as compatible with the purposes of investment protection. Investments depend to a large extent on financial stability, which is necessary for capital and current account transfers and for the preservation of the deposits of investors and their counterparties. Therefore, higher inflation risks might to a certain extent have to be accepted even if they were unexpected and might depreciate the value of certain investments in financial assets.

Investment tribunals do not need to fully defer to central banks to determine how much inflation risk is acceptable in the short term in order to ensure financial stability in the long term. But they might choose not to intervene as long as the decision of the central bank appears rationally justifiable in a monetary policy perspective, and as long as the central bank makes its reasons transparent.[98] This is because the deliberative approach also applies to central banks, not just to courts and tribunals. The latter need to check the reasonableness of central bank measures. This includes a scrutiny of the procedures in which they were adopted. In

---

96 See the chapter by Prabash Ranjan, 'Capital-Flow Management Measures and International Investment Law – Never the Twain Shall Meet?' (in this volume) 257.

97 Dolzer and Schreuer (n 75) 117.

98 Cf. *Gauweiler et al* (n 39) para. 70.

this way, central banks and investment tribunals might keep each other in check without unnecessarily interfering with the legal regime of the other.[99]

V. CONCLUSION

Some of these case studies might work better than others. In any event, I hope that they allow an illustration of how I imagine the relationship between investment law and other segments of international economic law as well as the institutions which govern them. The approach means a step away from the theory of functional separation, which still pervades much of contemporary practice. It requires investment tribunals to take into account the rationalities of other segments of international economic law in order to afford better protection against systemic risks. One might consider this solution unsatisfactory as investment tribunals appear misplaced to answer questions relating to sovereign debt sustainability, prudential regulation, and monetary policy, for which they have neither the expertise, nor the appropriate information or policy instruments at hand.

However, this approach does not require investment tribunals to replace the assessment of other, more competent institutions with theirs. It only requests investment arbitration to accommodate other perspectives to the extent possible *within* the purposes of international investment law. This presupposes understanding international investment law in a more holistic way as an integral part of financial regulation and of international economic law. Tribunals need to bring it in harmony with other segments of financial regulation and international economic law by way of systemic integration. But in doing so, investment tribunals should not and must not play the role of the super-regulator. They should only keep other decision-makers in check to the extent that their policies cannot be aligned with the purposes of investment law, broadly understood. This rationality check goes further than a mere control for arbitrariness, as it engages with the substance of the decision stemming from the other segment. But it does not substitute the judgment of other decision-makers with that of investment tribunals.

Of course, the deliberative approach suggested here is very broad and ambiguous. It does not claim that there is only one right answer to a

---

[99] On the relationship between central banks and domestic courts, see Goldmann (n 36); and further Matthias Goldmann, 'Constitutional Pluralism as Mutually Assured Destruction' (2016) 23 Maastricht JE&CL 119.

given legal dispute. The weight of international investment law relative to other segments of financial regulation is not fixed. At the same time, this relativity makes it adaptable to the rationalities of different segments of financial regulation. Like financial regulation, law is a fragmented, indeterminate, contested, and above all deliberative structure. It challenges us to continuously seek to understand other fields of society which follow different rationalities. As I tried to show, I see this as a virtue, not a vice.

PART II

Sovereign debt restructurings

4. Police powers of the state in sovereign debt restructurings

Hayk Kupelyants

I. INTRODUCTION

Sovereign debt defaults and restructurings are and have always been common phenomena in international finance.[1] A sovereign debtor, in the throes of a financial crisis or mismanagement of its public finance, often resorts to sovereign debt restructurings in its various manifestations: extensions of maturities, reductions of interest and/or principal, modification of the sovereign bond documentation and so forth.

Sovereign debt crises and restructurings, in their various forms, are often accompanied by references to various adverse consequences and external factors so as to create space for the State's budgetary and social needs. Such consequences and factors commonly include the duty of the borrower towards its population,[2] the consideration of human rights in sovereign financing,[3] the responsibility of the international community to

[1] Carmen Reinhart and Kenneth Rogoff, *This Time is Different: Eight Centuries of Financial Folly* (Princeton UP 2011).

[2] United Nations Conference on Trade and Development (UNCTAD) *Principles on Promoting Responsible Sovereign Lending and Borrowing* (United Nations 2012), Principle I.1 (Agency).

[3] Juan Pablo Bohoslavsky and Jernej Letnar Cernic (eds), *Making Sovereign Financing and Human Rights Work* (Hart 2014); Matthias Goldmann, 'Human Rights and Sovereign Debt Workouts' (2014) <http://papers.ssrn.com/sol3/papers.cfm?abstract_id=2330997> accessed 24 March 2016; Sabine Schlemmer-Schulte, 'Fragmentation of International Law: The Case of International Finance & Investment Law Versus Human Rights Law' (2012) 25 Pac McGeorge Global Bus & Dev LJ 409. The issue of impact of foreign financing on regimes involved in gross human rights violations may deserve better treatment, on which see Juan Pablo Bohoslavsky, 'Report on Financial Complicity: Lending to States Engaged in Gross Human Rights Violations' (2014) UN General Assembly A/HRC/28/59, especially para. 35.

fight global poverty and ensure socio-economic human rights in times of crises,[4] and the ethics of and fairness in dealing with an unsustainable debt burden.[5]

In this sense, the UN General Assembly – in spite of the opposition from major developed countries – adopted in September 2015 basic principles of sovereign debt restructurings driven by the idea that the existing system was inadequate to the State's obligations towards its population and insufficient to resolve the growing incidents of sovereign debt crises.[6] In the 1970s, developing countries (the Group of 77) expressed their commitment to the establishment of the New International Economic Order in the arena of sovereign debt, to alleviate the pressures of unsustainable stock of debt by sharing the financial burden with creditor countries and the international community.[7]

Against the background of this sentiment, the State in sovereign debt restructurings can thus be excused for acting under the general conviction that it takes its actions in the interest of the wider public and therefore the bondholders' interests have to succumb. This state of affairs, some may argue, is in principle capable of legitimising the use of coercive powers of the State under international law and validating the deployment of the arsenal of public acts in sovereign debt restructurings. In this sense, the Tribunal in *Continental Casualty v Argentina* seems to have reasoned on the assumption that the State has the right to regulate (police powers) in sovereign debt restructurings as a matter of international law:

> Expropriation, even indirect, requires a certain level of sacrifice of private property in order to be found. Minor losses that are an incidental consequence to a general regulation of the economy adopted in the public interest are not considered to be expropriation giving rise to indemnification as highlighted

---

[4] Margot Salomon, *Global Responsibility for Human Rights: World Poverty and the Development of International Law* (OUP 2007); Dimitris Chorafas, *Sovereign Debt Crisis: The New Normal and the Newly Poor* (Palgrave Macmillan 2011).

[5] Christian Barry, Barry Herman and Lydia Tomitova (eds), *Dealing Fairly with Developing Country Debt* (Blackwell Publishing 2007).

[6] United Nations General Assembly (UNGA) Res 319 (10 September 2015), 'Basic Principles on Sovereign Debt Restructuring Processes' A/RES/69/319.

[7] Milan Bulajic, 'Indebtness of Developing Countries and New International Economic Order' in Detlev Dicke (ed.), *Foreign Debts in the Present and a New International Economic Order* (Westview Press 1986) 64–5, 71. See also UNGA Res 3202 (1 May 1974), 'Programme of Action on the Establishment of a New International Economic Order' A/RES/S-6/3202, paras II.2.f. and g.

> before. This is applicable to the delays in payments of interest (that were subsequently made) and in the issuance of certain bonds (that were in any case delivered later to CNA) of which Continental complains. In the disarray Argentina was facing in 2002, these non compliances are covered in any case by the plea of necessity under the BIT.[8]

In this respect, the clarification of the scope of police powers that the State enjoys under international law in sovereign debt restructurings becomes of crucial interest. At the outset, an international tribunal might treat the police powers of the State as a question of capacity under the (domestic) law that applies to the sovereign debt contract (or perhaps the law of the sovereign debtor). This analysis cannot, however, supersede an investigation into the existence of police powers under international law, since the police powers of the State relate to the application of international standards of protection and may be regulated by international law.[9]

The focus of this chapter will thus be on the existence and deployment of the right to regulate (police powers) in sovereign debt restructurings as a matter of international law. Does the State have police powers in modifying its own financial obligations? What is the extent of these powers?

The risk of the use of police powers in sovereign debt restructurings is most apparent when sovereign bonds of the State are governed by the domestic law of the sovereign debtor. In such a case, the State may be tempted to modify its own domestic law and thus modify the extent of its financial obligations, subject to its domestic law. A clear example was the Greek debt restructuring of 2012 where the Greek Parliament introduced an act of Parliament modifying the terms of its own sovereign bonds on the basis that the bonds were governed by Greek law. Another example of the use of police powers is the purported cancellation of the Polish sovereign debt held by pension schemes in 2014.[10]

The all-important question is thus whether the State does possess police powers in the restructuring of its own financial obligations. If one subscribes to the view that the State does indeed enjoy police powers in

---

[8] *Continental Casualty v Argentina*, ICSID Case No ARB/03/9, Award (5 September 2008) para. 284.

[9] Zachary Douglas, *The International Law of Investment Claims* (CUP 2009) 81–90 ('The law applicable to the issue of liability for a claim founded upon an investment treaty obligation is the investment treaty as supplemented by general international law').

[10] Ralph Atkins, 'Poland Plays with Fire over Pension Reform' *Financial Times* (London 31 January 2014).

this context, then they are likely to be rather extensive under international law. The orthodox approach under customary international law is that the State has the power to modify the contractual obligations it has entered into[11] and would act in breach of international law only in cases where it repudiated the debt.[12] The repudiation of the debt can be accomplished through the adoption of legislative measures which may involve cancellations, excessive exchange controls and taxes, 'conversion of foreign debt into irredeemable local currency strip and other acts amounting to a constructive taking'[13] and possibly freezing of accounts and abrogation of indexation clauses.[14] Several factors, such as, for instance, the breakdown of negotiations or the unilateral suspension of payments, could evidence the coerciveness of sovereign debt restructurings and positively correlate with the creditor losses.[15]The temporary suspension of the service of the debt or mere non-payment, by contrast, are not considered generally breaches of international law *per se*,[16] unless accompanied by a denial of justice[17] or confiscation.[18] It would indicate

---

[11] Edwin Borchard, *State Insolvency and Foreign Bondholders* (Beard Books 1951) 158.

[12] Ibid., 119–20; Michael Waibel, *Sovereign Defaults Before International Courts and Tribunals* (CUP 2011) 278–97.

[13] Philip Wood, *Project Finance, Subordinated Debt and State Loans* (Sweet & Maxwell 1995) 146. For a similar definition, see International Law Association Sovereign Insolvency Study Group, *State Insolvency: Options for the Way Forward* (2010) 8 <www.ila-hq.org/download.cfm/docid/0A7ACEAC-94A3-4B47-B9E642CF4BEA5D81> accessed 9 April 2015.

[14] Carmen Reinhart and Kenneth Rogoff, 'The Forgotten History of Domestic Debt' (2008) NBER Working Paper 13946, 11, 38-39 <www.nber.org/papers/w13946.pdf> accessed 9 April 2015.

[15] Henrik Enderlein, Christoph Trebesch and Laura von Daniels, 'Sovereign Debt Disputes: A Database on Government Coerciveness during Debt Crises' (2011) 30 J Intl Mon & Fin 1, 4, 13.

[16] GC Christie, 'What Constitutes a Taking of Property under International Law' (1962) 38 BYBIL 307, 318; Ernst Feilchenfeld, 'Rights and Remedies of Holders of Foreign Bonds' in Sylvester Quindry (ed.), *Bonds and Bondholders: Rights and Remedies* (Burdette Smith 1934) 203–13; Covey Oliver, 'Judicial Decisions Involving Questions of International La (1962) 56 AJIL 1033, 1110 (Claim of Pietrzak).

[17] *Eagle Pencil Co, Inc*, 27 April 1959, (1966) 30 ILR 128 (the US Foreign Claims Settlement Commission found that the Soviet Russia barred the US claimant from enforcing its rights in the courts of Soviet Russia which gave rise to a denial of justice, thereby giving rise to claims against Soviet Russia under Section 305(a)(2) of the International Claims Settlement Act, 1949).

[18] Waibel (n 12) 193 (see, however, 203–6).

that in cases where the State *passively* refuses to pay its debt, international law would not sanction such default, whereas when the State repudiates the debt by adopting *positive* acts to renege on its debt, international legal liability is likely to come into play.[19]

Sometimes, an additional factor is introduced into the equation of international legal liability – the inability of the State to repay the debt. A State honestly unable to pay its debt should not be chastised for its default and is therefore not treated as acting in breach of international law.[20] Chances of successfully applying this latter criterion in practice, however, seem to be rather faint.[21]

Customary international law thus attaches different consequences when the debt is repudiated and when the State is merely in default. The repudiation of the debt, reminiscent of the standard of expropriation under Bilateral Investment Treaties (BITs) is, in contrast to mere default, usually made publicly and wilfully and the State takes some positive action to partially or entirely wipe its debt.[22] The trouble for creditors is that the repudiation in its pure form is rare in State practice.[23]

Whatever the precise provisions of the customary international law on sovereign debt are, BITs are capable of reinforcing the customary

---

[19] See, e.g., Christoph Schreuer, 'The Concept of Expropriation under the ECT and other Investment Treaties' in Clarisse Ribeiro (ed.), *Investment Arbitration and the Energy Charter Treaty* (Juris Publishing 2006) para. 118 (commenting on *Olguín v Paraguay*). In a similar vein, Reinisch, relying upon the duty under public international law to respect acquired rights, argues that the State would be in breach of international law when it directly or indirectly interferes with the contractual duties of private lenders through, among other things, a legislative loan annulment, a unilateral moratorium, obligatory transfer of the claims into domestic currency and so forth. According to him, the State would not incur liability for 'less extreme measures', such as exchange controls, devaluations or abrogations of gold clauses, that would neatly fit into the concept of monetary sovereignty and would not engage State responsibility, unless they are arbitrary or discriminatory. See August Reinisch, 'Debt Restructuring and State Responsibility Issues' in Dominique Carreau and Malcolm Shaw (eds), *La Dette Extérieure/The External Debt* (Brill 1995) 584–7

[20] Edwin Borchard, 'International Loans and International Law' (1932) 26 Proceedings of the American Society of International Law 157.

[21] Michael Waibel, 'Opening Pandora's Box: Sovereign Bonds in International Arbitration' (2007) 101 AJIL 711, 759.

[22] Borchard (n 11) 141–3.

[23] Florentino Feliciano, 'Report of the Director of Studies of the English-speaking Section of the Centre' in Carreau and Shaw (n 19) 45 (citing the examples of USSR, Cuba and the Third Reich).

protection of bondholders, to an extent yet to be determined through the incremental development of the case law.[24] In spite of strong opposition and criticism,[25] the adjudication of sovereign debt disputes in international investments arbitrations has become an undeniable part of our reality, much to the contentment of bondholders. This is of course subject to the exclusion of sovereign debt from the coverage of BITs, found in certain BITs[26] and proposed for others.[27] Three ICSID tribunals have so far accepted jurisdiction over disputes involving sovereign debt issuance and decided that holdings of sovereign bond do qualify as investment under the BIT in question and Article 25 of the ICSID Convention.[28] A more recent case against Greece has taken a contrary view.[29] In all of these cases, the State engaged in more or less compulsory measures, justified on the ground of public interest and pressing economic situation, to restructure the debt that it was unable to service in conformity with the terms of the sovereign bond documentation.This chapter will take a

---

[24] See *Continental v Argentina* (n 8) paras 220–222, 264–265 and 284–285 (finding that the restructuring was in breach of the fair and equitable treatment standard).

[25] Waibel (n 12) 212–50; Waibel (n 21) 718–36; Dissenting Opinion of Georges Abi-Saab in *Abaclat and others v The Argentine Republic*, ICSID Case No ARB/07/5 (28 October 2011); Dissenting Opinion of Santiago Torres Bernandez in *Ambiente Ufficio SpA and Others v The Argentine Republic*, ICSID Case No ARB/08/9 (2 May 2013).

[26] Annamaria Viterbo, 'Sovereign Debt Restructuring and Investment Protection' in Tullio Treves, Francesco Seatzu and Seline Trevisanut (eds), *Foreign Investment, International Law and Common Concerns* (Routledge 2014) 342–4.

[27] Daniella Strik, 'Investment Protection of Sovereign Debt and Its Implications on the Future of Investment Law in the EU' (2012) 29(2) J Intl Arb 183, 201–2.

[28] *Abaclat v Argentina* (n 25) Decision on Jurisdiction and Admissibility (4 August 2011); *Ambiente Ufficio v Argentina* (n 25) Decision on Jurisdiction and Admissibility (8 February 2013); *Giovanni Alemanni and Others v The Argentine Republic*, ICSID Case No ARB/07/8, Decision on Jurisdiction and Admissibility (17 November 2014). For a commentary, see, e.g., Stacie Strong, *Class, Mass, and Collective Arbitration in National and International Law* (OUP 2013); Stacie Strong, 'Mass Procedures in Abaclat v. Argentine Republic: Are They Consistent With the International Investment Regime?' (2013) 3 YB Intl Arb 261; Anna De Luca, 'Collective Actions in ICSID Arbitration: the *Argentine Bonds* Case' (2011) 21 Ital YB Intl L 211. See also *Fedex v Venezuela*, ICSID Case No ARB/96/3, Decision of the Tribunal on Objections to Jurisdiction (11 July 1997).

[29] *Poštová banka, as and ISTROKAPITAL SE v Hellenic Republic*, ICSID Case No ARB/13/8, Award (9 April 2015).

diametrically opposite view on the existence of police powers in sovereign debt restructurings as a matter of general international law. It will not discuss the specific standards of investment protection provided for in BITs as applied to sovereign debt restructurings.[30] Instead, it will address the more general and logically antecedent question of whether the State enjoys any police powers or the right to regulate (concepts which are used interchangeably for present purposes) in sovereign debt restructurings *in the first place*. The threshold question that this chapter will tackle is whether the State can rely on the police powers doctrine at all to preclude a finding of liability in international investment disputes. A positive answer would most certainly exclude State liability for breaches of the rights of bondholders, whereas a negative answer would constrain the powers of the State in sovereign debt restructurings.

As mentioned above, the question is likely to arise in circumstances when the State either blatantly seeks to overrule the provisions of the sovereign bond documentation through specific legislation or when it passes general legislation that affects, among other things, the extent of government's indebtedness. Normally, the police powers defence would be applicable when the bonds are subject to the law of the sovereign debtor, and hence the State may modify the governing law of sovereign bonds. External bonds subject to some foreign law will in most cases escape the application of domestic decrees of the sovereign debtor.

Part II of the chapter will briefly outline the doctrine of police powers under international law. Part III, where the main discussion will be concentrated, will test the application of the doctrine to sovereign debt disputes. Then the chapter will discuss the place of the doctrine in restructurings of private debt (Part IV) and restructurings of semi-public debt, that is to say the debt of State-owned enterprises (Part V). All parts of the chapter are predicated on the idea that the issue is addressed through the prism of general international law.

Before venturing upon the discussion of substantive matters, it is necessary to define the scope of the enquiry. For present purposes, the sovereign debt analysed is exclusively limited to private-to-State debt, to the exclusion of the State-to-State debt. The latter category is subject to

---

[30] See Waibel (n 21) 711; Reinisch (n 19) 537–605; Giorgio Sacerdoti, 'BIT Protections and Economic Crises: Limits to Their Coverage, the Impact of Multilateral Financial Regulation and the Defence of Necessity' (2013) ICSID Rev 1; Otto Sandrock, 'The Case for More Arbitration when Sovereign Debt is to be Restructured: Greece as an Example' (2012) 23(3–4) Am Rev Intl Arb 507, 536–7.

different procedures of restructuring, and considerations, often of political character, dominate the quest of reducing the sovereign debt owed to other States.[31] Also, the adjudication of State-to-State debt is unheard of in recent times and the restructuring of State-to-State debt is concentrated within the confines of the Paris Club.

II. THE DOCTRINE OF POLICE POWERS

The doctrine of police powers (the right to regulate) denotes the capacity of the State to regulate, excluding liability under international law for actions taken within its purview. In spite of the lack of mention in BITs, investment tribunals have shielded public regulation on the ground of the implicitly acknowledged doctrine of police powers.[32] It has been decided that:

> It is now established in international law that States are not liable to pay compensation to a foreign investor when, in the normal exercise of their regulatory powers, they adopt in a non-discriminatory manner bona fide regulations that are aimed at the general welfare.[33]

The recognition of the police powers and the balanced conduct of the State within the reach of such powers would generally disqualify any breach of international investment law.[34] Public regulations are nevertheless likely to cross the line if they are not made for a public purpose, are discriminatory and are accomplished without due process[35] and, additionally, if the State

---

[31] Gaston Jèze, 'Les défaillances d'Etat' (1935) 53 Recueil des cours 383–4.

[32] See, e.g., August Reinisch, 'Expropriation' in Peter Muchlinski, Federico Ortino and Christoph Schreuer (eds), *The Oxford Handbook of International Investment Law* (OUP 2008) 407–58; Stephan Schill, 'International Investment Law and the Host State's Power to Handle Economic Crises: Comment on the ICSID Decision in LG&E v. Argentina' (2007) 24(3) J Intl Arb 265, 277.

[33] *Saluka Investments BV v Czech Republic*, UNCITRAL, Partial Award (17 March 2006) para. 255.

[34] *LG&E v Argentina*, ICSID Case No ARB/02/1, Decision on Liability (3 October 2006) paras 194–196.

[35] *Methanex Corporation v United States of America,* UNCITRAL, Final Award of the Tribunal on Jurisdiction and Merits (3 August 2005) Pt IV, Ch. D, para. 15; *Azurix v Argentina*, ICSID Case No ARB/01/12, Award (14 July 2006) paras 310–312.

provided specific commitments to the investor to preserve the existing regulatory environment.[36]

Police powers are a rather elusive concept and the case law on the police powers in investment arbitration is impervious to easy categorisation. Article 10(5) of the Harvard Draft Convention on the International Responsibility of States for Injuries to Aliens lists the following matters as falling within the State's police powers under international law:

> An uncompensated taking of an alien property or a deprivation of the use or enjoyment of property of an alien which results from the execution of tax laws; from a general change in the value of currency; from the action of the competent authorities of the State in the maintenance of public order, health or morality; or from the valid exercise of belligerent rights or otherwise incidental to the normal operation of the laws of the State shall not be considered wrongful.[37]

To this list of police powers matters, one can add banking regulation,[38] gambling regulation,[39] environmental protection,[40] customs regulations,[41] protection of cultural property,[42] reductions or increases in tariff levels, imposition of zoning restrictions[43] and forfeiture for crime.

Aside from matters clearly falling within the State's police powers, certain matters are subject to controversy and their qualification might give rise to legal disputes before investment tribunals.[44] One such matter is clearly the unilateral modification of sovereign bonds. Is it a matter within the police powers of the State?

One way of approaching this question is to rely on the distinction between 'enterprise' and 'arbitral' capacities of the State triggering the police powers. Joseph Sax clarified the inconsistent case law of US courts on police powers by providing a standard for distinguishing

---

36 Andrew Newcombe and Lluis Paradell, *Law and Practice of Investment Treaties: Standards of Treatment* (Kluwer Law International 2009) 358.

37 Louis B Sohn and R R Baxter, 'Responsibility of States for Injuries to the Economic Interests of Aliens' (1961) 55 AJIL 545.

38 *Saluka v Czech Republic* (n 33) paras 266 ff.

39 *International Thunderbird Gaming Corporation v United Mexican States*, UNCITRAL, Award (26 January 2006) paras 123–127.

40 *Methanex v USA* (n 35) Part IV, ch. D, para. 9.

41 *Sea-Land Service Inc v Iran* (1984) 6 Iran-USCTR 149, 165.

42 *SPP v Egypt*, ICC Arbitration No YD/AS No 3493, Award (11 March 2003) (1983) 22 ILM 752, para. 158.

43 *Marvin Feldman v Mexico*, ICSID Case No ARB(AF)/99/1, Award (16 December 2002) para. 103.

44 *Saluka v Czech Republic* (n 33) para. 264.

between the uncompensated exercise of police powers and compensatory takings. A distinction is drawn between, on the one side, cases where the government is a participant to the relations it seeks to regulate ('enterprise capacity') and the public regulation adds to the assets of the State and, on the other side, where the government acts as a mediator and regulates competing private interests ('arbitral' or mediator capacity) and no direct benefit arises to the State. In the former cases compensation may be required, whereas in the latter case the regulation is in principle non-compensable.[45] If one were to adopt this distinction in the present context, sovereign debt restructurings would not fall under the police powers exception, given the State would be acting in the enterprise capacity and the measures would attract the duty to compensate.

At a different level, to justify the existence of police powers in cases of sovereign bankruptcy, academics have argued that municipal legal systems invariably afford protection to insolvent companies and individuals and, by extrapolation, international tribunals should be deferential to State insolvencies.[46] The analogy between domestic bankruptcies and defaults of sovereign States, it is submitted, is unconvincing. When the State enforces laws that regulate bankruptcies of private companies, it is acting in the mediator capacity and does not benefit from the resolution of a default (other than from the indirect benefit of efficiently regulating the national economy). On the other hand, the State unilaterally[47] affecting its own debt obligations places itself in the position of its own umpire and profits from its own actions taken in sovereign capacity.

Some awards and writers have suggested the intensity of interference with the property right as a ground for distinguishing between *bona fide* regulation and expropriation.[48] The intensity of interference is undoubtedly essential in passing a judgment upon the reasonableness of the exercise of police powers, but only after the existence of police powers has been established in the first place.

Another way of putting the argument might be that sovereign bonds contain a specific commitment by the State to exclude the exercise of police powers. The problem lies, of course, in that by subscribing to the

---

45 Joseph Sax, 'Takings and the Police Power' (1964–1965) 74 Yale LJ 36, 61–3.

46 Waibel (n 21) 750.

47 'Unilateral restructuring' is understood henceforth as a restructuring passed without the consent of bondholders, through the adoption of laws that modify the financial obligations under the sovereign bonds.

48 See, e.g., *Técnicas Medioambientales Tecmed, SA v The United Mexican States*, ICSID Case No ARB (AF)/00/2, Award (29 May 2003) para. 115.

bonds governed by the domestic law of the sovereign, the creditor may be assumed to accept the risk of unilateral modification.

Having said all this, clearly international law does not provide a 'mechanical test' that distinguishes between taking of property and the exercise of police powers[49] and various factors might be decisive in finding a non-compensable State regulation.[50] However, it is suggested that the standard for differentiating between matters that deserve the status of police powers and those that do not is the *general acceptance* of the State conduct in domestic legal contexts.[51] In other words, is the particular police power generally accepted in domestic legal systems? The crux of the following enquiry will thus be what 'is commonly accepted as within police power' in national legal systems. Through the examination of a number of domestic legal systems, it will be argued in the next part that police powers of the States in sovereign debt restructurings are nowhere close to being commonly accepted.

III. POLICE POWERS IN SOVEREIGN DEBT RESTRUCTURING

This section argues against the existence of police powers in sovereign debt restructurings by drawing on national case law examples, although very few and far between, which address the power of the State to amend its debt in a unilateral fashion. The inquiry is evocative of general principles of law,[52] although it is not suggested that it will lead to the crystallisation of a general principle of law *stricto sensu*, but rather the national case law should inform the decision of the arbitrators as to

---

[49] *Generation Ukraine, Inc v Urkaine*, ICSID Case No ARB/00/9, Award (16 September 2003) para. 20.29.

[50] Andrew Newcombe, 'The Boundaries of Regulatory Expropriation in International Law' (2005) 20(1) ICSID Rev 1, 40–54.

[51] See, e.g., Newcombe and Paradell (n 36) 358 ('evidence of consistent and general comparative practice in a variety of states is likely to be relevant'); *Too v United States* 1989) 23 Iran-USCTR 378, 387 ('commonly accepted as within the police power').

[52] August Reinisch conducted a comparative research on the state of necessity in sovereign debt restructurings as applied by municipal courts; however he came to the conclusion that crystallised general principles were still absent; see August Reinisch, 'Sachverständigengutachten zur Frage des Bestehens und der Wirkung des völkerrechtlichen Rechtfertigungsgrundes "Staatsnotstand"' (2008) 68 Zeitschrift für ausländisches öffentliches Recht und Völkerrecht (ZaöRV) 3, 37.

the inexistence of police powers through the 'commonality of acceptance' as a threshold standard for police powers. It will be claimed on the ground of such comparative research that the State, in issuing state debt and afterwards embarking on its restructuring, is deemed to be acting in its private capacity and should not be allowed to modify debt unilaterally.

It should be stressed that the purpose of this inquiry is not to find a commonly accepted standard in respect of sovereign debt restructurings. It is also rather unrealistic that investment tribunals in the determination of the consistent practice of a variety of States that would serve as a basis for the finding of police powers would engage in a broad and all-inclusive comparative survey of national jurisdictions. Municipal courts, as will be seen below, might take diametrically opposite stances in respect of sovereign debt restructurings (which is not surprising given the raft of implications that a particular stance might entail). The difference of treatment might be conditioned by the gravity of the financial crisis, the liberalism of the national economy, the independence of judges, and a whole array of other reasons.

The present inquiry is less ambitious: it is to show that there is no commonality of acceptance of police powers of the State in sovereign debt restructurings by relying upon some cases that deny such powers to the sovereigns in municipal legal systems. The showing of such a representative national case law would in principle defy efforts to establish a commonality of acceptance of police powers in national legal systems, thus rejecting the existence of commonly accepted police powers under international law. The US and Russian courts, and, less consistently, English courts, have frowned upon unilateral restructurings of sovereign debt.[53] The position of these three jurisdictions is in principle sufficient to frustrate the argument of the commonality of police powers.

The inquiry into the law of a multitude of States for the purpose of locating police powers can thus be dispensed with, but the case law of other jurisdictions – affirmative, to some extent, of the power of unilateral modification – will also be presented. Argentine and German courts have to varying degrees upheld the laws that allowed the State to restructure the sovereign debt through the adoption of legislative acts.

---

[53] Hints as to the recognition of the private character of sovereign debt are also found in international practice. The *Russian Indemnities Case* decided by the Permanent Court of Arbitration found 'no grounds for demanding an exception to this responsibility in the matter of monetary debts by pleading its character of public power'; *Russian Indemnities Case* (1925) 1 UNRIAA 529, II.4.

A. The United States

The United States is one of the jurisdictions where the State does not possess police powers unilaterally to modify its own financial obligations. The US Supreme Court in *Perry v United States*[54] was confronted with the unilateral modification of US government debt in the context of the Joint Resolution of 1933 which abrogated all gold clauses contained in, among others, sovereign bonds issued by the US Government. One affected bondholder, who held bonds issued by the US Government, brought an action that went up to the US Supreme Court. The Supreme Court, in the judgment delivered by Chief Justice Hughes, strongly affirmed that the US Government did not enjoy police powers in restructuring its own debt. The judgment of the Chief Justice written in 1935 has lost none of its cogency:

> There is a clear distinction between the power of the Congress to control or interdict the contracts of private parties when they interfere with the exercise of its constitutional authority, and the power of the Congress to alter or repudiate the substance of its own engagements when it has borrowed money under the authority which the Constitution confers … . By virtue of the power to borrow money 'on the credit of the United States,' the Congress is authorized to pledge that credit as an assurance of payment as stipulated, as the highest assurance the Government can give, its plighted faith. To say that the Congress may withdraw or ignore that pledge, is to assume that the Constitution contemplates a vain promise, a pledge having no other sanction than the pleasure and convenience of the pledgor. … When the United States, with constitutional authority, makes contracts, it has rights and incurs responsibilities similar to those of individuals who are parties to such instruments.

Chief Justice Hughes went on to emphatically confirm that there is a fundamental principle by virtue of which the validity of the public debt shall not be questioned. There are, nevertheless, difficulties in trying to square this pro-creditor pronouncement with the result of the case whereby the Court held that no damages were to be granted to the bondholder. The Supreme Court, with a strong dissent from four judges, found that the revocation of the gold clause did not result in any actual damages.[55] Gold coins had been already withdrawn from circulation – an action that the Supreme Court did not judge to be arbitrary or capricious

54 *Perry v United States*, 294 US 330 (1935).

55 A similar result reached in *Nortz v United States*, 294 US 317 (1935) 328-330. See also *Woodruff v Trapnall*, 51 US 190 (1850).

– which consequently barred the repayment of the debt in gold. Neither was the claimant able to establish the amount of currency equivalent to the promised gold coin for a simple reason that the market of gold was at the time subject to strict regulations. The claimant's action would therefore result in damages exceeding the nominal value of the bonds, which the Supreme Court refused to award. Nor did the claimant establish any loss in respect of the buying power as a result of the abrogation of the gold clause, for the value of bonds had soared due to the falling price level and thereby the bondholders would have been unjustly enriched.[56]

This part of the judgment effectively defeated the finding of unconstitutionality of the Joint Resolution of 1933 and in fact bolstered the Congress in its economic reforms, by denying effective relief to the bondholder.[57] The situation in *Perry v United States*, nevertheless, was not ordinary, because the gold clauses, though protected by the fundamental principle of the prohibition of the unilateral modification of State bonds, impeached the power of US Congress to exercise monetary regulation by withdrawing gold from the national economy.[58] By contrast, most sovereign debt restructurings, unconnected with the exercise of monetary regulation, would not be shielded by the doctrine of police powers. Furthermore, influential authorities contend that *Perry v United States* was ostensibly limited to the actions brought by local bondholders, who are subject to the compulsive gold regulation within the US territory, whereas foreign bondholders should be able to avail themselves of the action in damages against the government which unilaterally amended its bonds.[59]

The breadth of the pronouncement in *Perry v United States* is somewhat unclear. Francis Mann, referring to *Perry*, argued that '[t]here would seem to be no justification for founding upon this exception [*Perry v United States*] a general principle of law applicable to state loans',

---

[56] Richard H Timberlake, *Constitutional Money: A Review of the Supreme Court's Monetary Decisions* (CUP 2013) 198, 204.

[57] Henry Hart, 'The Gold Clause in United States Bonds' (1934-1935) 48 Harv L Rev 1057, 1080, 1087 and 1098–9; John Dawson, 'The Gold Clause Decisions' (1935) 33(5) Mich L Rev 647, 658.

[58] *Perry v United States* (n 54) 357; Hart (n 57) 1074; Dawson (n 57) 656–7.

[59] Borchard (n 11) 138, n 51; Martin Domke, *La clause 'dollar-o'": la non-application de la legislation américaine aux emprunts internationaux* (Les Éditions Internationales 1935); Charles Fenwick, 'The Gold Clause Decision in Relation to Foreign Bondholders' (1935) 29 AJIL 310; Georges Sauser-Hall, 'La Clause-Or dans le Contrats Publics et Privés' (1937) 60 Recueil des cours 762; Jèze (n 31) 414.

given that the decision in *Perry* was expressly based on the provisions of the US Constitution.[60] One has to disagree with the learned author's reading of *Perry*. It is true that the Supreme Court relied on various provisions of the US Constitution in its analysis of the constitutionality of the Joint Resolution of 1933, in particular the 14th Amendment of the US Constitution which provides that '[t]he validity of the public debt of the United States, authorized by law, … shall not be questioned'.[61] However, this provision, as the US Supreme Court expressly stated, merely confirms a 'fundamental' principle beyond the US Constitution, applying as well to bonds issued after, as to those issued before the adoption of the 14th Amendment. It was not a mere peculiarity or idiosyncrasy of the US constitutional regime. The principle was indeed fundamental, for it derived its force from the general framework of contract law which equally applied to contractual undertakings of the US Government, as well as from the implied ability of the sovereign to bind itself contractually, as a manifestation of its sovereignty.

Yet, one may still be perplexed that the Supreme Court did not accord any remedy to the bondholder affected by the Joint Resolution of 1933. However, other cases from the US Supreme Court confirm the pronouncement in *Perry* that the State does not enjoy police powers in restructurings of the debt to which it itself is party (although in a less extreme situation than the Great Depression). Thus, the US Supreme Court held in *United States Trust Co v New Jersey*: 'The instant case involves a financial obligation and thus as a threshold matter may not be said automatically to fall within the reserved powers that cannot be contracted away.'[62] The New York Court of Appeal in *Flushing Natl Bank v Municipal Assistance Corp for City of NY* decided that a moratorium on the short-term obligations of the city was illegal.[63]

In a similar vein, in *Murray v City of Charleston*, the Supreme Court stated that: 'A promise to pay, with a reserved right to deny or change the effect of the promise, is an absurdity.'[64] There the indebted municipality sought to increase the tax upon the interest on the bonds by 2 per cent. The Supreme Court held that while the municipality possessed a privilege

---

[60] Francis A Mann, 'State Contracts and State Responsibility' (1960) 54 AJIL 572, 586, 590.

[61] As well as the Fifth Amendment.

[62] *United States Trust Co v New Jersey,* 431 US 1 (1977) (concerning a repeal of a statutory covenant that provided a guarantee to the creditors).

[63] *Flushing Natl Bank v Municipal Assistance Corp for City of NY*, 40 NY2d 731 (1976).

[64] *Murray v City of Charleston*, 96 US 432, 445 (1877).

to tax, it could not be applied to lessen the interest rate prescribed in the debt instrument, for:

> States and cities, when they borrow money and contract to repay it with interest, are not acting as sovereignties. They come down to the level of ordinary individuals. Their contracts have the same meaning as that of similar contracts between private persons.[65]

This is a rather strong holding given that the power to tax is, in other contexts, ubiquitously recognised.

In litigation affecting foreign States, the US courts have since the 1990s consistently treated sovereign debt as a commercial activity not covered by State immunity. The US Supreme Court in *Weltover v Argentina* upheld the US courts' jurisdiction over Argentine debt, as the issuance of sovereign debt is a commercial activity within the meaning of the Foreign Sovereign Immunities Act.[66]

Equally, in the case law on the stay of actions, the US courts have consistently acted to preserve the rights of creditors and have effectively refused to stay their actions in deference to the sovereign debt restructuring processes.[67] In a few cases, which have led to much confusion and misunderstanding among academics,[68] New York courts have refused to issue interim measures when those would derail the sovereign debt restructuring.[69] These latter cases are exclusively applicable at the stage of interim measures and cannot be extended beyond.

The overall standpoint of US courts is that the State in principle does not enjoy police powers to modify its own financial obligations. This approach informs the finding of police powers at the international level in

---

[65] However, the Court recognised that the tax can be levied upon the lender who is subject to the jurisdiction of the municipality after the whole payment has been transferred to him.

[66] 28 US Code Title 28 Part IV Chapter 97 – Jurisdictional Immunities of Foreign States.

[67] See, e.g., *Pravin Banker Associates, Ltd v Banco Popular Del Peru and the Republic of Peru*, 109 F.3d 850 (1997); *Lightwater Corporation Ltd v the Republic of Argentina*, US Dist Ct SDNY (2003); *Allan Applestein Ttee Fbo D.C.A Grantor Trust v The Province of Buenos Aires*, 415 F.3d 242 (2005).

[68] See, e.g., Reinisch (n 52) paras 117–126.

[69] *Elliott Associates v the Republic of Peru and Banco de la Nacion*, 176 FRD 93 SDNY(1997)); *NML Capital Ltd v Republic of Argentina*, 699 F.3d 246 (2d Cir 2012), 727 F.3d 230 (2d Cir 2013); *EM Ltd v Republic of Argentina*, 695 F.3d 201 (2d Cir 2012); *Capital Ventures International v Republic of Argentina*, 443 F.3d 214 (2d Cir 2005); *Greylock Global Opportunity Master Fund v Province of Mendoza*, 162 Fed Appx 85 (2d Cir 2006).

that it dismantles the perception of commonality of acceptance of police powers in the context of sovereign debt restructurings in national legal systems.

B. The Russian Federation

In a manner similar to US courts, Russian courts have confirmed that the government does not in principle enjoy police powers to modify its own sovereign financial obligations. In the aftermath of the Russian sovereign debt crisis of 1998, the Government of the Russian Federation issued a decree which sought to restructure domestic bonds in a unilateral manner. A holder of Russian domestic bonds, OOO Rusatommet, sued the Ministry of Finance and the Government of the Russian Federation requesting payment under the terms of the Russian bonds and challenging the unilateral restructuring. The Federal Moscow District Arbitraj (Commercial) Court of the Russian Federation held that the restructuring decree was issued within the constitutional competence of the government to regulate the market of securities and the internal and external debt of the Russian Federation and should therefore prevail over the contractual obligations of the State.[70] However, the Presidium of the Supreme Arbitraj (Commercial) Court of the Russian Federation chastised the (lower) District Arbitraj court for the misplaced reliance on the governmental decree. It held that the government loan was subject to the contractual regime prescribed by Article 817 of the Civil Code of the Russian Federation which expressly provided that State loans can only be modified by mutual consent.[71] The application of the governmental decree with the effect of unilaterally modifying the State loans issued by the Russian Federation, the Court held, would result in breach of the right to property, protected by the Russian Federation Constitution.

The Court added the proviso that the lower courts should have enquired into the existence of a State-imposed moratorium, subject to a rather broad judicial review, and referred the case to the lower courts which failed to locate a moratorium.[72] It is not entirely clear why the Court was ready to grant legal effect, though subject to a judicial review, to the moratorium, while denying effect to a governmental decree purporting to restructure the sovereign debt. The difference in treatment might lie in the fact that the moratorium acts only as a temporary stay on

---

[70] Decision No KG-A40/723-00, 16 March 2000.
[71] Decision No 2453/00, 13 February 2002.
[72] Decision No KG-A40/6804-02, 28 October 2002.

legal claims, whereas the decree would have irreversible consequences on the rights of bondholders.[73]

Again, the approach of Russian courts belies the assumption of commonality of police powers in the context of sovereign debt restructurings in domestic contexts.

C. England and Wales

The position under English law is more complex. It is heavily informed by the doctrine of the absolute supremacy of the Parliament, which prevents a court from reversing a decision of the Parliament to modify the Crown's contractual obligations in a unilateral fashion. However, the desire to prevent a State from reneging on its commercial contracts and unilaterally modifying its contractual obligations has made inroads into the otherwise absolute supremacy of the Parliament.

English courts have not expressly decided on the power of the British Government or Parliament to amend State contracts unilaterally. The academic commentary is equally torn between two opposing views as to the (in)acceptability of such actions in English constitutional law. The orthodox view in English domestic law is that the English Parliament has absolute supremacy and any legitimate expectations can be overcome by a properly worded statute.[74] The conventional doctrine was expressed by Bowett as follows:

> Indeed, in English law not only is 'stabilization' impossible against future legislation but, because of the doctrine of Parliamentary supremacy, no English court could challenge the assertion that Parliament was acting in the public good.[75]

On the other hand, opinions are uttered with increasing frequency that the supremacy of the Parliament is no longer as absolute as it used to be historically.[76] Judge Higgins expressed her voice in favour of that development as early as 1977:

---

[73] See, in this sense, Jèze (n 31) 401.

[74] See, e.g., *R v Secretary of State for Education and Employment, ex parte Begbie* [2000] 1 WLR 1115, para. 53: 'It is common ground that any expectation must yield to the terms of the statute under which the Secretary of State is required to act.'

[75] Derek Bowett, 'State Contracts with Aliens: Contemporary Developments on Compensation for Termination or Breach' (1988) 59 BYBIL 49, 58.

[76] *Jackson v Attorney-General* [2006] 1 AC 262, 302–3; Trevor Allan, *Constitutional Justice: A Liberal Theory of the Rule of Law* (OUP 2003)

> [I]t is widely accepted that no compensation is due for government legislation which adversely affects individual contracts. The answer to this must surely be that there is no reason why that principle should apply to contracts to which the government itself is party.[77]

In *Page v Commissioners of Crown Lands*,[78] the Court of Appeal recognised that contracts with the Crown contained an implied term preserving the prerogative of the Crown to take measures for the public good. Nevertheless, Devlin LJ provided a caveat that this did 'not mean that the Crown can escape from any contract which it finds disadvantageous by saying that it never promised to act otherwise than for the public good'.

The Court of Appeal then drew a fundamental distinction between sovereign acts taken for the purposes of public good and those entered into 'for the purpose of achieving a particular result under the contract in question'.[79] As Lord Denning succinctly explained in *Czarnikow v Rolimpex,* the government would be acting for the latter purpose if it intends 'to avoid its own liabilities under a particular contract or contracts'.[80] The gloss on this pronouncement is that when the public good invoked is a mere subterfuge to avoid its own liabilities, then the court might be allowed to review the action of the State.[81] Conversely, if a certain course of action is entered into for public good, such as health, public morals or safety, then the action requires high deference (note that the actions in *Page* were taken under wartime powers which is a clear example of public good).

In the different context of foreign governments acting as defendants before English courts, the courts have shown no hesitation in following the commercial characterisation of State activities. In *Camdex v Bank of Zambia (No 2)*, the Court in an enforcement action against a central bank confirmed that:

201–42; Jaime Arancibia, *Judicial Review of Commercial Regulation* (OUP 2011) 144 (advocating review of commercial regulation on the ground of its proportionality).

77 Rosalyn Higgins, 'The Availability of Damages for Reliance by Government on Executive Necessity' in Werner Flume and others (eds), *International Law and Economic Order, Festschrift für F. A. Mann* (CH Beck 1977) 33.

78 [1960] 2 All ER 726, 736.

79 Ibid.

80 [1978] QB 176, 194.

81 See also *Smith Kline & French Laboratories (Australia) Ltd v Secretary to the Department of Community Services and Health* [1990] FSR 617, 651 where the distinction is well highlighted.

> If there was a recoverable debt available in the English courts to the bank from ZCCM, his Lordship saw no sufficient reason why a private litigant like Camdex should be disentitled on policy grounds from attaching it. … His Lordship was similarly unimpressed by the invocation of considerations of comity. Of course Zambia was a foreign friendly state and of course one recognised that state's acute need for hard currency. The rules of law, however, dictated that judgment debtors should pay their debts and that if they failed to do so all the usual methods of execution should be open to their creditors.[82]

While the position under English law is less certain than as a matter of US or Russian law, it still shows that the power of the State unilaterally to modify its own contractual obligations has limits.

D. Argentina

Argentinean courts clearly accord more deference to the regulatory powers of the government. However, even accepting in principle the police powers of the State in sovereign debt restructurings, they still impose constrains to the abusive exercise of such powers.

Argentina was struck by a severe economic crisis in 2001–02 which led the State, among other things, to a forceful debt restructuring. The crisis has sparked a series of cases before ICSID tribunals and courts in foreign countries. Interestingly for our purposes, local Argentinean courts have also been seised of the actions of dissatisfied bondholders, alleging the unconstitutionality of two measures of the Argentinean State: first, the pesification of sovereign bonds expressed in foreign currency and second, the statutory prohibition on the Argentinean Government to reach any kind of agreement with the holdout bondholders.

In respect of the constitutionality of the first measure, the compulsory pesification, the Argentine Supreme Court in *Galli*[83] upheld the pesification of Argentine bonds and found that it did not breach the right to property. The Supreme Court considered that the financial situation in the country was such as to justify wholly or partly suspending or modifying the payment under the external debt. In deciding that the pesification legislation did not confiscate sovereign bonds, the Supreme Court relied upon certain statutory mechanisms that sought to minimise the loss suffered by the bondholders from the forcible conversion of currency, in

---

[82] *Camdex International Ltd v Bank of Zambia and Others (No 2)* [1997] CLC 714.

[83] *Galli, Hugo Gabriel y otro* c/PEN-Ley 25.561-dtos.1570/01 y 214/02 s amparos ley 25.561 (5 April 2005).

particular the inclusion of a consumer-based inflation index and the option to participate in future public debt exchanges in foreign currency.

The analysis by the Supreme Court, and of lower courts in Argentina that were seised of the legality of the measures taken by Argentina to restructure its debt, was guided by the standard of reasonableness of the measures. In *Brunicardi, Adriano c/ Banco Central*, the Supreme Court held that a mere deferral of payment does not amount to a substantial degradation or concealed confiscation of the property and is reasonable considering the financial situation.[84] In *Civit Félix Guillermo v Poder Ejecutivo Nacional*, the Court of Appeal decided that the pesification of the bonds and diminution of the guarantee provided to the bondholder exceeded an acceptable limitation upon the bondholder's constitutional rights and held the decrees effecting such amendments unconstitutional, although holding the bondholder to the interest reduction.[85] The idea underlying the judicial scrutiny of sovereign debt measures was the reasonableness of measures.

As for the second major legislative measure contested by the creditors, the Law No 20,617 prohibited negotiating or reaching any type of agreement with the creditors who held out from the initial debt restructuring. In the challenges to the constitutionality of this law, the solution taken by Argentinean courts to this delicate issue was not uniform and, equally, the Supreme Court judges in *Galli* were divided in their *obiter* statements as to the constitutionality of the statute. The position of lower courts is divided – some of the courts deciding that the rights of bondholders subsisted in spite of the Law No 20,617,[86] whereas others applying it on its face.[87]

One should add that, although these holdings found that the bondholders' substantive rights subsisted in spite of the Law No 20,617, the payment under the bonds was held to be deferred given the budgetary regulations. This recognises the temporary constrains on the payment capacity of the State.

As this account shows, Argentinean courts recognise the existence of police powers, however they do institute limitations on the exercise of such powers.

---

[84] Rodrigo Olivares-Caminal, *Legal Aspects of Sovereign Debt Restructuring* (Sweet & Maxwell 2009) 342–9.

[85] Ibid.

[86] See, e.g., Belohlawek, Carlos Vicente y otros c/ PEN-Ley 25561-Dtos 1570/01 214/02 s/ proceso de conocimiento – ley 25561 (28 August2007).

[87] See, e.g., Di Nicolo Pietro c/ Poder Ejecutivo Nacional s/ sumarísimo – CNCIV Y COMFED (15 June 2006).

E. Germany

The position of German courts is somewhat fluctuating. They adopted a rather deferential stance towards the restructuring of the debt of the Third Reich, however took a slightly different approach to the debt of the Republic of Argentina.

The German Federal Constitutional Court in a 1962 judgment recognised the legislative cancellation of the government debt of the Third Reich without any compensation.[88] It held, inter alia, that the legislative cancellation of the debt did not violate the right to property protected in the German Basic Law (the German constitution). One is struck by the inconsistency of this judicial pronouncement with a much latter pronouncement of the same judicial instance on the Argentinean debt restructuring of 2001. In the latter case, the Court found that Argentina could not avail herself of the exception of the state of necessity to restructure the debt in times of a severe crisis.[89]

The rather peculiar facts of the first case explain the 1962 judgment by which the Federal Constitutional Court approved so draconian a measure as a legislative cancellation of the debt without any compensation. The legislative cancellation in question was based on the express provisions of the German Basic Law which, in Article 134(4) delegated the legislator with the task of regulating the debt of the Third Reich; furthermore, Article 135(a) ('Old obligations') stipulated that federal legislation might dispense the German State from complying with the obligations owed by the Third Reich. In the application of these constitutional provisions, the German Parliament in 1957 passed the Act on War Reparations that declared the debt owed by the Third Reich cancelled.

It transpires from this overview that the legislative annulment of the debt endorsed by the Federal Constitutional Court did not relate to the debt of the Federal Republic of Germany contracted during its existence, but rather was incurred by its predecessor, the Third Reich. The peculiarity of the Third Reich's debt justified its express regulation in the German Basic Law and it is far from clear what stance the Court would have taken, had the German Basic Law not expressly regulated the regime of the Third Reich.

---

88 Case 1 BvR 987/58, Judgment of 14 November 1962, BVerfGE 15, 126.

89 Joined Cases Nos 2 BvM 1-5/03 & 2 BvM 1-2/06, (2007) 60 Neue Juristische Wochenschrift 2610 in (2007) 101(4) AJIL 857.

Here again, the starting point of German courts is that the State enjoys police powers to modify or even repudiate its debt (however, mindful of the specific context of the case).

F. Interim Conclusions

The cases from the US, Russian and English courts, addressed hitherto, lead to the following conclusions:

1) sovereign debts are subject to the common regime of private contracts; and
2) the State cannot rely on the police powers doctrine to alter the obligations it has entered into in a unilateral manner.

The comparative analysis presented mostly the position of national courts in respect of the restructuring of the debt of their own government, which admittedly presents the highest degree of deference to the restructuring measures (compare the treatment of German debt with the treatment of Argentinean debt by German courts). It might be expected that investment arbitral tribunals which are external to the constitutional system of a State might show evidence a lesser degree of deference.

That said, the prohibition to modify sovereign bonds unilaterally is without prejudice to two distinct matters. First, the argument of this section extends at the very least to the modification of express provisions of sovereign debt only (such as maturities, interest rates, governing law, tax regime, provisions governing amendment of terms of bonds and so forth). By contrast, the modification of the legal system, when not expressly negotiated with the bondholder, might be argued to fall squarely within the police powers of the State, as long as the parties have not reached the agreement to embed the relevant rules in the bond documentation.

Examples of this sort of agreements abound. The sovereign bond documentation often explicitly elevates various parts of the legal system to the sovereign bond terms and conditions. A cursory overview of bonds shows that the following matters, among other things, are covered by the bond documentation: taxation, currency, interests, transfer of bonds, prescription, and so forth. For instance, in respect of the currency fluctuations, bonds can include provisions similar to the following one, included in the bond documentation issued by the Austrian Government:

> If the amount received or recovered is less than the amount expressed to be due to the recipient under any Note, Receipt or Coupon, the Republic shall

> indemnify it against any loss sustained by it as a result. In any event, the Republic shall indemnify the recipient against the cost of making any such purchase.[90]

Secondly, the mode of payment, and not the substance of the debt, can be modified by the State through general legislative measures. As a matter of example, the French *Conseil d'Etat* has judged that the conversion rate of the currency of payment can be decided by French law if the debt is payable in France, even though the obligations itself is governed by some other law.[91] This fits rather neatly into the principle of conflict of laws that the method of payment shall be governed by the place of performance.[92]

It should be added, to clarify the point made here, that police powers would not miraculously emerge when the State is in a financial or other crisis. The US gold clause cases were decided during the Great Depression of 1929 and the cases on Argentina's sovereign immunity were taken following the immensely hurtful crisis of 2001–02. The context in which State measures are taken would matter if the State's actions fall under the ambit of police powers in the first place,[93] and, logically, the context cannot be used if the adjudicator did not find police powers to be present in the event. This is of course without effect as to the application of the necessity defence which can apply to actions taken outside police powers too.

One can think of a number of possible counter-claims to the argument in this section. First, under public international law, the State is free to act in any way it wishes so far as it does not breach any obligations established by international law. As held by the PCIJ in the *Lotus* case:

> The rules of law binding upon States therefore emanate from their own free will as expressed in conventions or by usages generally accepted as expressing principles of law and established in order to regulate the relations between these co-existing independent communities or with a view to the achievement

---

[90] See, e.g., Condition 16 of the Offering Circular of the Medium Term Note Programme of the Republic of Austria, 23 March 2007, available at Thomson One Banker at <http://banker.thomsonib.com> accessed 25 January 2016.

[91] Conseil d'Etat 28 Nov 1958, Dame Langlois, Clunet 1960, 444.

[92] Art. 12(2) of the Regulation (EC) No 593/2008 of the European Parliament and of the Council on the Law Applicable to Contractual Obligations (Rome I) [2008] OJ L177/6; *Serbian and Brazilian Loans Cases*, PCIJ, Ser A, No 20 (1929); No 21 (1929).

[93] *Saluka v Czech Republic* (n 33) para. 264.

> of common aims. Restrictions upon the independence of States cannot therefore be presumed.[94]

Under this principle, the State would inevitably enjoy the right to regulate its sovereign debt, unless the claimant can establish the crystallisation of a customary rule of international law to the effect of limiting the right of the State to regulate its own financial obligations. The starting point would, therefore, be the existence of plenary powers of a sovereign.

It might be responded to such criticism that in the eyes of international adjudicators, sovereign debt is first and foremost a creation of private law and the measures taken by a State to restructure the unsustainable level of its debt have to fit into the paradigm of contractual renegotiation of financial obligations. By issuing sovereign debt, governed by domestic law, to foreign residents, the State is acting in its private capacity and should adjust its conduct to the principles of international financial transactions.

Second, it has been claimed, rather boldly, that sovereign debt restructurings are an instance of the exercise of international public authority, the implication being that they should be treated with high deference by international tribunals and national courts.[95] The argument seems to be completely detached from the position in at least the US, Russian and English courts. As shown above, these legal systems are aligned in treating sovereign debt as a sub-category of private financial obligations.

Having said all this, it remains true that, assuming the State is on the verge of bankruptcy, the extreme financial burden can seriously affect the proper function of the State. Financing – in aggregate, not bond by bond – goes to the heart of the State's public interest and its capacity to deliver a wide range of public goods. State infrastructures might not exist or might not be able to be maintained without what might seem to be a necessary, sovereign debt restructuring.

It is submitted here that certain more or less innocuous unilateral modifications may, nonetheless, call for the exercise of police powers. One such potential exclusion is the deferral of the payment maturities (although not beyond a reasonable term)[96] in the absence of payment

---

94 *SS Lotus (France v Turkey)* 1927 PCIJ (ser A) No 10, para. 44.

95 Armin von Bogdandy and Mathias Goldmann, 'Sovereign Debt Restructurings as Exercises of International Public Authority: Towards a Decentralized Sovereign Insolvency Law' in Carlos Espósito, Yuefen Li and Juan Pablo Bohoslavsky (eds), *Sovereign Financing and International Law: The UNCTAD Principles on Responsible Sovereign Lending and Borrowing* (OUP 2013) 39–70.

96 *Malysh and others v Russia* (App no 30280/03) ECtHR 11 February 2010.

capacity. It may be argued that the State does not enjoy police powers to reduce the volume of its financial obligations, but it may increase the maturities of its financial obligations.[97]

IV. RESTRUCTURINGS OF PRIVATE DEBT

Let us now turn to the restructuring of private-to-private debt. It is not uncommon for States to engage in compulsory restructurings of the debt owed by and to private parties, in an effort to regulate the national economy. A whole array of tools is at the service of the State: financial repression, capital controls, currency regulations and so forth. These situations present a stark contrast to the situation above where the State intends to restructure the debt it has contracted into. Given this fundamental difference, the State enjoys police powers in the restructuring of private debt and their reasonable exercise does not result normally in a finding of State liability. Restructurings of private debt fall squarely within police powers and are subject to the same standards of review as other areas of police powers which will not be treated in detail. For example, modifying exchange rates should not, absent special considerations, engage the liability of the State.[98]

Again, references to the US case law in the era of Great Depression in the context of the Joint Resolution of 1933 are well placed. In the two gold clause cases, *Norman v Baltimore & Ohio R Co* and *US v Bankers' Trust Co*, decided together,[99] the US Supreme Court had to decide on the validity of the Joint Resolution of 1933 abrogating gold clauses in the context of contracts between private companies. The Court upheld the Joint Resolution of 1933 in this context recognising that contracts between private parties could not fetter the constitutional authority of Congress when dealing with subjects within its control, such as monetary policy. Congress had the power to consider the enormous volume of existing obligations containing gold clauses in determining whether the existence of such clauses substantially obstructed its monetary policy so

---

[97] For elaboration and further examples of more or less innocuous modifications of sovereign bonds, see Hayk Kupelyants, 'Sovereign Defaults Before Domestic Courts' (PhD Thesis, University of Cambridge 2015).

[98] Robert Jennings and Arthur Watts (eds), *Oppenheim's International Law* (vol. I, OUP 1992) 930.

[99] *Norman v Baltimore & Ohio R Co* and *US v Bankers' Trust Co* 294 US 240 (1935).

as to warrant a statute abrogating them, accordingly such action would not be treated as arbitrary.[100]

The contrast with the holding in *Perry v United States* is suggestive. The US Supreme Court did not deny police powers to the State encroaching upon private obligations when the State was not itself a party to the obligations incurred by private parties. The reason underlying the difference lies in the fact that the power of the State to renege on its own obligations is contrary to the private law character of sovereign debt.

As a result, the State clearly enjoys police powers in the restructuring of private debt. But undoubtedly, there are limits to the exercise of police powers. A number of jurisdictions have shunned the application of foreign laws that had the effect of confiscating the property of lenders. The English courts in the *Kahler*[101] and *Zhivnstenska*[102] cases announced that they would not recognise foreign laws that are confiscatory or penal – in the event, foreign exchange regulations were not treated as such. The US court in *Libra v Banco Nacional de Costa Rica* considered that exchange control regulations that interfered with the loan owed by the banking concern wholly owned by the Costa Rican Government had the effect of confiscating the property of lenders and were repugnant to US policy.[103] By contrast, the US court in *Braka v Bancomer*[104] and *West v Multibanco Comermex*[105] held that exchange control regulations that targeted the debt payable within the foreign State were covered by the Act of State doctrine and were not confiscatory for the purposes of the Hickenlooper Amendment.

It should be emphasised that investment tribunals might be ready to hold a State liable for its actions or regulations that are limited to the territorial jurisdiction of the State concerned and would not be recognised by the courts chosen by the parties in the choice of forum agreement. Thus, in *Deutsche Bank v Sri Lanka*,[106] the hedging agreement in dispute was subject to the jurisdiction of the English courts and in a related case

---

100 For more detail, see Timberlake (n 56) 182–205.

101 *Kahler v Midland Bank* [1950] AC 24, 27.

102 *Zivnostenska Banka v Frankman* [1950] AC 57, 72.

103 *Libra v Banco Nacional de Costa Rica* 570 F Supp 870 (SDNY 1983). See also *Zeevi v Grindlays Bank* (at http://unisetca.ipower.com/other/css/371NYS2d892.html) where the New York Court of Appeals found foreign exchange controls confiscatory and conflicting with New York's public policy.

104 *Braka v Bancomer* 589 F Supp 1465, 1472–3 (SDNY 1984).

105 *West v Multibanco Comermex,* 807 F2d 820, 831–3 (2d Cir 1987).

106 *Deutsche Bank AG v Democratic Socialist Republic of Sri Lanka*, ICSID Case No ARB/09/2, Award (31 October 2012) paras 556–565.

English courts have held the Sri Lankan regulatory actions not applicable to the case before them. However, the investment tribunal, with the dissent of one of the arbitrators,[107] decided that the State measures gave rise to an action in damages, because the State-owned entity party to the hedging agreement was prevented from making payments to the other party to the hedging agreement as a result of the State decrees, territorial in nature.

The above analysis evidences that the standard of judicial review in the restructurings of private debt is set higher in comparison to the review of the restructuring of sovereign debt. The action of the State needs to rise to the level of confiscation to trigger the negative sanction from the court, whereas an act of a State materially affecting the (express) terms of the sovereign bonds is *per se* unacceptable.

V. RESTRUCTURINGS OF SEMI-PUBLIC DEBT

It is not rare for States to structure their debt borrowing through legally separate, although State-dependent entities. The resulting semi-public debt is held by formally private parties who are controlled by the State (e.g., State-owned banks). It is true that such debt is on its face private in nature, nevertheless, it is equally true that the presence of the State might temper its private character.

Independent State-owned enterprises as a matter of general domestic practice will not be assimilated to the State owning them.[108] When, however, the connection between the State and the State-owned enterprise is such that the latter is a mere instrumentality in the hands of the State and the former dominates the latter,[109] one is allowed to pierce the veil of incorporation[110] and hold the State liable for the debt of its instrumentality.[111] The US courts have set stringent requirements for piercing the corporate veil. Owning a company is not, in and of itself,

[107] Ibid., Dissenting Opinion of Makhdoom Ali Khan paras 83–86, 93, 98–99.

[108] *Czarnikow v Rolimpex* (n 80); *Democratic Republic of the Congo v FG Hemisphere Associates* [2012] UKPC 27.

[109] For US case law applying these criteria, see Robert McGreevey, 'Iranian Crisis and US Law' (1980) 2 Nw J Intl L & Bus 384, 394–6.

[110] *Mellenger v New Brunswick Development Corporation* [1971] 1 WLR 604.

[111] For more details on various techniques of piercing the veil, see, e.g., Stavros Brekoulakis, *Third Parties in International Commercial Arbitration*

sufficient to create an alter ego relationship between the sovereign and the enterprise.[112]

Recently, the Tribunal in *Deutsche Bank v Sri Lanka,* a dispute concerning a hedging agreement, was ready to accept that: 'While it may be unusual for a state enterprise to be considered an organ of the State, this is only the case where the state enterprise is genuinely independent – the fact that it takes the form of a separate legal entity is not decisive.'[113] Similarly, the European Court of Human Rights held that a Contracting State might be liable for loans of a State-owned company, even though the company is a separate legal entity, provided that the company does not enjoy 'sufficient institutional and operational independence from the State'.[114] The particularly strong link that State-owned enterprises have with the State in socialist economies might have established a rebuttable presumption in favour of the dependence of the banks of the State.

Once the attribution of the acts of State-owned enterprise to the State has been established, the prohibition of the unilateral modification of public debt, presented above, should apply. Similarly, frustration or *force majeure* defences of the State regulation should not be accepted in such a case. More generously, Mayer expands the list of circumstances when the State-owned enterprise cannot invoke the legislation of the State that seeks to modify its contractual obligations. Those instances are: the State's legislative intervention in the State-owned enterprise's contractual obligations gives rise to expropriation (e.g., unlimited moratorium on the repayment of debt); the State's legislative intervention infringes an expectation that the State had itself created; and lastly the contract entered into by the State-owned enterprise was by the order, and for the benefit, of the State.[115]

(OUP 2010); Karl-Heinz Böckstiegel, 'The Legal Rules Applicable in International Commercial Arbitration Involving States or State Controlled Enterprises' in International Chamber of Commerce, *60 Years of ICC Arbitration: A Look at the Future* (ICC Publishing 1984) 117.

[112] *Seijas v Republic of Argentina*, No 1:2004cv00401 – Document 113 (SDNY 2011)). Cf. *Kensington Int'l Ltd v Republic of Congo*, 2007 US Dist LEXIS 25282 (SDNY 2007), where the court found the Congolese enterprise to be an instrumentality of Congo.

[113] *Deutsche Bank v Sri Lanka* (n 106) para. 405.

[114] See *Mykhaylenky and others v Ukraine* (App no 35091/02) ECtHR 6 June 2005 paras 43–45; *Alisic v Bosnia and Herzegovina* (App no 60642/08) ECtHR 6 November 2012 paras 68 ff.

[115] Pierre Mayer, 'La neutralisation du pouvoir normative de l'Etat en matière de contrats d'Etat' (1986) 1 Journal du Droit International 5, 62–76.

A further distinction is to be drawn with quasi-sovereign debt[116] or subnational borrowing.[117] Quasi-sovereign debt is understood here as the debt issued by subnational political subdivisions, such as municipalities or federal states. The Foreign Claims Settlement Commission in the *Winget Claim* decided that the national government would not be liable for the default of municipalities.[118] The municipal bonds contained an express disclaimer of the liability of the national government for the municipal bonds and nothing indicated in the bonds that the national government undertook any payment obligations under the bonds. In another case, the Commission defined the Soviet Government as including 'any of its present or former constituent republics, other political subdivisions, and any territories thereof' to hold the Soviet Government liable for the bonds of the City of Kharkov.[119] The conclusion is perhaps that, absent any indication to the contrary in the bonds themselves or in the constitution of the State, the national government will be liable for the debt obligations of its political subdivisions as a matter of international law.

VI. CONCLUDING REMARKS

There is no denying that the State has a wide interest in regulating the volume and content of debt in the national economy. National sovereignty is unimaginable without economic independence and freedom in regulating national economy. However, such power needs to be carefully balanced against the fairness of the action of the State that seeks to interfere with its own obligations. In entering into loan obligations, the State is acting as a private contracting party with the ensuing obligation not to renege on its own obligations in a unilateral manner as a matter of international law. As an overarching principle, States borrowing from private creditors are subject to the common regime of contract law and conflict of laws. This is not to say, however, that, in exceptional

---

116 Lee Buchheit, 'Sovereign Debt Restructuring: The Legal Context' in William Cline and Guntram Wolff (eds), *Resolving the European Debt Crisis* (Peterson Institute for International Economics 2012) 19.1.

117 Lilu Liu and Michael Waibel, 'Managing Subnational Credit and Default Risks' in Carlos Primo Baga and Gallina Vincellete (eds), *Sovereign Debt and the Financial Crisis: Will This Time Be Different?* (The World Bank 2011) 273.

118 *Winget Claim* (1958-II) 26 ILR 255.

119 *Riis Claim* (1958-II) 26 ILR 274.

circumstances, States – facing a genuine financial crisis and ensuring an adequate protection for bondholders – should not be able to engage in more or less innocuous modifications of domestic-law bonds.

5. Restructuring sovereign debt on the basis of collective action clauses

Christoph Ohler

I. INTRODUCTION

This chapter argues that the introduction of Collective Action Clauses (CACs) in sovereign bond issues helps closing a *lacuna* in State insolvency law. In the Euro-area this step was taken in 2012 by the Member States together with the establishment of the European Stability Mechanism (ESM). These CACs do not form part of public international law but of domestic civil law. This means, however, that they can be tested under the standards of international investment law. It is suggested in this chapter that the existing CACs are compatible with these standards. The main argument is that CACs are of a procedural nature only and do not affect the substantive legal position of private creditors and public debtors. This could even be assumed if CACs were introduced with retroactive effect, as was the case in Greece.

II. THE NEED FOR AN INTERNATIONALLY WORKABLE RESTRUCTURING MECHANISM

For more than three decades, a vivid debate has been taking place on how to restructure sovereign debt adequately and what the role of international law in these processes should be. It started during the Latin American debt crisis of 1982–1994,[1] resulting in the Brady Initiative, accompanied

[1] Michael Bothe and Josef Brink, 'Public Debt Restructuring – The Case for International Economic Cooperation' (1986) German YBIL 86; Rudolf Dolzer, 'Staatliche Zahlungsunfähigkeit: Zum Begriff und zu den Rechtsfolgen im Völkerrecht' in Jürgen Jekewitz (ed.), *Festschrift für Karl Josef Partsch* (Duncker & Humblot 1989) 531; see also Christian Walter, 'Debt Crisis' in Rüdiger Wolfrum (ed.), *The Max Planck Encyclopedia of Public International Law*

the Heavily Indebted Poor Countries Initiative of the International Monetary Fund (IMF) and the World Bank in 1996,[2] and intensified during the Asian and Russian debt crisis of the late 1990s,[3] and, prominently, the Argentine crisis of 2001–02.[4]

Yet, the results of international practice on sovereign insolvencies are sobering, demonstrating a case-by-case approach without clear rules and procedures. Alternative proposals developed by international institutions like the IMF[5] and academic writers[6] mostly remained unanswered in Western capitals and financial centres. With the advent of the debt crisis in Europe, however, the legal problems surrounding the restructuring of sovereign debt returned to those capitals and financial centres themselves. Sovereign insolvency is no longer an issue for developing countries and emerging economies only.[7] It has become a fundamental challenge for the stability of States that, like the Member States of the European Union, seemed to have established strong market economies and modern forms of public governance under the rule of law. Hit by the immediate effects of the debt crisis they were forced to close a *lacuna* in their legal

---

(Online Version, OUP 2014) para. 7 <http://opil.ouplaw.com/home/EPIL> accessed 30 October 2015.

[2] See <http://www.imf.org/external/np/exr/facts/hipc.htm>. A legal analysis is provided by Leonie F Guder, *The Administration of Debt Relief by the International Financial Institutions* (Springer 2009).

[3] IMF, 'Recovery of the Asian Crisis and the Role of the IMF (June 2000) IMF Issue Brief 00/05 <https://www.imf.org/external/np/exr/ib/2000/062300.htm> accessed 6 June 2016.

[4] Bundesverfassungsgericht, Case 2 BvM 1/03, Decision of 8 May 2007, *Entscheidungen des Bundesverfassungsgerichts*, vol 118, 124; Jörn Axel Kämmerer, 'Der Staatsbankrott aus völkerrechtlicher Sicht' (2005) Zeitschrift für ausländisches öffentliches Recht und Völkerrecht 651; Christoph Ohler, 'Der Staatsbankrott' (2005) Juristenzeitung 590; Alexander Szodruch, 'Necessity and Beyond – the Legal Aftermath of the Argentine Financial Crisis before the German Constitutional Court' (2007) German YBIL 523.

[5] Anne O Krueger, *A New Approach to Sovereign Debt Restructuring* (IMF 2002) <http://www.imf.org/external/pubs/ft/exrp/sdrm/eng/> accessed 7 December 2016.

[6] Christoph G Paulus, 'Ein Regelungssystem zur Schaffung eines internationalen Insolvenzrechts' (2010) Zeitschrift für Gesetzgebung 313; Steven L Schwarcz, '"Idiot's Guide" to Sovereign Debt Restructuring' (2004) Emory LJ 1189.

[7] Kenneth Dyson, *States, Debt, and Power* (OUP 2014) 640.

orders that had made them extremely vulnerable, as the case of Greece demonstrates.[8]

A. The International Public Interest in Financial Stability

The main political answer given by the European Union in 2012 was the establishment of the ESM.[9] Even if it seemed to be a revolutionary step, at least in the eyes of the German Constitutional Court[10] and many commentators, its key concepts of how to overcome a modern debt crisis rely on patterns developed by the IMF and international State practice. The characteristics of a 'modern' debt crisis are: (i) a multitude of private international bondholders as creditors; and (ii) the spread of systemic risks in global financial markets if the sovereign debtor goes bankrupt in a disorderly fashion. In reaction to that, the ESM Treaty and the new Article 136(3) TFEU signal that the orderly settling of debt crises is in the international public interest,[11] not only of the debtor country but also of all other States forming part of the same economic or political environment and fearing contagion risks.[12]

The key concepts to restoring financial stability are: (i) public financial assistance for States that have lost access to private capital markets; (ii) a private sector involvement if and to the extent necessary to assure debt relief;[13] and (iii) a reform package imposed on the debtor by international financial institutions, often termed as 'conditionality'.[14] Public financial assistance may take different forms, e.g. bilateral or multilateral loan

---

[8] Cf. Antonio Sáinz de Vicuña, 'Legal Perspectives on Sovereign Default', (2013) Bank for International Settlements Paper Series No 72112 <http://www.bis.org/publ/bppdf/bispap72t.pdf> accessed 6 June 2016.

[9] Treaty Establishing the European Stability Mechanism (ESM Treaty), consolidated version available under <http://www.esm.europa.eu/about/legal-documents/index.htm> accessed 6 June 2016.

[10] Bundesverfassungsgericht, Case 2 BvR 1390/12, Decision of 12 September 2012, *Entscheidungen des Bundesverfassungsgerichts*, Vol. 132, 195, 247 para. 128.

[11] Cf. Kern Alexander, 'Sovereign Debt Restructuring in the EU: Lessons from the Recent Crisis' in Kern Alexander and Niamh Moloney (eds), *Law Reform and Financial Markets* (Edward Elgar Publishing 2011) 306, 307; see also Jörn Axel Kämmerer, 'State Bankruptcy' in Wolfrum (n 1) Vol. IX, 489, 491 para. 5, who considers threats to the interests of mankind or to basic human rights.

[12] Sáinz de Vicuña (n 8) 112, 115.

[13] ESM Treaty (n 9) para. 12 of the Preamble.

[14] Ibid., art. 12(1).

facilities,[15] covering rising budget deficits that result from the economic downturn in the country in question. Central banks provide emergency liquidity assistance to the banking system to assure the survival of illiquid credit institutions. In some jurisdictions, the strained budgetary situation is relieved by outright purchases of sovereign bonds by the Central bank. Yet, in order to assure a balanced public budget in the medium term, budgetary reforms are not sufficient. In most cases, the tax system and general economic policies need to be thoroughly revised, the main reason why conditionality is still considered as unavoidable in political reality.

B. Private Sector Involvement

It is in this wider context[16] that private sector involvement takes place as an additional contribution to restore fiscal sustainability. Due to the existing contractual relationship between public debtor and private creditors this involvement requires *bona fide* negotiations between the parties to come to a new arrangement.[17] Debtor-creditor negotiations are *the* standard instrument to restructure sovereign debt, as can be seen in the nineteenth century debt crises in Greece and Egypt,[18] the London Agreement on German External Debts of 1953,[19] and the long-lasting practice of the London and Paris Club.[20] Worldwide, it has become an accepted form of settling the diverging interests of the debtor and its

15 Ibid., art. 16.

16 Cf. Armin von Bogdandy and Matthias Goldmann, 'Die Restrukturierung von Staatsschulden als Ausübung internationaler öffentlicher Gewalt' (2013) Zeitschrift für ausländisches öffentliches Recht und Völkerrecht 61, 70 ff. English version published as 'Sovereign Debt Restructurings as Exercises of International Public Authority' in Carlos Espósito, Yuefen Li and Juan Pablo Bohoslavsky (eds), *Sovereign Financing and International Law* (OUP 2013) 39.

17 Matthias Goldmann, 'Good Faith and Transparency in Sovereign Debt Workouts' (2014) UNCTAD Working Group on a Debt Workout Mechanism Paper <www.unctad.info/upload/Debt%20Portal/DWM%20Good%20Faith%20and%20Transparency%2020131223.pdf> accessed 6 June 2016.

18 A good historical overview is provided by Lea Heimbeck, *Die Abwicklung von Staatsbankrotten im Völkerrecht* (Nomos 2013).

19 Detlev F Vagts, 'Sovereign Bankruptcy: In re Germany (1953), in re Iraq (2004)' (2004) AJIL 302; Marc Jacob, 'London Agreement on German External Debts (1953)' in Wolfrum (n 1).

20 Kämmerer (n 11) para. 16.

creditors.[21] The purpose of these negotiations is not to wind down the creditor or to extract as many assets as possible, as in many insolvency proceedings for private debtors.[22] Instead, these negotiations aim exclusively at restructuring the existing debt in order to lay the basis for a more stable future.[23] The sovereign debtor is not a company but a State that has the ability and power to levy taxes. This income is the main source of the public budget permitting the sovereign debtor to fund its expenditures and to repay its debts. The restructuring of the debt is, therefore, an attempt to re-balance income and expenditures of the public budget in the medium term. In a political sense this requires a balancing of conflicting financial obligations and interests of the debtor State. Accordingly, the purpose of such negotiations is to explore the budgetary room for manoeuvre in the short and medium perspective. The result will always be a compromise that requires the debtor to adapt its budgetary policy for potentially a long time and the creditors to waive a considerable portion of their claims.

C. The Role of Collective Action Clauses

In the Euro-area the legal basis of these negotiations is to be found in CACs as part of the terms and conditions of the original bond issue.[24] From the point of view of public international law it is arguable that CACs are an insufficient substitute for an international debt workout mechanism, as they provide only a solution on the basis of the private law relationship between the debtor and the creditors. The political decision to rely on CACs rather than on an international agreement finds, however, a basis in Article 12(3) of the ESM Treaty itself. The article provides that the Member States of the Euro-area shall include CACs, as of 1 January 2013, in all new Euro-area government securities, with a maturity above one year, in a way which ensures that their legal impact is identical. Therefore, the ESM Treaty establishes at least a harmonised

---

[21] Lee Buchheit, 'Sovereign Debt Restructurings: the Legal Context' (2013) Bank for International Settlements Paper Series No 72 107, 108.

[22] Kämmerer (n 11) para. 4.

[23] Bundesverfassungsgericht, Case 1 BvR 987/58, Decision of 14 November 1962, *Entscheidungen des Bundesverfassungsgerichts*, vol 15, 126, 141.

[24] See also Alexander (n 11) 317; Rodrigo Olivares-Caminal, *Legal Aspects of Sovereign Debt Restructuring* (Sweet & Maxwell 2010) para. 3-007.

legal practice, building on preliminary work by the G-10 in 2002[25] which experienced a broad international recognition in the years thereafter.[26]

Another argument against the use of CACs is that they put the fate of a nation in the hands of its creditors without considering the rights and interests of the population.[27] The application of CACs does not, however, exclude a participation of the domestic parliament in the negotiations with the creditors. Looking at the root of the problem, one should also not forget that a nation puts itself in the hands of its creditors once it decides to fund the public budget by debt. In practically all cases, a restructuring is the result of many years of public fiscal mismanagement leading to over-indebtedness. When considering the rights and interests of the population, it should, therefore, be taken into account that in a parliamentary democracy this development happens, normally, with the consent of a political majority. What then should be the alternative to a consensual restructuring of the unsustainable debt? At least, negotiations between the sovereign debtor and its creditors on the basis of CACs permit finding a compromise where both sides must make considerable concessions.

It must be admitted, however, that CACs do not provide a legal basis for the role to be played by other international actors in a sovereign debt restructuring. The international scene is made up mainly of public international donors, States and international financial institutions, who provide financial assistance, often with a view to the extent and conditions of private sector involvement. Accordingly, they play the role of watchdog for the negotiations of the debtor with its creditors, thereby protecting the legitimate interest of all parties. But, they may also exercise high political pressure to conclude the restructuring process as rapidly as possible, reducing the room for further political or economic discretion of the debtor and the creditors. In the Euro-area, some of these aspects are dealt with by Article 13 of ESM Treaty which, however, does not solve all of the problems involved. This is the reason why additional

---

[25] Group of Ten, *Report of the G-10 Working Group on Contractual Clauses* (26 September 2002) <http://europa.eu/efc/sub_committee/pdf/report_of_the_g-10_working_group_on_contractual_clauses.pdf> accessed 6 June 2016.

[26] Sean Hagan, Siddharth Tiwari and José Viñals, *Sovereign Debt Restructuring – Recent Developments and Implications for the Fund's Legal and Policy Framework* (2013) IMF Paper 13 ff <www.imf.org/external/np/pp/eng/2013/042613.pdf> accessed 6 June 2016; Buchheit (n 21) 110; critical about the legitimatory effect of the CACs von Bogdandy and Goldmann (n 16) 96.

[27] von Bogdandy and Goldmann (n 16) 96.

legal constraints have to be considered, including constraints under international investment law, as will be shown below.

III. DEBT RESTRUCTURING AND INTERNATIONAL INVESTMENT LAW

Private sector involvement requires creditors to waive some of their contractual claims under a bond. This may include a reduction of the principal amount of the debt, a reduction of the interest rates owed, or a rescheduling of the repayment terms. All these forms of restructuring conflict with the principle *pacta sunt servanda*[28] and have an adverse effect on the property rights arising out of the original claims of the creditors. This is the point where international investment law comes into play.[29] Assuming that bonds are an investment under the applicable investment treaty, and that Article 25 of the Convention on the Settlement of Investment Disputes Between States and Nationals of Other States (ICSID Convention) applies,[30] the restructuring procedures and their results may be seen as an expropriation, a violation of the fair and equitable treatment (FET) standard or, as the case may be, a discrimination against some creditors compared to others.[31] Yet, this is not necessarily the case, if certain conditions to be discussed below are met and the negotiations comply with these requirements.

Against this approach it could be objected that, at the current state of international law, universally recognised requirements for sovereign debt restructurings do not exist. It has been often noted that there is no coherent international legal regime that provides a set of internationally

---

[28] Engela C Schlemmer, 'The Enforcement of Sovereign Debt' in Mario Giovanoli and Diego Devos (eds), *International Monetary and Financial Law* (OUP 2010) 418, 421, 444. Doubts about the validity of this 'Grundnorm' are expressed by Robert Howse, 'Concluding Remarks in the Light of International Law' in Espósito and others (n 16) 385.

[29] See, e.g., Ioannis Glinavos, 'Haircut Undone? The Greek Drama and Prospects for Investment Arbitration' (2014) J Intl Disp Sett 1; Christian Tietje, 'Die Argentinien-Krise aus rechtlicher Sicht – Staatsanleihen und Staatsinsolvenz' (2005) 37 Beiträge zum Transnationalen Wirtschaftsrecht 13.

[30] Michael Waibel, 'Opening Pandora's Box: Sovereign Bonds in International Arbitration' (2007) 101 AJIL 711, 719. For the view that a bond does not come within the scope of investment protected under a BIT see the award in *Poštová banka, AS and Istrokapital SE v Greece*, ICSID Case No ARB/13/8, Award (9 April 2015) paras 276 ff.

[31] Ibid., paras 742 ff.

applicable standards on sovereign insolvencies.[32] This is all the more true with respect to restructuring negotiations with bondholders which are a matter of contractual provisions and/or domestic law. Yet, international law comes into play to assure minimum standards for the negotiation procedure and the procedural rights of the parties involved.[33] These international standards for restructuring negotiations can be derived from the common standards of Bilateral Investment Treaties (BITs), such as non-discrimination and FET standards. Further guiding principles can be found in customary international law, such as the prohibition of arbitrariness and the procedural guarantee of due process of law, and also in the past practice of the IMF and creditor States.[34] In addition, the UNCTAD Principles on Responsible Sovereign Lending and Borrowing can be considered as they refer to debt restructurings under CACs.[35]

The essential questions involved are: (1) When and under which conditions may a debtor State request the opening of restructuring negotiations? (2) Which provisions relating to the negotiations may be unilaterally adopted by the debtor State and which provisions must be subject to a majority voting of the creditors? (3) Can a majority decision of the creditors bind a non-consenting minority? and (4) Which means exist to ensure the international recognition of a majority decision? These questions will be discussed in the next section under the assumption that the restructuring negotiations take place on the basis of existing CACs as part of a bond issue. Additional questions occur when statutory domestic law provides the legal basis (see Section IV below).

A. Opening Restructuring Negotiations

It can happen that a State in severe financial difficulties simply defaults without further notice to the creditors. From a private law perspective, it is a breach of contract when the debt is not paid when due.[36] The same applies when a debtor repudiates an existing debt, be it tacitly or by an express declaration. To avoid this result, the theory of odious debt

---

[32] Buchheit (n 21) 107; Ross Buckley, 'The Bankruptcy of Nations: An Idea Whose Time Has Come' (2009) Intl L 1189, 1198; Kämmerer (n 11) para. 1.

[33] For a similar (but wider) approach cf. von Bogdandy and Goldmann (n 16) 83 ff.

[34] Cf. Bothe and Brink (n 1) 109.

[35] UNCTAD, Principles on Responsible Sovereign Lending and Borrowing, amended and restated as of 10 January 2012 <http://unctad.org/en/PublicationsLibrary/gdsddf2012misc1_en.pdf> accessed 6 June 2016, Principle 15.

[36] Buchheit (n 21) 108; Kämmerer (n 11) para. 2.

attempted to legitimise the repudiation of public debts under international law.[37] Yet, this theory does not form part of customary international law.[38] A similar argumentation was that a sovereign debtor should have the right to rely on the necessity defence in order to terminate its payments unilaterally to its creditors, as happened in the Argentine debt crisis of 2001.[39] This position clearly conflicts with the general principle that contracts are binding on both parties and that any amendment, even a moratorium, requires a re-negotiation of the contractual positions. Also a denunciation of the contract would not make the repayment obligation void as the debtor could not unilaterally cancel its debt. Accordingly, any attempt to restructure an existing debt requires the opening of negotiations with the objective of adapting or reducing the payment obligations.

From the point of view of international investment law this raises the question of whether the request to open negotiations is an act of sovereign authority. This could be doubtful, since the request is based on CACs, which constitute a legal relationship governed by private law. Apart from the request addressed to the creditors and its legal nature, there is a prior decision of the sovereign debtor to open restructuring negotiations. This decision is a highly political act, driven by a budgetary emergency situation, which falls under the ambit of international investment law. In this situation, the sovereign debtor is also bound by customary international law, in particular by the principle of good faith and the prohibition of arbitrariness.[40]

In the context of restructuring proceedings, the first principle means that the debtor must request opening *bona fide* negotiations with its creditors.[41] The request must be formal and public and must, accordingly, permit all creditors to take note of it. The second principle, the prohibition of arbitrariness, imposes an obligation on the debtor to

---

[37] For an overview see Robert Howse, 'The Concept of Odious Debts in Public International Law' (2007) UNCTAD Discussion Papers No 185 <http://unctad.org/en/docs/osgdp20074_en.pdf> accessed 4 June 2016.

[38] See Lee Buchheit, Mitu Gulati and Robert Thompson, 'The Dilemma of Odious Debts' (2007) 56 Duke LJ 1201, 1230; Thomas Kleinlein, 'Rechtsfragen staatlicher Auslandsanleihen: Odious Debts, Staatsnotstand und Immunität' (2006) 44 Archiv des Völkerrechts 405, 408.

[39] Matthias Herdegen, 'Der Staatsbankrott: Probleme eines Insolvenzverfahrens und der Umschuldung bei Staatsanleihen' (2011) Wertpapier-Mitteilungen 913, 914; Walter (n 1) para. 40.

[40] *Elettronica Sicula SpA (ELSI) v United States of America*, Judgement, ICJ Reports 1989, 65 para. 128.

[41] von Bogdandy and Goldmann (n 16) 84, who base this obligation on international law.

demonstrate that its debt has become unsustainable.[42] The meaning of the term 'unsustainable' is open to economic judgment and, accordingly, difficult to define *strictu sensu*. In the long-lasting practice of the IMF, various criteria have been developed that help understand when and why a sovereign debtor is unable to repay its debt.[43] These criteria include the fiscal deficit and the public debt, the public debt-to-GDP ratio, the primary fiscal surplus as well as contingent liabilities. If a State is indebted in a foreign currency, the sustainability of the external debt must be assessed with a view to private and official capital flows and by a projection of balance of payments developments. Provided that, applying these criteria, international organisations like the IMF or other financial institutions find that a debt is no longer sustainable, there is no reason to assume that the request of the debtor to open negotiations is arbitrary.

From the point of view of international investment law one could also ask whether the over-indebtedness of the sovereign debtor and its inability to fully repay result in an expropriation of the creditors. There is, however, no reason to assume that the economic loss to be suffered by the debtors constitutes expropriation. Each creditor-debtor relationship encompasses the economic risk for the creditor that the debtor may be unable to repay its debt when due. The inherent credit risk is an unavoidable part of any bond or other financial instrument. This means that when the debtor becomes insolvent the credit risk has materialised. In this respect, there is no difference between private and public debtors even if a sovereign should, normally, be subject to domestic budgetary rules preventing an over-indebtedness to occur.[44] Yet, the application of these rules does not form part of the contractual obligations under the bonds held by the creditors. Thus, the purpose of insolvency law cannot be to prevent creditors from suffering losses. Rather, its purpose must be to balance the interests of the creditors and the debtor.

B. Procedural Rules and Substantive Decisions

CACs pursue the same objective even if their legal effect is limited. In order to understand these limits, it is necessary to differentiate between procedural rules and substantive decisions in a debt restructuring. Of

---

42 Cf. ESM Treaty (n 9) art. 13(1)(b); see also Herdegen (n 39) 915.

43 Timothy Geithner (ed.), 'Assessing Sustainability' (2002) IMF Paper <www.imf.org/external/np/pdr/sus/2002/eng/052802.pdf> accessed 4 June 2016.

44 Cf. Art. 126 of the Treaty on the Functioning of the European Union [2012] OJ C326/47.

substantive character are all decisions that have an immediate impact on the outstanding principal amount of the debt, its legal character, the interest rates owed, the currency of the payments and the maturity. In contrast to that, procedural rules do not affect the substantive aspects of a debt restructuring, but attribute the procedural position of the debtor and the creditors within the restructuring negotiations. This is (or at least should be) the proper field of application for the CACs. They provide the legal basis for negotiations between the debtor and the bondholders, they define majorities and supermajorities and the right of the debtor to aggregate creditor groups for the purpose of calculating these majorities. Yet, the procedural rules must also be fair and prevent discrimination against some of the creditors. Basic fairness requirements include the right of all creditors to register their claims, to participate – at least indirectly via representatives – in the negotiations and to be informed of the compromise offered by the debtor.[45] If these conditions are met, it is suggested, procedural CACs should not be considered as violating the FET standard under a BIT.

The starting point for a legal analysis of a substantive decision is different. As a general principle of private law, any decision on the substantive aspects of a bond amending the original contract requires the consent of all creditors. Typically, this is effected by a debt exchange which revokes the original contract and replaces it by a new bond with different terms and conditions.[46] It is a new agreement between all creditors and the debtor that has a legally binding effect on both sides. The debt exchange does not violate international investment protection standards as the legal maxim *volenti not fit iniuria* applies. However, also the usual reservation, common to all legal orders, is applicable that the consent may not be the result of fraudulent conduct, threat or coercion by the debtor in the course of the negotiations.[47]

Another substantive issue is whether a restructuring must include all creditors of a sovereign under identical terms or not. Under international investment law this question requires considering the national treatment and most-favoured nation (MFN) treatment standards with respect to the various groups of investors. In practice, two main problems will occur. The first question is whether international financial institutions providing financial assistance, in particular the IMF and the ESM, may be exempt from a restructuring. The second question is whether specific groups of

---

[45] von Bogdandy and Goldmann (n 16) 86 ff.

[46] Group of Ten (n 25) 5.

[47] Cf. Arts 49–51 of the Vienna Convention on the Law of Treaties (1969) 1155 UNTS 331.

investors, e.g., small private households, may get better conditions than other groups. As far as international financial institutions are concerned, they normally claim not to participate in a debt restructuring, and accordingly invoke a preferred creditor status.[48] This legal standpoint seems to be justified as long as these international financial institutions have intervened in the international public interest, in particular when a sovereign debtor has lost access to the capital markets.[49] In this situation, only international financial institutions are prepared to refinance the debtor, whereas private investors refrain from taking further risks. A different justification is necessary for privileges in favour of specific investors like small private households. If the other investors give their consent to this special treatment, legal risks can be effectively avoided.

C. Binding Effect of Majority Decisions and Limitation on Suits

In practice, some holders of bonds will not consent to the compromise reached by the majority, including the decision to agree to a novation and exchange the old bonds against new bonds. But the purpose of CACs is also to extend the majority decisions to the non-consenting minority creditors. Substantive decisions (so-called reserve matters) require, under most CACs, a supermajority (e.g., more than 75 per cent) of holders, whereas procedural decisions can be made with a lower majority. The main legal effect is that the outcome of the negotiations, e.g., a novation, is binding also for non-consenting parties. Undoubtedly, the binding effect of majority decisions means a material change of the legal position of non-consenting bondholders. Under CACs existing as part of the terms and conditions of a bond purchased by the creditor, however, the purchase of the bond constitutes the consent also to be bound by a future majority decision of the holders of the same issue. This leaves no room to argue that a compromise reached by the majority creditors with the debtor violates contractual rights of the minority creditors. To this extent, CACs are the legal basis of a 'creditor democracy',[50] where majority decisions have a binding effect on all other creditors.

Furthermore, the legal position of individual holders of bonds is restricted by limitations on the right to enforce their claims and institute judicial proceedings against the debtor. The purpose of these limitations

---

[48] ESM Treaty (n 9) para. 13 of the Preamble; cf. also the standpoint of the European Central Bank referring to Article 123 TFEU, Sáinz de Vicuña (n 8) 117 ff.

[49] von Bogdandy and Goldmann (n 16) 92.

[50] Ibid., 85, comparing the creditors to members of a Parliament.

is to protect the restructuring negotiations against attempts of a creditor to improve unilaterally its individual economic position by initiating a lawsuit before a court or tribunal. These enforcement limitations keep all creditors in 'one boat' as long as the negotiations have not been concluded. The legitimacy of this measure should also be recognised[51] in international investment law and should, it is submitted, not be considered as a violation of the FET standard. After the successful conclusion of the negotiations or when they finally fail, an investor is not barred from filing a claim under a BIT against the sovereign debtor.

D. International Recognition of Restructuring Measures

When CACs meet the requirements and are applied as discussed above, there should, normally, not be a problem with the international recognition of restructuring measures in other jurisdictions than that of the sovereign debtor. The recognition is a matter of private international law, and the conflict of law provisions are to be found in domestic law or, in the EU, in the Rome-I Regulation.[52] According to these rules, the *lex contractus* of the debt exchange, which creates a new contractual obligation resolving the old contract should be applied in all legal orders. *Ordre public* aspects, which could hinder such application,[53] should, it is submitted, not come into play as long as the restructuring procedure complied with the conditions mentioned above. The same reasoning should be applied in investment arbitration dispute on the legality of the restructuring procedure. If debtor States comply with the principles described above, holdout creditors should not be successful when filing a claim under a BIT.

IV. RESTRUCTURING UNDER DOMESTIC LEGAL REGIMES

The legal problems are considerably different when bonds do not contain CACs. In this case, statutory domestic law can provide the necessary legal basis for a sovereign debt restructuring. From the point of view of the creditors, their legal position is not so different, since CACs are also

---

51 Ibid., 96 ff.

52 Regulation (EC) No 593/2008 of the European Parliament and of the Council on the law applicable to contractual obligations (Rome I) [2008] OJ L177/6.

53 Ibid., art. 21.

unilaterally adopted by the issuer (debtor). Even if CACs form part of the contractual relationship, the creditors are not in a position to negotiate the individual provisions with the debtor. In the Euro-area, this is underlined by Article 12(3) ESM Treaty, which provides that the legal impact of the CACs must be 'identical' in all participating Member States.

The situation becomes more complicated, however, when a statute is introduced only after the debt crisis breaks out. Then its provisions have a retroactive legal effect on the original contractual claims. This was the case in Greece in 2012.[54] It is suggested, that this retroactivity can be justified by the legitimate objective to restructure effectively the sovereign debt. The alternative would be a disorderly restructuring where all participants would suffer from a considerable lack of legal certainty. The necessity of retroactive provisions is even higher when the restructuring must take place as a prerequisite for further financial assistance by international lenders like the IMF or the ESM. Both arguments, it is suggested, apply to domestic law as well as to public international law, including international investment law.

Notwithstanding the general legitimacy of a national restructuring statute, its individual provisions must comply with international investment law standards. When the statutory provisions unilaterally amend the substantive elements of the bonds (principal amount, interest rates, currency, maturity, legal nature), there is sufficient reason to assume that this could constitute an expropriation. The legal analysis differs, by contrast, if the scope of the statutory provisions is confined to procedural rules for a consensual restructuring of the sovereign debt in cooperation with the creditors. Procedural rules aim at organising meetings of the holders of the bonds with the sovereign debtor, aggregating holders, defining majorities and empowering the majority to agree on an amendment of the original terms and conditions or to a debt exchange. In a general sense, procedural rules, even if they have retroactive effect, help establish a workable 'creditor democracy'. This is also true for a statutory provision that establishes a binding effect of majority decisions on all creditors, including the non-consenting creditors. With respect to the requirements of non-discrimination and FET standard, the statutory rules should be practically identical with internationally recognised CACs.

In this situation, however, the absence of a legal basis for the international recognition of national restructuring measures is painfully felt. Article VIII(2)(b) of the IMF Articles of Agreement does not apply,

---

[54] Hagan and others (n 26) 29 para. 38.

not even by analogy. In the EU, some relief could be, it is submitted, provided by Article 9(3) of the Rome I Regulation, which provides:

> Effect may be given to the overriding mandatory provisions of the law of the country where the obligations arising out of the contract have to be or have been performed, in so far as those overriding mandatory provisions render the performance of the contract unlawful. In considering whether to give effect to those provisions, regard shall be had to their nature and purpose and to the consequences of their application or non-application.

The recognition of foreign overriding mandatory provisions in other jurisdictions is nothing new in private international law, even if it is, in practice, rarely done. In the case of foreign restructuring statutes, however, there could be a field of application for Article 9(3) of the Rome I Regulation. These laws serve a common international interest, namely the maintenance of financial stability. Their application would protect the effectiveness of restructuring procedures, while leaving room for a detailed case-by-case analysis in the interest not only of the sovereign debtor, but also of the minority holders of bonds. Again, the same balancing of interests should apply in an investment arbitration dispute on the legality of the restructuring procedure.

V. CONCLUSIONS

So far, the legal validity of CACs has not been tested in international courts and tribunals. However, they promise to offer viable solutions for a complex and burdensome economic situation, provided that their content and their application are in conformity with international standards. To this extent, it is submitted that the legal analysis should distinguish between procedural rules and substantive decisions, where substantive decisions require the consent of a qualified majority of creditors, while the procedural framework for restructuring negotiations may be unilaterally adopted by the sovereign debtor, provided that the specific procedural rules are in conformity with the standards of non-discrimination and FET under a BIT. When these conditions are fulfilled, there is no room to assume that a debt restructuring violates international investment law.

6. Sovereign bond disputes before investment treaty tribunals: Safeguarding the exercise of collective action clauses with a single-limb voting mechanism

Yanying Li

I. INTRODUCTION

States often borrow from one or more of the following sources: commercial banks; bondholders; governments; and multilateral institutions such as the IMF and World Bank.[1] At present, there is no international insolvency regime governing sovereign debt crisis, and sovereign debt defaults are dealt with using an ad hoc, individual case-by-case approach. In practice, in order to avoid an eternal default, the sovereign debtor is compelled to seek debt relief from creditors before or shortly after the default, via an extension of maturity, and/or a reduction of the value of the claim. Such relief is obtained by renegotiating the relevant debt instruments with individual creditors, which is commonly referred to by the term 'debt restructuring'.

Renegotiations with multilateral creditors are often conducted in this ad hoc manner. Renegotiations with bilateral creditors who are members of the Paris Club are conducted through the Club's processes. The Paris Club is an informal group of official creditors with 19 permanent members and a small secretariat in Paris.[2] Countries that are not

---

[1] Anna Gelpern and Mitu Gulati, 'Public Symbol in Private Contract: A Case Study' (2006) 84 Wash U L Rev 1627, 1632–3; Lex Rieffel, *Restructuring Sovereign Debt: The Case for Ad Hoc Machinery* (The Brookings Institution 2003) 95.

[2] Paris Club's official website <www.clubdeparis.org/sections/composition/membres-permanents-et/membres-permanents> accessed 10 October 2014. See

members of the Paris Club renegotiate with the sovereign debtor on an ad hoc basis. Renegotiations with commercial banks are either purely ad hoc or conducted through the London Club, an informal group of commercial banks with no fixed membership and no secretariat.[3] Renegotiations with bondholders are conducted through exchange offers prepared by the sovereign debtor. Such exchange offers could take the form of either a single restructuring proposal or a menu of different restructuring options to reduce the value of the claim. Occasionally bondholder committees are formed on an ad hoc basis to facilitate the process.[4]

In the current debt market, traded securities such as bonds (instead of commercial bank loans) serve as the primary means of financing sovereign debt. Even though trading securities has improved the efficiency of the global financial market, it creates coordination problems for sovereign States trying to restructure their debts. Creditors have become increasingly numerous, anonymous and difficult to coordinate. Individual bondholders only relate to each other because they participate in bonds of the same series which share the same legal terms and payment mechanism. Given that bonds are easily tradable debt instruments, the identities of bondholders are constantly changing. In many cases, identifying and communicating with bondholders requires the help of clearance and settlement institutions. For some bonds that are bearer instruments, it is almost impossible to identify or communicate with unnamed individual bondholders.

Needless to say, the large number of bondholders makes it very hard for the sovereign issuer to organise debt renegotiations. It is likely that different kinds of creditors have different business interests and risk profiles. Investment banks have an interest in keeping the debt performing due to accounting issues. This is different from private investors who may have invested savings in the hope of capital gains. Matters become more complex if the outstanding bonds that need to be restructured are

---

generally Enrique Cosio-Pascal, 'The Emerging of a Multilateral Forum for Debt Restructuring: The Paris Club', (2008) UNCTAD Discussion Papers No 192 <http://unctad.org/en/Docs/osgdp20087_en.pdf> accessed 10 October 2014.

3 Rieffel (n 1) 103.

4 See for example Mark Richards, 'The Republic of Congo's Debt Restructuring: Are Sovereign Creditors Getting Their Voice Back?' (2010) 73 L & Contemp Probs 273. Creditors' committees were also organized in the Greek debt restructuring, see Jeromin Zettelmeyer, Cristoph Trebesch and Mitu Gulati, 'The Greek Debt Restructuring: An Autopsy' Peterson Institute for International Economics Working Paper Series, WP13-8 (2013).

subject to different applicable laws. Even though it may be in the interests of all bondholders to negotiate collectively to reach a debt restructuring agreement, some individual bondholders may choose to hold out for some additional time. By holding out, they expect the sovereign issuer to pay its obligation in full amount while other bondholders may only get partial payment. This presents the so-called collective action problem in sovereign debt restructuring.

In June 2014, a group of holdout creditors won a legal battle in US courts against Argentina in the context of Argentina's sovereign debt restructurings in 2005 and 2010 (*NML Capital v Argentina*).[5] Subsequently in October 2014, the Executive Board of the International Monetary Fund (IMF) approved a staff paper on 'Strengthening the Contractual Framework to Address Collective Action Problems in Sovereign Debt Restructuring',[6] which suggests a few contractual reforms to tackle collective action problems so as to achieve orderly sovereign debt restructurings.[7] Among other things, this staff paper promoted the use of Collective Action Clauses (CACs) with a menu of voting procedures, including:

(1) a series-by-series voting procedure, which enables a qualified majority of bondholders of a specific bond issuance to bind the minority of the same issuance to the terms of a restructuring if a minimum threshold of support is achieved in this specific issuance;
(2) a two-limb aggregated voting procedure, which enables a qualified majority of bondholders of multiple bond issuances to bind the minority of these multiple bond issuances to the terms of a restructuring if a minimum threshold of support is achieved in each issuance and across all issuances being restructured; or
(3) a single-limb voting procedure, which enables a qualified majority of bondholders of multiple bond issuances to bind the minority of these multiple bond issuances to the terms of a restructuring if a

[5] See *NML Capital, Ltd v Republic of Argentina*, 699 F.3d 246 (2d Cir. 2012) and *NML Capital, Ltd v Republic of Argentina*, 727 F.3d 230 (2d Cir. 2013).

[6] IMF Press Release No14/459 (6 October 2014) <www.imf.org/external/np/sec/pr/2014/pr14459.htm> accessed 5 June 2016.

[7] IMF, 'Strengthening the Contractual Framework to Address Collective Action Problems in Sovereign Debt Restructuring' (2014) <www.imf.org/external/pp/longres.aspx?id=4911>accessed 5 June 2016.

minimum threshold of support is achieved simply across all issuances being restructured.[8]

It should be stated at the outset that holders of sovereign bonds of the same issuance/series are parties to the same legal instrument, thereby enjoying the same legal rights and protection. By contrast, holders of bonds of different series may be subject to different payment terms and legal protections. As the purpose of CACs is to enable a qualified majority of bondholders to bind the minority bondholders to the terms of a restructuring, different voting procedures permit different levels of influence that minority bondholders could potentially exercise over the restructuring process. Under options (1) and (2), a creditor or a group of creditors could obtain a blocking position in a particular series and effectively prevent the operation of a CAC in that series. By contrast, a single-limb voting procedure in option (3) will enable contract terms to be amended on the basis of a single vote across all affected instruments, thereby limiting the ability of holdout creditors to undermine the restructuring process in a particular series.[9] To ensure an equitable treatment among creditors, the chapter suggests that, in a single-limb voting procedure, sovereign issuers should offer the same restructuring terms or the same menu of restructuring terms to all affected bondholders.[10]

This chapter analyses the mechanics of different types of CACs, in particular the nature of a single-limb voting mechanism. It explores the implications of a single-limb voting mechanism from the perspective of creditor protection, as under its rules, dissenting minority bondholders are forced to follow the decision of the majority bondholders. It is worth clarifying that the purpose of this chapter is not to find legal arguments for vulture funds but to analyse the level of protection for the remaining vast majority of individual bondholders, such as pensioners. More specifically, this chapter points out that a single-limb voting mechanism resembles the cram-down procedure under bankruptcy law. Based on a comparison between the single-limb voting mechanism and the cram-down procedure under the US bankruptcy law for municipalities, this chapter argues that the cram-procedure for municipality bankruptcy contains a better safeguard provision for the purpose of protecting the rights of dissenting minority bondholders. Having looked at the case law concerning fair and equitable treatment (FET) standard before investment

[8] Ibid., 22.
[9] Ibid., 20.
[10] Ibid., 21.

treaty tribunals, this chapter suggests that sovereign bond disputes could be brought before investment treaty tribunals in the event that dissenting minority bondholders suffer unfair discrimination and unfair treatment during the exercise of CACs with a single-limb voting mechanism.

The chapter is structured as follows: Part II provides a detailed explanation of the different types of CACs available and illustrates the difference between each voting mechanism through concrete examples. Part III introduces the cram-down procedure in US bankruptcy law, under which a dissenting class of creditors may be forced to accept a restructuring plan, and finds that the single-limb voting mechanism resembles the cram-down procedure. Part IV compares the safeguard provision for the single-limb voting mechanism and that for the bankruptcy cram-down procedure, and then concludes that the cram-down procedure provides better safeguard protection for the minority bondholders through the prohibition of unfair discrimination and the provision of fair and equitable treatment. Part V sets out the case law on the FET standard in investment arbitration and argues that, if sovereign bond disputes in connection with the operation of a single-limb voting mechanism were brought before investment treaty tribunals, those tribunals could use the case law from US bankruptcy courts concerning the safeguard element for the cram-down procedure as a tool to assist their interpretation of the FET standard under investment treaties in this particular context. Part VI presents the concluding remarks.

II. THE MECHANICS OF DIFFERENT TYPES OF CACS

This part sets out the mechanics of different types of CACs, including traditional CACs, aggregated CACs with a two-limb voting mechanism and aggregated CACs with a single-limb voting mechanism. Through the illustration of how each type of CACs differs from each other, this section demonstrates that aggregated CACs with a single-limb voting mechanism are a powerful tool for sovereign issuers to conduct a sovereign debt restructuring.

A. Traditional CACs

Traditional CACs enable a qualified majority of bondholders to bind all holders of the same bond issuance to a change of the contract terms, including the maturity date and the amount of interest and principal, on the basis of a series-by-series vote.[11] These CACs began to appear in bonds governed by English law in the 1980s.[12] In the wake of the 1995 Mexican crisis and the 2001–02 Argentine debt default, the IMF also began pushing for the adoption of such CACs in sovereign bonds governed by New York law, in order to facilitate the restructuring of sovereign bonds held by a large number of anonymous creditors.[13] Countries such as Mexico, Brazil, Belize, Guatemala, Venezuela and Uruguay were among the first to include traditional CACs in their New York law bonds.[14]

In 2004, following the shift to traditional CACs in the New York market, the International Capital Market Association (ICMA) promulgated a set of template CACs for sovereign bonds issued under English law.[15] Paragraph (e) of the template provides that:

---

[11] Strictly speaking, the term CACs includes two types of clauses: (1) 'majority restructuring' provisions, which enable a qualified majority of bondholders to bind all holders to the same bond issuance to the financial terms of a restructuring; and (2) 'majority enforcement' provisions, which allows a qualified majority of bondholders to limit the ability of a minority bondholders to enforce their rights following a default. The former type is most frequently employed in practice. See IMF, 'Collective Action Clauses in Sovereign Bond Contracts – Encouraging Greater Use' (prepared by the Policy Development and Review, International Capital Markets and Legal Departments) (2002) <www.imf.org/external/np/psi/2002/eng/060602a.htm> accessed 5 June 2016. The typical threshold for a qualified majority is 75 per cent. See Michael Bradley and Mitu Gulati, 'Collective Action Clauses for the Eurozone: An Empirical Analysis' [2013] Rev Fin 1.

[12] Mark Weidemaier and Mitu Gulati, 'How Markets Work: The Lawyer's Version' in Bettina Lange, Dania Thomas and Austin Sarat (eds), *Studies in Law, Politics, and Society* (Emerald Group Publishing 2013) 107. For a discussion of old English CACs, see Anna Gelpem and Mitu Gulati, 'A Modern Legal History of Sovereign Debt' (2010) 73(4) L & Contemp Probs viii.

[13] IMF (n 11); Bradley and Gulati (n 11) 17, 6 and 10; Mark Weidemaier and Mitu Gulati, 'A People's History of Collective Action Clauses' (2014) 54 Va JIL 1.

[14] Andrew Haldane and others, 'Optimal Collective Action Clause Thresholds', (2005) Bank of England Working Paper No 2497 and 9 <www.bankofengland.co.uk/research/Documents/workingpapers/2005/wp249.pdf> accessed 2 February 2016.

[15] International Primary Market Association, 'Standard Collective Action Clauses (CACs) for the Terms and Conditions of Sovereign Notes' (2004). The name has since been changed to the International Capital Market Association; see <https://www.icmagroup.org/ICMAGroup/files/3c/3cc80d90-da99-4562-8ef2-f604a8e5963e.PDF> accessed 2 February 2016.

> *Modifications*: Subject as provided in paragraph (d) (Matters requiring unanimity), any modification of any provision of these Conditions may be made if approved by an Extraordinary Resolution or a Written Resolution. In these Conditions, **'Extraordinary Resolution'** means a resolution passed at a meeting of Noteholders duly convened and held in accordance with the Fiscal Agency Agreement by a majority of at least:
>
> (i) in the case of a Reserved Matter, 75 per cent of the *aggregate principal amount of the outstanding Notes*; or
> (ii) in the case of a matter other than a Reserved Matter, 66 2/3 per cent of the aggregate principal amount of the outstanding Notes which are represented at that meeting.
>
> Any Extraordinary Resolution duly passed at any such meeting shall be binding on *all the Noteholders*, whether present or not and whether they voted in favour or not, and all Coupon holders.[16]

As stated in the template CAC, the decision of a qualified majority (75 per cent in respect of a Reversed Matter such as a change of payment terms) binds 'all the Noteholders' of the same bond series under such a collective action mechanism. To phrase it another way, they bind non-participating bondholders only on a series-by-series basis.[17] They are not considered as an effective restructuring tool for sovereign issuers because, if the minimum voting threshold is not reached within a single series, holders of bonds of that series will be forced to accept a restructuring proposal.

B. Aggregated CACs with a Two-Limb Voting Mechanism

In recent years, aggregated CACs with a two-limb voting mechanism have started appearing in the sovereign bond market, which would allow votes to take place across different series (i.e., not just within one series). So far, four countries have included aggregated CACs with a two-limb voting mechanism in their sovereign bonds—Argentina, the Dominican Republic, Greece and Uruguay.[18] The minimum voting thresholds contained in such a two-limb voting mechanism include:

---

16 Ibid., 2–3 (emphasis added).

17 Lee Buchheit and Mitu Gulati, 'Sovereign Bonds and the Collective Will', (2002) 51 Emory LJ 1317; Charles Schmerler, 'Restructuring Sovereign Debt' in James Silkenat and Charles Schmerler (eds), *The Law of International Insolvencies and Debt Restructuring* (OUP 2006) 461–2.

18 IMF, 'Sovereign Debt Restructuring—Recent Developments and Implications for the Fund's Legal and Policy Framework' (2013) para. 40 <www.imf.org/external/np/pp/eng/2013/042613.pdf> accessed 10 October 2014.

(1) 75 per cent (Greece) or 85 per cent (Argentina, the Dominican Republic and Uruguay) of the aggregated outstanding principal of *all* series to be affected; and
(2) 66.2/3 per cent of the outstanding principal of *each* individual series to be affected.[19]

To give an example, the aggregated CAC with a two-limb voting mechanism contained in the Uruguay Prospectus Supplement-Offer to Exchange of 10 April 2003 provides as follows:

- If Uruguay proposes any reserve matter modification to the terms and conditions of the debt securities of two or more series, or to the indenture insofar as it affects the debt securities of two or more series, in either case as part of a single transaction, Uruguay may elect to proceed pursuant to provisions of the indenture providing that such modifications may be made, and future compliance therewith may be waived, for each affected series if made with the consent of Uruguay and the holders of not less than 85 per cent in *aggregate principal amount of the outstanding debt securities of all series affected by that modification (taken in aggregate)*, and
- the holders of not less than 66.2/3 per cent in *aggregate principal amount of the outstanding debt securities of that series (taken individually)*.[20]

From a sovereign issuer's perspective, such aggregated CACs with a two-limb voting mechanism are more effective in conducting debt restructurings as they contain a lower threshold for votes to take place within a single series in respect of any reserve matter modification (66.2/3 per cent), such as a change of payment terms, as the following example illustrates. Let us assume that holders of 70 per cent in principal amount of outstanding bonds in a particular series have voted in favour of a restructuring proposal. Under traditional CACs, the sovereign issuer would not be able to restructure this series because the minimum threshold of 75 per cent is not reached. However, under Uruguay's aggregated CAC with a two-limb voting mechanism, Uruguay may still be able to restructure this series if holders of 85 per cent in principal

[19] Ibid.

[20] Cleary Gottlieb Steen & Hamilton LLP, 'Collective Action Clauses with Aggregation Mechanisms' (2 November 2011) <http://scholarship.law.duke.edu/cgi/viewcontent.cgi?article=3004&context=faculty_scholarship> accessed 10 October 2014 (emphasis added).

amount of outstanding bonds of all series affected by the proposed restructuring vote in favour.

Notably in the European bond market, the Treaty Establishing the European Stability Mechanism (ESM) requires the inclusion of CACs, as of 1 January 2013, in all Euro-area government securities with maturity above one year.[21] The model CAC prepared by the Sub-Committee on EU Sovereign Debt Markets of the EU Economic and Financial Committee includes an aggregation feature—referred to as cross-series modification—that permits changes to bind more than one series of bonds.[22] Compared with the Uruguay aggregated CAC, the aggregated CAC of the Eurozone model adopts a lower threshold (75 per cent) to calculate the affirmative vote of the aggregate principal amount of the outstanding debt securities of *all* the series that would be affected by the proposed modification.[23] As regards the nature of aggregated CACs with a two-limb voting mechanism, the EU Committee on EU Sovereign Debt Markets explains that these CACs can be understood as CACs that work at the series level, in that the decision of a specified majority binds all holders of all affected series, 'with the important further protection that holders of any individual series of affected bonds will not be bound by the decision of the group as a whole unless they also vote in favour of the proposed modification'.[24]

From a sovereign issuer's perspective, aggregated CACs are more effective than traditional CACs but they still have one key limitation—

---

21 Art. 12(3) of the Treaty provides that 'Collective action clauses shall be included in all new euro area government securities, with maturity above one year, from July 2013, in a standardised manner which ensures that their legal impact is identical'. See Treaty Establishing the European Stability Mechanism <http://ec.europa.eu/economy_finance/articles/financial_operations/2011-07-11-esm-treaty_en.htm> accessed 10 October 2014.

22 The model clause is available at <http://europa.eu/efc/sub_committee/cac/index_en.htm> accessed 30 September 2014. See 'Euro Area Member States Take Collective Action to Facilitate Sovereign Debt Restructuring' (2012) Clifford Chance Newsletter <www.cliffordchance.com/publicationviews/publications/2012/12/euro_area_memberstatestakecollectiveactiont.html> accessed 10 October 2014.

23 'Common Terms of Reference' of the Eurozone Model CAC (17/02/2012) para. 2.2 <http://europa.eu/efc/sub_committee/pdf/cac_-_text_model_cac.pdf> accessed 10 October 2014.

24 EFC Sub-Committee on EU Sovereign Debt Markets, 'Model Collective Action Clause Supplemental Explanatory Note' (2012) 3-4 <http://europa.eu/efc/sub_committee/pdf/supplemental_explanatory_note_on_the_model_cac_-_26_march_2012.pdf> accessed 10 October 2014.

they still enable a creditor or a group of creditors to obtain a blocking position in a particular series.[25] Here is another example. Let us suppose that holders of only 50 per cent in principal amount of outstanding bonds in a particular series have voted in favour of a restructuring proposal. Without reaching the minimum threshold of 66.2/3 per cent in respect of each series under Uruguay's aggregated CAC and the Eurozone model CAC, the sovereign issuer would still not be able to force the dissenting minority bondholders to participate in the restructuring.

C. Aggregated CACs with a Single-Limb Voting Mechanism

By contrast, a single-limb voting mechanism, as explained in the IMF paper, 'requires only a single vote calculated on an aggregated basis across all affected bond series'.[26]

It does not envisage any voting taking place within *each* individual series. Designed in this fashion, the collective action mechanism is activated simply when a qualified majority of the aggregate principal amount outstanding of all affected bond series is reached. As a result, a single-limb voting mechanism removes the possibility of creditors obtaining a controlling position within a particular series to block the restructuring of that series,[27] thereby rendering the restructuring process more debtor-friendly.

One example of a single-limb voting mechanism is the template ICMA clause published in May 2015, which sets out as follows:

> 'Multiple Series Single Limb Extraordinary Resolution' means a resolution considered at separate meetings of the holders of each affected series of Debt Securities Capable of Aggregation, duly convened and held in accordance with the procedures prescribed by the Issuer and the [Fiscal Agent/Trustee/other bondholder representative] pursuant to paragraph (a) (Convening Meetings of Noteholders; Conduct of Meetings of Noteholders; Written Resolutions), as supplemented if necessary, which is passed by a majority of at least 75 per cent *of the aggregate principal amount of the outstanding debt securities of all affected series of Debt Securities Capable of Aggregation (taken in aggregate).*[28]

---

25 IMF (n 18) para. 41.

26 IMF (n 7) 20.

27 Ibid.

28 ICMA English Law Standard CACs, Pari Passu and Creditor Engagement Provisions, May 2015, 4 <www.icmagroup.org/resources/Sovereign-Debt-Information/>, accessed 6 March 2016 (emphasis added).

Contrary to traditional CACs and aggregated CACs with a two-limb voting mechanism, CACs with a single-limb voting mechanism do not require any voting to take place within each single series. Thus, it is much easier for sovereign issuers to obtain sufficient votes to bind all creditors to a restructuring plan under a single-limb voting mechanism. Whereas insufficient votes within a single series would hinder the operation of traditional CACs and aggregated CACs with a two-limb voting mechanism, they do not have any impact on the single-limb voting mechanism.

Let us suppose that holders of only 50 per cent in principal amount of outstanding bonds in a particular series have voted in favour of a restructuring proposal. Under traditional CACs, the sovereign issuer would not be able to restructure this series because the minimum threshold of 75 per cent is not reached. The same holds true under Uruguay's aggregated CAC and the Eurozone model CAC as the minimum threshold of 66.2/3 per cent in respect of each series is also not reached, regardless of the outcome in respect of votes across all series. However, under this single-limb voting mechanism, the sovereign issuer may still be able to force the dissenting bondholders in this series to accept the restructuring proposal if at least 75 per cent of the aggregate principal amount of the outstanding debt of all affected series vote in favour of the restructuring proposal. This is a very powerful restructuring tool for sovereign issuers.

It is worth noting that the IMF and the ICMA did not promote the use of the single-limb voting mechanism as a standalone voting procedure in CACs contained in future sovereign bond issuances. Instead, they promoted the use of a single-limb voting mechanism as one of the three options for votes to take place in the context of CACs. They introduced the concept of 'Debt Securities Capable of Aggregation', which simply refers to those debt securities that allow votes to take place on an aggregated basis in the context of CACs, with either a two-limb voting mechanism or a single-limb voting mechanism.[29]

D. Market Practice

In September 2015, the IMF published a survey that set out the market practice in relation to its recommended type of CACs with a menu of different types of voting mechanisms. The survey covers international sovereign bonds whose issuances were announced between 1 October

---

[29] Ibid., 3.

2014 and 31 July 2015, except for Euro-area sovereign issuances (as they are required under law to include Eurozone model CAC).[30] During this period, there have been 73 international sovereign bond issuances, by 37 sovereign issuers, for a total nominal principal amount of approximately US$ 86 billion.[31]

According to this survey, a significant number of sovereign issuers have included the new CAC with a menu of three types of voting mechanisms (including a single-limb voting mechanism) as recommended in the IMF staff paper. These sovereign issuers are Kazakhstan, Vietnam, Mexico, Chile, Ethiopia, Indonesia, Colombia, Tunisia, Dominican Republic, Panama, Croatia, Armenia, Bulgaria, Montenegro, Ecuador, Costa Rica, Turkey, Gabon, Egypt, Zambia and Jamaica.[32]

III. CRAM-DOWNS IN BANKRUPTCY LAW AND SINGLE-LIMB VOTING MECHANISM

Having explained the mechanics of different types of CACs, this part explores the similarity between a single-limb voting mechanism and cram-down procedures in domestic bankruptcy law systems; for ease of reference, the comparison is made with the bankruptcy law for municipalities in the US.

It should be stated at the outset that cram-down procedures exist in US bankruptcy law for all kinds of debtors, including consumers, companies and municipalities. Among these debtors, the status of municipalities is most similar to that of States in the context of sovereign debt restructurings.[33] As a result, the bankruptcy law for municipalities—US Code Chapter 9 on municipality bankruptcy[34]—will be used as an example for our discussion on cram-down procedures.

---

30 IMF, 'Progress Report on Inclusion of Enhanced Contractual Provisions in International Sovereign Bond Contracts' (September 2015) 17.

31 Ibid., 4.

32 Ibid., 17–18.

33 A municipality's insolvency is determined on the basis of a cash-flow analysis, not budget deficiency analysis; a municipality is insolvent when it is unable to pay its debts as they become due. *In re Hamilton Creek Metropolitan District*, 143 F.3d 1381 (10th Cir 1998); *In Re City of Bridgeport*, 129 BR 332 (Bankr D Conn, 1991).

34 The US Bankruptcy Code defines a 'municipality' as a 'political subdivision or public agency or instrumentality of a state'. It includes cities and towns, villages, counties, taxing districts, municipal utilities, and school districts.

A. Cram-Down in US Municipality Bankruptcy

The US federal bankruptcy law Chapter 9 on municipality bankruptcy is designed to provide a financially distressed municipality protection from its creditors during the period when it develops and negotiates a restructuring plan for adjusting its debts. Adjustment of the debts of a municipality is typically accomplished by extending debt maturities, reducing the amount of principal or interest, or refinancing the debt by obtaining a new loan. The functions of bankruptcy courts in Chapter 9 cases generally include approving the petition (if the debtor is eligible), confirming a plan of debt adjustment, and ensuring implementation of the plan.

Under Chapter 9 on municipality bankruptcy, a restructuring plan is deemed to be accepted by *a* class of creditors if creditors holding at least two-thirds in amount and more than one-half in number of all claims in that class accept the plan.[35] With respect to all classes of creditors, a restructuring plan can be confirmed if *each* class of claims or interests 'has accepted the plan' or 'is not impaired under the plan'.[36] In the event of the failure of an impaired class (i.e., a class of creditors whose rights are impaired under the restructuring plan) to accept the plan, the plan can still be confirmed under the cram-down procedure in Section 1129(b)(1): 'the court, on request of the proponent of the plan, shall confirm the plan … If the plan does not discriminate unfairly, and is fair and equitable,

---

A municipality may be a debtor in a Chapter 9 case if: (a) it has been 'specifically authorized' to be a Chapter 9 debtor; b) is 'insolvent'; and (c) has either: (i) obtained majority approval of creditors in each class for the proposed plan of reorganisation; or (ii) negotiated in 'good faith' with creditors and failed to obtain such a majority; or (iii) is unable to negotiate with creditors because such negotiations are 'impracticable'. See 11 USC §101(40), United States Courts: Chapter 9 Municipality Bankruptcy; Zack A Clement and R Andrew Black, 'Important Issues in a Chapter 9 Case for a Municipality' (2014) 88(1) Am Bankr LJ 41.

[35] The US Code Title 11 Section 943(b) sets out the conditions when the court shall confirm the plan, which include that the plan complies with the provisions of this title made applicable by Section 901. Section 901(a) explicitly makes Sections 1126(c) dealing with the bankruptcy of companies applicable for municipalities, which provides that a class of claims has accepted a plan if such plan has been accepted by creditors 'that hold at least two-thirds in amount and more than one-half in number' of all allowed claims. See 11 USC §§943(b), 901(a) and 1126(c).

[36] 11 USC §1129(a)(8). It should be noted that Section 901(a) explicitly makes Section 1129(a)(8) dealing with the bankruptcy of companies applicable for municipalities.

with respect to each class of claims or interests that is impaired under, and has not accepted the plan'.[37] This is the so-called cram-down procedure.

B. Similarity Between a Single-Limb Voting Mechanism and the Cram-Down Procedure

As explained in Part II.C, a single-limb voting mechanism requires only a single vote to be calculated on an aggregated basis across all affected bond series. It does not envisage any voting taking place within each individual series. As a result, the collective action mechanism is activated simply when a qualified majority of the aggregate principal amount outstanding of all affected bond series is reached. It therefore removes the possibility of dissenting minority bondholders within a particular series to block the restructuring of that series.

Section A above shows that the purpose of the cram-down procedure in municipality bankruptcy is to force an impaired class that has not agreed to the terms of a restructuring to accept a proposed restructuring plan. Although a single-limb voting mechanism eliminates the power of dissenting minority bondholders within a particular series to block the restructuring of that series, the elimination of such power does not necessarily resemble the cram-down procedure, because the 'victim' of the cram-down procedure is an impaired class of creditors. The question is therefore whether a group of dissenting minority bondholders is equivalent to an impaired class of creditors under US municipal bankruptcy rules.

The UNCITRAL Legislative Guide on Insolvency Law provides some useful guidance on claims classification (i.e., what claims constitute a particular class by themselves). The purpose of classification of claims is to 'satisfy the requirements to provide fair and equitable treatment to creditors, treating similarly situated claims in the same manner and ensuring that all creditors in a particular class are offered the same menu of terms by the reorganization plan'.[38] Although the general rule is to put secured creditors in one class and unsecured creditors in another, the Legislative Guide mentions that ordinary unsecured creditors can be

---

[37] 11 USC §1129(b)(1). It should be noted that Section 901(a) explicitly makes Section 1129(b)(1) dealing with the bankruptcy of companies applicable for municipalities.

[38] See UNCITRAL, *Legislative Guide on Insolvency Law* (United Nations 2005) 218 <www.uncitral.org/pdf/english/texts/insolven/05-80722_Ebook.pdf> accessed 10 October 2014.

divided into 'different classes based upon their varying economic interests'.[39] In determining commonality of interest, the relevant criteria may include 'the nature of debts giving rise to the claims'.[40]

Arguably, the operation of a single-limb voting mechanism would resemble the cram-down procedure under municipality bankruptcy if a group of dissenting minority bondholders within a particular series could prove that compared with other bondholders they have very different economic interests. Plus, they could argue that the nature of debts giving rise to the claims of these minority bondholders differs from that of other bondholders subject to the same single-limb voting mechanism.

IV. SAFEGUARDS FOR CRAM-DOWNS AND FOR SINGLE-LIMB VOTING MECHANISM

This part compares the safeguard provision for the bankruptcy cram-down procedure for municipalities under US law and that for a single-limb voting mechanism. It concludes that the cram-down procedure for municipality bankruptcy provides better safeguard protection for the minority creditors through the prohibition of unfair discrimination and the provision of fair and equitable treatment, whereas the single-limb voting mechanism gives sovereign issuers the discretion to decide the holders of which series of bonds could receive the same restructuring terms or an identical menu of different restructuring options.

A. Safeguards for Cram-Downs in US Municipality Bankruptcy Law

Having argued that the single-limb voting mechanism could resemble the cram-down procedure in US municipality bankruptcy law, this section takes a closer look at how cram-down procedures work. A closer reading of Section 1129(b)(1) of the United States Code (applicable as a result of Section 901(a)) reveals that it provides a safeguard provision to ensure that each impaired dissenting class receives at least certain minimum protection in the context of a cram-down. To quote again the language of Section 1129(b)(1), the court shall confirm the plan under the cram down procedure 'if the plan does not discriminate unfairly, and is fair and

39 Ibid., 222.
40 Ibid.

equitable, with respect to each class of claims or interests that is impaired under, and has not accepted, the plan'.[41]

Section 1129(b)(1) provides minimum protection for each impaired dissenting class in two distinctive regards. It first addresses the interests of each impaired dissenting class and other creditor classes by prohibiting unfair discrimination, and then maintains a balance between the interests of each impaired dissenting class and that of the debtor by the application of a fair and equitable treatment test under US law. The following paragraphs will discuss both elements in turn.

i. Prohibition of unfair discrimination

Although Section 1129(b) does not provide a definition of unfair discrimination, the case law of US bankruptcy courts on this issue is quite straightforward, indicating that the prohibition against unfair discrimination requires equal treatment of similarly situated creditors.[42] In *re Barney & Carey Co*, the Court stated, 'the unfair discrimination language of section 1129(b)(1) prohibits a debtor from proposing unreasonably different treatment between classes of similar claims'.[43] The Court added that '[t]he burden is on the Debtor to show that unequal treatment between classes having the same priority does not constitute unfair discrimination'.[44] In *re Tucson Self-Storage, Inc*, the Court found that '[a] plan discriminates unfairly if it singles out the holder of some claim or interest for a particular treatment'.[45] Similarly, the court in *re Johns-Manville Corp* ruled that 'a plan proponent may not segregate two similar claims or groups of claims into separate classes and provide disparate treatment for those classes'.[46]

---

41 11 USC §§1129(b)(1). It should be noted that Section 901(a) explicitly makes Section 1129(a)(8) dealing with the bankruptcy of companies applicable for municipalities.

42 David Kupetz, 'Municipal Debt Adjustment Under the Bankruptcy Code' (1995) 27 *The Urban Lawyer* 531, 595, citing *In re Orfa Corp of Philadelphia*, 129 BR 404, 416 (BankrEDPa1991) and *In re AOV Indus, Inc*, 792 F.2d 1140, 1150 (DC Cir.1986).

43 Ibid., citing *In re Barney & Carey Co*, 170 BR 17, 25 (BankrDMass1994).

44 Ibid.

45 Ibid., n 292, citing *Oxford Life Ins Co v Tucson Self-Storage, Inc*, 166 BR 892, 898 (Bankr9th Cir1994).

46 Ibid., citing *In re Johns-Manville Corp*, 68 BR 618, 636 (BankrSDNY1986), aff'd, 78 BR 407 (BankrSDNY1987), aff'd, 843 F.2d 636 (2d Cir.1988).

ii. Fair and equitable treatment

Besides the prohibition of unfair discrimination, Section 1129(b)(2) sets out certain specified requirements for a plan to be fair and equitable. However, it leaves the substance of the terms 'fair and equitable' open to interpretation by US bankruptcy courts.[47] In Chapter 11 cases involving the bankruptcy of corporate entities, the phrase 'fair and equitable' has been interpreted to require that unsecured creditors be paid in full first before junior equity holders can be paid.[48] This interpretation is, however, not applicable in a Chapter 9 context, as a municipality does not have any equity holder. By contrast, US bankruptcy courts have construed a Chapter 9 plan to be fair and equitable if it is balanced and the debtor has taken reasonable steps to increase revenue and cut costs before proposing debt renegotiation.[49] In applying this standard, courts analyse whether the amount to be received by dissenting creditors under the plan is 'all that they can reasonably expect in the circumstances'.[50]

When interpreting the meaning of 'all that [dissenting creditors] can reasonably expect in the circumstances', some courts have required the debtor to exercise its taxing power to a greater extent with regard to the facts of the case presented.[51] Other courts have held that it is not necessary that all taxes collected go to the payment of creditors nor that

---

[47] Section 1129(b)(2)(A) provides that secured claims may be treated fairly and equitably if the plan: (a) allows the secured creditor to retain its lien and to receive cash payments over time which have a present value equal to the value of its collateral as of the effective date of the plan; (b) provides for a sale of the secured creditor's collateral at which it can credit bid; or (c) provides the secured creditor with the indubitable equivalent of its claim, including, among other things, returning the creditor's collateral to it. Section 1129(b)(2)(B) provides that unsecured creditors who are not paid in full are still treated fairly and equitably under a plan as long as any claim or interest that is junior will not receive or retain under the plan or on account of such junior claim or interest any property. See 11 USC §1129(b)(2).

[48] See *Case v Los Angeles Lumber Products*, 308 US 106 (1939).

[49] B Summer Chandler and Mark Kaufman, 'Maybe Taxes Aren't So Certain: What is "Fair and Equitable" in a Chapter 9 Plan?' 2013 XXXII(1) Am Bankr Inst J2, .

[50] See *Lorber v Vista Irrigation District*, 127 F.2d 628, 639 (9th Cir. 1942); *West Coast Life Insurance Company et al v Merced Irrigation District*, 114 F.2d 654 (9th Cir. 1940); *Moody v James Irrigation District*, 114 F2d 685 (9th Cir 1940); *Bekins v Lindsay-Strathmore Irrigation District*, 114 F.2d 680 (9th Cir. 1940), *Jordan v Palo Verde Irrigation District*, 114 F.2d 691 (9th Cir. 1940).

[51] In *Fano v Newport Heights Irrigation District*, the Court denied the proposed plan and stated that:

taxes be increased where evidence indicates that this would not be feasible.[52] Indeed, while raising taxes could help the municipality pay back its debt, it might be detrimental to attracting new residents and corporations and thus would adversely affect the municipality's long-term revenues.[53] The limited body of case law suggests that to what extent the debtor shall impose new or increased taxes should be determined on a case-by-case basis. Main factors to take into account when deciding whether a debtor shall impose new or increased taxes include: (1) the tax rates of neighbouring municipalities; (2) the employment market; (3) the local population and the potential impact of increased tax burden; (4) prospects for attracting new business with increased tax burden; and (5) any new financial needs of the municipality.[54]

Besides raising taxes, other reasonable steps the debtor shall take to increase revenue and reduce costs include: (1) checking existing contracts to look for inefficiencies; (2) negotiating modifications to collective-bargaining agreements and retiree benefits; (3) cutting labour costs; (4) selling or leasing municipal assets; (5) privatising or outsourcing certain services; and (6) securing financial support.[55]

> we are unable to find any reason why the tax rate should not have been increased sufficiently to meet the District's obligations or why it can be said that the plan is 'equitable' and 'fair' and for the 'best interest of the creditors' with no sufficient showing that the taxing power was inadequate to raise the taxes to pay them.

See *Fano v Newport Heights Irrigation District*, 114 F.2d 563 (9th Cir. 1940).

[52] In *Lorber* (n 50), the Court analysed the debtor's situation and found that '55 cents on the dollar was the maximum that the District could reasonably pay on outstanding bonds'. See *Lorber v Vista Irrigation District*, 143 F.2d 282 (9th Cir. 1944). In *Corcoran Hospital District*, the Court 'looked at the insolvency of the debtor and whether the debtor could, in fact, raise taxes sufficient to pay the bondholders in full' and concluded that 'the debtor Hospital District could not raise taxes sufficient to pay more to Class 5'. See *In re Corcoran Hospital District*, 233 BR 449, 459–60 (BankrEDCal 1999). In *Newhouse v Corcoran Irrigation District*, the Court stated that:

> [t]he bankruptcy of a public entity, however, is very different from that of a private person or concern. The operative assets of an irrigation district and the value of the land of the District, of course, have their evidentiary value as to the amount of money the District can reasonably raise to meet its indebtedness.

See *Newhouse v Corcoran Irrigation District*, 114 F.2d 690 (9th Cir. 1940).

[53] Chandler and Kaufman (n 49).

[54] Ibid.

[55] Ibid.

B. Safeguards for a Single-Limb Voting Mechanism

As noted in the IMF staff paper, it was generally recognised during the consultation process that a single-limb voting mechanism would only be feasible and desirable if it contained adequate safeguards to address potential abuse. Given that votes are calculated on the basis of the aggregated principal amount of outstanding debt across all series, there is a risk that, in the absence of a series-by-series voting requirement, holders of bond series with a larger principal amount could use their voting power to agree upon terms that discriminate against the holders of bond series with a smaller principal amount.[56] For example, in circumstances where there are several bond series issued by the same sovereign issuer (i.e., series A, B, C and D) and the size of series A, B and C is much larger than that of series D. In theory, there is a chance that the holders of series A, B and C could manipulate the vote with their larger combined voting powers and force the holders of series D to accept a restructuring plan where the holders of series A, B and C would receive much better terms than the holders of series D.

In order to address this concern, the IMF staff paper suggests that sovereign issuers could only use a single-limb voting mechanism if it offered all affected bondholders the same restructuring terms or an identical menu of restructuring options.[57] Accordingly, the ICMA template CAC requires that in circumstances where a single-limb voting procedure is chosen by the sovereign issuer to restructuring its debt, all holders of bonds that are affected by the vote must receive restructuring terms are 'uniformly applicable'.[58]

The 'Uniformly Applicable' condition will be satisfied if:

a. the holders of all affected series of Debt Securities Capable of Aggregation are invited to exchange, convert, or substitute their debt securities, on the same terms, for (i) the same new instrument or other consideration or (ii) a new instrument, new instruments or other consideration from an identical menu of instruments or other consideration; or
b. the amendments proposed to the terms and conditions of each affected series of Debt Securities Capable of Aggregation would,

---

[56] IMF, 'Strengthening the Contractual Framework to Address Collective Action Problems in Sovereign Debt Restructuring' (September 2014) 20.

[57] Ibid., 21.

[58] ICMA English Law Standard CACs, Pari Passu and Creditor Engagement Provisions, May 2015, 4.

> following implementation of such amendments, result in the amended instruments having identical provisions (other than provisions which are necessarily different, having regard to different currency of issuance).[59]

In short, the 'uniformly applicable' test is satisfied if: (i) bondholders are offered the same restructuring terms or the identical menu of restructuring options; or (ii) the restructuring proposal would result in the amended bonds having identical provisions (other than provisions which are necessarily different, such as currency of payment). Notably, the ICMA template CAC also provides in the same section that sovereign issuers could choose to include only some series of the Debt Securities Capable of Aggregation and, for the avoidance of doubt, the single-limb voting mechanism could be used for different groups of two or more series of Debt Securities Capable of Aggregation simultaneously.[60] It therefore gives sovereign issuers the discretion to decide holders of which series of bonds could receive the same restructuring terms or an identical menu of restructuring options, subject to no court supervision or scrutiny.

V. POSSIBLE CLAIMS BEFORE INVESTMENT TREATY TRIBUNALS ARISING FROM THE EXERCISE OF CACS WITH A SINGLE-LIMB VOTING MECHANISM

A comparison of the safeguards for the municipality bankruptcy cram-down procedure and those for a single-limb voting mechanism reveals that a single-limb voting mechanism without additional safeguards does not provide sufficient protection for dissenting minority bondholders because it allows the sovereign issuer to utilise a single-limb voting mechanism only in respect of some of the bond series at its own discretion, thereby treating the holders of these bond series equally. Problems may arise if the sovereign issuer decides to include the holders of different series with different economic interests and background in the same single-limb voting mechanism (i.e., when the sovereign issuer treats differently-situated creditors similarly). Alternatively, problems may also arise when the sovereign issuer does not include similarly situated creditors in the same single-limb voting mechanism. As the

[59] Ibid., 5.
[60] Ibid., 5–6.

sovereign issuer enjoys the sole discretion to make these decisions, there is no mechanism in place like that in the municipality bankruptcy cram-down procedure to ensure that the restructuring does not discriminate unfairly against the dissenting minority bondholders.

This section sets out case law concerning the FET standard as contained in international investment treaties and analyses how this standard could be interpreted in disputes arising when the single-limb voting mechanism under certain CACs is activated.

A. General Remarks

Over the past decade, investment treaty tribunals have struggled unsuccessfully to define the obligation of the FET standard included in a vast majority of over 3,000 bilateral investment treaties.[61] Recent case law indicates that most tribunals find it unnecessary to engage in an extensive discussion of the definition of the FET standard, and only analyse the meaning of FET when it is applied to a set of specific facts. For instance, the Tribunal in *Swisslion v Macedonia* did not provide a precise definition of the FET standard and limited itself to subscribe to 'the view expressed by certain tribunals that the standard basically ensures that the foreign investor is not unjustly treated, with due regard to all surrounding circumstances, and that it is a means to guarantee justice to foreign investors'.[62]

Among those tribunals that have made an attempt to define the FET standard, the Tribunal in *Deutsche Bank v Sri Lanka* confirmed the non-exhaustive definition of the FET standard offered by the *Waste Management* Tribunal and listed a few components of the FET definition:

- protection of legitimate and reasonable expectations which have been relied upon by the investor to make the investment;
- good faith conduct although bad faith on the part of the State is not required for its violation;

---

[61] Kenneth J Vandevelde, 'A Unified Theory of Fair and Equitable Treatment' (2010) 43 J Intl L & Pol 43, 44.

[62] *Swisslion DOO Skopje v The Former Yugoslav Republic of Macedonia,* ICSID Case No ARB/09/16, Award (July 6 2012) para. 273, citing *PSEG Global, The North American Coal Corporation, and Konya Ingin Electrik ve Ticaret Sirketi v Republic of Turkey,* ICSID Case No ARB/02/5, Award (19 January 2007) para. 239; *El Paso Energy International Co v The Argentine Republic,* ICSID Case No ARB/03/15, Award (31 October 2011) para. 373.

- conduct that is transparent, consistent and not discriminatory, that is, not based on unjustifiable distinctions or arbitrary;
- conduct that does not offend judicial propriety, that complies with due process and the right to be heard.[63]

In this context, the present author submits that while the maximum scope of the FET standard remains unclear, its minimum reach seems rather clear-cut. The FET standard covers at least the principle regarding the prohibition of unfair discrimination.

B. Prohibition of Unfair Discrimination

The most relevant case on unfair discrimination is *Saluka Investment BV v Czech Republic*, which concerned the gradual privatisation of the Czech banking sector.[64] In this case, the IPB, one of the banks that had been fully privatised, could not participate in a government assistance programme and subsequently collapsed, while three predominantly State-owned banks obtained assistance from that programme.[65] In explaining the meaning of FET and non-discrimination, the Tribunal stated that 'any differential treatment of a foreign investor must not be based on unreasonable distinctions and demands, and must be justified by showing that it bears a reasonable relationship to rational policies not motivated by a preference for other investments over the foreign-owned investment'.[66] The Tribunal further developed a test for the determination of discriminatory conduct, which provides that a conduct is considered discriminatory if similar cases are treated differently without reasonable justification.[67] Notably, such interpretation is very similar to the safeguard for cram-down in municipality bankruptcy, which as discussed above has been interpreted by US bankruptcy courts as prohibiting a debtor from proposing unreasonably different treatment between classes of similar claims.

---

63 *Deutsche Bank AG v Democratic Socialist Republic of Sri Lanka*, ICSID Case ARB/09/2, Award (31 October 2012) para. 420; *Waste Management, Inc v United Mexican States*, ICSID Case No ARB(AF)/00/3, Award (30 April 2004) para. 98.

64 *Saluka Investment BV v Czech Republic*, UNCITRAL, Partial Award (17 March 2006).

65 Roland Klager, *'Fair and Equitable Treatment' in International Investment Law* (CUP 2013) 193.

66 *Saluka v Czech Republic* (n 64) para. 307.

67 Ibid., para. 313.

In the context of the exercise of CACs with a single-limb voting mechanism, minority bondholders could bring a claim before investment treaty tribunals if they find that the holders of other series with similar terms are not included in the same single-limb voting process. For instance, claims may be initiated if the sovereign issuer includes the holders of its bonds due in 2016 and 2018 but not those bonds due in 2017, although they all contain similar terms and conditions. Furthermore, in 2012 Greece excluded the bond holdings of the European Central Bank (ECB) and other central banks from restructuring by swapping them into a new series with identical payment terms and maturity dates just before the publication of the exchange offer.[68]

Arguably, those bondholders who feel that they have been unfairly discriminated could request the sovereign issuer to provide an explanation or justification for its conduct. A look at the case law of FET standard of investment treaty tribunals suggests that there is no need to establish a new international court to fill this gap; it could be filled by granting sovereign bondholders access to investment treaty arbitration which could be done by an amendment of existing investment treaties to expressly include sovereign bonds as covered investments. Upon receipt of bondholders' claims, these investment treaty tribunals could assess whether the justification provided by the sovereign issuer for the differential treatment of a certain bondholder is reasonable. In this respect, the UNCITRAL Legislative Guide on Insolvency Law and the UNCTAD Principles on Responsible Sovereign Lending and Borrowing[69] could be useful references for the tribunal. Although the UNCTAD Principles do not specify the FET standard in the sovereign debt context as such, they could still provide some useful guidance for the development of this standard. It is worth noting that the dissenting arbitrator in *Ambiente Ufficio SpA and others v Argentine Republic* has referred to the UNCTAD Principles as relevant law.[70]

---

[68] As part of this swap arrangement, the ECB committed to return any profits made through its Greek government bond holdings to its shareholders. Hence, Greece received virtually no debt relief on these bonds, both because the bulk of the ECB's Greek bond holdings were bought during 2010 at relatively small discounts, and because of its small share in the ECB (about 2 per cent). See Zettelmeyer and others (n 4) 5.

[69] UNCTAD, Principles on Promoting Responsible Sovereign Lending and Borrowing (10 January 2012) <http://unctadxiii.org/en/SessionDocument/gdsddf2012misc1_en.pdf> accessed 29 May 2016.

[70] Juan Pablo Bohoslavsky, Yuefen Li and Marie Sudreau, 'Emerging Customary International Law in Sovereign Debt Governance?' (2013) 9(1) Capital

VI. CONCLUDING REMARKS

In the spring of 2013, the IMF began to revisit possible reforms for sovereign debt restructuring[71] and introduced the concept of a single-limb voting mechanism.[72] As explained in this chapter, a single-limb voting mechanism will enable contract terms to be amended on the basis of a single vote across all affected instruments, thereby disallowing a creditor or a group of creditors preventing the restructuring of a particular series. In the view of the author, a single-limb voting mechanism resembles the cram-down procedure in the US municipality bankruptcy law. Whereas the cram-down procedure contains a safeguard provision that ensures minimum protection for each impaired dissent creditor class through the prohibition of unfair discrimination and the application of a fair and equitable treatment, the single-limb voting mechanism only requires that bondholders in the same single-limb voting process be offered the same restructuring terms or an identical menu of different restructuring options but leaves it to the sovereign issuer to decide on the holders of which series to be included in the process.

According to the present author, investment treaty tribunals should be trusted to exercise their discretion and determine complex and delicate issues, such as which claims are similar and which groups of bondholders are similarly situated bondholders. In this connection, it is worth emphasising that one of the often-cited advantages of arbitration is the potential for choosing arbitrators with experience and expertise relevant to the dispute. As arbitration is merely a dispute resolution mechanism, it would be wrong to suggest that investment treaty tribunals lack the expertise to play the role of a bankruptcy court.[73] In practice, the parties

---

Markets LJ 55, 65, citing *Ambiente Ufficio SpA and others v Argentine Republic*, ICSID Case No ARB/08/9, Dissenting Opinion of Santiago Torres Bernardes (2 May 2013).

[71] IMF Press Release (n 6); IMF Public Information Notice 13/61, 'IMF Executive Board Discusses Sovereign Debt Restructuring—Recent Developments and Implications for the Fund's Legal and Policy Framework' (23 May 2013) <www.imf.org/external/np/sec/pn/2013/pn1361.htm> accessed 10 October 2014. For a discussion of the old reform proposal, see Sean Hagan, 'Designing a Legal Framework to Restructure Sovereign Debt' (2005) 36 Georgetown J Intl L 299; IMF, 'The Design of the Sovereign Debt Restructuring Mechanism-Further Considerations' (2002) <www.imf.org/external/np/pdr/sdrm/2002/112702.htm> accessed 10 October 2014.

[72] IMF (n 18) paras 38 and 42; IMF (n 7) 20.

[73] Michael Waibel, *Sovereign Defaults Before International Courts and Tribunals* (CUP 2013) 323.

to a dispute can appoint whomsoever they want as arbitrator and they certainly can choose someone with sovereign debt or bankruptcy law background.

As far as the amount of debt relief is concerned, US bankruptcy courts have construed a Chapter 9 restructuring plan for municipalities to be fair and equitable if it is balanced and the debtor has taken reasonable steps to increase revenue and cut costs before proposing debt renegotiation. In applying this standard, US bankruptcy courts analyse whether the amount to be received by dissenting creditors under the plan is all that they can reasonably expect in the circumstances. In the author's view, however, the phrase 'all that they can reasonably expect in the circumstances' is too vague and arbitrary to be transposed to the investment treaty context. Although US bankruptcy courts set out this principle, they do not provide sufficient detailed guidance as to its application. In the context of sovereign debt restructuring, it may thus seem more sensible for the international community to put in place a mechanism that ensures procedural fairness but leaves it to the parties to a restructuring to agree on the appropriate amount of debt relief. Giving investment treaty tribunals the authority to decide on the appropriate amount of debt relief is likely to create more legal uncertainty in this context.

7. Bilateral investment treaties and the principles on responsible sovereign lending and borrowing: Working together towards the provision of an international legal framework addressing sovereign debt issues?

Marie Sudreau

I. INTRODUCTION

In the wake of recent debt crises, talks about the supervision of sovereign debt issues in the form of a clearly defined legal framework at the international level have been the object of recurring discussions.[1] Sovereign debt is a field that is characterised, inter alia, by legal disputes stemming from a lack of supervision of both sovereign debt transactions and sovereign debt restructuring processes. The absence of international conventions on financial transactions led some legal practitioners and scholars to advocate the application of bilateral investment treaties (BITs) to sovereign debt issues. Provided they are interpreted to include financial obligations,[2] BITs would be, in their view, the only international legal instrument capable of addressing sovereign debt disputes.[3] This

[1] See, for instance, discussions at governing board of the International Monetary Fund (IMF) and resulting reforms <www.imf.org/external/pubs/ft/survey/so/2014/NEW100614A.htm> accessed 5 June 2016.

[2] For comment on the application of BITs *ratione materiae* to sovereign debt see the contribution by Charles N Brower and Alexandra Goetz-Charlier, 'International Investment Arbitration and the Global Financial System: Are They "Yin" and "Yang" or like Oil and Water?' (in this volume) 23, 27 ff.

[3] See for example Karen Halverson Cross, 'Arbitration as a Means of Resolving Sovereign Debt Disputes' (2006) 17(3) American Review of International Arbitration 335.

argument, however, is the object of questions and criticisms linked to the legitimacy of arbitration tribunals and their capacity to deal efficiently with sovereign debt issues.

At the same time, the United Nations Conference on Trade and Development (UNCTAD) has been working towards a set of internationally accepted rules and principles to guide sovereign debt contracting. The project on promoting responsible sovereign lending and borrowing started in the aftermath of the 2008 financial crisis and was carried out with the financial support of the government of Norway.[4] In 2012, the Principles on Responsible Sovereign Lending and Borrowing (PRSLBs) emerged as a result of this initiative.[5] The project on promoting responsible sovereign lending and borrowing started in the aftermath of the 2008 financial crisis; it has been promoted by member states and enjoyed the financial support of the government of Norway. So far, the PRSLBs remain, however, a set of soft law norms, without the means for judicial enforcement.

Given the support generated by the PRSLBs at the international level and the established judicial framework offered by BITs through the investor-State dispute settlement (ISDS) system, this chapter investigates the potential for integrating the PRSLB into the decision-making of investment treaty tribunals. It argues that, under certain conditions, through the application of a set of comprehensive, balanced and sovereign debt specific norms, such as the PRSLBs, investment treaty tribunals may provide a way to address some of the problems that arise in the field of sovereign debt, concerning the comprehensiveness and legitimacy of sovereign debt transactions and restructuring processes, by allowing more balanced and debt-specific investment arbitration decisions. However, this chapter ultimately suggests that, even with the integration of PRSLBs references in arbitral decisions, some aspects of sovereign debt disputes, such as collective action problems in restructuring processes, may still not be fully addressed under the investment arbitration system.

The chapter is structured as follows. Part II will briefly examine the main issues that must be dealt with at the international level in regard to sovereign debt to secure more coherent, comprehensive and legitimate

---

[4] The decision to begin the project was taken following consultation with UN Member States during an UNCTAD conference held in Xiamen, China in 2010. The outcome of the conference was a consensus on the need to regulate international lending and borrowing at the international level. See <http://unctad.org/en/Pages/MeetingsArchive.aspx?meetingid=20268> accessed 5 June 2016.

[5] See <http://unctad.org/en/PublicationsLibrary/gdsddf2012misc1_en.pdf> accessed 5 June 2016.

sovereign debt transactions and restructurings. Part III will introduce the PRSLBs and examine their value in light of the need to address the problems that require solution as regards sovereign debt. Part IV questions the potential for investment treaty arbitrations to deal with some of these sovereign debt issues.

II. SOVEREIGN DEBT: A COMPLEX AREA FOR INTERNATIONAL REGULATION

This part reviews the main sets of issues arising in the field of sovereign debt that require regulation at the international level. The first set of issues concerns the fragmented legal and institutional environment of sovereign debt transactions and restructuring processes (A.). The second set of issues includes the perceived legitimacy-deficit of debt restructuring practices and the necessity to take public interests into consideration (B.).

A. A Fragmented Area in Need of a Comprehensive and Consistent International Legal Framework

Sovereign debt is an area that involves a variety of different stakeholders[6] that are regulated by different legal norms at the domestic and international levels. So far no one entity exists to coordinate the practices in this fragmented landscape. In this section, two main areas of concern specific to fragmentation will be examined: the lack of consistently applied rules concerning international lending and borrowing; and the absence of a comprehensive legal framework for dealing with sovereign debt disputes at the international level.

While sovereign debt transactions are international transactions, their rights and obligations are solely defined by contracts governed by domestic law, without any internationally recognised statutory basis.[7] The lack of a common statutory basis effectively means that each State should regulate the conduct of their commercial lenders and public agencies (with the capacity to borrow) in relation to foreign lenders and borrowers, thereby opening its own legal system to foreigners seeking redress in

---

[6] These include commercial banks, hedge funds, private lenders, insurance companies, international financial institutions, development banks, national lending agencies and export credit agencies.

[7] The exceptions are sovereign debt contracted with international financial institutions like the IMF, which are subject to the institutions' statutory rules.

case of debt service problems. One can easily see that, unless the adoption of such regulation is multilateral, most States see no reason to expose their lenders and public borrowers to legal actions undertaken by foreigners on the basis of domestic laws that would recognise rights or duties owed to these foreigners.[8] The lack of effort to regulate foreign activities of lenders and borrowers affects their standards of conduct depending on the sovereign debt relation and the governing law in question.

An example of poor lenders' conduct stemming from the absence of international standards concerns the due diligence process. As in any prudent commercial transaction, one would expect lenders to carry out their due diligence and avoid lending under commercial terms to countries that do not fulfil basic criteria linked, inter alia, to the sustainability of the loan.[9] Yet, the examples of international loans that have been contracted by sovereigns in spite of serious debt sustainability issues are countless.[10] Political factors influencing the conclusion of these transactions cannot be ignored. However, it can be argued that one major contributing factor to bad lending decisions is the poor or improper conduct of due diligence by lenders, due to the absence of readily available information on the borrowing country's debt situation. This information is decentralised and extremely uneven across countries, as the laws governing borrowing and lending often reflect great disparities in the levels of sophistication of institutional settings as well as debt management practices.[11] Transparency and publication of data constitute

---

[8] There are some rare exceptions to the quasi-absence of unilateral regulation in regard to foreigners' conduct in sovereign debt transactions. States whose jurisdictions are used to dealing with international contracts, like the United States, may regulate the acts of their lenders with respect to foreign officials regarding certain issues, for instance, when lenders attempt to bribe these officials; see The Foreign Corrupt Practices Act of 1977 (FCPA) (15 USC § 78dd-1 et seq).

[9] This requirement is dealt with under Principle 4 (informed credit decisions) of the PRSLB.

[10] See generally James S Henry, *The Blood Bankers: Tales from the Global Underground Economy* (Basic Books 2005). Also Louis T Wells and others, *Making Foreign Investment Safe: Property Rights and National Sovereignty: Property Rights and National Sovereignty* (OUP 2006).

[11] Such disparities are evident in the World Bank's Debt Performance Management Assessment reports <http://documents.worldbank.org/curated/en/docsearch/collection-title/Debt%2520management%2520performance%2520

major concerns not only in developing countries.[12] The duty for lenders to conduct proper due diligence with adequate disclosure requirements[13] in lending to sovereigns could constitute a powerful tool to limit loans that would seem disproportionate in relation to the borrower's repayment or absorption capacity. In case of default or renegotiation of a sovereign debt, improper due diligence and disclosure could be arguments against the lender's claim for full repayment if it could be proved that the terms of the loans were abusive given the borrower's poor financial situation.[14] The absence of laws adopted across countries (either in the form of domestic laws with equivalent requirements or adopted multilaterally) clearly addressing such issues constitutes one of the factors contributing to debt crises.

The fragmented state of the current institutional framework for debt restructuring processes also suffers from coordination problems.[15] The manner in which sovereign debt restructuring is conducted depends on the type of lender and on the nature of the contract (multilateral, bilateral, commercial loan or bond issuance) binding the lender and the sovereign borrower. When debt is not governed by international agreements among States or between a borrowing State and an international organisation, such as an international development bank, the law of the contract will typically be that of a domestic jurisdiction chosen by the lender.[16] One of

assessment%2520%28DeMPA%29?colT=Debt%2520management%2520performance%2520assessment%2520%28DeMPA%29> accessed 3 March 2016.

[12] See Miranda Xafa, 'Sovereign Debt Crisis Management: Lessons from the 2012 Greek Debt Restructuring' (2014) 33 CIGI Papers 7. Also see Beat Balzli, 'Greek Debt Crisis: How Goldman Sachs Helped Greece to Mask Its True Debt' *Spiegel Online* (8 February 2010) <www.spiegel.de/international/europe/greek-debt-crisis-how-goldman-sachs-helped-greece-to-mask-its-true-debt-a-676634.html> accessed 11 January 2016.

[13] These due diligence process and disclosure requirements are specified in principles 3 and 4 of the PRSLBs.

[14] This is a principle derived from both domestic corporate laws and consumer laws. See, for example, the US Federal Truth in Lending Act 1968 (designed to promote the informed use of consumer credit, implemented by Regulation Z, amended in 2008, to protect consumers in the mortgage market from unfair, abusive, or deceptive lending and servicing practices).

[15] Jurgen Kaiser, 'Resolving Sovereign Debt Crises. Towards a Fair and Transparent International Insolvency Framework' Friedrich Ebert Stiftung, Dialogue on Globalization (2013) <http://library.fes.de/pdf-files/iez/07497.pdf> accessed 3 March 2016

[16] This is especially the case in developing countries; see Barry Herman, Jose Antonio Ocampo and Shari Spiegel, *Overcoming Developing Country Debt Crises* (OUP 2010) 3.

the main problems arises when the sovereign borrower is at risk of default, requiring the lenders to agree on repayment priorities and a restructuring deal.However, in order to conclude such a deal, all creditors, including the IMF (or other international financial institutions acting as lenders of last resort) and bilateral creditors (for example, through the Paris Club) need to be consulted.

Coordination among private creditors is already difficult, as witnessed by the propensity to holdout, whenever possible, from a restructuring agreement.[17] Yet, coordination between private creditors and multilateral or bilateral creditors is even more difficult, as shown by the difficulty of the Paris Club to implement the principle of comparable treatment, which holds that the debtor must seek comparable terms to the Paris Club agreement with its other creditors.[18] Similarly, creditors' holdouts create significant collective action problems that can stall sovereign debt restructuring processes. These problems are currently being dealt with through the inclusion of Collective Action Clauses (CACs) in sovereign bond contracts. While these clauses do not deal with the entirety of sovereign debt stock, as they are not applicable obviously to bonds that do not include them, they constitute quite an efficient way of deterring

---

[17] Udaibir S Das, Michael G Papaioannou and Christoph Trebesch, 'Restructuring Sovereign Debt, 1950–2010: From Process to Outcomes' (*Vox*, 28 November 2012) <http://voxeu.org/article/restructuring-sovereign-debt-1950-2010-process-outcomes> accessed 5 June 2016. In the article, the authors explain that coordination among creditors has been improving with the use of Collective Action Clauses (CACs) over the past decades. Creditor participation rates in restructuring deals are their main indicator for this finding. However, this only concerns private creditors who have bought sovereign bonds (excluding commercial loans for instance) and it does not account for bilateral and multilateral creditors. In addition, this improvement in participation rates is linked with the recent introduction of CACs in bond contracts, when about a trillion bonds around the world are still ungoverned by such clauses.

[18] See UNCTAD, 'Sovereign Debt Workouts: Going Forward – Roadmap and Guide (United Nations 2015) 43:

> Debtor states agree to seek debt restructuring terms comparable to those they obtained from the Paris Club from all its other private creditors and official bilateral creditors that are not part of the Paris Club. Comparability runs one way: the Paris Club itself does not consider itself to be bound in any way by private creditor concessions that precede a Paris Club agreement. Requests for 'reverse comparability' have been consistently rejected. Nor does the Club provide the debtor with any hint of how it should enforce comparable treatment against third parties.

less than a blocking minority of creditors from holding out and claiming full compensation through judicial avenues.[19]

Adding to the coordination problem witnessed in sovereign debt restructuring, the opportunistic behaviour of certain lenders who engage in distressed debt trading and use litigation as a strategy to obtain full repayment of their debt causes great concern.[20] These lenders/creditors generally benefit from the decisions of 'creditor-friendly' jurisdictions at the expense of the populations of foreign debtor countries.[21] Some jurisdictions, such as the UK and Belgium,[22] have taken action to prevent abusive behaviour with regard to distressed debt; however, in order to be fully effective, equivalent legislation would have to be adopted throughout the world using similar language and consistent legal interpretation.

All in all, under the present circumstances of fragmentation in the field of sovereign debt, clear formal international rules on the obligations of lenders/creditors and borrowers/debtors in the context of a sovereign debt transactions and restructuring would go a long way in establishing processes for the prevention and resolutions of sovereign debt crises.

---

[19] In general this blocking minority is not reached and the effect is that the terms of the sovereign debt restructuring deal negotiated by a supermajority of creditors (75 per cent) are imposed on all creditors holding bonds with CACs. For further detail on these and other aspects of CACs see the contributions by Christoph Ohler, 'Restructuring Sovereign Debt on the Basis of Collective Action Clauses' (in this volume) 120, and Yanying Li, 'Sovereign Bond Disputes Before Investment Treaty Tribunals: Safeguarding the Exercise of Collective Action Clauses with a Single-Limb Voting Mechanism' (in this volume) 135.

[20] See for example the Jubilee's campaign 'Stop the Vulture Funds' in the US, UK, Australia and many other countries. Also see Jonathan Blackman and Rahul Mukhi, 'The Evolution of Modern Sovereign Debt Litigation: Vultures, Alter Egos, and Other Legal Fauna' (2010) 73 Law and Contemporary Problems 47.

[21] Cephas Lumina, 'Thematic Report on Vulture Funds and Human Rights' (2010) A/HRC/14/21 para. 66 <www.un.org/ga/search/view_doc.asp?symbol=A/HRC/14/21> accessed 5 June 2016.

[22] See UK 2010 Debt Relief (Developing Countries) Act <www.legislation.gov.uk/ukpga/2010/22/contents> accessed 5 June 2016 and the 2015 Belgian 'Loi relative a la lutte contre les fonds vautours' <www.ejustice.just.fgov.be/cgi/article_body.pl?language=fr&pub_date=2015-09-11&numac=2015003318&caller=summary> accessed 5 June 2016.

B. An Area in Which Practices and Institutions Are in Search of Enhanced Legitimacy

The second set of issues examined in this chapter regards the legitimacy of sovereign debt restructurings and the need to take the public interest into account in this area. These issues are related to the fragmentation issues discussed above in the sense that fragmented practices resulting from the complexity of the regulatory environment in the sovereign debt arena may be seen as illegitimate, given that they introduce different rights and obligations depending on the identity of sovereign borrowers and lenders and hence lead to potential inefficiencies and unjustified differentiations. This notwithstanding, legitimacy issues in the sovereign debt area mostly stem from: (i) the public perception that private interests prevail over public interests in sovereign debt restructurings; and (ii) the absence of impartial institutions dealing with sovereign debt matters.[23] This section thus focuses on these two dimensions of legitimacy.

Civil society in debtor countries is becoming increasingly vocal on the duty resting on the State to secure its population's basic needs (social and human rights) during debt crises.[24] These perceptions are fed by the manner in which creditors' rights are privileged over the public interest, including the obligation of the State to protect the interests of all citizens (not just those of lenders) in sovereign debt transactions. Both borrowing States and lenders are responsible for this state of affairs, as having

---

[23] In this chapter, legitimacy is viewed as a political concept, the assessment of which results from public perceptions; it refers to people's beliefs about authority and obligations in the context of sovereign debt crises since they have become a matter of intense public contestation and debate.

See Robert Howse, 'Concluding Remarks in Light of International Law', in Carlos Espósito, Juan Pablo Bohoslavsky and Yuefen Li (eds), *Sovereign Financing and International Law: The UNCTAD Principles on Responsible Sovereign Lending and Borrowing* (OUP 2013). A legitimate sovereign debt governance system is one that the public can trust and accept as valid, as opposed to a system that generates massive public resistance as is sometimes the case with debt restructuring processes. See Max Weber's definition of legitimacy in Max Weber, *Politics as a Vocation* (Fortress Press 1965).

[24] As evidenced by the massive campaigns and protests in Iceland (Protests in Reykjavik in 2010), Spain (Podemos, los indignados), Portugal (geraçao a Rasca), Greece (Syriza and protests in Syntagma Square in Athens), US (Occupy Wall Street) in reaction to effects of the global economic crisis beginning in 2008, in particular against having to pay the debts of private banks; see the example of Iceland; 'Iceland Raises from the Ashes of Banking Collapse' *The Guardian* (6 October 2013) <www.theguardian.com/world/2013/oct/06/iceland-financial-recovery-banking-collapse> accessed 7 December 2016.

access to international bond markets has become, for a large number of States, a priority for financing their current expenditures As such, sovereign obligations to foreign creditors are easily confused with the obligations owed to the populations these States represent.

However, the real problems arise when the sovereign obligations to foreign creditors cannot be met, for reasons that may not even be linked with the State's capacity to manage its debts (e.g., exogenous shocks). In these situations, domestic populations generally have to incur severe economic and social adjustments in order to repay foreign creditors through higher taxes, who then benefit from the status of States as entities that cannot go bankrupt. For foreign creditors to count on this status of States for the purpose of sovereign debt repayment when, by law, these States are considered to be acting as economic agents (disregarding the fact that they owe a duty to protect the interests of their entire population), constitutes an incoherence leading to mistrust in the way sovereign lending, borrowing and restructurings are dealt with.[25] Other factors also contribute to this mistrust (and perception of illegitimacy), namely the reliance of many debt contracts on the laws of jurisdictions that are seen as protecting private property interests above any other interests. While the foundations of this perception are difficult to establish in a scientific way, one cannot ignore the general reluctance of courts and tribunals: (i) to use legal defences such as the state of necessity for sovereigns facing extreme social problems because of the restructuring process;[26] or (ii) to apply stays of litigation/proceedings

[25] The recognition of the State as an economic agent when raising finance on financial markets is confirmed through a number of sovereign immunity laws (such as the US *Foreign Sovereign Immunities Act* (*FSIA*) of 1976) as well as case law such as *Republic of Argentina v Weltover*, 504 US 607 or the European General Court's Joined Cases C-226/13, C-245/13, C-247/13 and C-578/13, Judgment of the Court (First Chamber) 11 June 2015.

[26] See European University Institute, Department of Law, '30 September 2015: General Court Confirms There is no EU Competence for Unilateral Member State Decision not to Pay Back Debts in State of Necessity' (2 October 2015) <http://eurocrisislaw.eui.eu/news/general-court-eu-no-competence-eu-for-unilateral-decision-not-to-pay-back-debts-in-emergency-situation/> accessed 5 June 2016. Also see German Federal Constitutional Court, Joined Cases 2 BvM 1-5/03, and 2BvM 1- 2/06, Decision of 8 May 2007, BVerfGE 118, 124. See also ICSID Decisions in *CMS Gas Transmission Co v Argentine Republic*, ICSID Case ARB/01/8, Award (12 May 2005); *Enron Creditors Recovery Corp (formerly Enron Corp) and Ponderosa Assets, LP v Argentine Republic*, ICSID Case ARB/01/3, Award (22 May 2007); *Sempra Energy International v Argentine*

preventing creditors from making a claim against the debtor State until after negotiations for restructuring the debt take place.[27] In addition to these factors contributing to the perception of illegitimacy, the application of a State's sovereign immunity laws to allow recovery by creditors against foreign States in their jurisdiction, undermines sovereign equality and thus reinforces the sentiment that some private interests are above international law.[28]

The second source of concern in regard to the legitimacy of sovereign debt restructuring processes and transactions is the dual and potentially conflicting role of creditor and adviser played by international financial institutions, such as the IMF.[29] These institutions face criticism for their constraining demands on sovereign debtors' economies and social policies in exchange for their lending in last resort.[30] Although sovereign debtors' commitments to implement structural adjustment programmes are voluntary, they often face pressures to comply with these programmes from institutional lenders who are only interested in full recovery of their loan.[31] Concerns for the borrowing country's recovery from debt problems and its sustainable growth may thus not be a priority for these institutions. This particular legitimacy issue highlights the need for institutions dealing with sovereign debt transactions and restructuring

---

Republic, ICSID Case ARB/02/16, Award (28 September 2007); *Metalpar SA and Buen Aire SA v Argentine Republic*, ICSID Case ARB/03/5, Award on the Merits (6 June 2008); *Suez, Sociedad General de Aguas de Barcelona SA and Interagua Servicios Integrales de Agua SA v Argentine Republic*, ICSID Case ARB/03/17, Decision on Liability (30 July 2010); *Total SA v Argentine Republic*, ICSID Case ARB/04/1, Decision on Liability (27 December 2010); *Suez, Sociedad General de Aguas de Barcelona SA and Vivendi Universal SA v Argentine Republic*, ICSID Case ARB/03/19, Award (9 April 2015).

27 See Matthias Goldmann, 'Necessity and Feasibility of a Standstill Rule for Sovereign Debt Workouts' (2014) Paper prepared for the first session of the Sovereign Debt Workout Working Group, UNCTAD 2014, 19 <http://unctad.org/en/PublicationsLibrary/gdsddf2014misc4_en.pdf> accessed 5 June 2016 (where the author shows that on many occasions US courts have denied stays on proceedings, for instance in the case of Argentina).

28 The Argentine case gives an illustration of the creative methods used by creditors to obtain the enforcement of a decision in foreign States. See Benedict Mander, 'Debt Holdouts Put Argentina on Spot' *Financial Times* (London 17 November 2013).

29 See Kaiser (n 15) 10.

30 See Eurodad 'World Bank and IMF Conditionality: A Development Injustice' (2006) <www.eurodad.org/uploadedfiles/whats_new/reports/eurodad_world_bank_and_imf_conditionality_report.pdf> accessed 5 June 2016.

31 See UNCTAD (n 18) 13.

processes to be fair and balanced in the policies or decisions they adopt. The PRSLBs, which are discussed next, have the potential to contribute to creating the type of institutions, the necessary procedures, and the substantive standards that are needed for a legitimate international framework for sovereign debt transactions, which applies both to lending transactions and restructurings, including to the judicial processes that may arise out of sovereign debt disputes both at the domestic level and in particular in investment treaty arbitration.

III. THE CONTRIBUTION OF THE PRSLBS TO SOLVING FRAGMENTATION AND LEGITIMACY ISSUES

The PRSLBs are a set of 15 non-binding principles dealing with the rights and obligations of lenders and borrowers in sovereign debt transactions. They also refer to the necessity of conducting sovereign debt restructurings under certain exceptional circumstances. Three main factors drove UNCTAD into the project of formulating the PRSLBs. First, the need to reduce the occurrence of debt crises presented itself as an obvious goal considering the probability that the 2008 global financial crisis would ultimately result in sovereign debt problems. The second driver was the need to restore the balance between the responsibilities of sovereign borrowers and those of their lenders. Indeed, the idea that the borrower is entirely responsible for the situation of the crisis in which it may find itself in the event of an imminent default prevailed until the subprime crisis, when financial institutions were called into question about their lending practices. The third driver was the need to address the legal gap existing at the international level concerning sovereign debt issues.[32] Indeed, despite numerous attempts to provide guidance in this field,[33] it was UNCTAD itself that flagged the absence of internationally

---

[32] The opinion that there is a legal gap in the regulation of sovereign debt governance is supported by the fact that disputes in the field are not resolved through an international convention or bankruptcy mechanism (which – other than in other fields of international economic relations, such as trade – simply does not exist). While the means required to fill the gap are much debated, the view that there is a gap is widely shared. See UNCTAD, 'Responsible Sovereign Lending and Borrowing' UNCTAD Discussion Papers No 198 (April 2010) <http://unctad.org/en/Docs/osgdp20102_en.pdf> accessed 5 June 2016.

[33] Previous guidelines by the Institute of International Finance, the Organisation for Economic Co-operation and Development, and Eurodad among others

recognised norms on sovereign debt to UN Member States by UNCTAD, which supported the idea that such principles should be developed.[34]

The PRSLBs have been designed by a widely representative expert group coordinated by UNCTAD[35] with the objective of reducing the occurrence and negative effects of debt crises. The expert group who formulated the PRSLBs gathered highly recognised representatives from civil society, the private sector (bondholder associations and private lawyers), academia and international organisations (IMF, World Bank, Paris Club). Following expert consultation, the PRSLBs were reviewed in regional consultative meetings by over 60 Member States. They are complemented by guidelines[36] to aid the interpretation and implementation of the principles.

A. How the PRSLBs Address Fragmentation

The PRSLBs contribute to reducing the fragmented landscape of sovereign debt regulation by providing a set of principles that cover all aspects of sovereign debt governance – from the contracting of sovereign debt to the resolution of sovereign debt crises. Hence, they offer guidance both for the prevention and resolution of debt crises. The principles are potentially applicable to sovereign borrowers at the national and subnational levels in both developing and developed countries, as well as to their lenders, be they bilateral, multilateral or private. This 'all inclusive'

---

either had a specific scope of application (emerging countries, low income economies) or were not submitted to political scrutiny (i.e., no Member States' involvement in the drafting process) and thus could not be seen as universal.

[34] This project and its Principles have never been the object of any opposition from Member States. They have been disseminated through conferences, regional consultative meetings and called for in General Assembly resolutions on a number of occasions. See Marie Sudreau and Juan Pablo Bohoslavsky, 'Sovereign Debt Governance, Legitimacy, and the Sustainable Development Goals: Examining the Principles on Responsible Sovereign Lending and Borrowing' (2015) 24 Washington International Law Journal 20.

[35] See UNCTAD, 'Promoting Responsible Sovereign Lending and Borrowing' UNCTAD Progress Report (January 2011) <http://unctad.org/en/PublicationsLibrary/gdsddf2011misc2_en.pdf> accessed 5 June 2016.

[36] The Guidelines on Responsible Sovereign Lending and Borrowing were elaborated by sovereign debt (legal, banking and debt management) experts under UNCTAD's coordination. They were then reviewed by a working group composed of field experts i.e. auditors, debt managers, former central bankers and lawyers. UNCTAD, 'Guidelines on Responsible Sovereign Lending and Borrowing' Draft Version (8 June 2014) <www.wgpd.org.mx/Anexos/141014/14UNCTAD_RSLB.pdf> accessed 5 June 2016.

coverage of sovereign debt matters makes the PRSLBs a comprehensive set of principles capable of guiding both lenders and borrowers in what are considered responsible practices at international level. This set of principles has recently been complemented by other principles specifically applicable to restructuring processes, which stem from Principles 7 and 15 of the PRSLBs, recognising the need to conduct sovereign debt restructurings in a timely, efficient and fair manner.[37]

Furthermore, the PRSLBs embrace a holistic approach that is based on domestic and international sound practices. Indeed, their formulation mirrors principles that exist in most legal orders in financial, constitutional, administrative, insolvency and contract law.[38] This approach is also reflected in Principles 1 and 8 of the PRSLBs, which postulate the existence of a fiduciary relationship between government officials and the State (as represented by its individuals). Not only are the PRSLBs formulated on the basis of both domestic and international legal sources, they also spell out the obligations of the State and of the lenders under both domestic and international law. Hence the holistic nature of these principles is reflected in: (i) its consideration of all legal sources in the formulation of the principles; and (ii) its inclusiveness of all the parties affected by sovereign debt issues at the domestic and international level.

The PRSLBs and its guidelines also systematise sovereign lending and borrowing standards and give contextual examples of sound practices on due diligence (Principles 3, 4, 5 and 10): (i) obliging lenders to establish whether the financing is duly authorised and valid under the relevant jurisdiction; and (ii) requiring borrowers to weigh costs and benefits when seeking loans. The broad disclosure of debt instruments' contractual terms and borrowers' economic situations is encouraged (Principles 10 and 11) and *ex-ante* and *ex-post* evaluations in the context of project financing are recommended (Principles 5 and 12). Transparency in the contracting process is sought through the disclosure and the publication of debt related information but also through the exercise of periodic public debt audits (Principle 13).

In line with their focus on crisis prevention, the PRSLBs establish that borrowers should implement adequate management strategies and monitoring systems for enhanced debt management practices (Principles 10

[37] See United Nations General Assembly (UNGA), 'Basic Principles on Sovereign Debt Restructuring Processes', Draft Resolution of 29 July 2015, UN Doc A/69/L84.

[38] Matthias Goldmann, 'Responsible Sovereign Lending and Borrowing: The View from Domestic Jurisdictions' (UNCTAD 2012) <http://unctad.org/en/PublicationsLibrary/gdsddf2012misc3_en.pdf> accessed 5 June 2016.

and 13). Principles 7 to 15 also promote the timely, efficient and fair resolution of debt crises through regulatory means.[39] Without undermining the necessity to abide by international contracts, the principles acknowledge the existence of extreme situations in which debt restructuring is necessary (Principle 9). The PRLSBs finally recall that lenders must not participate in transactions that violate, evade or hamper UN sanctions (Principle 6). Hence, in dealing with all aspects of sovereign debt matters and setting standards anchored in global practices the PRSLBs propose a comprehensive approach to sovereign lending and borrowing that is currently lacking in international law.

B. How the PRSLBs Address Legitimacy

Regarding legitimacy issues, it may be argued that the PRSLBs combine various dimensions of legitimacy stemming from, first, the way the content of the Principles was identified and chosen (legal sources); second, the way they were accepted at the international level (process/endorsement); and third, their substantive value (content).

First, the content of the PRSLBs is firmly grounded in public international law. Most of the principles are developed in such a way as to constitute general principles of law with the potential of becoming customary law.[40] This entails that they are not conjured out of thin air but find their sources in the laws and practices of most jurisdictions. The credibility (and thus legitimacy) of the PRSBLs is thereby reinforced. Through the systematic identification of domestic and international laws and practices, the PRSLBs also aim to reflect the public interest.

Second, the Principles find legitimacy in their widely representative formulation process, as well as in their effectiveness in generating substantive outcomes. Examples of such outcomes include, inter alia, the Principles' endorsement by a dozen UN Member States;[41] the mandate

[39] Juan Pablo Bohoslavsky and Yuefen Li, 'UNCTAD Principles on Responsible Sovereign Financing: The Intersection of Finance, Law and Politics' in Rosa M Lastra and Lee Buchheit (eds) *Sovereign Debt Management* (OUP 2013).

[40] Juan Pablo Bohoslavsky and Carlos Espósito, 'Principles Matter: On the Legal Status of the Principles on Responsible Sovereign Financing' in Espósito, Li and Bohoslavsky (n 23) 73; Goldmann (n 38).

[41] See UNCTAD, 'Principles on Sovereign Lending and Borrowing' Information Note (22 April 2012) <http://unctad.org/en/pages/InformationNoteDetails.aspx?OriginalVersionID=20> accessed 5 June 2016 and UNCTAD, 'Project on Promoting Responsible Sovereign Lending and Borrowing and Debt Workout Mechanism' Progress Report (December 2013) 3 <http://unctad.org/en/PublicationsLibrary/gdsddf2013misc2_en.pdf> accessed 5 June 2016.

granted by the UN General Assembly to work on responsible sovereign lending and borrowing, showing a widespread consensus of the international community on the necessity to strengthen debt crisis prevention and management on a global basis,[42] and the decision of the International Organisation of Supreme Audit Institution (INTOSAI) to integrate the principles into their auditing standards.[43] In line with Principles 7 and 15, the Principles on Sovereign Debt Restructuring were recently adopted at the UN General Assembly.[44]

Third, the content of the PRSLBs is based on principles, in particular that of co-responsibility, fiduciary duty and good faith, that aim to balance the interests of lenders and those of sovereign borrowers. The idea that the responsibility for a wrongful act may be shared among its perpetrators is deeply rooted in international law and, particularly, in the International Law Commission's Articles on the Responsibility of States for Internationally Wrongful Acts (ILC Articles).[45] Public international law focuses on the responsibility of States (including shared), in the context of breaches of international obligations.[46] Although the ILC Articles are not concerned with non-State actors, they pick up on a fundamental concept applicable to any field of law, namely, that when it comes to situations where harm is done, responsibility is often shared and it should not be ignored. The concept of co-responsibility inscribed in the PRSLBs shares this fundamental reasoning on responsibility and takes it further by considering the responsibilities of non-State lenders

---

[42] See UNGA Resolution 'External Debt Sustainability and Development' UNGA Res 65/144 (20 December 2010) para. 3.

[43] International Organization of Supreme Audit Institutions, 'Strengthening Public Oversight and Audit of Sovereign Lending and Borrowing Frameworks' (Presentation for WGPD Annual Meeting, 27–29 May 2013) <www.wgpd.org.mx/Anexos/100714/SovereingLending.pdf> accessed 19 February 2015.

[44] See UNGA (n 37). The Principles on Sovereign Debt Restructuring were inspired partly by UNCTAD's work on responsible sovereign lending and borrowing. The basis for UNCTAD's elaboration of further principles on sovereign debt restructuring was the inclusion of Principles 7–15 in the PRSLBs (on the sovereign right to conduct debt restructuring processes in certain circumstances).

[45] International Law Commission (ILC), 'Draft Articles on Responsibility of States for Internationally Wrongful Acts, with Commentaries' (2001) YBILC vol. II pt 2.

[46] It is interesting to note that during the formulation of the ILC draft, the possibility of transferring responsibility to private companies was discussed see Commentary to art. 28 (Crawford, Special Rapporteur) 87 (n 45).

towards their sovereign borrowers. While international law has not (yet) formally recognised non-State actors as subjects of international law, many signs concur to express the informal international recognition[47] of a co-responsible relationship between States and non-State contracting parties when public interests are at stake.[48]

The concept of co-responsibility is tightly linked to the fiduciary principle that sets the tone in regard to States' responsibilities towards their own population.[49] Fiduciary relationships are found in most States, whose governments act on behalf of their population as prescribed in most constitutional texts.[50] Pursuant to Principle 1 of the PRSLBs, foreign lenders have the duty to recognise that the governments they lend to have obligations towards their own population and that this duty must come first[51] not only for their populations' survival but also to maximise their chances following a crisis to return to foreign markets for profitable investments.[52] Should they fail to recognise this fundamental obligation

---

[47] To some extent, informal recognition may be considered as more effective than formal recognition because it is based on the actual conduct of State and their decisions at the domestic level. This is indeed the basis of output legitimacy; see generally Mijke Boedeltje and Juul Cornips, 'Input and Output Legitimacy in Interactive Governance' (2004) NIG Annual Work Conference 2004 Rotterdam No NIG2-01<http://repub.eur.nl/pub/1750> accessed 19 February 2015; Fritz Wilhelm Scharpf, *Governing in Europe: Effective and Democratic?* (OUP 1999).

[48] See the UN Principles on Business and Human Rights, which have been adopted unanimously by the Human Rights' Council (HRC), where both States and multinational enterprises have an obligation to respect and enforce human rights. UN HRC Res 26/22 'Human Rights and Transnational Corporations and Other Business Enterprises' (27 June 2014) A/HRC/26/L1.

For an elaboration of this idea see Theodor Meron, *The Humanization of International Law* (Martinus Nijhoff 2006). Also see Antônio Augusto Cançado Trindade, *The Construction of a Humanized International Law: A Collection of Individual Opinions (1991–2013)* (Brill 2014).

[49] For more information on the State as fiduciary, see Evan Fox-Decent, *Sovereignty's Promise: The State as Fiduciary* (OUP 2011).

[50] J.R. Oyola & M. Sudreau, 'Fiduciary Relations', in Espósito, Li and Bohoslavsky (n 23) 213, 234.

[51] This duty coming first may entail two outcomes: either the State regards the full service of the debt as essential to ensure its survival or it sees full payment as incapacitating the preservation of the bare minimum needs of its population.

[52] This logic is reflected in the practice of Debtor-in-Possession (DIP) financing adopted by the IMF to keep debtor countries afloat financially during and immediately after restructurings so that they avoid the risk of a second default. See also IMF, Paper, para. 33 <www.imf.org/external/np/pp/eng/2013/042613.pdf> accessed 19 February 2015.

of the State and extend loans knowing that it will not be in the public interest, they could face the loss of their credit and incur a claim for damages.[53] The message is thus clear for investors: they should carefully weigh the debt situation of the borrowing State in which they wish to invest before entering into a transaction.

Finally, good faith is a clearly established general principle of international law[54] that should be respected by both lenders and borrowers in any transaction. Although the PRSLBs generally rely on the application of this principle throughout the contractual process, it finds a specific relevance in the context of debt restructurings to ensure that both creditors and sovereign debtors enter into constructive and fair negotiations.[55] Indeed, the PRSLBs establish a duty to act in good faith that could, if breached, have consequences on the restructuring process both for sovereign debtors, should they act without creditor consultations, and for the creditors/investors, should they refuse to negotiate an agreement to the satisfaction of a supermajority of creditors. Although good faith is a difficult concept to reduce to technical definition, under international law, it gains all its meaning and importance when it influences behaviours that do not really respond to legal threats, but are rather motivated by political goals (such as regaining access to financial markets as quickly as possible).

Combined, the concepts of co-responsibility, fiduciary responsibility of the State and good faith give the PRSLBs an inherent balance between States, investors/lenders and the parties affected by their contractual transactions that has yet to be developed in BITs.

As with any set of soft norms, the PRSLB cannot be enforced by a dedicated judicial body. As general principles of law, they may be used by international as well as municipal courts for the purpose of substantiating legal reasoning in the context of sovereign debt disputes. Governmental and non-governmental institutions may also refer to them in order to justify political decisions, for instance, in the context of a change in proposed sovereign debt management practices. Because the PRSLBs can

---

53 Mitu Gulati, Lee Buchheit and Robert B Thompson, 'The Dilemma of Odious Debts' (2007) 56 Duke L J 1237.

54 Michel Virally, 'Review Essay: Good Faith in Public International Law' (1983) 77 AJIL 130; Steven Reinhold, 'Good Faith in International Law' (2013) 2 UCL J L & Jurisp 40.

55 Matthias Goldmann, 'Good Faith and Transparency in Sovereign Debt Workouts' (2014) Paper prepared for the Second Session of the UNCTAD Working Group on a Debt Workout Mechanism <http://unctad.org/en/PublicationsLibrary/gdsddf2014misc3_en.pdf> accessed 5 June 2016.

be implemented through various informal channels, these principles may face inconsistent applications depending on which institution uses them and for what purpose. Their interpretation through judicial channels thus contributes to adding a level of certainty and consistency in their use.

IV. INVESTMENT TREATY ARBITRATIONS: HOW CAN THEY CONTRIBUTE TO PROVIDE AN ENVIRONMENT WHERE SOVEREIGN DEBT ISSUES MIGHT BE BETTER REGULATED?

This part assesses the extent to which investment treaty arbitrations can deal with the issues identified in Part II and contribute to a judicial environment in which the resolution of sovereign debt issues may be dealt with. First, the investment treaty framework is reviewed in its relation to sovereign debt and current obstacles to the resolution of disputes involving sovereign debt issues (A.). Second, this part shows how some of these obstacles might be overcome (B.). In this subsection, it is argued that the integration of certain core PRSLB principles into the legal reasoning of investment treaty tribunals could be a solution.

A. The Investment Treaty Framework and Conditions for Progress Towards a Better Regulation of Sovereign Debt Issues at the International Level

Investment treaties generally provide for the resolution of disputes arising from the treaty by independent tribunals. Therefore, should 'investments' under BITs systematically cover sovereign debt, this area could be adjudicated under international law (including public international law), with the potential of offering more coherence in the interpretation of what could be considered adequate practices and norms governing sovereign lending and borrowing. Furthermore, BITs provide a unique opportunity at international level for investors-creditors to address their problems directly with host States outside the jurisdiction of a municipal court under a uniform set of rules. At first sight, one could thus argue that such features could have a positive impact on the above-mentioned fragmented landscape and its related issues. The positive impact would essentially be generated by the existence at international level of a single judicial framework guided by a uniform set of internationally recognised rules. There are, however, a few obstacles limiting both the use of BITs in the context of sovereign debt matters and the possibility for BITs to provide a comprehensive and legitimate legal framework for these matters.

First, there is no clear position on how sovereign debt would be dealt with by investment treaty tribunals. While investment treaty tribunals have already accepted jurisdiction for claims involving debt obligations (e.g., *Fedax*, *CSOB*, *Abaclat*, *Ambiente Ufficio*),[56] they have not yet made clear whether a sovereign default would be considered an act of expropriation or a breach of other standards such as fair and equal treatment under international law.[57] Furthermore, some tribunals, in particular the *Poštová banka* Tribunal, did not accept that sovereign bonds were covered investments, thus declining jurisdiction.[58] When a treaty leaves definitions open, it is generally history and usage that determine which meaning will prevail. However, neither the evolution of arbitration cases, nor the progress in the inclusion of sovereign debt matters in BITs seem to indicate a general willingness to expand the realm of BITs' interpretation to include sovereign debt matters, especially in regard to sovereign debt restructuring processes. If we consider the progression of investment treaty arbitration cases concerning sovereign debt matters, only a very few of them are being effectively heard by arbitration tribunals on the merits of the claims.[59] Furthermore, most

---

[56] See *CSOB v The Slovak Republic* ICSID Case No ARB/97/4, Decision of the Tribunal on Objections to Jurisdiction (24 May 1999), in which the Tribunal justified that on the basis that it was loan part of a larger transaction – a privatisation project – thereby putting the purpose of the transaction before the economic characteristics of the investment (as requested under art. 25 of the ICSID Convention); *Fedax NV v The Republic of Venezuela*, ICSID Case No ARB/96/3, Decision of the Tribunal on Objections to Jurisdiction (11 July 1997); *Abaclat and others v Argentine Republic*, ICSID Case No ARB/07/5, Decision on Jurisdiction and Admissibility (4 August 2011) paras 362–367 (the Tribunal held that the claimants' bonds and security entitlements fitted within the definition of investment under the relevant BIT, which expressly included financial obligations); *Ambiente Ufficio SpA and others v Argentine Republic*, ICSID Case No ARB/08/9, Decision on Jurisdiction and Admissibility (8 February 2013).

[57] Christoph Schreuer, *ICSID Convention: A Commentary* (2nd edn, CUP 2009) 122–5. (Schreuer noted that the ICSID Convention's drafters actually failed to agree on the definition of investment; part of the reason for this being the reluctance of certain States to include debt in the definition).

[58] *Poštová Banka, as and Istrokapital SE v The Hellenic Republic,* ICSID Case No ARB/13/8, Award (9 April 2015).

[59] *Abaclat v Argentina* (n 56); two other cases also concern bondholder claims against Argentina: *Giovanni Alemanni and others v The Argentine Republic*, ICSID Case No ARB/07/8), Decision on Jurisdiction and Admissibility

recent treaties exclude the coverage of bonds.[60] Most International Investment Agreements (IIAs) also do not explicitly mention sovereign debt and some even exclude it outright.[61]

Second, should sovereign debt be systematically accepted as being covered by BITs, it is important to highlight the current lack of rules in BITs that are necessary to deal efficiently with sovereign debt disputes stemming from restructuring processes. While BIT rules potentially cover creditor claims for breach of national treatment, most-favoured nation (MFN) treatment, fair and equitable treatment (FET), freedom of transfer of funds and expropriation without compensation, they do not deal adequately with collective action problems that lie at the heart of sovereign debt restructurings.[62]

BITs do not include rules applying a threshold under which dissenting creditors have to abide by the decision of the majority of creditors and refrain from using judicial channels to obtain the compensation of their claim. Indeed as few as 1 per cent of dissenting creditors to a restructuring offer might disrupt a negotiated sovereign debt restructuring agreement with the threat of litigation. Even in the case of a debt restructuring through the use of CACs, the minority creditors forced to accept the restructuring package by the sovereign debtor could still initiate an investment treaty dispute, since CACs only cover contractual rights that

(17 November 2014) and *Ambiente Ufficio v Argentina* (n 56) (agreeing to hear the claims).

[60] A few IIAs include an explicit annex on sovereign debt restructurings: Chile-US FTA, Uruguay-US BIT (with annex negotiated-specified majority-restructurings excluded).

[61] Canada-Colombia FTA (2008) art. 838; Australia-Chile FTA (2008) art. 10.1(j)(iii); Azerbaijan- Croatia BIT (2007); Chile-Japan FTA (2007), art. 105. Model BITs of Colombia (2008) and Ghana (2009), Germany (2005) art. 1.c, Bahrain-US, art. 1.d.2 exclude sovereign debt.

[62] The most common creditor claim would theoretically be that of assets expropriation for debt that cannot be recovered due to the sovereign debtor's decision to interrupt the service of its debt. BITs would also be used by holdout creditors who refuse an offer of debt restructuring. In the case of legislation passed by the sovereign debtor concerning the stock of domestic sovereign debts, creditors who feel discriminated against could claim a breach of the BIT National Treatment provision. In the case of a debt exchange, the FET clause could also be invoked against preferential status granted to certain creditors or against a unilateral procedure alleged to be in bad faith. Finally, if a debtor State decides to freeze assets or impose foreign exchange restrictions, creditors could invoke their right to freely transfer the funds invested. See Kevin P Gallagher, 'Financial Crises and International Investment Agreements: The Case of Sovereign Debt Restructuring' (2012) 3 Global Policy 362.

are governed by domestic law and not by international law.[63] Having holdout creditors bringing their claims under investment treaties could generate thousands of bondholder claims spread across many jurisdictions as well as investment treaty arbitrations, which do not allow class actions.[64] Bundling claims together under the umbrella of bondholders' association of same nationalities, as was done in *Abaclat*,[65] could potentially solve this problem but the procedure needs to be clearly established. The danger with this solution is that it is likely to shift the power away from bondholders participating in a sovereign debt agreement to the benefit of dissenting bondholders. In turn, this would be exacerbating the collective action problem of minority creditors attempting to block restructuring processes (in which a majority of creditors has already agreed to forgo a part of their claim) in order to satisfy their own claim for full compensation.

Third, the standards of protection in BITs do not offer internationally recognised and sovereign-debt-specific standards that apply to both lenders-creditors and borrowers-debtors. Instead, the requirements that these standards impose are left to be determined on the basis of domestic laws and practices which vary across jurisdictions and thus bring uncertainty for both investors and host States. Let us take the example of the transparency requirement expected under the FET clause.[66] This clause does not contain the type of information that should be published or made available for the protection of investors/creditors and, hence, it is left to be determined by investment tribunals which may, instead of developing a uniform international standard, rely on domestic laws' transparency requirements.[67]

---

[63] Michael Waibel, 'Opening Pandora's Box: Sovereign Bonds in International Arbitration' (2007) 101 AJIL 711, 715.

[64] Michael Waibel, *Sovereign Defaults Before International Courts and Tribunals* (CUP 2011) 278.

[65] *Abaclat v Argentina* (n 56).

[66] See for instance the 2004 US Model BIT the model treaty also includes a clause on publication of laws and decisions respecting investment but it only refers to 'laws, regulations, procedures, and administrative rulings of general application'.

[67] For instance, in *Genin*, the information demanded from the investors was an ad-hoc demand made by the central bank based on the power derived from its founding articles (Bank of Estonia Act, 17(5)). Here, the Tribunal decided that the investor should have known that any information request by a central bank should be complied with, even when not explicitly written in any domestic laws, Such decision was made on the basis of the founding articles of the Bank of Estonia and an interpretation of the requirements (standard of conduct) that these

Sovereign debt issues like over-lending and over-borrowing, involving a lack of acceptable standards of transparency, due diligence process,[68] data publication by the borrower, disclosure of information by the lender influencing the negotiation of sovereign debt contracts are hence unlikely to be addressed by investment treaty arbitrations in a way that would provide certainty to lenders and borrowers. Furthermore, BIT standards do not apply to investors and host States on an equal basis. The FET clause and its requirements for transparency, due process and disclosure apply to the State for the sake of guaranteeing the investors' protection. There is no equivalent obligation regarding, for instance, disclosure or transparency applying to investors. While investors' conduct constitutes a relevant factor in the analysis of FET claims by arbitral tribunals, such conduct only matters for defence purposes, it does not constitute an obligation that would then be considered as a proper standard of conduct.[69]

Fourth, settling disputes under BITs through arbitration suffers from inconsistencies in the decision-making of arbitral tribunals deriving from diverging interpretations in cases that are either similar or identical.[70] This lack of consistency could be quite damaging in the context of sovereign debt disputes, especially in relation to distressed debt creditors who seek redress in various jurisdictions in order to maximise the chances of obtaining a favourable judgment. Proposals for establishing an

---

articles entail for investors. See *Alex Genin, Eastern Credit Ltd, Inc and AS Baltoil v Estoni*a, ICSID Case No ARB/99/2, Award (18 June 2001) paras 357–358 and 362.

[68] This standard refers to the private standard of (commercial) due diligence which applies to investors/private corporations when they review the documents of a particular transactions before signing off on it. It differs from the standard of (administrative) due process owed by the State in its dealings with foreign investors. Due process is covered under minimum standards of treatment applied in investment tribunals' decisions, whereas due diligence process is not.

[69] *MTD Equity Sdn Bhd and MTD Chile SA v Republic of Chile*, ICSID Case No ARB/01/7, Award (25 May 2004), where the investor's lack of due diligence in assessing the lawfulness of its proposed property development was held to account for 50 per cent of its loss. See the duties implied in defences based on investors' conduct in Peter Muchlinski, '"Caveat Investor"? The Relevance of the Conduct of the Investor Under the Fair and Equitable Treatment Standard' (2006) 55 ICLQ 527.

[70] Susan D Franck, 'The Legitimacy Crisis in Investment Treaty Arbitration: Privatizing Public International Law Through Inconsistent Decisions' (2005) 73 Fordham L Rev 1545.

appellate body reviewing inconsistent decisions has been made but without success to this day.[71]

Fifth, investment treaty arbitrations suffer from legitimacy issues linked to: (i) the rules on the process of selecting arbitrators; and (ii) the original design of BITs, which both have an impact on the decisions made in these arbitrations with respect to the consideration of public interests. Indeed, like the field of sovereign debt, public concerns, such as social and human rights or environmental issues, tend to be disregarded by investors and, sometimes also by tribunals. The fact that investment arbitrators are in part selected among private law firms, which have clients in the private sector, is aggravated by the importance of their discretionary powers. In principle, there is nothing wrong in leaving some discretion to dispute resolvers. However, most domestic court judges are appointed within a national judicial framework, which makes them the representatives of the public interest and thus accountable to the people. International arbitral tribunals, on the contrary, lack representative legitimacy in dealing with issues relating to States and their exercise of public authority.[72] Even though pro-investor bias precluding complete impartiality cannot be scientifically verified, arbitrators' (lack of) representativeness combined with a lack of public participation in an arbitration system that has an influence on public policies remains a significant problem. On questions of transparency, the rules applicable to investment arbitrations have evolved in light of recent reforms.[73] However, since the choice of being more transparent is still primarily in the hands of the disputing parties, the confidential dimension of investment arbitration

---

[71] See the proposal for the establishment an appellate body for investment treaties (inconsistent) decisions, e.g. at <http://kluwerarbitrationblog.com/2014/05/01/appellate-structure-and-need-for-legal-certainty-in-investment-arbitration/> accessed 7 December 2016.

[72] A worrying factor for sovereign debt further lies in the increasing penetration of investment arbitrations by investment funds helping finance investor-State disputes in exchange for a share in any granted award or settlement strategies deployed by distressed debt funds are especially at stake, see Pia Eberhardt and Cecilia Olivet, 'Profiting from Injustice' (Transnational Institute and Corporate Europe Observatory 2012) 9.

[73] ICSID rules of arbitration now include the following provisions under art. 12:

> 12.1 Except where one of the parties object, the oral hearings in an ICSID arbitration can be attended by members of the public;
>
> 12.2 ICSID tribunals may, following consultation with the parties, permit submissions from third parties; and
>
> 12.3 With both parties' consent, any award may be published by ICSID.

may remain unchanged in a lot of cases with minimal access to the parties' pleading and evidence, little opportunity for *amicus curiae*-participation and decisions not available to the public.[74]

Furthermore, the use of arbitration to resolve BIT disputes effectively creates a situation whereby private arbitrators make decisions entailing public interests without necessarily having the instruments to pursue public policy oriented decisions. This situation can only be redressed through a major integration of social concerns in the interpretation of BITs. This option may, nevertheless, not be encouraged by private investors and creditors who count on this forum to ensure their property rights are enforced.

In order for investment treaty arbitrations to offer an environment able to deal with sovereign debt issues at the international level the obstacles identified above must be overcome: (i) jurisdiction of investment treaty tribunals on debt restructuring issues must be clearly established to reflect whether debt restructuring processes may be covered; (ii) BITs should include CACs or an equivalent rule so as to match current contractual practices and make it impossible for smaller than blocking minorities of creditors to bring claims related to sovereign debt restructuring under investment arbitration rules. Moreover, investment treaty tribunals should be in a position to deal with mass claims through clearly identified procedures if they are to embark in sovereign debt restructuring disputes; (iii) sovereign-debt-specific standards applying to both creditors and debtors need to be identified and sourced from internationally recognised norms so as to promote coherence and consistency in the interpretation of BIT rules in the field of sovereign debt. In the spirit of promoting interpretative coherence, the establishment of an appeal procedure may be a good thing; and (iv) the legitimacy of investment treaty arbitrations needs to be improved through more representative procedures for the selection of arbitrators and increased reference in arbitral awards to legal principles reflecting public interests, namely general principles of public law. In regard to the third and fourth conditions, it may be argued that the PRSLBs may play an active role if they were used, where relevant, as a basis of the legal reasoning backing the decisions of investment tribunals. The following section examines the extent to which this option may be feasible.

---

[74] Franck (n 70) 1545.

B. Meeting the Conditions for Progress Towards an Enhanced Sovereign Debt Regulation Framework for Investment Treaty Arbitrations: What Role for the PRSLBs?

A possible source of legitimacy in applying BITs to sovereign debt matters could stem from the integration of public interest notions in investment treaty decisions through the use of public law. Since some of the PRSLBs already embody general principles of law, backing the legal reasoning of investment treaty tribunals, where appropriate, with such principles should not represent an impossible task. Nonetheless, such principles should be compatible (not conflicting) with BITs core principles in order to be used. This section examines the extent to which core BITs' principles, such as national treatment and FET can be interpreted in line with the PRSLBs.

National treatment implies that foreign investments are to be treated no less favourably than their domestic counterparts. In the field of sovereign debt, where national savings are at stake, sovereigns need to be able to make decisions that may imply (or not) a differentiation between domestic and foreign creditors in order to protect their economy in times of crisis. The reason behind this differentiation, if made, between foreign and domestic creditors lies in the sovereign's fiduciary duty to protect its population, which also constitutes its tax basis and the only resource to recover from a debt crisis when all foreign lenders have disappeared (that is as soon as they have suspicions about economic troubles). Protectionist attitudes are indeed common practice when dealing with an excessive debt burden and slow growth. As shown by reactions across developed countries to the recent financial crisis, keeping the domestic financial sector afloat constitutes a number one priority in distressed times.[75] Debt restructuring situations constitute a striking example of the problems that may arise in applying national treatment. National treatment could be claimed when a foreign bondholder receives different terms during a restructuring than do domestic counterparts.[76] In theory, national treatment profoundly conflicts with the fiduciary principle present in the PRSLBs because this principle intends, inter alia, to protect a country's

[75] On the rationale for keeping the private sector afloat in times of crisis see <www.vox.com/2015/10/20/9571349/blinder-zandi-stimulus-bailout> accessed 3 March 2016.

[76] Gallagher (n 62) 367.

given population, if necessary, against third parties when their claims menace the public interests of a society.[77]

Although equality of treatment between domestic and foreign investors may be desirable in order to ensure predictability and a level playing field for business transactions, it could be argued that transparent rules for foreign investors (even if they are different to those applying to domestic investors) are sufficient to ensure this predictability. Non-discrimination principles are important when it comes to protecting the assets of individuals (irrespective of their nationality) who reside in a given host country as they indeed equally suffer from economic and social adjustments in times of crisis. This is not true, however, for lending institutions incorporated outside the host countries as they do not have to face the austerity measures generally imposed in a debt crisis stricken country. States thus have to make a choice between foreign investors who often do not pay taxes in their countries and the others to whom they owe a fiduciary responsibility. As seen earlier, the fiduciary responsibility of the State constitutes a core principle of the PRSLBs entailing that protectionist measures that may infringe the national treatment standard must be balanced so as to ensure both the economic health and the basic social needs of its population. An increasing number of economists and lawyers support the view that the ability to treat domestic and foreign creditors differently is a necessary policy option for government during financial crises.[78]

The FET standard may be the most important principle in BITs because its interpretation often has implications on the extent to which host States may adopt policies in the public interest. The varying interpretations given by tribunals to the FET standard offer a non-negligible diversity of requirements including '[a] State's obligation to act consistently, transparently, reasonably, without ambiguity, arbitrariness or discrimination, in an even-handed manner, to ensure due process

[77] Evan Fox-Decent, 'The Fiduciary Nature of State Legal Authority' (2005) 31 Queen's LJ 271 (where it is argued that fiduciary relationships are inherent in the State as they arise from the natural vulnerability of the people of a territory with respect to the institution ensuring impartiality among them. A society thus exists in relation to a higher entity, which is embodied in the rule of law enforced by governing institutions. This situation induces a delegation process whereby the government has a responsibility to protect the interests of the citizens otherwise known as the public interest).

[78] Anna Gelpern and Brian Setser, 'Domestic and External Debt: The Doomed Quest for Equal Treatment' (2004) 35 Georgetown J Intl L 795, 796.

in decision-making and respect investors' legitimate expectations'.[79] The FET standard in BITs may be pegged to customary law[80] or interpreted more broadly by tribunals on the basis of the treaty's language. Sometimes, BITs borrow from customary law's more restrictive language so as to avoid limiting the scope of sovereign States' discretion to act in the public interest.[81]

Applied to the sovereign debt context, the FET standard could be invoked if lenders perceived the sovereign borrower's actions as altering their legitimate expectations (including non-compliance with the debt contract between a lender and a borrower). Non-compliance might for example include legislating to alter the terms of a bond or restructure its sovereign debts unilaterally. In the context of a debt restructuring, creditors who do not agree with a restructuring offer may claim that the FET standard has been breached on the grounds that the debt negotiation process lacked transparency or due process[82] or that the debt exchange was imposed unilaterally and was not proposed in good faith.[83] Transparency constitutes another important principle of law that is derived from interpretation of the FET standard.[84] Several tribunals have considered transparency and participation as part of an investor's legitimate expectations.[85] Transparency is found in both investment treaty jurisprudence and the PRSLBs insofar as it creates an obligation for the borrower to provide investors with the necessary documents that will allow them to make a more informed decision about the decision to lend. In *Tecmed v*

---

[79] UNCTAD, *Fair and Equitable Treatment* (UNCTAD Series on Issues in International Investment Agreements) (United Nations 2012) vol II, xiii.

[80] The FET standard, if viewed as reflecting custom, is usually traced back to the arbitral practice of various claims commissions operating in the inter-war period; it mostly refers to the minimum standard of treatment of aliens. See NAFTA Free Trade Commission, 'Notes on Interpretation of Certain Chapter 11 Provisions' (31 July 2001) <www.sice.oas.org/tpd/nafta/Commission/CH11understanding_e.asp> accessed 19 February 2015.

[81] UNCTAD (n 18) 28.

[82] Waibel (n 63) 752.

[83] Good faith constitutes one of the FET standard's components; see Deyan Draguiev, 'Bad Faith Conduct of States in Violation of the "Fair And Equitable Treatment" Standard in International Investment Law and Arbitration' (2014) 5 Journal of International Dispute Settlement 273. See further Goldmann (n 55) 12 ('duty not to obstruct').

[84] See for instance *Glamis Gold Ltd v United States*, NAFTA/UNCITRAL, Award (8 June 2009) para. 605.

[85] See the review of relevant case law (including cases such as *Tecmed*, *Pope & Talbot, Metaclad*) in Andrew Newcombe and Lluis Paradell, *Law and Practice of Investment Treaties. Standards of Treatment* (Kluwer 2009) 291–4.

Mexico,[86] the transparency requirement was highlighted with respect to rules applicable to the investment in question so as to protect the legitimate expectations of the investor.

About a decade ago, investment tribunals started to take into account investors' behaviour to justify the measures taken against the investor by the respondent country.[87] Such behaviours naturally include outright fraud and misrepresentation but also lack of due diligence (e.g., *MTD Equity*)[88] or bad management (e.g., *Noble Ventures*).[89] These cases certainly indicate a more balanced interpretative direction on the path to reinforcing the legitimacy of investment arbitration, which could be extended further with the PRSLBs by integrating principles such as co-responsibility (of investors-lenders and sovereign borrowers) as well as by relying on standards (embedded in the principles) coming from an observation of the soundest practices seen in the field of sovereign debt. As highlighted before, the current BITs standards of interpretation in regard to due diligence process, transparency and disclosure could be further defined.[90] As an example, in sovereign debt transactions lenders cannot simply rely on the documents that they are handed out and assert the due diligence process was thus properly conducted; the PRSLBs (Principle 3) require not only that lenders should rely on the 'best available information' but also that they should ensure that sovereign borrowers understand the implications of the transactions into which they enter. This is particularly important when an unsophisticated sovereign borrower is dealing with foreign commercial lenders who may not want to emphasise certain aspects of the deal. Applying co-responsibility in this case, entails disclosing information that may not be in the sovereign borrowers' commercial interest, so that the borrower is in a position to make an informed decision about accepting a debt. Here again, the PRSLBs reflect a commitment to consider both sides of the equation

---

[86] *Técnicas Medioambientales Tecmed SA v The United Mexican States*, ICSID Case No ARB/AF/002, Award (29 May 2003) para. 154.

[87] Ibid., paras 3, 14 and 83 (and paras 7, 16 quoting *Methanex*, in which the Tribunal held that 'the regulatory and political environment may be a factor that the investor should take into account, and to anticipate regulatory change in areas where high levels of regulation can be foreseen, unless the host country has given assurances that no regulatory changes will take place'). See *Methanex Corporation v United States of America,* NAFTA/UNCITRAL, Final Award on Jurisdiction and Merits (3 August 2005), Part IV – Chapter D, paras 9–10.

[88] *MTD Equity* (n 69).

[89] *Noble Ventures Inc v Romania*, ICSID Case No ARB/01/11, Award (12 October 2005). Also see UNCTAD (n 18) 83–86.

[90] See Section II.A of this chapter.

(investors' and host States') so as to produce the fairest and most legitimate outcomes.

In summary, the analysis of the use of the PRSLBs in interpreting BITs in the context of sovereign debt matters shows a mixed picture. Both sets of instruments rely on legal concepts and principles such as good faith, transparency, comparability of treatment/non-discrimination and others entailing some degree of compatibility between them. These legal concepts however sometimes need elaboration into standards that are specifically related to the area to which they apply in order to maximise their efficiency. Hence, the expertise of investment arbitrators would only be reinforced by the use of the PRSLBs. Moreover, in sovereign debt restructuring, applying BIT rules as they stand may prove counterproductive in relation to collective action issues and complicate the process rather than facilitate it.[91] In order to change this, BITs would have to include the equivalent of the CACs, which are now found in most Eurobond contracts.[92] Arbitration tribunals would also have to clarify the procedural ways of dealing with a large number of claims if they accepted such cases. Hence, arbitration tribunals would really be of added value where debt restructuring negotiation processes have taken place and the vote on the debt exchange governed by domestic law is insufficient to secure a 'cram-down' on dissenting investors-creditors (i.e., when a supermajority of creditors – generally gathering at least 75 per cent of the votes in favour of the restructuring agreement – is not reached). As argued in the Roadmap and Guide for Sovereign Debt Workouts,[93] an independent and impartial arbitration process could deal with holdout creditors' claims and possibly result either in an obligation to accept the restructuring deal if this is deemed legitimate (i.e., the negotiations are conducted in good faith and the restructuring deal allows the debtor country to recover a sustainable debt situation), or, in case of bad faith negotiations, in the demand of a new negotiation round with a binding outcome. In this context, the question of independence, impartiality and expertise of the tribunal in question is of significant importance and it remains questionable as to whether investment treaty tribunals could perform this function.[94]

---

91 Ibid.

92 The design of such clause into BITs goes beyond the scope of this chapter, but its effect would have to be the recognition of creditors supermajority votes having already taken place in the context of a sovereign debt restructuring.

93 Released in April 2015; see UNCTAD (n 18).

94 See section II.B.

V. CONCLUSION

This chapter has examined the potential for the use of the PRSLBs in the context of investment treaty arbitrations with a view to providing a comprehensive, consistent and legitimate framework for the regulation of sovereign debt matters at the international level. On the one hand, the use of an international arbitration system, such as the one provided for by BITs, could be useful in enforcing international sovereign debt restructuring agreements and resolving sovereign debt disputes. On the other hand, BITs are not (yet) equipped to address a number of issues ranging from collective action matters in sovereign debt restructuring to issues stemming from disregard for standards of transparency, due diligence process and disclosure in relation to sovereign debt transactions. Moreover, should BITs be systematically applied to sovereign debt issues, the questions revolving around the legitimacy of such instruments still have to be addressed.

Despite the recognition of defences based on the investors' (poor) conduct in investment disputes, BITs remain instruments designed to protect investors' property rights and as such, they lack balanced legal tools to ensure a legitimate regulation of both host States' and investors' conduct. We have seen that concepts such as co-responsibility, fiduciary duty and good faith stemming from the PRSLBs could find their way into investment arbitrations through a more comprehensive integration of public international law into the interpretation of BITs.[95] Such integration could bring more balance and more legitimacy to decisions of investment treaty tribunals. Of course, this would also entail having to find a way to accommodate potential conflicts with some of BITs' core principles such as national treatment. A general recognition that, in times of crises, States may have to make strategic choices in the public interest of their nationals with possible discriminatory consequences on foreigners would go a long way in dealing with national treatment conflicts.

Nevertheless, despite clear legal space for the use of PRSLBs within the investment treaty framework challenges remain with respect to the institutional settings needed to address both fragmentation and legitimacy issues. First, the lack of representativeness of the investment treaty

---

[95] Here 'public international law' is meant to include the laws (treaty based, principles of international law or customary international law) that bring public interests (e.g., social, human rights, environmental) at the centre of investors' rights discussions. This also includes concepts such as the co-responsibility of lenders and borrowers, which have the potential of being recognised as general principles of international law.

system makes its decisions questionable in regard to their intention of taking into account the States' fiduciary responsibility. In addition, the absence of an appellate body or other mechanism dealing with inconsistent legal interpretations could be quite problematic if sovereign debt dispute claims were submitted to more than one tribunal. Finally, sovereign debt restructuring processes need an institutional structure that is capable of coordinating the interests and functions of international actors (creditor committees, IMF, Paris Club, etc.) during negotiations and is sufficiently flexible to intervene only if these negotiations fail. It thus remains to be seen whether the current dispute resolution framework for international investment could adapt its rules to perform this role. Notwithstanding these remaining challenges, the PRSLBs constitute a useful tool to make investment dispute resolutions more equipped for the purpose of addressing sovereign lending and borrowing issues.

PART III

Bank rescue measures

8. Bail-ins and international investment law: In and beyond Cyprus

Maurice Mendelson QC and Martins Paparinskis*

I. INTRODUCTION

It would be unfair to say that there is no international law of money; there is.[1] But international financial law is relatively underdeveloped in comparison to international trade and investment law,[2] particularly as far as rules providing for formalised dispute settlement go.[3] This chapter considers the legal issues which may arise from bail-ins of depositors of banks from the perspective of international investment treaty law. The

* Except where otherwise indicated, this chapter does not take into account developments subsequent to March 2014.

[1] E.g., Charles Proctor, *Mann on the Legal Aspects of Money* (7th edn, OUP 2012) Part IV ('Exchange Controls, Exchange Rates, and Sanctions'), Part V ('Public International Law of Money') and Part VI ('Monetary Unions and Other Forms of Monetary Organisation').

[2] Thomas Cottier and Rosa M Lastra, 'The Quest for International Law in Financial Regulation and Monetary Affairs: Introduction' (2010) 13 JIEL 527; Michael Waibel, 'Two Decades Lost: Reinvigorating the Weak Cousin of WTO Law' (2010) 3 Select Proceedings Eur Society Intl L 353.

[3] Rules of international law that discipline the discretion of States in this area are more likely to come from, as it were, contiguous disciplines of international economic law that deal with international investment and international trade; see for example Michael Waibel, *Sovereign Defaults Before International Courts and Tribunals* (CUP 2011); Thomas Cottier, John H Jackson and Rosa M Lastra (eds), *International Law in Financial Regulation and Monetary Affairs* (OUP 2012); Claus D Zimmermann, *A Contemporary Concept of Monetary Sovereignty* (OUP 2013) particularly Ch. 3. Direct engagement with international financial law is often characterised precisely by the absence of binding rules and procedures, Carlos Espósito, Yuefen Li and Juan Pablo Bohoslavsky (eds), *Sovereign Financing and International Law: The UNCTAD Principles on Responsible Sovereign Lending and Borrowing* (OUP 2013).

focus is consciously narrow: it may be the case that, in addition to bail-ins of depositors, other measures are applied to depositors, bondholders, shareholders, or banks, raising further questions not only under investment law, but also the law of the European Union (EU) and the European Convention on Human Rights (ECHR) (or indeed the domestic law).[4] However, these issues are outside the scope of this chapter.

Bailing-out a State or institution means bringing in money from the outside to assist it, in particular to avoid insolvency. 'Bail-in' is essentially the opposite technique, though with a similar objective. Deposits are converted, against the depositors' will, into equity, recapitalising the failing bank without the use of public money. In recent years, the bail-in tool has achieved particular prominence in a number of ways. It was included in proposed amendments to the relevant Directives of the EU, with the particular provisions intended to be applied from 1 January 2018.[5] The amendments define bail-ins as the power of the relevant authorities to write down the claims of unsecured creditors of a failing institution and convert debt claims into equity, also setting out a

---

[4] The possible relevance of various regimes of domestic and international law for these matters is neither new nor unusual; see Maurice Mendelson, 'Compensation for Expropriation: the Case-Law' (1985) 79 AJIL 414; Maurice Mendelson, 'Correspondence' ibid., 1041; Maurice Mendelson, 'International Law and the Valuation of Nationalised Shares: Two French Decisions' (1985) 34 ICLQ 284; Maurice Mendelson, 'The United Kingdom Nationalization Cases and the European Convention on Human Rights' (1987) 57 BYBIL 33; Nicolas Jansen Calamita, 'The British Bank Nationalizations: An International Law Perspective' (2009) 58 ICLQ 119. In relation to the subject-matter of this chapter, the Supreme Court of Cyprus refused jurisdiction over challenges to decisions of the Cypriot Resolution Authority, inter alia, regarding bail-ins, sending the claimants to civil courts, Jenny Giotaki, 'The Cypriot "Bail-in Litigation": a First Assessment of the Ruling of the Supreme Court of Cyprus' (2013) 28 Butterworths J Intl Banking Financial L 485. The Court of Justice of the European Union has rejected a claim of non-contractual liability, brought by depositors against the European Commission and the European Central Bank, emphasising the importance of the objective of ensuring the stability of the banking system of the euro area, CJEU, Joined Cases C-8/15 to C-10/15 P, *Ledra Advertising Ltd and Others v EC and ECB* [2016] ECLI:EU:C:2016:701 paras 63–76.

[5] Proposal for a Directive of the European Parliament and of the Council establishing a framework for the recovery and resolution of credit institutions and investment firms and amending Council Directives 77/91/EEC and 82/891/EC, Directives 2001/24/EC, 2002/47/EC, 2004/25/EC, 2005/56/EC, 2007/36/EC and 2011/35/EC and Regulation (EU) No 1093/2010, COM/2012/0280 final – 2012/0150 (COD), arts 37–51.

detailed hierarchy of claims. The recitals explain that bail-ins achieve the purpose of minimising the costs of resolution of failing institutions to taxpayers by ensuring that shareholders and creditors suffer appropriate losses. The proposals were approved by the Council of the EU at the end of June 2013,[6] and have now been adopted as the Bank Recovery and Resolution Directive (BRRD).[7] Bail-ins are already available under US law in certain circumstances, pursuant to the 2010 Dodd-Frank Act.[8]

Conversion of deposits into shares was an important and controversial element of the response to the banking crisis in Cyprus. In late March 2013, the Central Bank of Cyprus intervened in the two largest banks in the country, the Bank of Cyprus (BoC) and the Cyprus Popular Bank (also known as the Laiki Bank), applying a range of measures to their restructuring. These measures left deposits subject to the standard EU Government guarantee of €100,000 untouched, but provided for conversion of 37.5 per cent of uninsured deposits of BoC into shares, and freezing of a further 22.5 per cent with the possibility of a further bail-in after an independent valuation of BoC assets.[9] On 30 July 2013, the Central Bank of Cyprus issued a decision that an additional 10 per cent

---

[6] Council of the European Union, 'Council agrees position on bank resolution' (27 June 2013) 2–3 <www.consilium.europa.eu/uedocs/cms_data/docs/pressdata/en/ecofin/137627.pdf> accessed 7 December 2016; 'Statement of Commissioner Barnier following agreement in ECOFIN on bank recovery and resolution' MEMO 13/601 (27 June 2013) <www.europa.eu/rapid/press-release_MEMO-13-601_en.htm?locale=en> accessed 7 December 2016.

[7] Directive 2014/59/EU of the European Parliament and of the Council of 15 May 2014 establishing a framework for the recovery and resolution of credit institutions and investment firms and amending Council Directive 82/891/EEC, and Directives 2001/24/EC, 2002/47/EC, 2004/25/EC, 2005/56/EC, 2007/36/EC, 2011/35/EU, 2012/30/EU and 2013/36/EU, and Regulations (EU) 1093/2010 and (EU) 648/2012, of the European Parliament and of the Council Text with EEA relevance, [2014] OJ L173/190, arts 43–58.

[8] Dodd-Frank Wall Street Reform and Consumer Protection Act', Pub L 111-203, HR 4173.

[9] See IMF, 'Cyprus: Letter of Intent' (29 April 2013) <www.imf.org/external/np/loi/2013/cyp/042913.pdf> accessed 29 March 2015; IMF, 'Cyprus: Memorandum of Economic and Financial Policies' (29 April 2013) ibid., 2, 9 and 10; IMF, 'Cyprus: Technical Memorandums of Understanding' (29 April 2013) ibid., 26.27; IMF, 'Financial Assistance Facility Agreement between European Stability Mechanism, Cyprus and Central Bank of Cyprus' (8 May 2013) <http://esm.europa.eu/pdf/ESM%20FFA%20Cyprus%20publication%20version%20final.pdf> accessed 29 March 2015; IMF, 'Cyprus: Memorandum of Economic and Financial Policies' (29 August 2013); press release at <www.imf.org/external/np/loi/2013/cyp/082913.pdf> accessed 29 March 2015 3 [5], [14].

of the frozen deposits would be bailed-in, bringing the total bail-in to 47.5 per cent.[10] According to news sources, foreign, mainly Russian, depositors have been particularly affected by the bail-in, in view of their substantial deposits. For instance, a depositor of €1m with €100,000 covered by deposit insurance, would have been bailed-in initially for 37.5 per cent of €900,000 (€337,500), with an additional 10 per cent subject to further bail-in (€90,000). The Managing Director of the International Monetary Fund (IMF) praised Cyprus for having taken 'bold steps to address the crisis, including the upfront resolution and restructuring of the two largest and insolvent banks at no fiscal cost, while protecting insured depositors'.[11]

But how far are measures of this type consistent with investment protection law? This legal regime is mainly embodied in international treaties, largely bilateral investment protection treaties (BITs) (around 3,200 at the end of 2013), but also some important multilateral treaties (e.g., the North American Free Trade Agreement and the Energy Charter Treaty). These treaties provide substantive and procedural protection to foreign 'investors' regarding the treatment of 'investments', as defined in each particular agreement. The boilerplate substantive standards set out in the investment treaties include compensation for expropriation, fair and equitable treatment, freedom of transfers and non-discrimination, whether by comparison with the host State's nationals (the national treatment standard) or by comparison with nationals of other States (the most-favoured-nation (MFN) standard).

However, the particular importance of investment treaties lies in the procedural rights that are usually granted to investors: they are entitled to bring a direct arbitral claim against the State in which the investment has been made, regarding breaches of investment treaties, and without having to procure specific consent or exhaust local remedies. In most treaties, investors are offered a choice between arbitration under the auspices of the International Centre for the Settlement of Investment Disputes (ICSID, an affiliate of the World Bank) and under other rules of arbitration—ad hoc proceedings under the Arbitration Rules of the UN Commission for International Trade Law (UNCITRAL) being the most

---

[10] 'Recapitalisation Through Bail-in and Resolution Exit Bank of Cyprus Announcement' <www.bankofcyprus.com/en-GB/Start/News_Archive/Recapitalisation-through-Bail-in-and-Resolution-Exit-Bank-of-Cyprus-Announcement/> accessed 29 March 2015.

[11] 'IMF Executive Board Approves €1 Billion Arrangement Under Extended Fund Facility for Cyprus' (Press Release No 13/175) (15 May 2013) <www.imf.org/external/np/sec/pr/2013/pr13175.htm> accessed 29 March 2015.

common alternative option.[12] Cyprus has concluded 27 BITs, of which 21 are in force,[13] and is a party to the ICSID Convention.[14]

The next sections will consider whether investment protection rules, particularly the right to compensation for expropriation, might be relied on by foreign investors affected by bail-ins, considering in turn certain preliminary issues of applicability of investment treaties, then focusing on legal and factual aspects of expropriation and bail-ins, and finally giving a brief overview of the possible relevance of other investment protection obligations. It is not the purpose of this chapter to provide definitive answers, but rather, to identify some of the multifarious thorny legal questions that could arise. This is partly because the law in certain respects remains unsettled, and partly for professional reasons of the first-named author.

II. SETTING THE SCENE FOR INVESTMENT PROTECTION LAW

The applicability of and the degree of protection provided by investment protection law to depositors subject to bail-ins may differ from case to case. The Cyprus bail-ins provide a good case study for analysing the conditions for the application of investment protection law, particularly in view of the controversial application of bail-in to all uninsured depositors,[15] and the apparent consensus—even if articulated with different degrees of elegance—that depositors and bondholders from Russia were particularly heavily hit by these measures (rightly so, according to those who maintain that the funds were in many cases the result of money-laundering and other dubious conduct). Could foreign depositors rely on investment protection law to challenge the measures taken by Cyprus'

---

[12] See generally UNCTAD, *World Investment Report 2014: Investing in the SDGs: An Action Plan* (United Nations 2014) 114–33; Zachary Douglas, *The International Law of Investment Claims* (CUP 2009); Rudolf Dolzer and Christoph Schreuer, *Principles of International Investment Law* (2nd edn, OUP 2012).

[13] For a list see UNCTAD's website at <http://investmentpolicyhub.unctad.org/IIA/CountryBits/54#iiaInnerMenu> accessed 29 March 2015.

[14] See <https://icsid.worldbank.org/ICSID/FrontServlet?requestType=ICSIDDocRH&actionVal=ShowDocument&language=English> accessed 29 March 2015.

[15] Charlemagne, 'A Better Deal, but still Painful: The Cyprus Bail-Out' (*The Economist*, 25 March 2013) <www.economist.com/blogs/charlemagne/2013/03/cyprus-bail-out> accessed 29 March 2015; 'Second Time Unlucky', *The Economist* (30 March 2013); 'Cyprus One Year on: Injured Island', *The Economist* (8 March 2014).

Central Bank? In answering this question, it may be convenient to distinguish two types of preliminary legal issues: matters relating specifically to the criteria of 'investors' and 'investments', and other preliminary issues. These issues will be addressed in turn.

A. 'Investors' and 'Investments'

Investment protection law gives investors procedural rights to bring arbitral claims against States regarding investments; the existence of 'an investor' and 'an investment' is therefore a necessary jurisdictional requirement for such a claim.[16]

The first jurisdictional aspect may be disposed of relatively briefly: the relevant question is whether the definition of 'investor' in an international treaty binding upon Cyprus is satisfied. While the BIT between Cyprus and Russia is not yet in force, and investments by Russian nationals would therefore not be directly covered,[17] investments by Russian-controlled companies incorporated in States that do have binding BITs with Cyprus would normally qualify.[18]

Deposits are undoubtedly 'possessions' and 'property' under e.g., the ECHR;[19] but BITs speak in terms of 'investments', which is arguably a narrower concept. Most treaties define 'investments' in broad and non-exhaustive terms, often explicitly mentioning bonds and claims to money.[20] While one might expect that to be the end of the matter, there has been some disagreement between tribunals and scholars about the general contours of the definition of 'investment': in particular, whether a putative investment has to satisfy only the definition provided in the particular treaty, or also certain additional criteria regarding commitment

---

[16] UNCTAD, 'Scope and Definition' in *UNCTAD Series on Issues in International Investment Agreements II* (United Nations 2011).

[17] The Russia-Cyprus BIT has been signed but is not in force, therefore only certain obligations under the law of treaties, particularly the obligation not to defeat the object and purpose of the treaty, may be applicable. But they would not include all the full substantive protections and certainly not consent to arbitration.

[18] E.g., the 1991 Belgium and Luxembourg-Cyprus BIT art. 1(1)(b) defines 'investors' as juridical persons only by reference to the place of constitution and registered office, without requiring business presence in the particular State.

[19] See the recent confirmation by the Grand Chamber in *Ališi and Others v Bosnia and Herzegovina, Croatia, Serbia, Slovenia and the Former Yugoslav Republic of Macedonia*, App no 60642/08 (Grand Chamber, 16 July 2014) para. 80.

[20] E.g., the 1991 Belgium and Luxembourg-Cyprus BIT (n 18) art. 1(2)(c).

of funds, duration, profit, risk, and contribution to development. Some have argued that these additional criteria are inherent in the notion of 'investment' under, at any rate, the ICSID Convention (Art. 25 of which contains no definition of the concept); others disagree.[21] Debate centres on whether such criteria are jurisdictional requirements or merely typical features of investments;[22] and whether these criteria would apply to investment treaty claims brought in arbitral fora other than ICSID.[23] There has also been some disagreement between arbitrators, sitting in recent cases brought against Argentina, as to whether governmental bonds qualify as investments made within the territory of the borrower State[24]—a discussion that could potentially throw some light, by analogy, on the 'investment' status of deposits. While a number of investment treaty arbitrations have dealt with claims relating to alleged mistreatment of banks,[25] the narrower question of whether deposits qualify as

---

[21] Cf. *Malaysian Historical Salvors Sdn Bhd v Malaysia,* ICSID Case No ARB/05/10, Decision on the Application for Annulment (16 April 2009) paras 56–79; ibid, Dissenting Opinion of Arbitrator Shahabuddeen, paras 5–47.

[22] Cf. *Philip Morris Brands Sarl and Others v Oriental Republic of Uruguay,* ICSID Case No ARB/10/7, Decision on Jurisdiction (2 July 2013) paras 204–209; *KT Asia Investment Group BV v Kazakhstan,* ICSID Case No ARB/09/8, Award (17 October 2013) paras 160–173.

[23] Cf. *Romak SA (Switzerland) v Uzbekistan,* PCA Case No AA280, Award (26 November 2009) paras 192–196; *Guaracachi America, Inc and Other v Bolivia,* PCA Case No 2011-17, Award (31 January 2014) para. 364.

[24] *Abaclat and Others v Argentina,* ICSID Case No ARB/07/5, Decision on Jurisdiction and Admissibility (4 August 2011) paras 347–387; ibid., Dissenting Opinion of Arbitrator Abi-Saab (8 October 2011) paras 34–119; *Ambiente Ufficio SpA and Others v Argentina,* ICSID Case No ARB/08/9, Decision on Jurisdiction and Admissibility (8 February 2013) paras 405–520; ibid., Dissenting Opinion of Arbitrator Torres Bernárdez (2 May 2013) paras 146–330; *Giovanni Alemanni and Others v Argentina,* ICSID Case No ARB/07/8, Decision on Jurisdiction and Admissibility (17 November 2014) para. 296.

[25] *Genin, Eastern Credit Ltd, Inc and AS Baltoil v Estonia,* ICSID Case No ARB/99/2, Award (25 June 2001); *Saluka Investment BV v Czech Republic,* UNCITRAL, Partial Award (17 March 2006); *OKO Pankki Oyj and Others v Estonia,* ICSID Case No ARB/04/6, Award (19 November 2007); *Deutsche Bank AG v Sri Lanka,* ICSID Case No ARB/09/02, Award (31 October 2012); *Standard Chartered Bank v Tanzania,* ICSID Case No ARB/10/12, Award (2 November 2012); *Rafat Ali Rizvi v Indonesia,* ICSID Case No ARB/11/13, Award on Jurisdiction (16 July 2013); *Renée Rose Levy de Levi v Peru,* ICSID Case No ARB/10/17, Award (26 February 2014); *Belokon v Kyrgyzstan,* UNCITRAL, Award (24 October 2014); *British Caribbean Bank Ltd v Belize,* PCA Case No 2010-18, Award (19 December 2014); *Poštová banka, as and ISTROKAPITAL SE v Greece,* ICSID Case No ARB/13/8, Award (9 April 2015);

investments does not seem to have been properly dealt with.[26] A definition of 'investment' focusing on the language of BITs, or applying more general criteria in a flexible manner would be easy to satisfy, while a strict reading of requirements of e.g., duration of contribution may arguably exclude at least short- to medium-term deposits.

B. Other Preliminary Issues

The case of Cyprus also raises a challenge that is simultaneously obvious and atypical: should any significance be attached to the broader context within which the bail-ins took place, when Cyprus was apparently nudged in the direction of applying bail-ins to a broad category of depositors by the so-called Troika, formed by the IMF, the European Commission (EC) and European Central Bank (ECB)?[27] This fact might be significant in three ways.

Ping An Life Insurance Company of China and Other v Belgium, ICSID Case No ARB/12/29, Award (30 April 2015). A number of cases relating to banking services are pending: *BV Belegging-Maatschappij 'Far East' v Austria,* ICSID Case No ARB/15/32; *City-State NV and Others v Ukraine,* ICSID Case No ARB/14/9; *Cyprus Popular Bank Public Co Ltd v Greece,* ICSID Case No ARB/14/16; *Guardian Fiduciary Trust, Ltd and Other v Former Yugoslav Republic of Macedonia,* ICSID Case No ARB/12/31; *JSC BTA Bank v Kyrgyzstan,* UNCITRAL; *Marfin Investment Group Holdings SA, Alexandros Bakatselos and Others v Cyprus,* ICSID Case No ARB/13/27; *LSF-KEB Holdings SCA and Others v Korea,* ICSID Case No ARB/12/37; *State General Reserve Fund of the Sultanate of Oman v Bulgaria,* ICSID Case No ARB/15/43; *Valle Verde Sociedad Financiera SL v Venezuela,* ICSID Case No ARB/12/18.

[26] The Iran-US Claims Tribunal accepted in an early case that unreasonable interference with or taking of a bank account could constitute expropriation or other measures affecting property rights, *Harza Engineering Company v Iran,* Award No 19-89-2 (1982) 1 Iran-US CTR 499, para. IV, and has confirmed this position in several subsequent decisions, e.g., *Edgar Protiva and Eric Protiva v Iran,* Award No 566-316-2 (1995) 31 Iran-US CTR 89, para. 50. Whether 'a claim' for the purpose of jurisdiction in the Iran-US Claims Tribunal is quite the same thing as 'an investment' in a BIT case is a question that will not be pursued here.

[27] The Executive Director for Cyprus described the background to the adoption of bail-in measures in the following terms:

> The authorities' concern, even dissatisfaction, regarding the chosen type of the unconventional financing method of 'bailing-in' depositors and particularly the extent to which this took place, is no secret. However, a variety of reasons, some of which are explained in the staff paper, necessitated the use of this alternative. Furthermore, the delays in concluding an agreement

First, in factual terms, if an arbitral tribunal takes the view that the particular conduct reflects not merely the policy of Cyprus, but also the shared preference of the IMF, EC and ECB, it might be less inclined to view it as arbitrary, capricious, or unreasonable in a way that breaches, e.g., the standard of fair and equitable treatment or the requirements for lawful expropriation.

Second, in legal terms, there may be some uncertainty about the manner in which the legal order of the post-Lisbon Treaty EU, which now possesses competence over direct investments, fits together with pre-existing investment protection treaties between Member States[28] (Cyprus is a Member State of the EU, as are some of the States of nationality of direct investors, or of subsidiaries of non-EU—e.g., Russian—investors). The EC has tended to take a negative view about various aspects of the competence of investment treaty tribunals to rule on disputes raising matters of EU law and practice;[29] again, one imagines that a similar argument might be made in this case.

Third and finally, the question might arise in terms of admissibility: Cyprus might invoke precedents from the International Court of Justice and assert that it is impermissible to decide a case in the absence of necessary and proper third parties.[30] The question of the admissibility of

---

> between all parties involved, worsened the situation and magnified the size of the financing need that is now seeked out from the uninsured depositors, which the authorities accept some responsibility for. Even so, they would have hoped that the negotiations were dealt with a more sensitive and fair manner for the benefit of Cyprus, the euro area, the EU and for the programme in general

Statement by Mr Menno Snell, Executive Director for Cyprus [at IMF] and Mr Ektoras Kanaris, Adviser to the Executive Director (15 May 2013) <www.imf.org/external/pubs/ft/scr/2013/cr13125.pdf> 2, accessed 30 March 2015.

28 See Philip Strik, *Shaping the Single European Market in the Field of Foreign Direct Investment* (Hart 2014) Ch. 5.

29 *Achmea BV (formerly Eureko BV) v Slovakia,* UNCITRAL, PCA Case No 2008-13, Award on Jurisdiction, Arbitrability and Suspension (26 October 2010) paras 217–291; *Electrabel SA v Hungary,* ICSID Case No ARB/07/19, Decision on Jurisdiction, Applicable Law and Liability (30 November 2012) paras 4.111–4.199 and 5.31–5.60; European Commission, 'State aid SA.38517(2014/C) (ex 2014/NN)—Romania: Implementation of Arbitral award Micula v Romania of 11 December 2013' (1 October 2014) <http://ec.europa.eu/competition/state_aid/cases/254586/254586_1595781_31_11.pdf> accessed 30 March 2015.

30 *Monetary Gold Removed from Rome in 1943 (Italy v France, UK, and US)* (Preliminary Question) Judgment, ICJ Reports 1954, 19, 31-3. Contrast *Certain*

a claim before an international tribunal against a State regarding conduct that was required as a precondition for obtaining credit[31] in a memorandum of understanding with international organisations raises a number of complicated legal issues.[32] Still, the relevant authorities of international law may provide the best frame of reference for capturing possible uneasiness about this case, in which the scope and manner of application of bail-in tools by a particular State may be causally linked to the position of international organisations providing credit.[33] There can be no certainty as to how tribunals will react.

Phosphates Land in Nauru (Nauru v Australia) Preliminary Objections, Judgment, ICJ Reports 1992, 240 paras 50–57; *Philippines v China,* PCA Case No 2013-19, 29 October 2015 (Award on Jurisdiction and Admissibility) paras 179–188.

[31] Or was similar to a precondition.

[32] Some of the issues of possible relevance are: (1) the scope and content of the *Monetary Gold* doctrine; Martins Paparinskis, 'Procedural Aspects of Shared Responsibility in the International Court of Justice' (2013) 4 J Intl Disp Settlmt 295, 308–17, in particular (2) the applicability of *Monetary Gold* to international arbitration, *Larsen v Hawaiian Kingdom,* PCA, Award (5 February 2001) para. 11.17; and (3) the relevance of *Monetary Gold* for absent international organisations, *Application of the Interim Accord of 13 September 1995 (the former Yugoslav Republic of Macedonia v Greece)* Judgment, ICJ Reports 2011, 644 paras 42–44; and (4) ultimately, whether a case against Cyprus could be decided without attributing conduct to, identifying breach by, or establishing secondary responsibility of entities other than Cyprus. In *Ping An v Belgium* (n 25), the parties raised the issue of *Monetary Gold* in their written pleadings but it was not addressed by the tribunal, paras 127–128, 238.

[33] The Minister of Finance of Cyprus answered the question of the European Parliament's Committee on Economic and Monetary Affairs about his leeway in deciding upon the design of the necessary measures in the following terms:

> Negotiations regarding the MoU did not proceed in a timely and effective manner. ... the new government had only very limited time and scope to further negotiate aspects of the MOU. The most controversial aspect of the final negotiation was the application of the bail-in instrument on bank deposits. The Cyprus government was forced to accept this measure under duress.

See <www.europarl.europa.eu/document/activities/cont/201401/20140114ATT77319/20140114ATT77319EN.pdf> accessed 30 March 2015. The law of international responsibility provides for rules on responsibility of States and international organisations in connection with acts of other States, due to aid or assistance, direction and control, or coercion; see International Law Commission, 'Draft Articles on Responsibility of States for Internationally Wrongful Acts' YBILC (2001) Vol. II Part Two, arts 16–18; International Law Commission, 'Draft Articles on the Responsibility of International Organizations' YBILC

III. BAIL-INS AND EXPROPRIATION

If the hurdles of jurisdiction and admissibility can be overcome, the question also arises whether the relevant BIT's provisions on expropriation have been breached. This analysis may be divided into three parts: the international legal standards relating to expropriation; application of these standards to bail-ins; and the consequences.

A. Law of Expropriation

Investment protection treaties almost invariably contain rules on expropriation that, while differing at the level of small print, usually define expropriation (as both direct and indirect); formulate criteria of lawfulness of expropriation (legitimate public purpose, non-discrimination, compensation, and sometimes also due process); and spell out certain elements in more detail (the criteria for calculation of compensation, conditions of transfer of compensation, rights of review under due process, additional assurances of non-discriminatory treatment, etc.).[34]

Determination of whether direct expropriation has occurred should be fairly straightforward: the title to property is taken away from its private owner by a public act (and either vested in the State or another person).[35] Nationalisations of the last century were mostly clear-cut cases of direct expropriation, with the debate mainly focusing on compensation.[36] Indirect expropriation is more challenging to define.[37] One might draw a

---

(2011) art. 14-6; James Crawford, *State Responsibility: The General Part* (CUP 2013) Ch. 12.

[34] E.g., the 1991 Belgium and Luxembourg-Cyprus BIT (n 18) art. 4. More recent treaties tend to be more elaborate, e.g., Consolidated Comprehensive Economic and Trade Agreement Text (26 September 2014), art. X.11, Annex X.11 <http://trade.ec.europa.eu/doclib/docs/2014/september/tradoc_152806.pdf> accessed 30 March 2015.

[35] *Bernandus Henricus Funnekotter and Others v Zimbabwe,* ICSID Case No ARB/05/6, Award (22 April 2009) paras 96–97; *Venezuela Holdings, BV and Others v Venezuela,* ICSID Case No ARB/07/27, Award (9 October 2014) para. 288.

[36] Rudolf Dolzer, 'New Foundations of the Law of Expropriation of Alien Property' (1981) 75 AJIL 553; Mendelson (n 4); Oscar Schachter, 'Compensation Cases—Leading and Misleading' (1985) 79 AJIL 420.

[37] Martins Paparinskis, 'Regulatory Expropriation and Sustainable Development' in Marie-Claire Cordonnier-Segger, Markus W Gehring and Andrew Newcombe (eds), *Sustainable Development in International Investment Law* (Kluwer Law International 2010) 298, 300–19.

distinction between decisions that focus on the effect of measures on the investments, and those that take the public character of the measures as the starting-point; two awards dealing with alleged mistreatment of banks may illustrate the difference. According to the *Deutsche Bank v Sri Lanka* Tribunal:

> [M]any tribunals in other cases have tested governmental conduct in the context of indirect expropriation claims by reference to the effect of relevant acts [e.g. of major unilateral increases in royalties], rather than the intention behind them. In general terms, a substantial deprivation of rights, for at least a meaningful period of time, is required.[38]

Conversely, the *Saluka v Czech Republic* Tribunal suggested that:

> It is now established in international law that States are not liable to pay compensation to a foreign investor when, in the normal exercise of their regulatory powers, they adopt in a non-discriminatory manner bona fide regulations that are aimed at the general welfare.[39]

Each strand of the law of expropriation—direct and indirect—would thus formulate the definitional question in different terms. For direct expropriation, one would ask whether the title to the investment has been lost. For the *Deutsche Bank* version of indirect expropriation, one would ask whether, despite the title not being lost, the substantial and temporal effect on property has reached the level of direct expropriation. On the *Saluka* approach, one might ask whether the regulations, whatever their effect might be, have been non-discriminatory, aimed at public welfare, and adopted in a non-arbitrary manner in accordance with due process. Finally, an intermediate position might take into account all considerations by articulating an inquiry in terms of proportionality, considering the effect, purpose, and formal and procedural quality of the measures.

B. Applying the Law of Expropriation to Bail-Ins

The legal inquiry may be conducted in two steps: first, has expropriation taken place? Second, if it has, have the criteria of lawfulness been satisfied? There is considerable force in the argument for viewing bail-ins as direct expropriations. It is uncontroversial that taking shares in a company would be a direct expropriation. Why should one reach a different conclusion if it is title to deposits in a banking company that is

38 *Deutsche Bank v Sri Lanka* (n 25) para. 503.
39 *Saluka v Czech Republic* (n 25) para. 255.

lost, even if the former depositors get shares in return for their loss, a part of the deposits remains untaken, and furthermore, some of the deposits may be returned in due course (as the memoranda on Cyprus suggested regarding future bail-ins)?[40] The fact that shares are provided in place of deposits does not affect the initial proposition that deposits are, in fact, lost. One might reasonably be cautious about characterising *partial and indirect* taking or destruction of a business as an expropriation for the purposes of investment law;[41] but a direct expropriation of a clearly identifiable part of an investment, such as a part of a deposit, would probably still be treated as an expropriation.[42]

The application of bail-in tools may also be characterised as indirect expropriation, resulting from a regulatory process regarding bank restructuring and insolvencies. The *Deutsche Bank* standard would consider the permanence of bail-ins, and the degree to which they deprive depositors of their rights (in some cases, other measures depriving investors of their rights e.g., taxation or exchange controls, may be applied in parallel, making the argument for expropriation on the basis of effect even stronger).

The *Saluka* standard would ask questions of a different nature. The proposition that measures aimed at the recovery of banks, particularly in circumstances of severe financial crisis, are designed for the general welfare would seem fairly uncontroversial. But whether the measures were discriminatory would require an examination of particular factual circumstances: have the bail-ins been formulated and applied in a formally even-handed manner? If they have not, are the distinctions (e.g., exempting insured deposits, deposits below or above a certain amount, or deposits by particular types of depositors) justifiable by reference to legitimate purposes? In the case of Cyprus, the IMF acknowledged the concern, 'caution[ing] against exemptions from conversions into equity, which could lead to unequal treatment among uninsured depositors'.[43] Similarly, the possible provision of compensation for measures affecting pension funds may raise questions of the justifiability of distinctions

---

[40] IMF (29 April 2013) (n 9) 3 para. 10.

[41] *Venezuela Holdings and Others v Venezuela,* ICSID Case No ARB/07/27, Award (9 August 2014) paras 286–287.

[42] *GAMI Investments, Inc v Mexico,* UNCITRAL, Final Award (15 November 2004) para. 126.

[43] IMF, 'Cyprus: Request for Arrangement under the Extended Fund Facility' (May 2013) 20 <www.imf.org/external/pubs/ft/scr/2013/cr13125.pdf> accessed 30 March 2015.

between different types of depositors.[44] In any event, even if the bail-ins are non-discriminatory on their face, are they *de facto* discriminatory, disproportionately affecting a particular group of depositors (e.g., foreign depositors as a whole, or depositors from a particular State or a State that is not a member of a particular international organisation)? If the origin of capital in particular States and its allegedly dubious nature have been explicitly used in the policy discussion about the scope of bail-ins, this—it might be argued—demonstrates an underlying discriminatory *animus*.

Requirements of non-arbitrariness and due process would require an examination of the formal aspects of the bail-in tools: are they formulated in sufficiently clear and predictable terms and not introduced and applied in a sudden or arbitrary manner? For example, in Cyprus, recapitalisation measures applied by the BoC on 29 March 2013 used powers granted by a law that had been adopted only on 22 March (based on EU legislative proposals that themselves considered it too hasty to apply bail-ins before 2018). Have the necessary procedural guarantees (e.g., appropriate information and consultation) been complied with?

The intermediate method of determining whether there had been indirect expropriation would draw together all the considerations identified and ask whether an ultimate relationship of proportionality has been maintained between the very severe deprivation of rights, very important public interests, and the form and procedure through which the measures have been formulated and implemented. A possible criticism of this approach, however, is that it uses criteria for determining whether indirect expropriation has taken place similar to those applicable in deciding whether the expropriation has been *lawful*, as we are about to see.

C. Substantive Legal Consequences

If expropriation is held to have occurred, it may have been lawful or unlawful. As previously indicated, expropriation is not unlawful if it is carried out with due legal process, for a legitimate public purpose, and in a non-discriminatory manner, providing also that compensation is paid—as to which see further below. If these criteria are not met, then the taking is unlawful and the property has either to be returned or damages paid for its taking—which will also be discussed shortly.

---

[44] IMF (29 August 2013) (n 9) 3 para. 14.

Cyprus might try to rely on the defence of necessity, and argue that this meant that what would otherwise be illegal was not. Under general international law, necessity can preclude wrongfulness, even if not expressly provided for in the treaty. The defence is, however, intended to apply only in narrow circumstances when essential interests of States have to be safeguarded against grave and imminent peril.[45] The invocation of necessity in the disputes arising out of the Argentine crisis of the early 2000s has somewhat muddied the waters, because many of the awards take into account the Argentine Government's own contribution to the crises which befell it.[46] But more generally, one might point to arbitral or doctrinal authority for nearly every imaginable construction of necessity in investment treaties or the general international law of State responsibility. Still, in the absence of explicit treaty exception, necessity has never so far been recognised as precluding wrongfulness for breaches of investment obligations.[47] Arguably, though, the crisis in Cyprus may provide a stronger case for applying the doctrine. Cyprus was perceived as being not very far from a sovereign default, with grave implications for itself, the Euro, and the EU as a whole, and the particular solution was found to be the most appropriate (or perhaps even suggested) by the EU and IMF.

The Cyprus case is also somewhat unusual in another respect. If a going concern, for instance, is expropriated, there is a significant difference in *quantum* between the compensation payable for a lawful taking and the damages (which can include lost future profits) payable if

---

[45] 2001 ILC Articles (n 32) art. 25; Crawford (n 33) 305–15; cf. Robert D Sloane, 'On the Use and Abuse of Necessity in the Law of State Responsibility' (2012) 106 AJIL 447.

[46] Cf. *LG&E Energy Corporation and Others v Argentina,* ICSID Case No ARB/02/1, Decision on Liability (3 October 2006) paras 226–261; annulment decisions in *CMS Gas Transmission Company v Argentina,* ICSID Case No ARB/01/8, Decision of the *Ad Hoc* Committee on the Application for Annulment (25 September 2007) paras 119–136, 144–150; *Sempra Energy International v Argentina,* ICSID Case No ARB/02/16, Decision on Argentina's Application for Annulment of the Award (29 June 2010) paras 192–209; *Enron Corporation and Ponderosa Assets, LP v Argentina,* ICSID Case No ARB/01/3, Decision on the Application for Annulment of Argentina (30 July 2010) paras 355–405, and the Tribunals' awards in the same cases (*CMS, Sempra* and *Enron*).

[47] Attila Tanzi, 'Necessity, State of' (February 2013) Max Planck Encyclopaedia of Public International Law <http://opil.ouplaw.com> paras 8–11; Crawford (n 33) 313–4.

the taking was unlawful.[48] Where the investment is a money claim, however, the difference may be hard to detect. Compensation for an otherwise lawful taking will require the payment of the sum (or something close to it) plus interest; if on the other hand the conduct is unlawful, repayment of the sum in question comprises the restitutionary element, while interest is the normal way of compensating for the loss of opportunity to utilise the money in question.[49] Where the financial difference is marginal, respondent States may not be unduly troubled by the characterisation of their measures, and so might not rely (or rely not too heavily) on necessity to demonstrate the lawfulness of their conduct. But a plea of necessity could make considerable sense in some serious crises, providing States with breathing space until the extraordinary circumstances are over and when the obligation will be reactivated (further questions could arise as to when that would be the case here: is it when Cyprus no longer requires emergency credit; when it has repaid the credit; or when it has recovered from the crisis?). Article 27(b) of the 2001 ILC Articles on State responsibility addresses the issue of compensation and circumstances precluding wrongfulness, but does not provide a clear solution for this case. In the words of the annulment committee in *CMS v Argentina*,

> Article 27 itself is a 'without prejudice' clause, not a stipulation. It refers to 'the questions of compensation' and does not attempt to specify in which circumstances compensation could be due, notwithstanding the state of necessity.[50]

Finally, to return to issues of *quantum*, further delicate questions could arise. The *quantum* of compensation for a lawful taking is normally

---

[48] *Factory at Chorzów (Germany v Poland)* (Merits) [1928] PCIJ Series A no 17 47; *Funnekotter v Zimbabwe* (n 35) paras 108–111; *Yukos Universal Ltd (Isle of Man)*, PCA Case No AA 227, Final Award (18 July 2014) paras 1585–1591, 1763–1769.

[49] See generally Irmgard Marboe, *Calculation of Compensation and Damages in International Investment Law* (OUP 2009) Ch. 5; Borzu Sabahi, *Compensation and Restitution in Investor-State Arbitration* (OUP 2011) Chs 5–8.

[50] *CMS Gas Transmission Company v Argentina*, ICSID Case No ARB/01/8, Decision on the Application for Annulment (25 September 2007) para. 147. Legal writings have addressed the question as part of the broader debate about the coherence of the concept of circumstances precluding wrongfulness. Solutions suggested are somewhat varied, cf. Sandra Szurek, 'The Notion of Circumstanced Precluding Wrongfulness' in James Crawford, Alain Pellet and Simon Olleson (eds), *The Law of International Responsibility* (OUP 2010) 427, 435–7; Crawford (n 33) 318–20.

calculated on the basis of the value of the asset before the expropriation occurred or the intention to expropriate became known. One argument in the present case might be that deposits with an insolvent bank are worthless: it would be odd to require compensation for full nominal value if uninsured depositors would be unlikely to get anything at all in the event of insolvency, and the bail-in might both save the bank and give at least some possibility of a return for shareholders and bondholders. Another view might be that deposits are better analogised to contracts, where the benchmark for compensation might be the sum agreed as a matter of contractual obligation, rather than the fair market value of a contractual right at a particular point.[51] Unlike shares, where the correlation between the market value and shares is an underlying assumption, depositors do not expect the right to repayment of their deposit to be affected by such changes (at least to the extent that they are not included as part of the contract itself, e.g., calculation of interest by reference to changes in the lending rates).

IV. OTHER SUBSTANTIVE INVESTMENT RULES

Investors will naturally plead as many different breaches as they can. Often a finding of expropriation will yield a higher level of compensation or damages than a claim for breach of, e.g., the fair and equitable treatment standard, so there is an additional incentive for investors to concentrate on expropriation. Still, in many cases investors will find it easier to prove that the State has acted in a discriminatory or unfair manner than that expropriation has occurred (e.g., in the *Saluka* case cited above), and substantial damages have also been awarded in disputes where no expropriation has been found.

Some of the considerations sketched in the previous sections dealing with expropriation will also be relevant for other substantive investment protection rules. For discrimination, the question is whether the State has treated investors (or some of them) in an unjustifiably less favourable manner than others. In the absence of *de jure* discrimination, has indirect discrimination taken place, affecting e.g., foreign investors in general, or

---

[51] Abby Cohen Smutny, 'Some Observations on the Principles Relating to Compensation in the Investment Treaty Context' (2007) 22 ICSID Rev—FILJ 1, 19–21. This is, of course, not to deny the variety of approaches to contractual breaches, which may also lend support to other analogies, see Herfried Wöss and others, *Damages in International Arbitration Under Complex Long-term Contracts* (OUP 2014).

foreign investors from certain States in particular, in a disproportionate manner?[52] Consideration of other elements of the fair and equitable treatment standard focus on the formal and procedural characteristics of the measures: e.g., whether the rules regarding bail-ins have been sufficiently transparent and predictable; their consistency with due process, and whether reasonable expectations have been complied with.[53] The complexity and fluidity of the factual circumstances surrounding the crisis in Cyprus make it quite challenging to provide clear answers, with both the fine print and the broader themes—sudden and apparently unexpected introduction and application of the regime, severity of the crisis, and support by the IMF and the EU of the policies—pulling in different directions.

V. CONCLUSION

Bail-ins may be an effective and neat way of recapitalising important financial institutions without spending a penny of taxpayers' money, but their lawfulness from the perspective of investment law is—as we have seen—a highly complex question. This chapter has outlined some relevant considerations of a procedural and substantive character that a tribunal might need to take into account in deciding a claim that a bail-in constitutes a breach of the applicable investment treaty. No clear answer has been provided here to all of the questions: there are legal issues on which reasonable people may disagree (e.g., the definition of investments and of indirect expropriation); specific treaty provisions vary; factual circumstances are complex and may raise different issues in different situations in Cyprus the situation is still evolving; and finally, different forensic strategies might formulate the issue in different terms. Still, investment protection law certainly has to be accepted and accounted for as an important element in the complex web of legal rules and procedures framing the responses by States to financial crises (both the present one in Cyprus and those that will be covered by EU and US rules in the future), and will form an important part of the background to any resolution.

---

[52] Nicolas F Diebold, 'Standards of Non-Discrimination in International Economic Law' (2011) 60 ICLQ 831.

[53] Martins Paparinskis, *The International Minimum Standard and Fair and Equitable Treatment* (OUP 2013) Ch. 9.

9. Bank rescue measures under international investment law: What role for the principle of causation?

Anna De Luca

> We have ... used an exceptional set of non-standard policy tools. These tools, combined with the bold action taken by the euro area governments over recent months, have played an essential role in preventing a collapse of the financial system and in bolstering confidence.
> (Jean-Claude Trichet, Former President of the European Central Bank)[1]

> States have always resorted to extraordinary measures to save themselves from imminent dangers and the injuries to foreigners resulting from these measures do not generally afford a basis for claims ... The foreigners, residing in a country which, by reasons of natural, social or international calamities is obliged to adopt those measures, must suffer the natural detriment to his affairs, without any remedy, since Governments, as expressed by a distinguished jurist, are not insurers against every event.
> (*Dickson Car Wheel Company (USA) v United Mexican States,* July 1931)[2]

I. INTRODUCTION

National banking systems of advanced economies were heavily impacted by the global financial crisis of 2008–13.[3] As has been observed, 'the last

[1] Jean-Claude Trichet, Former President of the European Central Bank (ECB), ceremony conferring the honorary title of Doctor Honoris Causa at the University of National and World Economy, Sofia, 12 June 2009 quoted in Stéphanie Marie Stolz and Michael Wedow, 'Extraordinary Measures in Extraordinary Times – Public Measures in Support of the Financial Sector in the EU and the United States' European Central Bank Occasional Paper Series No 117/July 2010, 7 <www.ecb.europa.eu/pub/pdf/scpops/ecbocp117.pdf> accessed 8 April 2015.

[2] RIAA, Volume IV, 669–91, 681–2.

[3] The author wishes to thank Michael Waibel and all the colleagues who took part in the 2013 Programme ('The Legal Implications of Global Financial

global financial crisis has given rise to the largest wave of banking crises seen since the Great Depression'.[4] The last financial crisis endangered the existence and financial stability of not only banks with risky credit strategies but of the entire banking system and thus the real economy. States had little choice but to react promptly to pass legislation in support of their banking systems in an attempt to maintain financial stability.

An overview of the State measures enacted in order to confront the short- and long-term effects of the systemic banking crisis experienced by many advanced economies in recent years[5] shows that States adopted exceptional measures supporting individual banks and financial institutions as well as the financial and banking systems at large. The list of such exceptional measures includes measures aimed at avoiding the failure of individual institutions of systemic importance[6] (such as selected liquidity assistance by Central Banks, ad-hoc recapitalisation, non-recourse

---

Crises') of the Centre for Studies and Research of The Hague Academy of International Law, for their helpful comments and suggestions during the preparation of this work. Furthermore, the author is grateful to the Hague Academy of International Law for the support during the research period spent at Centre for Studies and Research in The Hague.

[4] Luc Laeven and Fabian Valencia, 'Systemic Banking Crises Database: An Update', (2012) IMF Working Paper) 6 <www.imf.org/external/pubs/ft/wp/2012/wp12163.pdf> accessed 20 February 2015.

[5] See the list of advanced economies encountering systemic banking crises and borderline banking crises in Laeven and Valencia, ibid.

[6] For a definition of systemically important financial institutions (SIFIs) See Financial Stability Board, 'Policy Measures to Address Systemically Important Financial Institutions' (4 November 2011) para. 3, which defines SIFIs as 'financial institutions whose distress or disorderly failure, because of their size, complexity and systemic interconnectedness, would cause significant disruption to the wider financial system and economic activity.' See <www.financialstabilityboard.org/wp-content/uploads/r_111104bb.pdf?page_moved=1> accessed 8 April 2015. See also Rosa Maria Lastra, 'Systemic Risk, SIFIs and Financial Stability (2011) 6(2) Capital Markets L J 197. For a definition of systemic risk see also European Central Bank (ECB), 'Financial Stability Review' (June 2010) 138, going on to observe that '[t]he literature has identified three "forms" of systemic risk, namely contagion risk, the risk that widespread imbalances that have built up over time unravel abruptly, and the risk of macro shocks causing simultaneous failures'. See <www.ecb.europa.eu/pub/fsr/html/index.en.html> accessed 8 April 2015 See also ECB, 'Financial Stability Review' (December 2009) 134–5 <www.ecb.europa.eu/pub/fsr/html/index.en.html> accessed 15 April 2015 and International Monetary Fund, Bank for International Settlements and Financial Stability Board 'Guidance to Assess the Systemic Importance of Financial Institutions, Markets and Instruments: Initial Considerations' (October 2009) 2, which defines systemic risk as 'a risk of disruption to financial services that is

loans, government guarantee on bank bonds, asset relief, and bail-in of banks' capital investors and depositors) and general measures of systemic character (such as deposit insurance, guarantee schemes, and national financial support schemes for financial institutions).[7]

The exceptional measures to support both individual institutions and the entire system, which were adopted by States under the urgent need to restore financial stability (even resorting to disused legal tools such as nationalisations or emergency legislation),[8] impacted on various stakeholders: shareholders, bondholders and depositors. The present chapter proceeds from the assumption that all these actors and, generally speaking, secured and unsecured creditors, are protected investors under Bilateral Investment Treaties (BITs):[9] BITs (at least the BITs of Member

---

(i) caused by an impairment of all or parts of the financial system and (ii) has the potential to have serious negative consequences for the real economy'. <www.imf.org/external/np/g20/pdf/100109a.pdf> accessed 8 April 2015. According to the Report, there are three key criteria for identifying the systemic importance of markets and institutions; these are '*size* (the volume of financial services provided by the individual component of the financial system); *substitutability* (the extent to which other components of the system can provide the same services in the event of a failure); and *interconnectedness* (linkages with other components of the system)'. The Report notes that as far as concerns financial institutions:

> [T]he size of exposures, volumes of transactions or assets managed are indicative of the extent to which clients and counterparties could be disrupted. Clusters of institutions can be individually small but collectively significant because they fall into distress at the same time. Some institutions, for example those providing key services such as clearing and settlement, lack immediate substitutes for this role. Interconnectedness captures situations when distress in one institution raises the likelihood of distress in others.

[7] For an overview of the measures supporting the banking systems in the US and EU see Stolz and Wedow (n 1); EU Commission, 'Communication from the Commission – The Application of State Aid Rules to Measures Taken in Relation to Financial Institutions in the Context of the Current Global Financial Crisis [2008] OJ C270/8.

[8] For instance, the nationalisation of Northern Rock by the UK government in 2008; the nationalisation of SNS BANK and SNS REAAL, by the Netherlands on 1 February 2013; Iceland's Act on Authorization for the Treasury Disbursements due to Unusual Financial Market Circumstances (No 125/2008); Cyprus's Resolution of Credit and Other Institutions Law (L 17(I)/2013).

[9] For more on these issues see the contributions by Maurice Mendelson and Martins Paparinskis, 'Bail-Ins and International Investment Law: In and Beyond Cyprus' (in this volume) 193 and Phoebus Athanassiou, 'BITs and Pieces: Reflections on the Relevance of BITs in Resolution-Related Litigation' (in this volume) 240.

States) cover 'any kind of asset' having an economic value, and list as protected investments a wide range of tangible and intangible assets. Among these are 'shares in and stocks and debentures of a company and any other form of participation in a company', and 'claim to money or to any performance under contract having a financial value'.[10] These broad definitions of 'investment', overcoming the uncertainties as to the international protection of foreign creditors under customary law,[11] cover claims of both secured and unsecured foreign creditors of host states' companies.[12]

---

[10] See, for example, the UK Model BIT of 2005, art. 1(1) protecting as investment 'every kind of asset', and in particular listing as protected investments 'any property rights such as mortgages, liens and pledges', 'shares in and stocks and debentures of a company and any other form of participation in a company', and 'claim to money or to any performance under contract having a financial value'; and the Italian Model BIT of 2003, art. 1(1), protecting as investment 'any kind of asset invested' and in particular:

> a) movable and immovable property and any ownership rights in rem, including real guarantee rights on a property of a third party, to the extent that it can be invested; b) shares, debentures, equity holdings and any other instruments of credit, as well as Government and public securities in general; c) credits for sums of money connected with an investment as well as reinvested incomes and capital gains or any service right having an economic value as integral part of an investment.

See also the German Model BIT of 2008, art. 1(1); France Model BIT of 2006, art. 1(1). All instruments at <http://investmentpolicyhub.unctad.org/IIA> accessed 8 April 2015.

[11] David J Bederman, 'Creditors' Claims in International Law' (2000) 34 *The International Lawyer* 235, 235–41, observing that the status of creditors' claims under customary international law has been 'one of the most vexing issues in the international law of state responsibility', and their eligibility to international protection disputed particularly with regard to unsecured creditors, if one looks at the pre-World War I and inter-war practices. See also Lucius C Caflisch, 'Indirect Injuries to Foreign Creditors in International Law' (1967) Revue belge de droit international 404.

[12] See Bederman ibid., 246-–8. The case *Poštová banka, AS and ISTRO-KAPITAL SE v Hellenic Republic*, ICSID Case No ARB/13/8, Award (9 April 2015) para. 335 also supports the position of a BIT's asset-based definition of investment, which includes 'shares in and stocks and debentures of a company and any other form of participation in a company, covers bonds, and debt instruments issued by a local company'. Conversely, the Tribunal excluded sovereign bonds from the BIT protection (paras 331–335), thus reopening the issue, which will not be discussed here, of whether sovereign/governmental bonds are protected under the ICSID Convention and BITs. As is well known,

If seen in this light, shareholders, creditors, and depositors of a rescued bank could challenge the various exceptional State measures taken in response to the global financial crisis. More specifically, they could claim to have been subject to a direct or indirect expropriation, to a prohibited discrimination, and to a denial of fair and equitable treatment and full security and protection in an investment treaty arbitration against the State that enacted the rescue package. In fact, such claims have been brought[13] in response to bank rescue measures adopted by the Republic of Cyprus from June 2012 onwards, and the 2013 bail-in of the distressed banks' capital investors and depositors.[14]

This brief introductory survey highlights the relevance of investment law as a potential limit to State measures designed to secure financial stability. It also points to some of the peculiar features of disputes

---

the issue was consistently answered in the positive by previous tribunals (albeit not unanimously).

[13] See *Marfin Investment Group Holdings SA, Alexandros Bakatselos and others v Republic of Cyprus*, ICSID Case No ARB/13/27, Notice of Dispute (23 January 2013); *Cyprus Popular Bank Public Co Ltd v Hellenic Republic*, ICSID Case No ARB/14/16, Notice of Arbitration (16 July 2014); *Theodoros Adamakopoulos and others v Republic of Cyprus*, ICSID Case No ARB/15/49. Some information on the last case is available at <www.ajot.com/news/greek-investors-bring-legal-action-against-republic-of-cyprus> accessed 10 April 2016. See also Ping An Life Insurance Company of China and Other v Belgium, ICSID Case No ARB/12/29, Award (30 April 2015), where the investors' claims relating to the Belgian government's financial rescue of Fortis were, however, dismissed by the Tribunal for lack of jurisdiction ratione temporis.

For a fuller discussion of the legal issues raised by bail-ins see Maurice Mendelson and Martins Paparinskis, 'Bail-Ins and International Investment Law: In and Beyond Cyprus' (in this volume) 193, as well as Maurice Mendelson and Martins Paparinskis, 'Bail-Ins and the International Investment Law of Expropriation: In and Beyond Cyprus' (September 2013) Butterworths J Intl Banking and Financial L 475.

[14] The country, experiencing both a systemic banking crisis and a sovereign debt crisis between 2012–13, introduced a new law in March 2013, The Resolution of Credit and Other Institutions Law (English draft text at <www.centralbank.gov.cy/media/pdf/17_I_2013_EN_Resolution.pdf> accessed 10 April 2016). The government then proceeded to restructure the two largest banks of the island, Laiki Bank and the Bank of Cyprus, which were already subjected to various intervention measures by the Central Bank of Cyprus as of 2012, through a depositor bail-in. For comment see Jan Jack and Tom Cassels, 'Cyprus: An Analysis of the Impact of the Resolution Methodology on Stakeholders' Claims Including the Emergency Liquidity Assistance' (2013) 8 Capital Markets L J 450; and Alexander Apostolides, 'Beware of German Gifts Near Elections: How Cyprus Got Here and Why it is Currently More Out Than in the Eurozone' (2013) 8 Capital Markets L J 300.

brought in response to bank rescue measures. Contrary to what occurs in a typical investment case, in proceedings brought against rescue measures it is by no means certain whether the claimants actually suffered losses: the rescue measures were after all taken to save banks and financial institutions that already were technically insolvent (or very close thereto), if not failed. This, in turn, raises the preliminary issue of whether the investment of a claimant investor in the affected bank had any value at all regardless of the rescue measures.[15] What is more, losses that have been sustained may be the result, not of State conduct, but of the bank's exposure to strongly distressed segments of the financial market and sovereign debts, or other external factors. Put differently, investment cases concerning bank rescue measures require tribunals and commentators to ascertain the role of economic losses within international investment disputes, and to specify the required causal link between such economic losses and the challenged State measures.

Seeking to shed light on the peculiar features of cases concerning bank rescue measures, the present chapter begins by addressing the threshold

[15] Damages claims, brought by investors before domestic courts in response to governmental rescue measures have raised the very same issue, as the American case on the US government's financial rescue and takeover of AIG shows: see *Starr International Company v The United States*, No 11-779C (United States Court of Federal Claims, 15 June 2015) <https://ecf.cofc.uscourts.gov/cgi-bin/show_public_doc?2011cv0779-443-0> accessed 9 April 2016 where the American court, on the one hand, found that the government's taking of the controlling equity stake in AIG as a part of its bailout was beyond the boundaries of its legal authority under the applicable domestic law; on the other, having looked to the property owner's loss (not the government's gain), as the 'just compensation analysis' under the Fifth Amendment provides for, the Court found that the claimants were not entitled to recovery any damages (65–6). The 'inescapable conclusion' was drawn by the court that, had the government not intervened, 'AIG would have filed for bankruptcy, most likely during the week of September 15–19, 2008. In that event, the value of the shareholders common stock would have been zero'. In fact, '[b]y loaning AIG $85 billion under the September 22, 2008 Credit Agreement, the government significantly enhanced the value of the AIG shareholders' stock. While the taking of 79.9 per cent equity ownership and the running of AIG's business were not permitted under the Federal Reserve Act, the government did not cause any economic loss to AIG's shareholders, because as Mr Studzinski said, '[20] percent of something [is] better than [100] percent of nothing'. (66). On the basis of the above, the court concluded that: 'the Credit Agreement Shareholder Class shall prevail on liability due to the Government's illegal exaction, but shall recover zero damages, and that the Reverse Stock Split Shareholder Class shall not prevail on liability or damages' (67).

issue of economic loss: it does so by asking whether economic loss is a necessary element of a BIT breach (section II). Having concluded in the affirmative, the analysis turns to questions of causation proper, which is first addressed in general terms (section III), and then with a particular focus on intervening causes potentially breaking the causal link between State conduct and economic loss (section IV). The final section concludes and highlights the possible relevance of newly emerging prudential standards on bank resolution and recovery for investment disputes (section V).

II. ECONOMIC LOSSES AND PECUNIARY DAMAGES

The preceding discussion has presumed that, in order for an investment tribunal to find that a BIT has been breached, the protected investor must have suffered an economic loss. This presumption clearly accords with the traditional understanding of the law of claims. For example, during the International Law Commission's (ILC's) pre-1963 work on State responsibility (then still focused on the 'customary law rules on (foreign) investor protection'[16]), Special Rapporteur Garcia Amador noted that '[t]he injury in question here is invariably pecuniary, originating in the non-performance on the part of the State of residence of an obligation towards a particular alien'.[17] More generally, at no stage during the ILC's work on State responsibility for injury to aliens was it disputed that an act or omission of a State would have to entail pecuniary injury to the property or other economic interests of the alien in order to amount to a violation of international law.[18] More specifically, in classifying the relevant categories of injuries for international law purposes, the Special Rapporteur distinguished between 'injuries caused to the State' and those 'caused to private persons (aliens)'. In respect of the latter category, he

[16] Such a definition in respect of the pre-1963 work of the International Law Commission on State Responsibility is borrowed from James Crawford and Tom Grant, 'Responsibility of States for Injuries to Foreigners' in John P Grant and J Craig Barker (eds), *The Harvard Research in International Law: Contemporary Analysis and Appraisal* (William S Hein 2007) 77, 105–6.

[17] See F V Garcia-Amador, 'Second Report' YILC (1957) Vol. II, 117, para. 1 (Garcia Amador II) with reference to the international protection of economic interests and rights of foreigners; F V Garcia-Amador, 'Third Report' YILC (1958) Vol. II, 69, para. 10 (Garcia Amador III); F V Garcia-Amador, 'Sixth Report', YILC (1961) Vol. II, 29, para. 113 (Garcia Amador VI).

[18] Some criticisms were addressed to Garcia-Amador's Draft Articles on State Responsibility of 1961 because of their pro-investor bias. See Crawford and Grant (n 16) 95–6.

added that a further distinction between injuries to the person and injuries to the property had to be drawn.[19] While the discussion centred on the methods of quantifying reparation,[20] the ILC at the time simply took for granted that an injury to the property (and other economic interests) of aliens presupposed an economic loss or damage.

The same, traditional, approach persists under BITs: economic loss to the claimant investor in respect to her investments is an implicit (if not explicit[21]) requirement of any claim under a BIT,[22] alongside the causal relationship between the pecuniary injury and the impugned State conduct.[23] To use the words of the NAFTA Tribunal in the *Merrill case*, since the damages and the investment treaty breach (namely, the fair and equitable treatment standard of Article 1105(1) NAFTA) are inextricably

---

[19] Garcia-Amador VI (n 17) paras 29 and 146–65.

[20] Ibid., 29, para. 113, where the Special Rapporteur observes that 'international law provides no precise methods of measurement for the award of pecuniary damages', quoting Clyde Eagleton, *The Responsibility of States in International Law* (New York UP 1928) and Abraham H Feller, *The Mexican Claims Commissions 1923–1934* (MacMillan 1935).

[21] See, for example, art. 24.1 of the US model BIT of 2012, and art. X.17 of the CETA between Canada and the EU, explicitly requiring the existence and proof of losses and damages arising from treaty breaches for investors to make their claims under the treaty.

[22] For instance, see *Achmea BV v The Slovak Republic*, UNCITRAL, PCA Case No 2008-13 (formerly *Eureko BV v The Slovak Republic*), Final Award (7 December 2012) para. 320, where the Tribunal implicitly considers financial losses and the causal link between such losses and the State measures challenged as relevant in respect of both liability and causation, and the determination of compensation payable; *SD Myers, Inc v Government of Canada*, NAFTA/UNCITRAL, Partial Award (13 November 2000) para. 315, referring to the general principle of international law according to which 'compensation should undo the material harm inflicted by a breach of an international law', and mentioning, as also applicable, the following principles, advanced by Canada:

> [T]he burden is on SDMI to prove the quantum of the losses in respect of which it puts forward its claims; compensation is payable only in respect of harm that is proved to have a sufficient causal link with the specific NAFTA provision that has been breached; the economic losses claimed by SDMI must be proved to be those that have arisen from a breach of the NAFTA, and not from other causes; damages for breach of any one NAFTA provision can take into account any damages already awarded under a breach of another NAFTA provision; there must be no 'double recovery'.

[23] The economic loss of the claimant investor might be regarded as either a condition of admissibility of the investor's claim or a condition for the jurisdiction of the Tribunal, depending on the drafting of the specific BIT at stake, and/or the arbitration rules selected.

related, and liability is 'inextricably associated with the occurrence of damages',[24] 'an international wrongful act will only be committed in international investment law if there is an act in breach of an international legal obligation, attributable to the Respondent that also results in damages'.[25] Therefore in the absence of an economic loss sustained by the foreign investor, there simply is no breach of the BIT. For instance, it is difficult to envisage how an asset having no economic value can be, reasonably, the object of an indirect expropriation, given that for a tribunal to find an indirect expropriation under international law an effective deprivation of the investment implying an almost total loss in value is required.[26]

Importantly, the ILC's more recent work on State responsibility does not affect this approach. Admittedly, in formulating general concepts of State responsibility, the ILC moved away from the traditional understanding that linked damage and wrongfulness.[27] However, in line with the

---

[24] *Merrill & Ring Forestry LP v The Government of Canada*, NAFTA/UNCITRAL, ICSID Administered Case, Award (31 March 2010) paras 244 (where the citation is located) and 245.

[25] Ibid., para. 266.

[26] On the concept of indirect expropriation under international law see Anna De Luca, 'Indirect Expropriations and Regulatory Takings: What Role for the "Legitimate Expectations" of Foreign Investors?' in Giorgio Sacerdoti and others (eds), *General Interests of Host States in International Investment Law* (CUP 2014) 58, 59–60, and references therein. The contrary position was taken by the Tribunal in *Biwater Gauff (Tanzania) Ltd v United Republic of Tanzania*, ICSID Case No ARB/05/22, Award (24 July 2008) paras 466 and 804. According to the Tribunal an indirect expropriation might be found (and was found in the case) without economic damages being suffered by the investor. In the view of the Tribunal, economic damage is not a necessary requirement of a claim of being victim of an indirect expropriation (paras 463–464). To support this position the Tribunal relied exclusively on an inapposite passage of the Commentary to art. 2 of the ILC's Draft Articles on State Responsibility. The passage restates that, on the one hand, whether a damage is required depends on the content of the primary obligation, and, on the other hand, refers to the case of a treaty obligation to enact a uniform law as an illustrative example of a primary obligation which clearly does not provide damage as a necessary requirement.

[27] See ILC, 'Draft Articles on Responsibility of States for Internationally Wrongful Acts' (ILC Draft Articles) YBILC (2001) Vol. II, Part Two, notably art. 2, pursuant to which wrongfulness depends on two general conditions, the breach of an obligation and attribution. The ILC's approach has met with some criticism. See, for instance, Gilbert Guillaume, 'Overview of Part One of the Articles on State Responsibility', in James Crawford, Alain Pellet and Simon Olleson (eds), *The Law of International Responsibility* (OUP 2010) 187, 191, arguing that, although the original project of ILC Articles de-linked damage and

focus of the ILC's work after 1963 (which sought 'to codify the rules governing the responsibility of States for internationally wrongful acts *in general*, and not only in regard to certain particular sectors such as responsibility for acts causing injury to the person or property of aliens'[28]), that position was adopted in an attempt to formulate general conditions of wrongfulness that had to be present in all instances. Conversely, while not required in all instances, damage or economic loss could still be required by particular rules of international law. As noted by the ILC in its Commentaries to the Articles, whether damage to a protected interest is a necessary element of a breach of international law 'is a matter which is determined by the relevant primary rule'.[29] In this

---

wrongfulness with the view to sanctioning international crimes of States and of legitimating counter-measures, the ILC:

> was not able to achieve these aims, and indeed one may well question the continued relevance of the audacious intellectual construction initiated by Ago … it is necessary to retain the more secure conceptions of the International Court which has for its part never ceased to distinguish carefully between: – unlawful conduct which every State with a legal interest may call on a judge to determine as such; – responsibility itself, which is only engaged in the event of moral or material damage caused to a State injured in its rights.

[28] See ILC, Report of the Commission to the General Assembly, Doc A/9010/REV.1, Report of the Commission International Law Commission on the work of its twenty-fifth Session, 7 May–13 July 1973, State Responsibility, YILC (1973) Vol. II 165, para. 42, where the ILC also goes on to state: 'The draft Articles accordingly deal with the *general rules* of the international responsibility of the State for internationally wrongful acts …' [Emphasis in the original]. See also ILC Draft Articles (n 27) 31, paras 1–2.

[29] See ILC Draft Articles (n 27), Commentaries to art. 2, 36, para. 9, and art. 31, 92, para. 6. In any case, one should avoid, in principle, understanding the dichotomy primary rules-secondary rules in the ILC Articles as a rigid distinction; otherwise the distinction would appear to be rather artificial. See, for instance, Rosalyn Higgins, 'Overview of Part Two of the Articles on State Responsibility', in Crawford and others (n 27) 537, 539:

> [t]he Commission has at all times eschewed embarking upon the substantive content of obligations, the breach of which could cause responsibility. But the reality is that some consequences of breach have developed into vast bodies of substantive law, generating their own norms. If a State takes the property of a foreigner unlawfully, compensation is due …

and ibid., 540:

> Inter-State disagreements about the compensation methods employed in the event … constitute disagreements on substantive law. The expropriating State whose compensation is being challenged may be violating a secondary rule, but the fall-out may not so different from a violation of a primary rule.

respect, it is worth noting that the ILC itself acknowledged that, within particular areas, international law continued to require 'damage' (or 'economic injury'), and that among those areas, it specifically mentioned the international rules on the protection of foreigners' property rights and economic interests.[30]

The general picture emerging from this analysis is that, under contemporary international law, the establishment of economic losses remains necessary if the primary rules in question seek to protect assets having an economic value. This is the case for the provisions of a BIT.[31] As a consequence, as a threshold issue, claimants in investment treaty arbitrations will be required to establish that they have suffered economic loss. Beyond this threshold issue, as noted above, they will also need to show that the loss in question has been sustained as a result of the impugned State measure. This second aspect – the question of causation – is the focus of the subsequent considerations.

III. THE INTERNATIONAL RULES GOVERNING CAUSATION

For the purpose of State liability for damages arising from wrongful acts causing injury to aliens, it is well established that there must be three elements: a) there must be a State act; that is b) unlawful under international law; and c) it must be shown that the act caused the damages claimed.[32] The third of these elements, causation describes the

---

[30] ILC Draft Articles (n 27), Commentaries to art. 3, para. 12, and n 94. By contrast, the Commission referred to human rights obligations, State obligations under international labour conventions, and treaty obligations to enact a uniform law to support its view that the element of 'damage' is not among 'the constituent elements without which there can in no case be an internationally wrongful act': ibid.

[31] See, inter alia, *Rompetrol Group NV v Romania*, ICSID Case No ARB/06/3, Award (6 May 2013) paras 189–190 where the Tribunal states (not without some ambiguities) that it 'is in no doubt that those provisions [the fair and equitable treatment standard, and the guarantees of non-impairment, and physical protection and security] have principally in mind "disputes" over breaches which occasion actual (and therefore assessable) loss or damage to the investor', although the issue was immaterial in the case at stake because the claimants' claim was framed 'in terms of monetary damages'.

[32] Art. 1(1) of the 1961 Harvard Draft Convention on the International Responsibility of States for Injuries to Aliens: 'A State is internationally responsible for an act or omission which, under international law, is wrongful, is

required link between conduct and injury.[33] As has been observed, '[i]n determining liability for a loss international law requires simply that there be a causal connection between an unlawful act and such loss, and once such nexus is established, compensates all proximately caused loss …'.[34]

The question of causation involves both factual and legal considerations. The two lines of inquiry can be distinguished in the abstract;[35] however in practice, whether a cause is factually relevant can only be determined in light of the nature, scope, and purpose of the obligation at stake.[36] Causation further interacts with rules of evidence, including the burden of proof, and its allocation among the disputing parties, informed by the generally accepted principle '*alleganti probatio incumbit*'. As a result, factual causation and legal causation are so closely intermingled in practice that they are hardly ever clear-cut.[37]

---

attributable to that State, and causes an injury to an alien.' A causal link between the wrongful act and the injury is also required by art. 31 ILC Draft Articles (n 27): 'The responsible State is under an obligation to make full reparation for the injury caused by the internationally wrongful act. Injury includes any damage, whether material or moral, caused by the internationally wrongful act of a State.' In legal literature see Michael Straus, 'Causation as an Element of State Responsibility' (1984) 16 L & Pol in Intl Business 893.

33 See Andrea Gattini, 'Breach of the Obligation to Prevent and Reparation Thereof in the ICJ's Genocide Judgment' (2007) 18 EJIL 695, 708, who mentions the two common standards used to operationalise causation, viz the standards of proximity and '*conditio sine qua non*'.

34 Richard B Lillich and Charles N Brower, 'Opinion Regarding the Jurisdiction and Powers of the United Nations Compensation Commission February 10, 1992' (1997–1998) 38 Va JIL 25, 35 (where the quote is located) and 40–41.

35 See Ilias Plakokefalos, 'Causation in the Law of Responsibility and the Problem of Overdetermination: In Search of Clarity', (2015) 26 EJIL 471, 486–9, and 492 calling for the application by international tribunals of a two-step causal inquiry: a causal analysis at a factual level, and a normative analysis on the scope of responsibility.

36 ILC Draft Articles (n 37) Commentary to art. 31, para. 10:

> [t]he allocation of injury or loss to a wrongful act is, in principle, a legal and not only a historical or causal process … the requirement of a causal link is not necessarily the same in relation to every breach of an international obligation. In international as in national law, the question of remoteness of damage is not a part of the law which can be satisfactorily solved by search for a single verbal formula.

37 For instance, the *Lauder* Tribunal and the *CME* Tribunal although judging on the basis of the same set of facts and similar provisions, took diverging decisions. See *Ronald S Lauder v Czech Republic*, UNCITRAL, Final Award

In operationalising the rules of causation, the test of proximity (or the analogous test of '*conditio sine qua non*') is of crucial relevance. While terminology is not uniform, there is broad agreement that the claimed damage and loss must be the *proximate* result of an act of the Respondent. To use the words of the United States-Germany Mixed Claims Commission,

> [a]ll indirect losses are covered, provided only that in legal contemplation Germany's act was the efficient and proximate cause and source from which they flowed. The simple test to be applied in all cases is: has an American national proven a loss suffered by him, susceptible of being measured with reasonable exactness by pecuniary standards, and is that loss attributable to Germany's act as a proximate cause?[38]

Proximity, in turns, depends on reasonableness and foreseeability. In other words, the losses and damage 'must be the "normal" or "natural" (or "necessary and inevitable") consequence of the original injury or of the act or omission by which it was occasioned'.[39] In applying these

---

(3 September 2001); *CME Czech Republic BV v Czech Republic*, UNCITRAL case, Partial Award (13 September 2001) para. 580, and Final Award on Damages (14 March 2003) para. 450. Such outcome, rather than being the result of the application of a different causation standard, can be explained by the different legal analysis by the two Tribunals of the acts of a third party as possible intervening causes. Having found a BIT breach without damage, the *Lauder* Tribunal, practically reversing the ordinary burden of proof, said that the claimant did not demonstrate that 'there existed no intervening cause for the damage', and, consequently that the State's conduct in breach of the BIT was the proximate cause (para. 234). Conversely, the *CME* Tribunal refused to consider the acts of a third party as intervening causes relevant at least as mitigating factors at the compensation level on the basis of the legal argument that:

> [a]s the United Nations International Law Commission in its Commentary on State responsibility recognizes, a State may be held responsible for injury to an alien investor where it is not the sole cause of the injury; the State is not absolved because of the participation of other tortfeasors in the infliction of the injury.

For the *CME* case see also Stephan Wittich 'Joint Tortfeasors in Investment Law' in Christina Binder and others (eds), *International Investment Law for the 21st Century: Essays in Honour of Christoph Schreuer* (OUP 2009) 708, 722.

38 Mixed Claims Commission (*United States and Germany*) (1 November 1923–30 October 1939), Administrative Decision No II, November 1, (1923) II RIAA 1, 30.

39 Garcia-Amador VI (n 17) para. 160, referring to the above criterion for determining the casual link as the objective rule, which had generally been applied by international tribunals.

tests, tribunals enjoy a wide measure of discretion; and much turns on the specific facts and circumstances of each case, which are matters for tribunals' discretionary appreciation.

Particular problems arise if – as is often the case – losses occur as the result of complex processes, and as a consequence of different factors. In assessing causation, tribunals have often drawn distinctions between direct and indirect consequences, or pure and transitive losses.[40] While those distinctions have a certain explanatory value, it is important to note that they do not absolve tribunals from applying the general tests for causation as set out in the preceding paragraphs.[41] Notably, and despite some variations in the use of terminology, indirect losses are compensable as long as they result from the State initial wrongful act. In the words of the United States-Germany Mixed Claims Commission,

> [i]t matters not whether the loss be directly or indirectly sustained so long as there is a clear, unbroken connection between Germany's act and the loss complained of. – It matters not how many links there may be in the chain of causation connecting Germany's act with the loss sustained, provided there is no breach in the chain and the loss can be clearly, unmistakably and definitely traced, link by link, to Germany's act.[42]

By the same token, '[t]ransitive causal links do not exclude the responsibility of the wrongdoer',[43] when the claimant is able to prove, link by

---

[40] As to the distinction between pure and transitive causal links see Brigitte Bollecker-Stern, *Le prejudice dans la théorie de la responsabilité international* (Pedone 1973) 186. See also *Charles Lemire v Ukraine*, ICSID Case No ARB/06/18, Award (29 March 2011) para. 164 where the Tribunal, relying on the seminal book of Professor Stern on the subject-matter, clarifies that:

> [p]ure causal links exist when the damage derives directly from the wrongful act, without intermediary elements. In practice, this situation is rare, because it is difficult to prove that a certain factor is the immediate and unique cause of a result. Normally, the link between wrong and damage is more complex, and additional elements intervene to form a chain of events.

[41] Put differently, the requirement of 'directness' merely illustrates the application of the general rules of causation: see Lillich and Brower (n 34) 35–41, and references cited therein. Among the cited legal authorities see *Amco Asia et al v Republic of Indonesia*, ICSID Case No ARB81/1, Award (20 November 1984), (1985) 24 ILM 1022, 1037, where the Tribunal states that '[t]he requirement of directness is but a consequence of the requirement of a casual link between the failure and the prejudice …'.

[42] Mixed Claims Commission (n 38) 29–30.

[43] See *Lemire v Ukraine* (n 40) para. 166 with reference to Mixed Claims Commission, ibid.

link, the chain of causation between the legally relevant cause, its consequential effects and the economic losses suffered as an ultimate effect. That chain is broken, not if the losses are indirect, but if they are no longer sufficiently connected to the initial wrongful act (e.g., because they are hypothetical, remote, speculative, imaginative or incapable of estimation), or loss was caused 'not by the wrongful acts, but rather by intervening causes, such as factors attributable to the victim, to a third party or for which no one can be made responsible (like *force majeure*)'.[44]

To apply these standards requires not only a factual analysis but also an assessment of the scope and purpose of the obligation breached.[45] This aspect – viz. (in the ILC's words) 'whether the harm caused was within the ambit of the rule … , having regard to the purpose of that rule' – has a particular significance in international proceedings on public support measures for banks and investors' protection.[46] With respect to

---

[44] Ibid., para. 163. On *force majeure* in particular see the contribution by Anastasios Gourgourinis, 'Financial Crisis as *Force Majeure* Under International Law and EU Law: Defending Emergency Measures, *à l'Européenne*, in Investment Arbitration Under Intra-EU BITs' (in this volume) 281.

[45] See ILC Draft Articles (n 27), Commentary to Art. 31, para. 10, observing also that, leaving the elements of directness, foreseeability, and proximity aside, other elements connected with the causation assessment as a legal process might be relevant; for instance, 'whether the harm caused was within the ambit of the rule which was breached, having regard to the purpose of that rule'.

[46] See, for instance, *Hesham T M Al Warraq v Republic of Indonesia*, UNCITRAL, Final Award (15 December 2014) para. 527, where some rescue measures of Indonesia (inter alia a short-term emergency loan provided by the Bank of Indonesia and a bail-out) addressing Bank Century, a virtually failed bank of systemic importance under foreign control, were at stake. Among the arguments of the claimant, a foreign shareholder controlling the bank, was the argument that his legitimate expectations had been frustrated by Indonesia by means of the Bank of Indonesia's negligent supervision of Bank Century in breach of its duties as banking regulator. In rejecting the above argument of the claimant, the Tribunal held:

> that a central bank's primary duty of care is to the depositors of a bank, not to portfolio investors who buy shares of the bank, or of other financial institutions through intermediate corporate entities on the stock market. Thus, the Claimant could not have legitimately expected that the central bank owes him a duty in the circumstances. (para. 619).

Similar observations have been made by the ECtHR in the case *Dennis Grainger and others v UK*, App no 34940/10 (ECtHR, 10 July 2012) paras 39 and 42 where the ECtHR observes that the lender of last resort assistance provided by the Bank of England to Northern Rock, as well as its nationalisation afterwards, were aimed at protecting (instead of shareholders and individual depositors) 'the

international standards for the protection of property rights, the European Court of Human Rights, for example, has held that Article 1 of Protocol No. 1 ECHR 'cannot be interpreted as imposing any general obligation on the Contracting States to cover private debts' with the consequence that a shareholder in a distressed bank cannot have any legitimate expectation that public money will be injected into the concerned bank to save it.[47] Similarly, as many investment arbitral tribunals have acknowledged, BITs are not 'insurance policies against bad business judgments', and even less are they designed to guarantee the success of an investment.[48] The latter principle clearly echoes the words of the Arbitral Tribunal in the case *Dickson Car Wheel Company (USA) v. United Mexican States* quoted at the beginning of this contribution:

> The foreigners, residing in a country which, by reasons of natural, social or international calamities is obliged to adopt those measures, must suffer the natural detriment to his affairs, without any remedy, since Governments, as expressed by a distinguished jurist, are not insurers against every event.[49]

In the light of these considerations, it is possible to apply international rules governing causation to the particular problems of bank rescue measures.

IV. ASPECTS OF CAUSATION ARISING IN RELATION TO BANK RESCUE MEASURES

The requirement of causation between the challenged State measure and the economic loss suffered 'is an essential element in any international claim or exercise of diplomatic protection under the law of state

---

financial sector in the United Kingdom from the contagion that might spread to other key institutions if Northern Rock [a bank of systemic importance] were allowed to fail', and restoring 'the depositor confidence in the safety of placing money with banks', respectively.

[47] See *Grainger v UK* ibid., para. 42. See also *Kotov v Russia*, App no 54522/00 (ECtHR, 3 April 2012) paras 111 and 116. With specific reference to States' measures addressing a distressed bank and investors' expectations see *de Levi v Republic of Peru*, ICSID Case No ARB/10/17, Award (26 February 2014) paras 319–321 and 325.

[48] See, inter alia, *Emilio Agustín Maffezini v Kingdom of Spain*, ICSID Case No ARB/97/7, Award (13 November 2000) para. 64.

[49] *Dickson Car Wheel Company (USA) v United Mexican States,* July 1931, RIAA, Vol. IV, 669–91, 681–2.

responsibility, except where an international agreement alters the requirement of such a casual link'.[50] BITs do not generally alter the ordinary international law requirement of causation; as a consequence, questions of causation are to be addressed on the basis of the general principles outlined in the preceding section.

Where these general principles are applied to a State's bank rescue measures, a number of problems of causation arise acutely, as is highlighted below.

A. Testing the Chain of Causality: Intervening Factors

Disputes about bank rescue measures typically require a particularly careful application of the rules of causation, which has regard to potential intervening factors.

In line with the general principles outlined above, the chain of causation will be broken if losses were caused by intervening factors, 'such as factors attributable to the victim, to a third party or for which no one can be made responsible'.[51] It follows that if a respondent State is able to show that an extraneous event is the real cause of the losses suffered or, in the alternative, that the losses suffered are the direct result of the claimant's own conduct (which need not have been imprudent or faulty[52]), liability will be excluded. This will notably lead tribunals to reject liability for damages that are actually the result of an extraneous event, such a systemic banking crisis.[53] Similarly, a State will not be held liable for measures that are triggered by (and constitute a reasonable response to) inadequate, or deficient behaviour of the claimant, who e.g., may have failed to cooperate with the competent supervisory authorities of the respondent State, or to implement its prudential regulations.

It is worth noting that, while not strictly a question of causation, the conduct and behaviour of the claimant investor can also influence the

---

[50] Bederman (n 11) 249, going on to identify the Algiers Accords and the UK-Poland 1947 Exchange of Notes as examples of international agreements altering the normal requirement of causation.

[51] *Lemire v Ukraine* (n 40) para. 163.

[52] Brigitte Stern, 'The Obligation to Make Reparation' in Crawford and others (n 27) 563, 570.

[53] Such rule has been applied also by the ECtHR as to the protection of a creditor of an insolvent company put into 'extraordinary liquidation' by the Italian ministry of economic development. See *Alfio Saggio v Italy*, App No 41879/98 (ECtHR, 25 October 2001) para. 35.

assessment of whether or not there has been a breach of the BIT.[54] This holds particularly true with respect to claims of breach of the fair and equitable treatment standard. As is clear from the case law, a lack of due diligence on the part of the claimant investor in cooperating with the banking and financial supervisory authorities of the respondent State, or in implementing its prudential regulations can exclude State liability,[55] even if the challenged measures are found by the arbitral tribunal to be contrary to international standards (such as a generally accepted banking and regulatory practice).[56]

---

[54] In legal literature see, inter alia, Mara Valenti, 'The Protection of General Interests of Host States in the Application of the Fair and Equitable Treatment Standard' in Sacerdoti and others (n 26) 26, and references therein.

[55] See, inter alia, with specific reference to State measures affecting a bank owned by a foreign investor (mainly the revocation by the Central Bank of the host State of the concerned bank's licence to operate) *Alex Genin, Eastern Credit Ltd, Inc and AS Baltoil v The Republic of Estonia*, ICSID Case No ARB/99/2, Award (25 June 2001) paras 361–363, where the Tribunal excluded that Estonia had breached the fair and equitable treatment standard and non-discriminatory and non-arbitrary treatment due to the reasonable misgivings, regarding the management of the bank concerned, its operation, its investments and its soundness as a financial institution, as well as the lack by the bank (and its controlling shareholder) of prudent cooperation in providing the information required by the Central Bank in the exercise of its duties as banking supervisory authority (para. 352). This is notwithstanding, according to the Tribunal, the fact that the overall conduct of Estonian authorities was contrary to generally accepted banking and regulatory practice (para. 364). A similar outcome has been reached by the Tribunal in the case *Al Warraq v Indonesia* (n 46) paras 634–648, where the Tribunal first listed six types of fraud in which the claimant was engaged, and then concluded that the claimant could not benefit from the protection of the investment agreement because of his fraudulent conduct, although Indonesia's conduct in the prosecution and conviction of the claimant was found in breach of the fair and equitable treatment standard. More specifically, the Tribunal held that the investor committed acts prejudicial to the public interest in breach of art. 9 of the Organisation of Islamic Cooperation Investment Agreement, and for this reason was not entitled to any damages in respect of the respondent's breaches of the fair and equitable treatment standard. Art. 9 of the Organisation of Islamic Cooperation Investment Agreement provides that:

> The investor shall be bound by the laws and regulations in force in the host state and shall refrain from all acts that may disturb public order or morals or that may be prejudicial to the public interest. He is also to refrain from exercising restrictive practices and from trying to achieve gains through unlawful means.

[56] See *Genin v Estonia* (n 55) para. 364.

As is clear from these considerations, in some instances the question of causation defy clear-cut solutions; quite often, a challenged State measure is not the sole cause of an economic loss, but one of a number of concurrent factors. In this case, the relevant question is how close or effective the connection between the State measure and the loss should be. When a claimant shows a reasonable and sufficient causal connection, it is for a respondent State to show that the damage claimed is partly due to the acts of the claimant (or a third party) and/or the result of an extraneous event. If a respondent State succeeds in discharging its burden of proof, its international liability for losses can be reduced because of claimant's contribution.[57]

To bring about such a reduction of damages, international tribunals have developed a number of conceptual tools. First of all, there is the principle of unjust enrichment, which, albeit not one-sided,[58] requires that the amount of damages awarded does not put the claimant in a better position than he would have been, if not for the challenged measures[59]

[57] Anaïs Moutier-Lopet, 'Contribution to the Injury' in Crawford and others (n 27) 639, 643–4.

[58] The principle of unjust enrichment may also operate in favour of the damaged investors. States should not (and cannot) benefit from their internationally wrongful acts. Although not unanimously accepted in the case law and literature, the above principle has been regarded as part of the principle of full compensation in case of unlawful expropriation. See *Factory at Chorzów, Merits (Germany v Poland)*, Judgement (13 September 1928) 47, where, after having found an unlawful expropriation by Poland, the PCJ stated that:

> the compensation due to the German Government is not necessarily limited to the value of the undertaking at the moment of dispossession, plus interest to the day of payment. This limitation would only be admissible if the Polish Government had had the right to expropriate, and if its wrongful act consisted merely in not having paid to the two Companies the just price of what was expropriated; in the present case, such a limitation might result in placing Germany and the interests protected by the Geneva Convention, on behalf of which interests the German Government is acting, in a situation more unfavourable than that in which Germany and these interests would have been if Poland had respected the said Convention. Such a consequence would not only be unjust, but also and above all incompatible with the aim of Article 6 and following articles of the Convention-that is to say, the prohibition, in principle, of the liquidation of the property, rights and interests of German nationals and of companies controlled by German nationals in Upper Silesia – since it would be tantamount to rendering lawful liquidation and unlawful dispossession indistinguishable in so far as their financial results are concerned.

[59] Garcia-Amador VI (n 17) 43–4, paras 170–175.

and the connected duty of investors to mitigate their losses. The investor's duty to take any reasonable action necessary to minimise the losses caused by wrongful conduct in turn would seem to derive from the general principle of unjust enrichment, and has been widely acknowledged in investment case law as mitigating factor in calculating damages. Otherwise '[i]t would be patently unfair to allow Claimants to recover damages for loss that could have been avoided by taking reasonable steps. In other words, the injured party must be held responsible for its own contribution to the loss'.[60] Alternatively, damages have been reduced if claimants themselves had acted wrongfully;[61] similar considerations can apply under the emerging concept of loss of

[60] See *EDF International SA and Other v Argentine Republic*, ICSID Case No ARB/03/23, Award (11 June 2012) paras 1301 and 1306 where the Tribunal further observes that '[w]hether the aggrieved party has taken reasonable steps to reduce the loss is a question of fact, not law. What is reasonable depends largely upon the facts of the individual case'. See also *Achmea BV v The Slovak Republic* (n 22) paras 319–320, although the Tribunal also acknowledged that the claimant had indeed discharged its duty to mitigate its losses in the case.

[61] In investment case law see, inter alia, *MTD Equity Sdn Bhd and MTD Chile SA v Republic of Chile*, ICSID Case No ARB/01/17, Award (25 May 2004) paras 168 and 178, and Decision on Annulment (21 March 2007) paras 99–100; *Yukos Universal Ltd (Isle of Man) v The Russian Federation*, PCA Case No AA 227, Final Award (18 July 2014) paras 1594 (where the Tribunal re-states the principle of contributory fault according to which 'Claimants may not recover from the Russian Federation the fruits of their own wrongdoing') and 1596 (where the Tribunal found it 'must therefore decide, on the basis of the totality of the evidence before it, whether there is a sufficient causal link between any wilful or negligent act or omission of the Claimants (or of Yukos, which they controlled) and the loss Claimants ultimately suffered at the hands of the Russian Federation through the destruction of Yukos'), while pointing out that 'not any contribution by the injured party to the damage which it has suffered which will trigger a finding of contributory fault. The contribution must be material and significant. In this regard, the Tribunal has a wide margin of discretion in apportioning fault' (para. 1600). After having found the abuse by the claimants of the low tax regions, and its questionable use of the Cyprus-Russia DTA, as having contributed in a material and significant way to the prejudice which they subsequently suffered caused by the conduct of Russian Federation in breach of the ECT, the Tribunal decided to reduce the amount of damages to be paid by the respondent by 25 per cent (paras 1633–1637). For the *Yukos* cases see Andrea K Bjorklund and Lukas Vanhonnaeker, 'Yukos: The Clean Hands Doctrine Revisited' (2015) 9 Diritti Umani e Diritto Internazionale 365, 381–4.

opportunity.[62] These considerations underline the wide margin of discretion enjoyed by tribunals in determining questions of causation, and in appreciating the relevance of particular causal factors. That having been said, the existing case law does yield some insight into how tribunals are likely to evaluate questions of proximity, contributory fault, and other potential intervening causes – i.e., questions likely to arise in litigation

[62] The concept of loss of opportunity has been very rarely applied in investment treaty-based arbitration since it pertains to both the assessment of damage and causation, and the assessment of the extent of reparation. As a general concept widely recognised in both common law and civil law legal systems, the loss of opportunity approach is mainly applied to professionals' malpractice, irregular bid procedures, and lastly the breach of certain types of contract. In the latter case the concept is applied as a default rule for calculating damages as lost profits, and generally implies the application of a less-demanding standard of causation, than proximity and condition *sine qua non*. The same holds true in cases of professionals' malpractice and irregular bid procedures. In fact the loss of opportunity approach applies when the existence of damage is uncertain: the damage consists in the loss of attaining a business opportunity (or any other economic benefit), rather than the loss of the business opportunity (or the economic benefit) itself. Art. 7.4.3(2) of the UNIDROIT Principles of International Commercial Contracts also confirms the above as to international contracts, providing that '[c]ompensation may be due for the loss of a chance in proportion to the probability of its occurrence'. The official comment of the UNIDROIT Principles to art. 7.4.3(2) makes the following example: 'thus, the owner of a horse which arrives too late to run in a race as a result of delay in transport cannot recover the whole of the prize money, even though the horse was the favourite'. (See UNIDROIT Principles of International Commercial Contracts (2010 Edition) 270). As has been authoritatively observed the loss 'of opportunity (or chance) is a subcategory of lost profits where not only the magnitude but even the existence of the monetary prejudice is doubtful'. See Jan Paulsson, 'The Expectation Model' in Yves Derains and Richard H Kreindler (eds), *Evaluation of Damages in International Arbitration*, (Wolters Kluver 2006) 57, 57. The concept of loss of opportunity requires only that damage would have occurred with a sufficient probability (rather than with reasonably certainty) but for the breach. See, for instance, *Sapphire International Petroleum, Ltd v National Iranian Oil Company*, Arbitral Award (15 March 1963) (1963) 35 ILR 136, where an oil exploration contract was at stake and NIOC breached the contract before the investor had actually found oil. The above observations explain why the concept can be (and has been) only exceptionally applied in investment treaty arbitration. For an example of application of the concept of loss of opportunity in investment case law see *Gemplus SA, SLP SA, Gemplus Industrial SA de CV v The United Mexican States*, ICSID Case No ARB(AF)/04/3, Award (16 June 2010) part XIII, paras 13.83–13.91 where the Tribunal applied the lost of opportunity approach just as a device for limiting the amount of damages awarded.

about bank rescue measures. It is to this particular aspect of causation that the analysis now turns.

B. In Particular: Case Law on Prior Insolvency and Imprudent Claimant Conduct

While litigation about bank rescue measures taken during the recent global financial crisis is on-going, international courts and tribunals have in the past addressed questions of prior (near-)insolvency and imprudent claimant conduct – factors that, in light of the preceding analysis, could very well preclude State liability or significantly reduce it. A review of some of the more prominent decisions reveals a rather cautious approach.

In the *ELSI* case, decided by the International Court of Justice (ICJ) the United States (US) claimed that Italy had breached the international standards of protection of investments included in the Treaty of Friendship, Commerce and Navigation (FCN Treaty) between the two countries, in relation to the Italian company Elettronica Sicula S.p.A. (ELSI), wholly owned by two US corporations, Raytheon and Machlett.[63] The claims of the US were based on the allegation that the requisition by an Italian local authority of the plant and related assets of ELSI had frustrated the orderly liquidation of the company (as planned by its shareholders), led to its bankruptcy and left the shareholders with significant losses. According to US, Italy had violated treaty rights of the US investors 'to organize, control, and manage' their investment (i.e., ELSI); furthermore, its conduct was said to amount to an 'indirect expropriation' and 'arbitrary and discriminatory'.

In its judgment, the ICJ dismissed these claims, finding that no sufficient causal link between the impugned measure (the requisition) and the effect (economic loss) had been established. According to the court, what really deprived the US investors of their treaty rights to control and manage their investment, as well as their treaty rights to dispose of the assets of ELSI, 'was not the requisition but the precarious financial state of ELSI, ultimately leading inescapably to bankruptcy'.[64]

The central passage of the judgment on questions of causation is instructive. In the view of the court:

> [O]ne feature of ELSI's position stands out: the uncertain and speculative character of the causal connection, on which the Applicant's case relies,

---

[63] *Elettronica Sicula SpA (ELSI) (US v Italy),* Judgment (20 July 1989) ICJ Reports 1989, 15.

[64] Ibid., para. 135.

> between the requisition and the results attributed to it by the Applicant. There were several causes acting together that led to the disaster to ELSI. No doubt the effects of the requisition might have been one of the factors involved. But the underlying cause was ELSI's headlong course towards insolvency; which state of affairs it seems to have attained even prior to the requisition. There was the warning loudly proclaimed about its precarious position; there was the socially damaging decision to terminate the business, close the plant, and dismiss the workforce; there was the position of the banks as major creditors. In short, the possibility of that solution of orderly liquidation, which Raytheon and Machlett claim to have been deprived of as a result of the requisition, is purely a matter of speculation.[65]

Similarly the Court dismissed the claim that the interests of shareholders in the assets of the company and in their residual value on liquidation, had been expropriated. In the court's view, the requisition could not amount to a taking under the FCN Treaty: the requisition could not be regarded as a significant cause, as the precarious financial state of ELSI *before* the requisition made its bankruptcy inevitable.[66]

The BIT case of *de Levi v Republic of Peru* also illustrates the relevance of a company's prior financial state of a bank for the assessment of claims.[67] The proceedings were brought by the majority shareholder of a Peruvian bank, Banco Nuevo Mundo (BNM), according to whom Peru had arbitrarily and illegally subjected the bank to a series of measures that ultimately resulted in its dissolution and liquidation. The claimant contended that, by several acts and omissions (such as the refusal of the Central Bank of Peru to provide an emergency loan to the BNM, the arbitrary refusal to authorise a planned merger with another bank, and the intervention by the Banking Supervisor), Peru impaired its BIT rights and expropriated its investment. The Tribunal's award supports the proposition that the precarious financial state (or a state close to insolvency) of a bank before the State's intervention, as well as the conduct of the bank's shareholders, can interrupt the chain of causation.

In the circumstances of the case and based on the principle that 'no investment treaty is an insurance or guarantee of investment success,

[65] Ibid., para. 101.

[66] Ibid., para. 119.

[67] *Renée Rose Levy de Levi v Republic of Peru*, ICSID Case No ARB/10/17, Award (26 February 2014).

especially when the investor makes bad business decisions',[68] the Tribunal concluded that the precarious financial state of the bank and certain acts of the investor in violation of Peru's bank regulation and sound credit and lending policies, made the intervention and subsequent dissolution and liquidation of the bank inevitable; these prior factors thus had caused the collapse of the investment.[69] In the words of the award, 'although there were several causes that led to the failure of BNM (including, and to a significant degree, the economic crisis in Peru during 1999 and 2000), it was ultimately the actions of its shareholders and employees that brought it to ruin.'[70] Among these 'actions of its shareholders and employees' the Tribunal particularly mentioned the following: accounting mismanagement; risky and inadequate credit and lending policies on the basis of the condition of the State's economy (lack of a sound credit policy in time of financial and banking crisis); non-compliance with Peru's regulation on lending activities of banks; the elaboration of inadequate development plans for financial and economic crises; the implementation of bad banking practices (such as favouring companies affiliated to the shareholders of the bank); and providing inaccurate financial information and statements to supervising authorities.[71]

In December 2014 the Tribunal in the case *Al Warraq v Indonesia* reached similar conclusions to those of the *de Levi* Tribunal with

---

[68] Ibid., para. 478, relying on *Maffezini v Spain* (n 48) para. 64; *MTD v Chile* (n 61) para. 178; *CMS Gas Transmission Company v Republic of Argentina*, ICSID Case No ARB/01/8, Decision on Jurisdiction (17 July 2003) para. 29; *Eudoro Olguín v Republic of Paraguay*, ICSID Case No ARB/98/5, Award (26 July 2000) para. 73.

[69] *de Levi v Peru* (n 67) para. 478, where, in dismissing the claim of the investor of being victim of an expropriation, the Tribunal stated that;

> it is not true that there was an expropriation in the case of BNM, as affirmed by the Claimant. What happened was a repeated non-compliance with the banking regulations by BNM, which moreover took risks in times of a considerable liquidity crisis that affected it, causing it to fail to perform its obligations and to close its offices. These acts made its intervention and subsequent dissolution and liquidation inevitable;

and para. 483, where the Tribunal states that, '... BNM's own breaches of the banking regulations led to SBS's intervention in the Bank. Once SBS had confirmed the improper accounting practices, it determined the total losses incurred by the bank and, according to the Banking Law requirements, its dissolution and liquidation were inevitable;'.

[70] Ibid., para. 488.

[71] Ibid., paras 490–500.

reference to the bailout of a failed bank owned by a foreign investor (Bank Century). Contrary to the investor's claims, the Tribunal held the bailout did not amount to an unlawful taking under the applicable BIT since:

> the value of Bank Century at the time of the bailout was negative, and thus the shares likewise were of no value. It is the view of the Tribunal that the bailout was within the discretion and authority of the government and was completely justified, particularly since Bank Century at a ratio below 10% at the time of the bailout, could have caused a systemic risk to the entire Indonesian financial system. Bank Century represented the 0.73% of the banking deposits and 0.68% of the commercial banks activities.[72]

While the afore-mentioned cases concern the treaty protection of shareholders, the case *Olguín v Paraguay*[73] implicated a debt interest of an investor in a financial institution, La Mercantil. The investor was a depositor in La Mercantil and had received investment instruments in return for his deposits.[74] During the 1995 economic crisis in Paraguay and the related crisis of its financial system, La Mercantil suspended its operations and stopped paying its dues. In accordance with Paraguay's domestic rules governing banks and financial institutions, this led the Central Bank to withdraw its licence to operate, and to eventually proceed to its dissolution and liquidation.

According to the claimant, Peru's Financial Supervisory authorities had failed to exercise their duty of supervision; this in its view had led to the suspension of the operations of La Mercantil and its liquidation, which in turn had caused the claimant's losses.

Although there were considerable omissions on the part of the Financial Supervisory authorities,[75] the Tribunal concluded that these had not caused the claimant's losses. In its assessment, the bankruptcy of La Mercantil, occurring within the broader context of a national financial crisis, was primarily the consequence of irregular conduct by its managers.[76] In addition, the imprudent conduct of the claimant making a speculative investment, as well as his irregular conduct (such as his improper links with a public officer of the Central Bank of Paraguay, as

72 *Al Warraq v Indonesia* (n 46), para. 526.
73 *Olguín v Paraguay* (n 68).
74 Ibid., paras 49 and 65(a).
75 ibid., para. 70.
76 Ibid., paras 68–69.

well as one of the managers of La Mercantil), contributed to the occurrence of the facts causing his losses.[77]

This brief review, it is submitted, is indicative. It illustrates that in applying the general principles of causation, the ICJ and investment tribunals have accorded great weight to the imprudent conduct of investors and the critical financial situation of an investment. In all of the reviewed cases, these factors were sufficient to break the chain of causation, even where the host State's conduct had been found to be deficient.

V. CONCLUSIONS

On the basis of this review of the case law, it may be difficult for shareholders of a rescued bank to establish a sufficient causal link between the rescue measures and the losses suffered, in circumstances in which the bank was insolvent or in a precarious financial situation before the measures were enacted. The same holds true where the bank and its shareholders acted in breach of the host State's banking regulation, or conducted the bank's affairs in an unsound manner.

As regards foreign creditors of a rescued bank, it has been observed that 'the weight of authority is to the effect that such losses as a creditor may suffer as a result of the wrongful act committed against his debtor are too remote or indirect connected to sustain an award to the creditor'. A creditor could only prevail, according to the US Foreign Claims Settlement Commission (FCSC), where 'the debt forming the basis of [the creditors' claim] would have been paid, *but for* the actions of the Government … of which it complains'.[78] This statement, while made in the 1950s, retains much of its pertinence; it highlights the difficulties of

---

[77] Ibid., paras 75–82. For a similar pronouncement on the investor's lack of due diligence see the case of *Aldair Ross Anderson et al v Republic of Costa Rica*, ICSID Case No ARB(AF)/07/3, Award (19 May 2010) para. 58, which concerned the deposits, by Canadian investors, of funds with a Ponzi scheme managed by two nationals of Costa Rica engaging in financial intermediation without authorisation by the Central Bank of Costa Rica, in violation of Costa Rica's law. In that case, the lack of due diligence of the investors in assuring themselves that their investments were in accordance with the law of the host State, as required by the BIT, led the Tribunal to decline jurisdiction.

[78] Bederman (n 11), 235 observing that creditors' claims 'implicate problems of attribution and causation in the international law of state responsibility', and 243, referring to the *European Mortgage Series B Corp* decision of the FCSC, and 252–3.

satisfying the requirement of causation in respect of foreign creditors' claims. After all, States cannot be generally held *directly* responsible for private companies' debts; neither can they be generally considered as *directly* responsible for mismanagement or fraud committed by the managers of distressed or failed companies.[79]

Furthermore, the failure of host State regulatory bodies to preserve the integrity and stability of its financial and banking systems can hardly be considered a plausible basis for a BIT claim.[80] The 2001 award in *Olguín*, which found negligence on the part of the Paraguayan financial and banking supervisory bodies, supports this position.[81] According to the Tribunal:

> [a]lthough, as explained elsewhere in this ruling, the establishment, in the future, of strict rules that impose economic sanctions on States that fail to closely monitor their financial entities is desirable, the truth is that these rules do not now exist in either Paraguayan law or in the BIT. The Tribunal adds that they do not exist in the majority of the countries in the region either.[82]

That said, while intended to support the orthodox view, this statement might also be taken to point to a novel approach to the handling of causation issues. Whereas the tribunal in *Olguín* considered 'the establishment … of strict rules that impose economic sanctions on States that fail to closely monitor their financial entities [to be] desirable', but a matter for 'the future', the recent financial crisis may have catalysed developments. Notably, States, international organisations and regulatory bodies have elaborated a number of common prudential standards on bank resolution and recovery. Prominent among them is the 'burden-sharing by the shareholders and subordinated creditors' principle, pursuant to which shareholders and creditors have to bear the losses arising from maintaining the insolvent institution as a going concern (as far as possible) for financial stability reasons, in order to minimise public financing.[83] This principle, in turn, is tempered by the 'no creditor worse

---

[79] As observed by the ECHR in the case *Kotov v Russia* (n 47) para.116, 'by depositing his money with a private bank the applicant assumed a certain risk, including those related to mismanagement and even fraud'.

[80] The same holds true in respect of similar complaints before other international courts. See also *Grainger v UK* (n 46), para. 41.

[81] *Olguín v Paraguay* (n 68) paras 73–74.

[82] Ibid., para. 74.

[83] See Basel Committee on Banking Supervision, 'Consultative Document, Report and Recommendations of the Cross-border Bank Resolution Group' (September 2009) 42, Recommendation 10, according to which 'National

off principle', which clarifies that creditors affected by rescue measures should not receive less in economic terms than they would have received if no public support had been granted and the bank had been wound up under normal insolvency proceedings.[84]

While developments are still on-going, the emergence of generally accepted prudential standards might strengthen the international protection of foreign creditors of banks affected by State measures aimed at protecting financial stability. This would notably be the case if tribunals, in proceedings concerning bank rescue measures, gave effect to the 'no creditor worse off principle' in relation to foreign creditors. Should

---

authorities should adopt crisis management and resolution strategies that reduce moral hazard by minimising public expenditures. Losses should be allocated among shareholders and other creditors, where possible …' <www.bis.org/publ/bcbs162.pdf> accessed 8 April 2015; Basel Committee on Banking Supervision, 'Report and Recommendations of the Cross-border Bank Resolution Group' (March 2010) 43, Recommendation 10 <www.bis.org/publ/bcbs169.pdf> accessed 15 April 2015. See also Financial Stability Board (n 6) para. 4i); Financial Stability Board, 'Key Attributes of Effective Resolution Regimes for Financial Institutions' (October 2011) Preamble:

> The objective of an effective resolution regime is to make feasible the resolution of financial institutions without severe systemic disruption and without exposing taxpayers to loss, while protecting vital economic functions through mechanisms which make it possible for shareholders and unsecured and uninsured creditors to absorb losses in a manner that respects the hierarchy of claims in liquidation

and para. 3.5 <www.financialstabilityboard.org/wp-content/uploads/r_111104cc.pdf?page_moved=1> accessed 8 April 2015; European Commission, 'EU Bank Recovery and Resolution Directive (BRRD): Frequently Asked Questions' MEMO/14/297, 3 <http://europa.eu/rapid/press-release_MEMO-14-297_en.htm> accessed 8 April 2015.

[84] EU Commission, ibid., para. 46; Directive 2014/59/EU of the European Parliament and of the Council of 15 May 2014 establishing a framework for the recovery and resolution of credit institutions and investment firms and amending Council Directive 82/891/EEC, and Directives 2001/24/EC, 2002/47/EC, 2004/25/EC, 2005/56/EC, 2007/36/EC, 2011/35/EU, 2012/30/EU and 2013/36/EU, and Regulations (EU) No 1093/2010 and (EU) No 648/2012 of the European Parliament and of the Council [2014] OJ L173/190, Preamble at 5:

> The regime should also ensure that shareholders bear losses first and that creditors bear losses after shareholders provided that no creditor should incur greater losses than it would have incurred if the institution had been wound up under normal insolvency proceedings in accordance with the no creditor worse off principle as specified in this Directive.

and art. 34.1(g).

respondent States not respect this principle when enacting and implementing the bank rescue measures, tribunals might well award the difference (if any) between the losses actually suffered and the losses that the claimant would have in any case suffered but for the State measures. Similarly, the 'no creditor worse off principle' could be also regarded as a new manifestation of the principle of unjust enrichment, widely considered as a general principle of law.[85]

More generally, the newly emerging prudential standards on bank resolution and recovery might be taken to reflect generally accepted benchmarks of State conduct during and following economic crises. Judged against such benchmarks, insufficient actions or gross omissions by the host State's financial supervisory bodies could provide at least a plausible basis for BIT claims advanced by foreign creditors of distressed banks. In this respect, it is worth noting that the *Al Warraq* case,[86] which is more recent than the *Olguín* case, accepts that allegedly negligent supervisory actions of Central Banks and other supervisory authorities are not, in principle, shielded from the scrutiny of investment tribunals,[87] unless limited or excluded by the treaty itself.[88] Seen in this light, gross omissions by the host State's financial supervisory bodies in violation of newly emerged international prudential standards – while so far dismissed as a basis for a claim of breach of international provisions on foreign property rights protection – might in future proceedings be qualified as breaches of BIT standards of protection.

[85] In case of an unlawful expropriation the claimant investor might also ask for the application of the principle that States should not (and cannot) benefit from their internationally wrongful acts, and claim, therefore, any successive gain obtained by the respondent State from its internationally unlawful expropriation as compensation. See *Factory at Chorzów* (n 58) 47.

[86] *Al Warraq v Indonesia* (n 46).

[87] Ibid.

[88] See, for instance, art. 110 Mexico-Japan FTA of 2004, and art. 20(1) and (3) US BIT Model of 2102.

10. BITs and pieces: Reflections on the relevance of BITs in resolution-related litigation

Phoebus Athanassiou*

I. INTRODUCTION

This chapter will discuss selected aspects of two contributions to this volume. The focus of the first of these two contributions, authored by Maurice Mendelson QC and Martins Paparinskis, is on the relevance of international investment law, in general, and bilateral investment treaties (BITs), in particular, to the protection of depositors in the context of litigation arising from bank resolution measures decreed by the competent national authorities in a crisis situation.[1] This chapter will seek to determine under which conditions depositors prejudiced by national bail-in measures can rely on international investment law as a source of legal constraints to the exercise of statutory resolution powers by the competent national authorities. The second contribution, authored by Anna De Luca, addresses much the same issue (that of depositor protection, under international investment law, against national resolution measures), but from a broader perspective and from a somewhat different angle, focusing on issues of causation in the context of damage claims arising from national resolution measures.[2] The second part of this chapter will concentrate on the relevance and relative weight of the causal link between the damage/loss to depositors and the actions of the

* The views represented here are those of the author, and need not reflect those of the ECB or the Eurosystem.

[1] Maurice Mendelson and Martins Paparinskis, 'Bail-Ins and International Investment Law: In and Beyond Cyprus' (in this volume) 193.

[2] Anna De Luca, 'Bank Rescue Measures Under International Investment Law: What Role for the Principle of Causation?' (in this volume) 211.

competent national authority, issues aptly drawn attention to by Anna De Luca in her contribution.

II. BACKGROUND TO THE TWO CONTRIBUTIONS AND TO THIS COMMENT

The Cypriot authorities' bail-in of uninsured deposits, as part of the restructuring and resolution of Cyprus' two largest banks, the Bank of Cyprus and the Cyprus Popular Bank (otherwise known as 'Laiki Bank'), were among the most significant events to affect depositors since the start of the European sovereign debt crisis. Several of the affected depositors were foreign nationals, some of whom hailed from jurisdictions with which the Republic of Cyprus (RoC) had concluded BITs. As the Cypriot bail-in of uninsured deposits provides the background for both of the above contributions, a few words are apposite on the events leading up to it, on its features and consequences.

All of the leading economic performance indicators of the RoC began deteriorating soon after the adoption of the euro. In particular, GDP growth slowed in the period between 2008 and 2013 (to the point of contracting), while Cyprus' debt-to-GDP and unemployment ratios grew constantly and considerably. A combination of fiscal mismanagement, declining competitiveness, continuous downgrades of the RoC's sovereign ratings, and the onset of the financial crisis, which exposed the vulnerabilities of an over-sized,[3] poorly managed and inadequately supervised banking sector,[4] contributed to Cyprus' predicament in the run-up to its sovereign debt crisis.

On 25 June 2012, the Cypriot Government decided to issue a request for stability support to the President of the Eurogroup, in line with Article 13(1) of the Treaty establishing the European Stability Mechanism[5]

---

[3] The rapid expansion of the Cypriot banking sector between 2005 and 2012 had led to the build-up of significant vulnerabilities. The Bank of Cyprus and Laiki Bank had expanded considerably in Greece, which exposed their loan portfolios to the deteriorating macroeconomic conditions there.

[4] The reader is referred, in particular, to the findings of the Independent Commission on the future of the Cypriot Banking Sector, Interim Report, June 2013 <www.centralbank.gov.cy/media/pdf/ICFCBSInterimReport_EN.pdf>, accessed 30 December 2015.

[5] Treaty establishing the European Stability Mechanism between the Kingdom of Belgium, the Federal Republic of Germany, the Republic of Estonia, Ireland, the Hellenic Republic, the Kingdom of Spain, the French Republic, the Italian Republic, the Republic of Cyprus, the Grand Duchy of Luxembourg,

(ESM Treaty), citing, inter alia, spill-over risks from the exposure of its banking sector to the Greek economy, as well as urgent budgetary needs. Cyprus' application had been preceded by the adverse developments described in the preceding paragraph, and was no doubt precipitated by the fallout of Greece's voluntary debt-restructuring process in February–March 2012, which cost the Cypriot banking sector an estimated €4,5 billion (or 20 per cent of GDP) in write-downs to its Greek Government bond holdings. In a statement dated 27 June 2012, the Eurogroup declared that the European Financial Stability Facility or the ESM would provide financial assistance to the RoC within the framework of a comprehensive adjustment programme. As provided by Article 13(1) and (3) ESM Treaty, the Commission, in liaison with the ECB and the IMF, would negotiate the programme with the Cypriot authorities.

With negotiations on-going, on 16 March 2013 the Eurogroup agreed with the Cypriot authorities on a financial assistance envelope of up to €10 billion. The Eurogroup and the Cypriot authorities also agreed that the RoC would introduce a one-off stability levy applicable to resident and non-resident depositors alike in all Cypriot banks, to be levied at the rate of 6.75 per cent for deposits of up to €100,000 and 9.9 per cent for deposits above that amount.[6] The imposition of a levy on insured deposits drew sharp criticism from various quarters across Europe.[7] On 19 March the Cypriot House of Representatives rejected the levy. In anticipation of the parliamentary vote, the Central Bank of Cyprus (CBC) had declared a bank holiday for 18 March, motivated by fears of a

---

Malta, the Kingdom of the Netherlands, the Republic of Austria, the Portuguese Republic, the Republic of Slovenia, the Slovak Republic and the Republic of Finland, concluded in Brussels on 2 February 2012 <www.esm.europa.eu/>, accessed 30 December 2015.

[6] Eurogroup Statement on Cyprus, 16 March 2013 <www.google.de/url?sa=t&rct=j&q=&esrc=s&frm=1&source=web&cd=1&ved=0ahUKEwj6_Im9lJDKAhWFbRQKHSF0ANgQFggcMAA&url=http%3A%2F%2Fwww.consilium.europa.eu%2Fpress%2Fpress-releases%2F2013%2F03%2Fpdf%2FEurogroup-Statement-on-Cyprus(1)%2F&usg=AFQjCNEJfftVqLs60VMQ9GND-mHVX_4D8Q> accessed 30 December 2015.

[7] See, by way of example, Mario Draghi, Introductory Statement to the ECB Press Conference (with Q&A), 4 April 2013 <www.ecb.europa.eu/press/pressconf/2013>, accessed on 30 December 2015; and Sharon Bowles, Chair, European Parliament Economic & Monetary Affairs Committee, 'The Cyprus Bailout Deal is a Disaster for EU Rules and Single Market Principles' 16 March 2013 <http://sharonbowles.org.uk/en/article/2013> accessed 30 December 2015.

bank-run.[8] On 22 March, the Cypriot House of Representatives adopted the Resolution of Credit and Other Institutions Law of 2013 which, inter alia, authorised the CBC to bail-in by decree the debts of credit institutions under resolution, with the exception of insured deposits.[9] On 25 March the Eurogroup agreed with the Cypriot authorities' plan for the restructuring of the Cypriot banking sector, specifically safeguarding all deposits of up to €100,000.[10]

Acting under the Resolution of Credit and Other Institutions Law of 2013, the CBC adopted certain decrees restructuring the Bank of Cyprus and resolving Laiki Bank. The restructuring and resolution process was accomplished in two main steps. First, by way of a purchase and assumption transaction, Laiki Bank was required to transfer all deposits of up to €100,000, together with certain other deposits, its CBC loans and most of its assets to the Bank of Cyprus, receiving, in return, shares in the Bank of Cyprus. Many uninsured deposits were left behind in what remained of Laiki Bank.[11] Second, to restore the capital adequacy of Bank of Cyprus, uninsured deposits in the Bank of Cyprus were 'bailed-in', with the compulsory conversion of the depositors' claims into a combination of shares and longer-term deposits.[12]

---

[8] European Commission, 'The Economic Adjustment Programme for Cyprus' (2013) Occasional Papers 149, 39.

[9] The Resolution of Credit and Other Institutions Law of 2013, Law 17(I)/2013, arts 2 and 12(1).

[10] Eurogroup Statement on Cyprus, 25 March 2013, <http://eurozone.europa.eu/newsroom/news/2013> accessed December 2015.

[11] Central Bank of Cyprus, Sale of Certain Operations of Cyprus Popular Bank Public Co Ltd Decree of 2013, *Official Gazette of the Republic of Cyprus*, 3rd Annex, Part I, Regulatory Administrative Acts Issue No 4645/ Fri Mar 29, 2013/ p. 781, Regulatory Administrative Act No 104; Central Bank of Cyprus, Issuance of Share Capital of Bank of Cyprus for Compensation of Cyprus Popular Bank Decree of 2013, *Official Gazette of the Republic of Cyprus*, 3rd Annex, Part I, Regulatory Administrative Acts Issue No 4703/ Tue Jul. 30, 2013/ p. 1772, Regulatory Administrative Act No 279.

[12] Central Bank of Cyprus, Bailing-in of Bank of Cyprus Public Co Ltd Decree of 2013, *Official Gazette of the Republic of Cyprus*, 3rd Annex, Part I, Regulatory Administrative Acts Issue No 4645/ Fri Mar. 29, 2013/ p 769, Regulatory Administrative Act No 103; Central Bank of Cyprus, Bailing-in of Bank of Cyprus Public Co Ltd Decree (Amended) (No 3) of 2013, *Official Gazette of the Republic of Cyprus*, 3rd Annex, Part I, Regulatory Administrative Acts Issue No 4703/ Tue Jul. 30, 2013/ p 1767, Regulatory Administrative Act No 278; Minister of Finance of Cyprus, Decree under the Cypriot Enforcement of Restrictive Measures on Transactions in Case of Emergency Law of 2013, *Official Gazette of the Republic of Cyprus*, 3rd Annex, Part I, Regulatory

Soon after the depositor bail-in, aggrieved *domestic* depositors presented damage claims before the Supreme Court of Cyprus (SCC). The SCC issued its landmark ruling on the Cypriot 'bail-in litigation' on 7 June 2013.[13] In a nutshell, the SCC refused jurisdiction over applications filed against the CBC's resolution decrees, treating the relationship between the aggrieved depositors and the resolved banks as one of private law, and referring the aggrieved depositors' compensation claims to the civil courts. Echoing section 3(2)(d) of Cyprus' Resolution of Credit and Other Institutions Law of 2013, the SCC noted, *obiter*, that to succeed before the civil courts, claimants had to establish that their position after resolution was worse than it would have been had the bank gone into liquidation (the 'no-creditor-worse-off-than-in-insolvency' or 'NCWO' principle).[14]

As the aggrieved depositors in the Cypriot 'bail-in litigation' were *domestic*, an obvious question is how courts would approach the predicament of *foreign* depositors, hailing from jurisdictions with which the RoC maintains a BIT: how, if at all, would the existence of a BIT affect the decision of the Cypriot authorities to subject the deposits of those foreign investors to a bail-in, and what, if anything, would international investment law have to say about the legitimacy of the bail-in measures decreed by the Cypriot authorities? It is, essentially, this question that the two contributions commented on in this chapter seek to answer, approaching that question from different viewpoints.

Administrative Acts Issue No 4702/ Tue Jul. 30, 2013/ p 1763, Regulatory Administrative Act No 277; Joint Notice of the Ministry of Finance and the Central Bank of Cyprus, 30 Jul. 2013.

[13] Judgment of the Supreme Court of Cyprus, 7 June 2013, Case 551/2013 *Christodoulou and others v Central Bank of Cyprus and others*. For an account of the Supreme Court's ruling in this case see Jenny Giotaki, 'The Cypriot "Bail-in Litigation": A First Assessment of the Ruling of the Supreme Court of Cyprus' (2013) 28(8) Butterworths J Intl Banking and Financial L 485.

[14] The provision in question enshrines the 'no-creditor-worse-off-than-in-insolvency' among the overarching principles applicable in resolution. This requires that the creditors of an institution under resolution not be placed in a less favourable financial position on account of the implementation of the resolution measures, compared to the position they would have been in if the affected institution was, instead, put into liquidation. For an account of the NCWO principle and the parameters relevant to its application see Phoebus Athanassiou, 'Valuation in Resolution and the "No-Creditor-Worse-Off Principle"' (2014) 29(1) Butterworths J Intl Banking and Financial Law 16.

III. OBSERVATIONS ON MENDELSON'S AND PAPARINSKIS' CONTRIBUTION: IS THERE AN ELIGIBLE CLAIMANT UNDER A BIT?

In their contribution, Mendelson and Paparinskis essentially argue that bail-ins of the drastic type performed in Cyprus raise questions of compliance with international investment law in general and BITs in particular (in those cases where a BIT is in place). While highlighting the uncertain state of the law (as applied by tribunals), the authors engage with the merits of BIT-based compensation claims, premised on the assumption that bail-ins could be directly or indirectly expropriatory, notwithstanding the various questions of jurisdiction and admissibility to which they would inevitably give raise, and the hurdles that these questions would represent for successful claims against sovereigns whose competent authorities have mandated the offending bail-in.

Taking a step back, this author would argue (somewhat unspectacularly) that for aggrieved depositors to plausibly claim against the national resolution authorities that their depositor bail-in measures are in breach of a BIT, it is essential that depositors should qualify as protected 'investors', and that their deposits should qualify as protected 'investments'. Whether this is the case will depend on the applicable BIT's definition of protected 'investor' and 'investments'.[15] To take the example of the RoC's BITs, what a cursory examination reveals is that their definitions of 'investor' and 'investment' differ from one BIT to another, and that there is a substantial degree of ambiguity about many of the available definitions.[16] What is more, none of the BITs that this author has come across expressly includes 'deposits' within the scope of the definition of 'investment'. Assuming that the text of a given BIT leaves the above questions without a clear answer, and that national law lends

[15] See Mendelson and Paparinskis (n 1) 198–200.

[16] Cyprus is a signatory to numerous bilateral treaties for the promotion and reciprocal protection of investments, the text of which is available on the website of the UNCTAD. The BITs in question define the term 'investment' fairly broadly: the term is generally defined to comprise every kind of asset connected with direct or indirect participation in companies, associations and joint venture, whether such participation is taken in cash, in kind or in services. The term includes, inter alia, title to money, goodwill and other assets and to any performance having economic value.

no assistance in this matter, it is to first principles and to conceptual considerations that one would need to turn for clarity on the treatment of deposits as protected investments. It is to those principles and considerations that tribunals would presumably turn if faced with an actual investment dispute.

As it happens, there are arguments both ways, depending on the perspective from which the question is approached. The author has presented those arguments in some detail in one of his earlier works.[17] Suffice it, nevertheless, to make the following observations here.

There are, clearly, a number of similarities between bank deposits and investments. They include the following: (i) both bank deposits and investments in equity/transferable securities, bonds or shares in mutual funds/unit trusts are assets from the point of view of their holder/owner and liabilities from that of their debtor; (ii) both bank bonds and deposits in excess of the deposit insurance threshold are unsecured claims of the bondholder or the depositor, respectively, on the bank; (iii) both cash deposits and investments are intended as income-producing or capital generating assets, and both carry a certain measure of risk, although the differences between deposits and investments can be substantial in terms of their risk profile; and finally, (iv) bank deposits are one of a number of 'investment' options available to the holders of excess cash, meaning that saving products (such as bank deposits) are in competition with (or can be substitutes for) investment products, depending on the risk aversion and economic needs of different economic agents. However, there are also a number of considerable differences between bank deposits and investments, some of which are legally significant. For instance: (i) investments typically involve the transformation of capital into an asset: this element of transformation of cash or cash-equivalents into other assets is altogether lacking in the case of bank deposits;[18] (ii) the return on deposits is guaranteed, whereas that on investments is not: the absence of risk (in terms of return) undermines the claim of equivalence between deposits and other investments;[19] (iii) bank depositors do not intend, nor do they perceive, their investments as risk-taking activities:

[17] Phoebus Athanassiou, 'Are Bank Deposits Investments? A Legal and Economic Analysis' (2014) 29(12) J Intl Banking L and Regulation 713.

[18] Thus, the purchase of bank shares, bank bonds or certificates of deposit would qualify as an investment, because of the element of transformation of cash into another valuable instrument, which such purchases entail, while the opening of a bank account would not.

[19] Because investments involve risk, there is no guarantee of the return promised on them. Deposits, on the other hand, represent monetary claims of the

risk-taking with a view to wealth-generation is one of the hallmarks of investment business, and its distinguishing feature compared to custody business and speculation; save in exceptional circumstances, i.e., when a bank is resolved or becomes insolvent, deposits are not perceived nor are they intended by depositors to involve risk-taking (if anything, what bank deposits are generally thought of as is risk-elimination tools, since cash deposited with a bank is safer than cash under the mattress);[20] (iv) the regulatory treatment of deposits is different from that of investment products;[21] and (v) unlike investors in a bank, bank depositors do not own an identifiable asset: cash deposits are inverted by banks in their lending business, being co-mingled (mixed) with those of other depositors, as a result of which one's cash deposits are no longer identifiable as one's own; with investments, by contrast, investors own an identifiable asset[22] (hence, the failure of the fund manager administering that asset

---

depositor against the bank for the redemption of principal, incremented by the contractually agreed interest rate.

[20] Inflation is the only risk acceptable to most depositors in the natural course of things. This element of *perception* may be crucial from a legal point of view (however irrelevant it may be in economic terms), as perceptions may give rise to (justiciable) legitimate expectations.

[21] The difference in treatment is reflected, for instance, in the Market in Financial Instruments Directive's definitions of 'investment services' and 'investment activities', which, subject to minor exceptions are silent on deposits, in the different (lesser) degree of protection that the Investor Compensation Schemes Directive affords to investors, as compared with the level of protection afforded to depositors under Directive 94/19/EC, as amended, and in the many exceptions to investor protection under the Investor Compensation Schemes Directive (for which there is no equivalent in the case of deposit protection). These differences reflect, in all probability, the lower risk profile of deposits, which warrants a greater level of coverage and which sets them apart from investments. See Directive 2004/39/EC of the European Parliament and of the Council on Markets in Financial Instruments [2004] OJ L145/1.

[22] The following excerpt from the SCC ruling of 7 June 2013 (n 13) is revealing:

> The relationship between a depositor and the Cyprus Popular Bank is a creditor-debtor relationship. Creditors essentially deliver their money to the bank, and this money is absorbed into the bank's assets, becoming those of the bank from then on, with the bank owing to the depositor the amount of his deposit in accordance with the conditions of the contract of deposit. Depositors' bank accounts do not grant them a right over a specific sum of money: instead, they represent their exact give-and-take, by way of an account, with the bank, in the form of a written statement of their contractual relationship. The position of a depositor to a bank safe deposit box is entirely different, as

should have no incidence on the investor's ownership of it).[23] There are other differences between certain types of deposits and investments, which are also worth mentioning in passing: *first*, deposits tend to be more liquid and readily accessible compared to most forms of investments (with the exception of transferable securities traded in a regulated market or liquid commodities), even fixed-term deposits can be withdrawn on demand, despite the substantial fees and penalties applied by banks to their withdrawal prior to the agreed maturity; *second*, investments often have a higher degree of permanence compared to bank deposits; *third*, investment products are treated differently, from a revenue law perspective, compared to investment products (which attract tax liability and, in the case of transferable security-type investments, may also attract stamp duty); and *finally*, investment products are treated differently from deposits from the point of view of prudential capital adequacy requirements.

It follows that, unless national law or a BIT explicitly provide so, there is no clarity as to whether deposits qualify as investments.[24] Much will depend on the point of view from which the question is approached. In economic terms deposits may well qualify as investments. In legal or financial terms they may not. Much will also depend on the *type* of deposits at stake (an overnight deposit is unlikely to qualify as an investment, and the same is probably true of a deposit that is remunerated at a negative rate; conversely, a high-yielding deposit or a fixed-term

---

the depositor maintains ownership over the specific sums of money or other objects placed in that safe deposit box (author's translation).

[23] This difference is (or may be) legally significant in a bank insolvency scenario, where assets identifiable as those of a given natural or legal person may need to be separated from the bank's insolvency estate before the bank is put into liquidation.

[24] The same would, incidentally, be true of *other* types of assets, as a 2015 International Centre for Settlement of Investment Disputes (ICSID) tribunal award would suggest, in connection with sovereign bonds. The reference is to *Poštová Banka, as and Istrokapital SE v The Hellenic Republic,* ICSID Case No ARB/13/8, Award (9 April 2015), where an ICSID Tribunal dismissed, for lack of jurisdiction, a claim brought against the Hellenic Republic, as issuer of sovereign bonds, purchased, in the secondary market, by private claimants, and subsequently subjected to a haircut, on the occasion of the Greek Private Sector Initiative of February-March 2012. The haircut led the claimants to initiate arbitration in May 2013 under the Slovakia–Greece and the Cyprus–Greece BITs. The claims were dismissed, inter alia, on the basis that neither one of the claimants held a protected 'investment' within the meaning of the BITs in question.

deposit are closer to an investment) and on their *amount* (deposits may not be investments up to the amount guaranteed by deposit insurance; they may, however, qualify as investments for the unsecured amount).

Faced with litigation brought by depositors claiming a breach of a BIT, where the BIT in question does not explicitly treat depositors as protected 'investors' and their deposits as protected 'investments', one would expect the State (as defendant) to raise some of the arguments presented above to challenge the claimants' standing as 'investors' and, consequently, their right to bring a claim under the terms of a BIT that their country of origin may have entered into with the defendant State. Herein lies the less compelling point in what is an otherwise very lucid contribution to this volume by Mendelson and Paparinskis: without clarity on the key question of whether or not the deposits of parties hailing from jurisdictions that the home country of a prospective defendant has entered into a BIT with will qualify as 'investments', it is somewhat difficult to meaningfully discuss the, admittedly, very important, follow-up question of whether, and to what extent, bail-ins might amount to breaches of the terms of the relevant BIT and, through it, of international investment law. As explained above, this key question is one to which no universal answer is possible and in connection with which many BITs are singularly unhelpful (even if one would, instinctively, expect otherwise).

The above observations do not diminish the originality of the contribution of Mendelson and Paparinskis, nor do they undermine its basic premise that investment protection law has an important role to play in framing the response of States to crisis situations. What they do is to shed light on a pre-condition for their analysis to be relevant in the context of litigation initiated by foreign depositors against national bail-in measures (and, possibly, to an issue that may inform the contents of future BITs, especially those involving highly indebted sovereigns).

IV. OBSERVATIONS ON DE LUCA'S CONTRIBUTION: CAUSAL LINK BETWEEN THE DAMAGE AND THE ACT OF THE COMPETENT NATIONAL AUTHORITY

In her contribution, De Luca looks at bank rescue measures from a particular angle: in essence, she seeks to ascertain whether foreign depositors or shareholders can claim to be prejudiced by rescue measures when the bank itself had already been in dire financial straits. The conclusion to which De Luca comes is that the near-insolvency of a bank, which subsequently becomes subject to resolution measures, and any wrongful or imprudent conduct by its managers or shareholders (or, even, by the claimant-creditor), can be a proximate cause for any losses suffered by the creditor-claimant, thus breaking the chain of causation between the measures taken by the resolution authority and the damage suffered by the claimant.[25] The same would apply, *a fortiori*, where the damages claimed are the results of an extraneous event (e.g., a systemic crisis). In either of the above cases, depositor or shareholder claims for damages against the resolution authorities and, through them, against the State, would be doomed to fail. As a consequence, shareholder or depositor claims ought to be directed not against the State but against the distressed bank itself.

This author would agree that the appropriate defendant in an action brought by an aggrieved depositor may well be the distressed bank itself, and would, in this regard, draw attention to the ruling of the SCC of 7 June 2013, and to the hierarchy of potential respondents that it establishes, which, in the author's view, was intended.[26] The author would also agree with De Luca that the competent national authorities and, through them, the State, should only be brought into the picture if the claimants can establish a clear case of supervisory failure to which their alleged loss/damage is directly attributable.[27] For the reasons explained by this author in an earlier work,[28] it can be very difficult for claimants to substantiate claims against supervisors under domestic law, except in the most flagrant cases of failed supervision. Turning to the issue of the impact of European Union (EU) law on the third-party liability of financial supervisors, the conclusion reached by this author in his earlier research is that, to the extent that prudential supervisory standards are derived from obligations enshrined in EU law, deficient

[25] De Luca (n 2) 232 ff.

[26] The SCC, inter alia, stated in its ruling of 7 June 2013 (n 13) that: '[C]ertainly, one should not forget that the object of civil proceedings can only be the financial loss suffered by the depositors due to the actions of the banks, the state or the European Union bodies involved (in the depositor's bail-in)' (author's translation).

[27] For thoughts on whether such supervisory duties have hardened in recent years, see De Luca (n 2) 239 ff.

[28] Phoebus Athanassiou, 'Bank Supervisors' Accountability: A European Perspective', ECB Legal Working Paper Series, No12, August 2011 <www.ecb.europa.eu/pub/pdf/scplps/ecblwp12.pdf> accessed 30 December 2015.

supervision could, in principle, provide a basis for claims for damages based on EU law. However, to date, there has been no successful claim against financial supervisors brought on the basis of the *Francovich*[29] doctrine, despite the wide scope for successful claims against negligent supervisors that this appears to allow.[30]

At the same time, and without prejudice to the merits of De Luca's causality argument, and its common-sense appeal, it could be argued that the core issue here is not so much one of causality but one of the substantive rights guaranteed under a BIT, which makes it essential to examine claims against States and their national authorities first from the point of view of the compliance of national action with the terms of a BIT, taking into account both the safeguards that international investment law provides in the case of foreign nationals, benefiting from the protection of a BIT.

Another perspective from which the legality of national action can be examined, causality considerations aside, is that of the fairness of the treatment that depositors have received, and the consistency of such treatment with the property rights protections accruing to individuals, whether under the relevant national Constitution or under the European Convention on Human Rights (ECHR) and international standards of human rights protection.[31] The wording of Article 1 of the First Additional Protocol to the ECHR (on the right to the peaceful enjoyment by individuals of their possessions) leaves no doubt that the rights protected under it are *not* absolute. Moreover, as the case law of the European Court of Human Rights (ECtHR) readily demonstrates, measures restricting an individual's property rights may be taken in the public interest. As

---

[29] Joined Cases C-6/90 & 9/90 *Francovich and Bonifaci v Italy* [1991] ECR I-5357.

[30] The full scope of the principle of State liability was clarified in another landmark ruling of the Court of Justice of the European Union, Joined Cases C-46/93 and C-48/93 *Brasserie du Pêcheur and Factortame* [1996] ECR I-1029 *(Factortame III),* where the Court (33) held that:

> [T]he full effectiveness of EC law would be impaired and the protection of the rights which they grant would be weakened if individuals were unable to obtain redress when their rights are infringed by a breach of Community law for which a Member State can be held responsible

and that it did not matter *which* State organ was responsible for the breach (ibid 31–32).

[31] Property right guarantees also appear in art. 6 of the Treaty on the European Union (TEU) and art. 17 of the Charter of Fundamental Rights of the EU.

the ECtHR has stated, '[the Contracting States] enjoy a wider margin of appreciation [of public interest] in delicate areas such as the stability of the banking system'.[32] The ECtHR has given public interest a wide interpretation, and where the legislature intervenes in an area of economic or social policy, the ECtHR will respect the State's assessment unless this is manifestly flawed. The case law of the ECtHR has also recognised proportionality as a second condition for the lawful restriction of property rights. Proportionality effectively requires that a fair balance be struck between the demands of the community and the protection of individual interests.[33] Finally, it follows from the case law of the ECtHR that the possibility of obtaining compensation is an important element in assessing the proportionality (and, ultimately, the legitimacy) of restrictions imposed on the enjoyment, by individuals, of their property rights. In its decision in *Dennis Grainger and Others v UK*,[34] the ECtHR assessed the legitimacy, from a property rights protection perspective, of zero compensation awards and, in the circumstances of that case, found them to be consistent with human rights protection.

Similarly, the importance of the NCWO principle, as the ultimate yardstick against which to measure the legitimacy of any bail-in measure, and the burden of proof it places on applicants, should not be underestimated in assessing the legality of national resolution action: even assuming the resolution authority and, through it, the State to be the appropriate defendant, no resolution-related claim in damages against them will succeed unless aggrieved depositors can substantiate that their financial position has become less favourable on account of the implementation of the resolution measures, compared to what it would have been if the affected institution was, instead, put into liquidation. Several of the national recovery and resolution regimes currently in place treat compliance with the NCWO principle as the key substantive and procedural safeguard to be observed in resolution.[35] Unless it can be shown that this principle has, in a given case, been disregarded, the key

---

[32] *Camberrow MM5 AD v Bulgaria*, App no 50357/99 (EctHR, 1 April 2004).

[33] See, for instance, ECtHR judgements of 1 March 2001 in *Malama v Greece* (App No 43622/98) and 2 February 2010 in *Aizpurúa Ortiz et al v Spain* (App No 42430/05).

[34] App no 34940/10 (ECtHR, 10 July 2012).

[35] The UK, Greece, Spain and Cyprus are among the jurisdictions where an explicit statutory right to compensation applies for creditors that are worse off in resolution than they would have been in a liquidation scenario. For an account of the relevant national laws, see Athanassiou (n 14) 16–18.

legal question would not so much be whether the chain of causality between the acts of the resolution authority and the loss sustained by depositors has been broken by the acts or omissions of the failed bank and/or its management, but whether resolution was a legitimate choice for the resolution authority, also from the point of view of the protection of creditor/depositor rights. For, one of the benefits of compliance with the NCWO principle is precisely that it obviates the need for other, more disruptive, procedural safeguards to be observed as part of the recovery and resolution process, including the *ex ante* judicial review of resolution decisions: the obligation to provide compensation to creditors receiving lower returns compared to those they would expect to receive in a liquidation scenario replaces such other procedural safeguards (while at the same time guaranteeing the efficiency of resolution).

It is, therefore, submitted that while causality is one of the important issues at stake in the context of litigation pitting aggrieved depositors against States – and, to that extent, De Luca rightly draws attention to it – there are certain other, no-less important issues, that a court would be expected to examine if faced with litigation arising from a depositor bail-in. These are: first, the compliance of resolution measures with the substantive rights guaranteed under a BIT (where the interests of foreign depositors are at stake); second, their consistency with human rights law, whether nationally or under the ECHR (with an emphasis on the protection of property rights); and, third, their compliance with the NCWO principle as the litmus test of their legitimacy. What is fair to say is that the probative demands that human rights law and the NCWO principle place on applicants are so high that, even if national resolution authorities were to be the appropriate respondents in an action in damages brought by depositors prejudiced by national resolution measures, the probability of success of a legal challenge brought against them would appear remote, save in cases of egregious breaches of human rights law or manifest misuse of the resolution authorities' discretion to mandate the resolution of a bank (instead of its liquidation). But it need not be the same of a claim premised on the substantive rights recognized under a BIT, which, depending on its concrete provisions, as well as on its definitions of protected 'depositor' and 'protected deposit', may well represent a potent tool in the hands of an aggrieved depositor.

V. CONCLUDING REMARKS

International investment law is one of the areas that national governments faced with a banking crisis and national resolution authorities will need to have regard to, in deciding how to respond and in assessing the legal risks that resolution action may entail. The contributions commented on here have the merit of bringing this point to the fore, attributing to it the prominence it would deserve, but which it has not, so far, received either in the literature or in the public debate surrounding bank resolution in crisis situations. The contributors thus merit recognition for rendering a service to policy-makers and lawyers alike in what is the fairly litigious environment of bank resolution and bank bail-ins.

At the same time, international investment law is only one piece of the puzzle. For the reasons briefly touched on in this chapter, conceptual considerations, of relevance to the fundamental nature of deposits and their treatment in a bail-in scenario, human rights law and the NCWO principle predictably occupy centre stage in the legal and policy debate surrounding bank resolution. This chapter has sought to draw attention to these consideration, less by way of an original contribution to the academic debate (such as those that the contributors to this volume can rightfully boast) and more as a useful and, inevitably, modest reminder, lest the reader be carried away by the force of some of the original thinking propounded by the contributors to this volume.

PART IV

Alternative claims and defences: New actors

11. Capital-flow management measures and international investment law: Never the twain shall meet?

Prabhash Ranjan[1]

I. INTRODUCTION

BITs are bilateral treaties to protect investments made by investors of both countries.[2] There are more than 3000 Bilateral Investment Treaties (BITs) currently in force[3] and these treaties are the most important source of modern international investment law. This network of treaties has been described as the BIT regime.[4] The first BIT was signed in 1959 between Germany and Pakistan as a 'Treaty for the Promotion and Protection of Investments'.[5] Since 1959 to the end of 2013, a total of

[1] The author is extremely grateful to Christian J Tams for his very useful comments on the draft chapter and to Haris Jamil of the South Asian University for his very able research assistance.

[2] Jeswald W Salacuse, 'BIT by BIT: The Growth of Bilateral Investment Treaties and Their Impact on Foreign Investment in Developing Countries' (1990) 24 Intl Lawyer 503. For a general discussion on BITs see, M Sornarajah, *The International Law on Foreign Investment* (CUP 2004) 204–314; Rudolf Dolzer and Christoph Schreuer, *Principles of International Investment Law* (2nd edn, OUP 2012) 13; Andrew Newcombe and Lluís Paradell, *Law and Practice of Investment Treaties: Standards of Treatment* (Kluwer Law International 2009) 1–73; Jeswald W Salacuse, *The Law of Investment Treaties* (OUP 2010) 21; Kenneth J Vandevelde, *Bilateral Investment Treaties: History, Policy and Interpretation* (OUP 2010)

[3] Dolzer and Schreuer (n 2); Jeswald W Salacuse, 'The Treatification of International Investment Law' (2007) 13 Law & Bus Rev Am 155, 157.

[4] Salacuse, *The Law of Investment Treaties* (n 2) 21.

[5] Vandevelde (n 2) 1.

3236 BITs have been concluded.[6] These BITs contain numerous substantive provisions, including on the criteria for lawful expropriation; the obligation to treat foreign investments fairly and equitably; the obligation not to discriminate against foreign investments in favour of domestic investments or in favour of investment from some other foreign investor; and, and most importantly, the possibility for foreign investors to bring cases against host States via international arbitration for breaches of the BIT, in order to obtain compensation.[7]

The focus of this chapter is on another important substantive provision contained in BITs, the monetary transfer provision (MTP). MTPs in BITs regulate the transfer of funds related to investment in and out of the host country.[8] Broadly speaking, one can classify MTPs into two categories or types: 'Type I' imposes a broad and unqualified obligation on host countries to guarantee transfer of funds in and out of the country without any exceptions. In other words, such clauses do not explicitly recognise

[6] This includes 2902 stand-alone investment treaties and 334 investment chapters in Free Trade Agreements, see UNCTAD, *World Investment Report 2014: Investing in the SDGs: An Action Plan* (United Nations 2014) 114.

[7] Dolzer and Schreuer (n 2); Salacuse *The Law of Investment Treaties* (n 2).

[8] For comment see Michael Waibel, 'BIT by BIT – The Silent Liberalization of the Capital Account' in Christina Binder and others (eds), *International Investment Law for the 21st Century: Essays in the Honour of Christoph Schreuer* (OUP 2009) 497; Salacuse, *The Law of Investment Treaties* (n 2) 256–71; Abba Kolo and Thomas Wälde, 'Capital Transfer Restrictions under Modern Investment Treaties' in August Reinisch (ed.), *Standards of Investment Protection* (OUP 2008) 205; Rudolph Dolzer and C Schreuer *Principles of International Investment Law* (1st edn, OUP 2008) 212–15; Kevin P Gallagher, *Policy Space to Prevent and Mitigate Financial Crises in Trade and Investment Agreements* (UNCTAD G-24 Discussion Paper No 58, 2010); Sarah Anderson, 'Policy Handcuffs in the Financial Crisis: How U.S. Trade and Investment Policies Limit Government Power to Control Capital Flows' (Institute for Policy Studies, Washington DC 2009) <www.bilaterals.org/IMG/pdf/Policy_Handcuffs_in_the_Financial_Crisis.pdf> accessed 2 March 2016; Alejandro Turyn and Facundo Perez Aznar, 'Drawing the Limits of Free Transfer Provision' in Michael Waibel and others (eds), The *Backlash Against Investment Arbitration* (Kluwer Law International 2010) 51–78; Peter T Muchlinski, 'Trends in International Investment Agreements: Balancing Investor Rights and the Right to Regulate: The Issue of National Security' (2009) 1 Yrbk Intl Invest L& Pol 35, 59–61; Vandevelde (n 2) 316–33.

the imposition of capital-flow management measures (CFM measures)[9] by host States. A good example of Type I MTP is Article V of the United States-Argentina BIT,[10] which obligates the host country to permit 'all transfers related to an investment', 'freely' and 'without delay'. There is no mention of any exception to this obligation.[11]

Type II MTPs, while imposing an obligation to permit all transfers related to investment, do mention exceptions: they identify circumstances under which the host country is allowed to deviate from its obligations.[12] A good example of Type II MTP is Article 12 of the Japan-Korea BIT.[13] This Article imposes the same obligations as Article V of the US-Argentina BIT, i.e., the obligation to allow transfers of all funds

---

[9] MTPs in BITs should not to be confused with admission requirement clauses where a host State is under an obligation to admit new investments: see UNCTAD, 'Transfer of Funds' (2000) UNCTAD/ITE/IIT/20, 32 <http://unctad.org/en/docs/psiteiitd20.en.pdf> accessed 2 March 2016.

This term is borrowed from Kristin Forbes and others, 'Capital Controls and Macroprudential Measures: What Are They Good For?' (DIW Berlin, Discussion Paper No 1343, 2013) <www.diw.de/documents/publikationen/73/diw_01.c.433707.de/dp1343.pdf> accessed 2 March 2016. In simple terms, CFM measures refer to controls adopted by host States to regulate the inflow and outflow of funds. For more detail please see below, section II.

[10] Article V of the Treaty between United States of America and the Argentine Republic Concerning the Reciprocal Encouragement and Protection of Investment (US-Argentina BIT) (signed 14 November 1991, entered into force 20 October 1994) IC-BT 384 (1991):

> Each Party shall permit all transfers related to an investment to be made freely and without delay into and out of its territory. Such transfers include: (a) returns; (b) compensation pursuant to Article IV; (c) payments arising out of an investment dispute; (d) payments made under a contract, including amortization of principal and accrued interest payments made pursuant to a loan agreement directly related to an investment; (e) proceeds from the sale or liquidation of all or any part of an investment; and (f) additional contributions to capital for the maintenance or development of an investment.

[11] It is worth noting that MTPs impose obligations on host States for inward investment and not outward investment. Thus, the discussion in this chapter is with regard to transfer of funds related to inward foreign investment.

[12] See the discussion on such BITs in Salacuse, *The Law of Investment Treaties* (n 2) 266–70.

[13] Agreement Between the Government of the Republic of Korea and the Government of Japan for the Liberalisation, Promotion and Protection of Investment (Japan-Republic of Korea BIT) (signed 22 March 2002, entered into force 1 January 2003) IC-BT 855 (2002).

related to an investment freely and without delay.[14] However, Article 17(1) of the same BIT allows the host State to maintain measures not conforming with the obligation imposed by Article 12 in certain situations, e.g., when there exists a 'serious balance of payment and external financial difficulties or threat thereof'.[15] Thus, this BIT allows host States to deviate from the obligation to permit free transfer of funds related to an investment in certain situation of macroeconomic crisis. Also, Article 17(3)[16] provides that nothing in the BIT alters the rights enjoyed and obligations undertaken by both countries under the Articles of the

---

[14] Article 12(1) of Japan-Republic of Korea BIT provides:

> Each Contracting Party shall ensure that all payments relating to an investment in its territory of an investor of the other Contracting Party may be freely transferred into and out of its territory without delay. Such transfer shall include, in particular, though not exclusively: (a) the initial capital and additional amounts to maintain or increase an investment; (b) profits, interest, dividends, capital gains, royalties or fees; (c) payments made under a contract including a loan agreement; (d) proceeds of the total or partial sale or liquidation of investments; (e) payments made in accordance with Articles 10 and 11; (f) payments arising out of the settlement of a dispute under Article 15; and (g) earnings and remuneration of personnel engaged from the other Contracting Party in connection with an investment.

[15] Article 17(1) of the Japan-Republic of Korea BIT provides:

> A Contracting Party may adopt or maintain measures not conforming with its obligations under paragraph 1 of Article 2 relating to cross-border capital transactions and Article 12 of this Agreement: (a) in the event of serious balance-of-payments and external financial difficulties or threat thereof; or (b) in cases where, in exceptional circumstances, movements of capital cause or threaten to cause serious difficulties for macroeconomic management, in particular, monetary and exchange rate policies.

Article 17(2) provides:

> Measures referred to in paragraph 1 of this Article: (a) shall be consistent with the Articles of Agreement of the International Monetary Fund so long as the Contracting Party taking the measures is a party to the said Articles of Agreement; (b) shall not exceed those necessary to deal with the circumstances set out in paragraph 1 of this Article; (c) shall be temporary and shall be eliminated as soon as conditions permit; and (d) shall be promptly notified to the other Contracting Party.

[16] Article 17(3) of the Japan-Republic of Korea BIT provides: 'Nothing in this Agreement shall be regarded as altering the rights enjoyed and obligations undertaken by a Contracting Party as a party to the Articles of Agreement of the International Monetary Fund.'

International Monetary Fund (IMF Articles).[17] In other words, the BIT purposefully does not 'interfere' with the approach to monetary transfers taken in the IMF Articles.

While MTP clauses of Type II raise particular problems going to the interpretation of exceptions, Type I clauses implicate CFM measures directly. Accordingly, this chapter tackles the question whether the imposition of such measures (not just in situations of severe economic crisis but also in situations related to achieving various macroeconomic objectives like stabilising appreciating domestic currency following massive inflows) will violate Type I MTPs. This question arose in the *Continental Casualty v Argentina*[18] case, which involved the abovementioned Type I MTP clause of the US-Argentina BIT. Argentina had imposed certain restrictions on the transfer of funds out of the country[19] due to a severe economic crisis;[20] these measures were challenged by the foreign investor,[21] who alleged that they violated the MTP in the US-Argentina BIT.[22] As will be shown below, an analysis of these questions involves intricate questions of norm conflict and systemic interpretation.

In addressing these questions, the chapter starts by introducing CFMs and the different ways by which international law regulates the freedom of States to impose them (section II). It then analyses the relationship between the different approaches adopted under the IMF Articles on the one hand, and BITs on the other; this involves an inquiry into questions of norm conflict as well as systemic treaty interpretation (section III).

---

[17] Articles of Agreement of the International Monetary Fund (adopted 22 July 1944, came into force 27 December 1945) 2 UNTS 39 <www.imf.org/external/pubs/ft/aa/pdf/aa.pdf> accessed 2 March 2016.

[18] *Continental Casualty Company v Argentine Republic*, ICSID Case No ARB/03/9, Award (5 September 2008).

[19] Argentina issued Decree 1570 of 2001 (*Corralito*) which forbade withdrawals from banks and transfers of funds out of Argentina – See para. 237.

[20] For a detailed description of the Argentine economic crisis, see Jim Saxton, 'Argentina's Economic Crisis: Causes and Cures' (Joint Economic Committee, United States Congress, Washington, DC, 2003) <www.hacer.org/pdf/Schuler.pdf> accessed 2 March 2016; IMF, The IMF and Argentina: 1991-2001 (IEO-Evaluation Report 2004) <www.imf.org/external/np/ieo/2004/arg/eng/pdf/report.pdf> accessed 2 March 2016; 'Argentina's Collapse: A Decline Without Parallel' *The Economist* (Special Report) (2 March 2002); Paul Blustein, *And the Money Kept Rolling In (and Out): Wall Street, The IMF and the Bankrupting of Argentina* (Public Affairs 2005) 23–4.

[21] See *Continental Casualty* (n 18) paras 62, 237.

[22] Ibid.

Having discussed rules specifically addressing CFM measures, the chapter moves on to discuss alternative options for host countries to respond on the basis of generally available defences (section IV). The chapter finally concludes by observing that the method to resolve the conflict is through the legislative route where countries enter into Type II MTPs that recognise the right of countries to impose CFM measures (section V).

II. INTRODUCING CFM MEASURES AND MTPS

In order to appreciate their interaction, it is first necessary to introduce CFM measures and monetary transfer provisions potentially limiting the power of States to impose them.

A. CFM Measures

The Permanent Court of International Justice (PCIJ) in the *Serbian Loans* case,[23] in 1929, stated that it is generally accepted principle that a State is entitled to regulate its own currency.[24] In other words, a State has sovereignty over its currency; it enjoys monetary sovereignty, which includes sovereignty over internal and external monetary and financial systems.[25] More specifically, it means a State's monetary sovereignty under general international law extends to regulating how much capital comes in or goes out of the country because this could have an impact on the State's currency.[26] Indeed, under general international law States are not required to permit foreign investors to freely transfer currency into or out of their boundaries.[27]

---

[23] *Case Concerning the Payment of Various Serbian Loans Issued in France (France v Serbia)* PCIJ Rep Series A Nos 20–21 (12 July 1929).

[24] Ibid., 44. Also see, *Julliard v Greenmann* 110 US 421 (1884).

[25] Charles Proctor, *Mann on the Legal Aspect of Money* (6th edn, OUP 2005) 500; Claus D Zimmermann, 'The Concept of Monetary Sovereignty Revisited' (2013) 24 EJIL 797; Rosa Maria Lastra, *Legal Foundations of International Monetary Stability* (OUP 2006) 22; Asif H Qureshi and Andreas Ziegler, *International Economic Law* (Sweet & Maxwell 2011) 147–8; Jeswald W Salacuse, *The Three Laws of International Investment* (OUP 2013) 76–7. Michael Waibel, *Sovereign Defaults Before International Courts and Tribunals* (CUP 2011) 58–60.

[26] Salacuse (n 25) 76.

[27] Vandevelde (n 2) 317.

CFMs are one way for States to regulate the entry or exit of currency or capital, or more broadly, transfer of funds. Absent specific agreements to the contrary, international law permits countries to impose CFMs, including in situations such as balance of payment crisis, macroeconomic difficulty or instability caused by volatile financial markets.[28] CFMs have been variously categorised, e.g., by distinguishing capital controls that discriminate based on residency from macroprudential measures relating to cross-border or foreign-currency exposure and lending that do not discriminate based on residency.[29] They include restrictions such as requiring that foreign capital invested should stay in the host country for a minimum period,[30] or imposing taxes on inward investment.[31] Countries can also impose exchange controls, such as restricting the ability to convert domestic currency into foreign currency.[32]

Many countries have successfully adopted CFM measures as a policy tool to regulate the inflow or outflow of capital in accordance with their policy priorities. For example, during the 1990s Chile adopted CFM measures to stem the short-term volatile inflow of capital and was successful in altering the composition of the capital inflow to medium- and long-term capital inflows.[33] During the Asian financial crisis of 1998,[34] Malaysia adopted a variety of capital regulation measures, such

---

[28] Mahvash S Qureshi and others, 'Managing Capital Inflows: Role of Capital Controls and Prudential Policies' (2011) NBER Working Paper 17363 <http://www.nber.org/papers/w17363.pdf> accessed 2 March 2016; Forbes and others (n 9). Also see, Nicholas Magud and Carmen M Reinhart, 'Capital Controls: An Evaluation' (2006) NBER Working Paper 11973 <www.nber.org/chapters/c0157.pdf> accessed 2 March 2015.

[29] Forbes and others (n 9) 1–6.

[30] Gallagher (n 8) 4.

[31] Andrew Yianni and Carlos De Vera, 'The Return of Capital Controls?' (2010) 73 L & Contemp Prob 357, 358. Brazil used this control measure against short-term capital inflows in order to discourage these flows. Markus Jaeger, 'Brazil Fights Capital Inflows' (Deutsche Bank Research, 15 December 2009) <www.dbresearch.com/PROD/DBR_INTERNET_EN-PROD/PROD0000000000251631.pdf> accessed 2 March 2016.

[32] Yianni and De Vera (n 31) 358.

[33] Guillermo Le Fort and Sergio Lehmann, 'The Unremunerated Reserve Requirement and Net Capital Flows: Chile in 1990s' (2003) 81 Cepal Review 33, 50.

[34] Five countries in East Asia – South Korea, Thailand, Malaysia, Indonesia and Philippines – faced a financial crisis in 1997 when there was a turnaround of $86 billion of capital flows from a net inflow of $66 billion in 1996 to a net outflow of $20 billion in 1997. This volatility in capital flows resulted in depreciation of the currencies of these countries against the US dollar and

as imposing a one-year ban on outflows and charging taxes on outflows (graduated taxes based on length of stay).[35] Colombia's capital controls helped it to mitigate some of the adverse effect of the global financial crisis of 2008.[36] It has also been stated that countries that adopted capital controls in the years leading to the financial crisis of 2008 were among the least hard hit by the crisis.[37]

B. Regulating CFMs: The IMF Articles

Various rules of international law deal with CFMs. Before addressing MTP provisions found in BITs, it may be useful to outline the position taken by the International Monetary Fund (IMF). As regards its political stance, the IMF had for some time argued for outlawing controls on capital account transactions.[38] However, more recently, it has recognised that in certain situations countries may have to impose CFM measures like capital controls;[39] thus, capital controls are now generally seen as an

---

combined with other factors resulted in drastically reducing the growth rate of these countries. For more on the crisis see – Chakravarthi Rangrajan, 'Capital Flows – Another Look' (2000) 35 EPW 4421; Masahiro Kawai, Richard Newfarmer and Sergio L Schmukler, 'Crisis and Contagion in East Asia: Nine Lessons' (2001) World Bank Policy Research Working Paper WSP2610.

[35] Ricardo French-Davis and others, 'Financial Stability and Trans Pacific Partnership: Lessons from Chile and Malaysia' (2013) GEGI Working Paper No 2 <www.bu.edu/pardee/files/2013/09/Working-Paper-October-13.pdf> accessed 2 March 2016.

[36] Bruno Coelho and Kevin P Gallagher, 'Capital Controls and 21st Century Financial Crises: Evidence from Colombia and Thailand' (2010) PERI Working Paper Series No 213 <www.peri.umass.edu/fileadmin/pdf/working_papers/working_papers_201-250/WP213.pdf> accessed 2 March 2016.

[37] Jonathan D Ostry and others, 'Managing Capital Inflows: What Tools to Use?' (IMF Staff Discussion Paper, Washington, D.C. 5 April 2011) <www.imf.org/external/pubs/ft/sdn/2011/sdn1106.pdf> accessed 2 March 2016. Recently, Brazilian President, Dilma Rousseff, rebuked industrialised countries for creating a 'liquidity tsunami' of speculative capital, which is being tackled by Brazil by extending the tax on speculative inflows of capital in Brazil – See, Kevin Gallagher, 'Taming the Liquidity Tide' *The Financial Times* (8 March 2012). The global financial crisis of 2008 has brought CFM measures like capital controls 'back into focus as a means to respond to a crisis', Yianni and De Vera (n 31) 357.

[38] Stanley Fischer, 'Globalization and Its Challenges' (2003) 93 Am Ec Rev 1, 9. See also Waibel (n 8) 501; Qureshi and Ziegler (n 25) 217.

[39] IMF, 'The Liberalisation and Management of Capital Flows – An Institutional View' (14 November 2012) <www.imf.org/external/np/pp/eng/2012/

important tool in a country's policy arsenal.[40] This view is in line with the IMF Articles, which allow (and have always allowed) its member countries to impose restrictions on their capital account transactions. More specifically, Article VI.3 of the Articles provides that member countries may impose controls as are necessary to regulate international capital movement.[41] According to Sir Joseph Gold, Article VI.3 was necessary 'because of the destabilising effects that flows of "hot money" had in the period before the IMF came into existence'.[42] However, member countries, while exercising control on international capital movement, have to ensure that these controls are not exercised in a manner that will restrict payments on current accounts, since the IMF Articles prohibit such restrictions. Article VIII.2 (a) of the IMF Articles provides that subject to certain provisions[43] no member country shall impose restrictions on the payment of transfers for current international transactions.[44] Article VIII.2 (a) covers only outflows.[45] If a member country has to impose restrictions on current account restrictions, then it will have to obtain permission from the IMF.[46]

111412.pdf> accessed 2 March 2016; Claus D Zimmermann, *A Contemporary Concept of Monetary Sovereignty* (OUP 2013) 42–3.

[40] Jonathan D Ostry and others, 'Capital Inflows – the Role of Controls' (IMF Staff Position Note SPN/10/04, 19 February 2010) <www.imf.org/external/pubs/ft/spn/2010/spn1004.pdf> accessed 2 March 2016.

[41] Andreas F Lowenfeld, *International Economic Law* (2nd edn OUP 2008) 608.

[42] Joseph Gold, '"Exchange Contracts", Exchange Control, and the IMF Articles of Agreement: Some Animadversions on *Wilson, Smithett & Cope Ltd. v. Terruzzi*' (1984) 33 ICLQ 777, 778–9.

[43] These provisions are – art. VIII.3(b) and art. XIV.2 of the IMF Articles (n 17). It is also important to note that once a country notifies the IMF of its willingness to accept the obligations contained in art. VIII, there is no going back; see Lowenfeld (n 41) 607.

[44] IMF Articles (n 17) art. VIII (2) (a) provides: 'Subject to the provisions of Article VII, Section 3(*b*) and Article XIV, Section 2, no member shall, without the approval of the Fund, impose restrictions on the making of payments and transfers for current international transactions.' A majority of membership of IMF is now under art. VIII regime; see Qureshi and Ziegler (n 25) 205. For a detailed analysis of the IMF Articles and capital and current account transactions see Joseph Gold, 'The Fund's Concepts of Convertibility' (1971) Pamphlet Series of the International Monetary Fund No 14; Richard W Edwards, *International Monetary Collaboration* (Transnational Publishers 1985); Qureshi and Ziegler (n 25) 202–25; Lowenfeld (n 41) 606–22.

[45] Zimmermann (n 39) 50.

[46] IMF Articles (n 17) art. VIII.2.

C. Regulating CFMs: Monetary Transfer Provisions Contained in BITs

MTPs in BITs, as mentioned before, regulate the transfer of funds related to an investment. MTPs in BITs cover transfers related to investments that have been made (such as allowing entry of new capital to augment existing investment or to allow outflow of incomes derived from the investment made). A typical MTP in a BIT identifies the 'transfer' or 'payment' to which the provision applies and also provides the conditions governing such transfers, such as whether the transfer is to be made in foreign currency and whether the transfer can be made promptly.[47] In most BITs, MTPs cover all 'transfers' or 'payments' related to investment.[48] Further, depending on the treaty language, MTPs can cover both inflows and outflows of funds.[49] The 'transfers' include both current transfers (such as the transfer of income derived from investments[50]) and capital transfers (e.g., the transfer of proceeds of liquidation of foreign investment.[51]). Moreover, MTPs also cover additional capital to maintain and increase an investment; net operating profits including dividends; repayment of any loan including interest; proceeds from sales of their shares, etc.[52]

MTPs are an integral part of the protection offered to foreign investment by host States in BITs. They are important for foreign investors because they provide the freedom to transfer all funds related to investment for a number of business-related needs.[53] For example, a foreign investor may need to bring in additional capital to support the existing investment or might need to repatriate capital back to the home country in order to service debts or to pay dividends or to repatriate proceeds of sale of investment, etc.[54] Restrictions on the transfer of funds related to an investment may result in investment not being made in the first place, because foreign investors will be deprived of the benefits accruing from the investment (such as repatriating profits) and will also

---

[47] Vandevelde (n 2) 317.

[48] Ibid.

[49] Ibid., 319.

[50] Zimmermann (n 39) 48.

[51] Ibid., 48. Art. V(e) of the US-Argentina BIT, which provides for transfers related to 'proceeds from the sale or liquidation of all or any part of an investment', will fall in the category of capital transfers.

[52] See US-Argentina BIT (n 10) art. V.

[53] Dolzer and Schreuer (n 8) 191.

[54] Salacuse, *The Law of Investment Treaties* (n 2).

not have the freedom to develop their investment (like bringing in additional capital to support the existing investment).[55]

D. The Relationship Between MTPs and CFMs: 'Contracting Out'

As is clear from the foregoing, MTPs affect the monetary sovereignty of the host State: there is a tension between a State's desire to impose CFMs and its obligations under MTPs. More specifically, for the foreign investor to freely transfer funds out of the country, it is necessary to draw on the host country's foreign exchange reserve (for example, by converting earnings in the local currency into an international currency by drawing from the foreign exchange reserve).[56] However, the host country's foreign exchange reserve is finite and also serves other significant purposes like paying for imports and maintaining the value of the domestic currency.[57] Thus, if the freedom to transfer funds out of the country severely impacts the finite foreign exchange reserve of the host country, the country might be tempted to impose restrictions on the conversion of local currency into foreign currency,[58] which, in turn, impacts the right of the foreign investor to transfer funds out of the country. Similarly, large infusions of capital by the foreign investor can have adverse macroeconomic consequences, such as the appreciation of the country's currency, the consequent reduction of export competitiveness and the widening of the current account deficit; it can also result in inflation by increasing the monetary supply, which can have other adverse macroeconomic consequences.[59] These might also compel the host State to impose restrictions on inflows, which could impact the rights of foreign investors. This brings the imposition of certain kind of CFMs like capital controls in direct potential confrontation with the MTPs in BITs.

Of course, treaty provisions regularly interfere with aspects of State sovereignty.[60] By agreeing to be bound by a treaty provisions, States are

---

[55] Waibel (n 8) 498; Kolo and Wälde (n 8) 213–14.

[56] Vandevelde (n 4) 316.

[57] Ibid.

[58] Ibid.

[59] Salacuse, *The Law of Investment Treaties* (n 2) 256.

[60] There are many examples of treaties contracting out of customary international law. For instance, the Statutes of the International Criminal Tribunal for the former Yugoslavia and the International Criminal Tribunal for the former Rwanda contract out of international law with regard to the immunities traditionally provided to heads of State and members of government. Similarly, the WTO

typically seen to have deviated (as between themselves) from the general legal position. International law allows such contracting out, unless it affects *jus cogens* norms.[61] However, as the *ELSI* case demonstrates, contracting out of customary international law should not be tacit; in other words, in the absence of express provisions, it cannot be presumed that the treaty concerned has contracted out of customary international law.[62] The reason for this is that in international law, there is a presumption that unless or until a treaty expressly contracts out, general international law continues to exist and apply.[63]

In light of this, it might be asked whether Type I MTPs in BITs an example of a treaty 'contracting out' of the general legal position protecting the monetary sovereignty of States? A quick glance at the text of the relevant provisions seems sufficient to answer the question in the affirmative. To illustrate, pursuant to Article V of the US-Argentina BIT:

Agreement's dispute settlement provisions contract out of customary international law of countermeasures. By the same token, most BITs allow foreign investors to directly bring claims against the host State, where the State has consented to investor-State arbitration, without necessarily exhausting domestic local remedies, which would be required under customary international law rules governing diplomatic claims.

[61] Vienna Convention on the Law of Treaties (adopted 23 May 1969, entered into force 27 January 1980) 1155 UNTS 331 (VCLT). Art. 53 of the VCLT clearly states; 'A treaty is void, if at the time of its conclusion, it conflicts with a peremptory norm of general international law.' For comment see Roozbeh B Baker, 'Customary International Law in the 21st Century: Old Challenges and New Debates' (2010) 21 EJIL 173, 176–7; Joost Pauwelyn, *Conflict of Norms in Public International Law* (CUP 2004) 391. Also see Christian J Tams, *Enforcing Obligations Erga Omnes in International Law* (CUP 2005) 261–2. The Appellate Body of the WTO in *United States – Anti Dumping Measures on Certain Hot Rolled Steel Products From Japan* in footnote 40 recognised the possibility of States to 'contract out' of general international law. *United States – Anti-Dumping Measures on Certain Hot-Rolled Steel Products from Japan – Report of the Appellate Body* (24 July 2001) WT/DS184/AB/R.

[62] *Case Concerning Elettronica Sicula SPA (Elsi) (United States of America v Italy)* (Judgment) [1989] ICJ Rep 15, 42, para. 50. Also see, *Legal Consequences for States of the Continued Presence of South Africa in Namibia (South West Africa) notwithstanding Security Council Resolution 276 (1970)* (Advisory Opinion) [1971] ICJ Rep 16, 47, para. 96.

[63] Joost Pauwelyn, 'The Role of Public International Law in the WTO: How Far Can We Go?' (2001) 95 AJIL 535, 541; Campbell McLachlan, 'The Principle of Systemic Integration and Article 31(3)(c) of the Vienna Convention' (2005) 54 ICLQ 279, 313; Jürgen Kurtz, 'Adjudging the Exceptional at International Investment Law: Security, Public Order and Financial Crisis' (2010) 59 ICLQ 325, 354.

'Each party shall permit all transfers related to an investment to be made freely and without delay into and out of its territory'.[64] Thus, the obligation on the host State is to permit 'all' transfer of funds related to a foreign investment across borders (without distinguishing between current account transfers or capital account transfers) 'freely' and 'without delay'. There is no mention of imposition of CFMs by the host State in case of 'transfers related to an investment'. The usage of these words shows that, on the face of it, these two countries have 'contracted out' of customary international law as far as imposing CFMs on transfer of funds related to foreign investment between themselves. Countries still retain their right under customary international law to impose CFMs on those transfers of funds that are not related to foreign investment; however, where the BIT applies, this right is restricted.

III. DIFFERENT APPROACHES TO REGULATING CFMS: THE INTERRELATIONSHIP BETWEEN BITS AND THE IMF ARTICLES

The preceding considerations highlight that different treaties regulate CFMs rather differently. While Type I MTPs found in BITs contract out of a State's monetary sovereignty, the IMF Articles allow States to impose CFMs, at least with respect to capital account transactions. Against this background, it is useful to assess the interrelationship between MTP provisions and the IMF Articles. This interrelationship can be looked at in two different ways: first as a question of norm conflict; and second, as a question of treaty interpretation in light of a treaty's normative context. The following sections addresses these two questions in turn.

A. Normative Conflict?

Given their different approaches to the regulation of CFMs, it may first be asked whether MTPs in BITs are compatible with the IMF Articles. In light of the distinction drawn above, MTPs do not appear to be inconsistent with Article VIII.2(a) of the IMF Articles, which restricts the right of member States to impose restrictions on *current account transactions*. As a result, a host State is under an obligation not to impose

[64] See US-Argentina BIT (n 10).

CFMs on current account transactions related to inward investment, both under the IMF treaty and the MTPs in BITs.

However, MTPs in BITs that cover transfers related to the *capital account*, such as guaranteeing the transfer of proceeds after the liquidation of investment, appear to be inconsistent or in conflict with Article VI.3 of the IMF treaty, which, as mentioned before, allows countries to impose capital controls. In other words, if a host State imposes capital controls on capital account transactions relying on the IMF treaty, such an imposition could be challenged as a violation of MTPs in BITs that obligate the host State to guarantee transfers of capital account nature (not just transfers of current account nature).

This potential conflict between BITs and IMF Articles can be better understood by situating it within the general academic debate on conflict between treaties. Wilfred Jenks, writing in 1953, provided a technical and narrow definition of conflict of norms: 'A conflict in the strict sense of direct incompatibility arises only where a party to the two treaties cannot simultaneously comply with its obligations under both treaties.'[65] Jenks refused to acknowledge divergences between the norms as conflicts even if they defeat the object of one or both treaties.

In other words, as per this narrow definition, there is no conflict (but only incompatibility or divergence) between a Type I MTP clause requiring host States to permit the transfer of funds and the IMF rule that allows countries to impose CFMs on capital account transactions. This is because the two norms do not impose *mutually exclusive obligations*: by complying with the MTP clause, States do not violate the IMF Articles, they merely choose not to make use of a right recognised by the IMF Articles.

Pauwelyn has argued that this strict definition of conflict of norms will indirectly favour the stricter norm, i.e., the one imposing a prohibition:[66] under it, the BIT MTP prohibition will trump the IMF rule because the latter is permissive whereas the former is obligatory. This result is perhaps too straightforward, though, and ignores the different ways in which treaties can ensure States' freedom of action. A broader notion of norm conflict would avoid such a straightforward outcome. For example, according to Pauwelyn and others, norm conflicts exist not only when the

---

[65] Wilfred Jenks, 'Conflict of Law Making Treaties' (1953) 30 BYBIL 401, 426. Also see, Wladyslaw Czaplinski and Gennady Danilenko, 'Conflicts of Norms in International Law' (1990) 21 NYIL 3, 12–13; Gabrielle Marceau, 'Conflicts of Norms and Conflicts of Jurisdictions: The Relationship Between the WTO Agreement and MEAs and Other Treaties' (2001) 35 JWT 1081, 1082–6.

[66] Pauwelyn (n 61) 170.

performance of two obligations is mutually exclusive, but also when one norm explicitly or implicitly prohibits something which is permitted by another norm.[67] Under this approach, there would be a norm conflict between Type I MTP clauses on the one hand, and the IMF Articles on the other: the former after all obligate host States to allow the free transfer of funds related to investment, while the latter permit it to impose capital controls on outflows including funds related to investment.[68]

The broader definition of norm conflicts emphasises the role of conflict resolution principles that permit law-appliers to identify which of two competing norms prevails. Such conflict resolution techniques can reflect the different status of norms (e.g., giving priority to a hierarchically higher provision), their chronology (*lex posterior derogat legi priori*) or their degree of specificity (*lex specialis derogat legi generali*). With respect to MTP clauses and the IMF Articles, the latter of these techniques is commonly held to apply. As BITs address only transfers relating to an investment, their content is more specific in nature. To the extent that MTPs apply, they could therefore be taken to not apply the general rule relating to transfers found in the IMF Articles. In a similar manner, the *Continental* Tribunal said that the MTP in the US-Argentina

---

[67] Erich Vranes, 'The Definition of Norm Conflict' in International Law and Legal Theory' (2006) 17 EJIL 395. Also see, Jasper Finke, 'Regime Collisions: Tension Between Treaties (and How to Solve Them)' in Christian J Tams and others (eds), *Research Handbook on the Law of Treaties* (Edward Elgar Publishing 2014) 415; ILC, 'Report of the Study Group on Fragmentation of International Law: Difficulties Arising from the Diversification and Expansion of International Law' 58th session (2006) UN Doc No A/CN.4/L.682 <http://legal.un.org/ilc/documentation/english/a_cn4_l682.pdf> accessed 2 March 2016.

[68] Pauwelyn (n 61) 180–88 has further developed this broad definition of conflict recognising different situations of conflict out of which two situations are relevant for the current purposes. These two conflict situations are: (i) conflict between a command and a right; and (ii) conflict between a prohibition and a right. The conflict between MTPs in BITs and the IMF rule recognising the right of countries to impose restrictions on capital account transactions can be classified either as a conflict between a command and a right or a prohibition and a right. This will depend on how one construes MTPs in BITs. For example, the MTPs in most BITs states the following: 'Each Contracting Party shall guarantee to the investors of the other Contracting Party the transfer of their investments and returns …' This can be read as a command, since it requires a country to 'guarantee' to foreign investors the free transfer of their investments. At the same time, this can also be read as prohibiting the host State from imposing restrictions on transfers by foreign investors.

BIT was *lex specialis*[69] compared to the IMF regime and also more liberal than the IMF regime, because the IMF Articles distinguish between current and capital transactions whereas such a distinction is missing in the MTP in US-Argentina BIT.[70] In other words, while under the broader approach the relationship between the IMF Articles and MTP clauses found in BITs is characterised as one of conflict, the *lex specialis* principle means that the MTP will prevail over the conflicting IMF Articles.[71] This approach is in line with Muchlinski's view that, where the MTPs in BITs do not mention the IMF regime, the presumption is that countries wanted to keep the IMF regime outside the BIT.[72]

B. Avoiding Conflicts: Promise and Limits of Systemic Integration

Given the above discussion regarding the conflict between MTPs in BITs with IMF rules on imposition of capital controls, it will be worthwhile to examine whether there is any possibility of avoiding this conflict. The reason for this is that in international law the presumption is that countries do not undertake conflicting obligations by entering into different treaties on different subjects.[73] In this regard, Article 31(3)(c) of the VCLT is very important because this rule of treaty interpretation expresses a more general principle, i.e., the principle of systemic integration within the international legal system.[74] In other words, this

---

69 According to this rule, *lex specialis* – one norm deals with the same subject matter more directly and precisely in comparison to another norm – prevails over the more general norm. Also see, ILC Report on Fragmentation (n 67).

70 See *Continental Casualty* (n 18) paras 243–244.

71 See also Annamaria Viterbo, *International Economic Law and Monetary Measures: Limitations to State's Sovereignty and Dispute Settlement* (Edward Elgar Publishing 2012) 281.

72 Muchlinski (n 8) 60.

73 Melanie Samson, 'High Hopes, Scant Resources: A Word of Skepticism about the Anti Fragmentation Function of Article 31(3)(c) of the Vienna Convention on the Law of Treaties' (2011) 24 Leiden J Intl L 701, 712. See Michael Akehurst, 'The Hierarchy of the Sources of International Law' (1974) 47 BYBIL 273, 275: '[J]ust as there is a presumption against the establishment of new customary rules which conflict with pre-existing customary rules, so there is a presumption against the replacement of customary rules by treaties and *vice versa*.' Sir Robert Jennings and Sir Arthur Watts (eds), *Oppenheim's International Law* (9th edn Longman 1992) 1275; ILC Report on Fragmentation (n 67) 25.

74 Arnold D McNair, *The Law of Treaties* (Clarendon Press 1961) 466; Campbell (n 63). See also Philippe Sands, 'Treaty, Custom and the Cross

rule reflects the proposition that no treaty originates outside the international legal system and that the international legal system will continue to be relevant for the purposes of interpreting the international treaty.[75] This premise makes the use of Article 31(3)(c) attractive for finding out whether MTPs in BITs can be systematically integrated with non-BIT norms such as Article VI.3 of the IMF treaty that allows countries to impose 'controls as are necessary to regulate international capital movements'.

Article 31(3)(c) provides that: 'There shall be taken into account, together with the context: (c) any relevant rules of international law applicable in the relations between the parties.'

According to the wording of the provision (which is widely held to reflect customary international law), the treaty interpreter is under an obligation to take into account those relevant rules of international law that are applicable in the relations between the parties. There is some divergence on the issue whether 'parties' refers to all parties to a treaty or only to parties to the dispute.[76] This divergence will play a very important role in deciding the applicability of Article 31(3)(c) in situations where a multilateral treaty norm is being interpreted by having recourse to a bilateral treaty norm or to another multilateral treaty norm where the number of parties is lower than the parties to the primary treaty. However, for all practical purposes, this divergence does not matter much in the kind of situations envisaged in this chapter, where in order to interpret the a norm in a bilateral treaty, recourse is being sought to a multilateral treaty like the IMF.

By indicating that account be taken of 'relevant rules of international law', Article 31(3)(c) covers not just rules of customary international law but also international treaty law,[77] as long as these relate to the same

Fertilization of International Law' (1998) 10 Yale HR & Devet L J. 3; Duncan French, 'Treaty Interpretation and the Incorporation of Extraneous Legal Rules' (2006) 55 ICLQ 281; ILC Report on Fragmentation (n 67) 206–43.

[75] For full discussion on art. 31(3)(c) of the VCLT, See Richard K Gardiner, *Treaty Interpretation* (OUP 2008) 256–81.

[76] For different views on this, see Samson (n 73). On the other hand, see David Palmeter and Petros Mavroidis, 'The WTO Legal System: Sources of Law' (1998) 92 AJIL 398; Gabrielle Marceau, 'A Call for Coherence in International Law: Praises for the Prohibition Against Clinical Isolation' (1999) 33 JWT 125. For a discussion on this topic, see Ulf Linderfalk, 'Who Are "The Parties"? Art. 31, Para 3(c) of the 1969 Vienna Convention and the "Principle of Systemic Integration" Revisited' (2008) 55 NILR 343.

[77] Ian Sinclair, *The Vienna Convention on the Law of Treaties* (2nd edn, Manchester UP 1984) 119; Pauwelyn (n 61) 255.

subject matter as the treaty rule that is being interpreted. In this respect, it is worth noting that the IMF treaty norm on imposition of capital controls covers the same subject matter as the MTPs in BITs, namely the regulation of monetary transfers.[78] More specifically, the subject matter of Article VI.3 of the IMF Articles, regulating international capital movements by imposing controls, is same as the subject matter of those transfers of funds in MTPs that relate to international capital movements. Thus, the IMF rule on imposition of capital controls is a 'relevant' rule for the purpose of Article 31(3)(c).

However, the important and difficult question is how does one take this relevant rule into account when interpreting the MTPs in BITs? This issue has not been dealt specifically in context of MTPs. However, it has been argued, in the context of the US-Argentina BIT, that despite the BIT stating that: 'each party shall permit all transfers related to an investment to be made freely and without delay into and out of its territory', the customary norm and other treaty norms that recognise the right of countries to impose capital controls in situations of balance of payment crisis should be read into the BIT.[79]

Can Article 31(3)(c) be used to import the IMF treaty norm into the primary treaty in such a manner that it effectively replaces the norm to be interpreted? Alternatively, does Article 31(3)(c), which has been widely hailed as an instrument to bring about systemic integration of international law,[80] allow for the importation and application of another treaty norm into the treaty being interpreted in a manner that blurs the distinction between the two norms? The answer to these questions is 'no'. The chapeau of Article 31(3), which states that while interpreting a treaty there shall be 'taken into account' 'together with the context', is important in this regard. In other words, the weight of the IMF rule on capital controls in the interpretative process will be decided using the chapeau.[81] The

---

[78] The understanding of 'relevance' by reference to the subject matter of the rules can be found in Pauwelyn (n 61) 260; Marceau (n 65) 1087. See also *Peru – Additonal Duty on Imports of Certain Agricultrural Products – Appellate Body Report* (20 July 2015) WT/DS457/AB/R, paras 5.100–5.105.

[79] Turyn and Aznar (n 8) 71–5.

[80] Campbell (n 63) 279–320.

[81] Martins Paparinskis, 'Investment Treaty Interpretation and Customary Law: Preliminary Remarks' in Chester Brown and Kate Miles (eds), *Evolution in Investment Treaty Law and Arbitration* (CUP 2011) 73. In this regard see also *Certain Questions of Mutual Assistance in Criminal Matters (Djibouti v France)* (Judgment) [2008] ICJ Rep 177, para. 114, where the ICJ said that 'relevant' rules only 'have a certain bearing on interpretation' and that it cannot possibly come in the way of particular rules in the treaty which is being interpreted.

interpretative materials introduced by Article 31(3)(c) 'carry (only) the same interpretative weight as the context'.[82]

Article 31(3)(c) is limited to giving meaning to explicit and undefined treaty terms or to fill 'gaps' that exist in the primary treaty.[83] Its role is to guide the task of interpreting the norm in the primary treaty and not to incorporate legal rights set out in other treaty norms, which are not part of the clear meaning of the terms of the treaty norm to be interpreted.[84] In this case, if the right to impose capital controls under IMF norm is read into the primary treaty, it would mean that the following provision: 'each party shall permit all transfers related to an investment to be made freely and without delay into and out of its territory', would change to countries permitting free transfers only of current account transactions and not of capital account transactions. Such an interpretation would be desirable from the host country's perspective, to the effect that the imposition of restrictions on transfer of funds related to capital account would be consistent with its obligations under the BIT. However, such an interpretation goes against the 'ordinary' meaning of the MTP in the BIT. Reliance on Article 31(3)(c) would therefore do far more than filling a 'gap' in the primary treaty or throwing light on a term not defined in the primary treaty. As Philippe Sands has argued, Article 31(3)(c) cannot be used to apply the foreign norm instead of the treaty norm or to override it.[85] The treaty norm to be interpreted retains its primary relevance. If the application of Article 31(3)(c) leads to the conclusion that a State's reliance on outside norms (customary or treaty) does constitute a breach of the primary treaty norm, then it means that the potential conflict situation cannot be resolved by treaty interpretation.[86]

The above discussion is not to suggest that the IMF Articles shall have no role to play in the interpretation of broad and unqualified MTPs in BITs. The role that Article 31(3)(c) will play in context of a broad and unqualified MTP is to help define those terms that are not defined in the BIT, such as 'freely convertible currency'. The *Continental* Tribunal

---

82 Paparinskis (n 81).

83 Pauwelyn (n 61) 262.

84 Ibid.

85 Sands (n 74) 102. Also see, French (n 74); Alexander Orakhelashvili, 'Restrictive Interpretation of Human Rights Treaties in the Recent Jurisprudence of the European Court of Human Rights' (2003) 14 EJIL 529, 537.

86 Pauwelyn (n 61) 272. See also Christopher J Borgen, 'Resolving Treaty Conflicts' (2005) 37 Geo Wash Intl L Rev 573, 639.

relied on Article XXX of the IMF Articles, which defines current account transactions, to find out whether the transfer in question was a fund related to investment.[87] However, Article 31(3)(c) does not mandate an interpretation that goes against the ordinary meaning of an MTP clause.

IV. ALTERNATIVE OPTIONS FOR IMPOSING CFM MEASURES

The preceding discussion suggests that, notwithstanding the different approach adopted under the IMF Articles, Type I MTPs in BITs significantly restrict the ability of host countries to impose CFM measures. It also clarifies that the principle of systemic integration reflected in Article 31(3)(c) of the VCLT is of little help in avoiding the conflict. Against this background, the subsequent section will briefly explore if there are other options available to host States seeking to impose CFMs. It does so by assessing to what extent CFM measures can be taken under provisions that recognise the host State's general regulatory freedom.

One option would be for host countries to rely on Non Precluded Measures (NPM) clauses found in BITs.[88] Such clauses, which are contained in a considerable number of (though not all) BITs, provide the necessary regulatory latitude to host countries to deal with threats to important national interests.[89] Whether the country will be able to use the NPM provision will depend on the wording of the provision. Notably, the applicable clause will need to stipulate that measures taken to redress balance of payments crises or monetary or macroeconomic difficulties (or a similarly defined purpose) come within the scope of its permissible objectives.[90] In other words, the host country will first have to show that its regulatory measure, such as imposing CFM measures, is aimed at fulfilling an objective for which the treaty permits it to deviate from its BIT obligations. As a second step, the host country will have to show that

87 *Continental Casualty* (n 18) para. 244.

88 These are also known as General Exception Clauses.

89 See William Burke-White and Andreas von Staden, 'Investment Protection in Extraordinary Times: The Interpretation and Application of Non-Precluded Measures Provisions in Bilateral Investment Treaties' (2008) 48 Va JIL 314; Kurtz (n 63) 343.

90 Permissible objectives mean those non-investment objectives that are listed in NPM provisions and for which the host country can deviate from BIT obligations.

it has satisfied the nexus requirement[91] given in the NPM provision. The nexus requirement is the link between the regulatory measure adopted and the non-investment objective that is sought through that measure.[92] Typically, this means that the host country will have to show that imposing CFM measures is 'necessary'[93] to achieve the monetary or other regulatory objective identified as a permissible objective in the NPM provision. Under the approach adopted in the *Continental Casualty* case, this will require showing that the CFM measure imposed makes a contribution to the permissible objective and that this objective cannot be achieved through any other alternative measure reasonably available to the host State and consistent with the BIT.[94] Some tribunals have interpreted 'necessary' in the NPM provision (in the US-Argentina BIT) by drawing upon the customary defence of necessity in customary international law.[95] This shows that the term 'necessary' in NPM provisions has been subjected to different interpretations by arbitral tribunals. Consequently, how successfully a country will be able to use the NPM provision to impose CFM measures will, to a great extent, depend on the interpretation of 'necessary' in the NPM provision.

This brings us to the second option that the host country can use to impose CFM measures. The host State can rely on the customary international law defence of necessity given in Article 25 of the Draft

---

[91] For more on different kinds of nexus requirements found in NPM provisions in BITs see Burke-White and von Staden (n 89).

[92] Ibid.

[93] For WTO jurisprudence on 'necessary' as the nexus requirement in art. XX of GATT see *Korea – Measures Affecting Imports of Fresh, Chilled and Frozen Beef – Appellate Body Report* (11 December 2000) WT/DS 161 and 169/AB/R; *Dominican Republic – Measures Affecting the Importation and Internal Sale of Cigarettes [Dominican-Republic – Cigarettes] – Appellate Body Report* (25 April 2005) WT/DS320/AB/R; *United States – Measures Affecting the Cross-Border Supply of Gambling and Betting Services – Appellate Body Report* (7 April 2005) WT/DS285/AB/R; *Brazil Measures Affecting Imports of Retreaded Tyres – Appellate Body Report* (17 December 2007) WT/DS332/AB/R.

[94] See *Continental Casualty* (n 18) paras 196–198.

[95] See *CMS Gas Transmission Co v The Republic of Argentina*, ICISD Case No ARB/01/8, Award (12 May 2005); *Enron Creditors Recovery Corporation and Ponderosa Assets, LP v The Republic of Argentina,* ICSID Case No ARB/01/3, Decision on the Application for Annulment (30 July 2010); *Sempra Energy International v The Republic of Argentina*, ICSID Case No ARB/02/16, Award (28 September 2007).

Articles on Responsibility of States for Internationally Wrongful Acts.[96] Article 25 states '[T]his defence can be invoked if the adopted measure is the "only way" for the state to safeguard an essential interest against a "grave and imminent peril"'.[97] Furthermore, the necessity defence is subject to three more stringent conditions. First, the adopted measure should not impair the essential interest of the other State(s) or of the international community as a whole.[98] Second, the international obligation in question should not exclude the possibility of invoking necessity.[99] Third, the invoking State should not have contributed to the situation of necessity.[100] These conditions make the customary international law defence of necessity a very stringent exception to preclude wrongfulness.[101] Indeed, this was recognised by the tribunal in *CMS v Argentina* when it said:

> While the existence of necessity as a ground for precluding wrongfulness under international law is no longer disputed, there is also consensus to the effect that this ground is an exceptional one and has to be addressed in a prudent manner to avoid abuse. The very opening of the Article to the effect that necessity 'may not be invoked' unless strict conditions are met, is indicative of this restrictive approach of international law ... The reason is not difficult to understand. If strict and demanding conditions are not required or are loosely applied, any State could invoke necessity to elude its international obligations. This would certainly be contrary to the stability and predictability of the law.[102]

V. CONCLUSIONS

The chapter started by asking the question whether MTPs in BITs which impose broad and unqualified obligation on host States to freely allow transfer of all funds related to investment in BITs restrict the ability of country's to impose CFM measures especially capital controls on capital account transactions. The analysis in the chapter shows that the answer to

---

96 ILC, 'Articles on Responsibility of States for Internationally Wrongful Acts' 53rd session (2001) UN Doc. no. A/56/10, art. 25.

97 Ibid., art. 25(1)(a).

98 Ibid., art. 25(1)(b).

99 Ibid., art. 25(2)(a).

100 Ibid., art. 25(2)(b).

101 James Crawford, *The International Law Commission's Articles on State Responsibility: Introduction, Text and Commentaries* (CUP 2002) 160–86.

102 *CMS Gas* (n 95) para. 317. See also, *Enron Creditors* (n 95); *Sempra Energy* (n 95).

this question is 'yes'. MTPs are an example of a treaty contracting out of customary international law of monetary sovereignty. Although MTPs in BITs are in line with the IMF rules in prohibiting imposition of restrictions on current account transactions (art. VIII.2), they are in conflict with Article VI of the IMF Articles, which allows member countries to impose capital controls. The chapter discussed whether Article 31(3)(c) of the VCLT, which is often presented as a tool of 'systemic integration' in international law, could be used to interpret MTPs in BITs in light of Article VI of the IMF treaty. It found that reference to the IMF Articles would not resolve this conflict. In other words, if a country were to impose capital controls under the IMF Articles,[103] it will end up breaching its MTP obligation in the BIT. Alternative options of course remain, but they are not lightly available: not all BITs contain NPM clauses; and both NPM clauses and in particular the necessity defence are subject to very stringent conditions.

Critics will argue that based on the analysis given in this chapter, the host country's imposition of restrictions on transfer of funds will result in a violation of the BIT, which, in turn, will leave the host country without many options. Unfortunately, one cannot escape from such a conclusion. Even the IMF has recognised that the limited flexibility in BITs in respect of liberalisation obligations will impose challenges for the management of capital flows.[104]

Against this background, host countries may ultimately consider a further option, viz. renegotiating BITs in order to make sure that MTPs are not in conflict with the customary international rules of monetary sovereignty and the IMF Articles. In other words, countries should not 'contract out' of general international law when they think that such 'contracting out' will be inimical to them. Increasingly, countries have started doing this: they have begun to adopt Type II MTPs, i.e., MTPs that expressly preserve the host country's rights under the IMF Articles.

---

[103] On this see also Kevin P Gallagher and Yuan Tian, 'Practicing What They Preach: The IMF and Capital Controls' (13 June 2014) <http://triplecrisis.com/practicing-what-they-preach-the-imf-and-capital-controls/> accessed 2 March 2016.

[104] IMF, 'Liberalizing Capital Flows and Managing Outflows' (13 March 2012) <www.imf.org/external/np/pp/eng/2012/031312.pdf> accessed 2 March 2016.

The most recent example is the Indian Model BIT adopted in 2015,[105] which provides in Article 32.3 that:

> Nothing in this Treaty shall affect the rights and obligations of Parties as members of the International Monetary Fund under the IMF Articles of Agreement, as applicable from time to time, including the use of exchange actions which are in conformity with the IMF Articles of Agreement. In case of any inconsistency between the provisions of this Agreement and the IMF Articles of Agreement, the latter shall prevail.[106]

A provision of this nature makes it very clear that the Tribunal shall give precedence to the IMF treaty in case of any conflict of the kind that this chapter has discussed. Provisions like these will allow host States to strike a balance between protecting the rights of the foreign investor with their right to regulate.

---

105 Model text for the Indian Bilateral Investment Treaty (28 December 2015) <http://finmin.nic.in/the_ministry/dept_eco_affairs/investment_division/ModelBIT_Annex.pdf> accessed 2 March 2016.

106 Ibid., art. 32.3.

12. Financial crisis as *force majeure* under international law and EU law: Defending emergency measures, *à l'européenne*, in investment arbitration under intra-EU BITs

Anastasios Gourgourinis

I. INTRODUCTION

The doctrine of *force majeure* is well known in most, if not all, domestic legal systems, expressive of the venerable maxim *ad impossibilia nemo tenetur* ('nobody is held to the impossible').[1] In public international law, *force majeure* has traditionally enjoyed a role as a general exception for non-performance in the law of treaties,[2] as an exception at the level of specific primary rules themselves,[3] but also, and prominently, as a defence in the context of secondary rules of State responsibility for internationally wrongful acts.[4] Historically, sovereigns invoked *force*

[1] See inter alia, Matti S Kurkela, *Comparative Report on the Force Majeure in Western Europe* (Union of the Finnish Lawyers Publishing Co 1982); Theo Rauh, 'Legal Consequences of *Force Majeure* Under German, Swiss, English and United States' Law' (1996) 25 Denv J Intl L& Pol 151; Martin Schmidt-Kessel and Katrin Mayer, 'Supervening Events and *Force Majeure*' in Jan M Smits (ed.), *Elgar Encyclopedia of Comparative Law* (Edward Elgar Publishing 2006) 689.

[2] Vienna Convention on the Law of Treaties, 1155 UNTS 331, 8 ILM 679, art. 61.

[3] E.g., United Nations Convention on the Law of the Sea, 1833 UNTS 3; 21 ILM 1261 (1982), arts 18(2) and 39(1)(c).

[4] For the distinction between primary and secondary rules in international law, see Eric David, 'Primary and Secondary Rules' in James Crawford, Alain Pellet and Simon Olleson (eds), *The Law of International Responsibility* (OUP 2010) 27–33; Anastasios Gourgourinis, 'General/Particular International Law and

majeure as a circumstance precluding wrongfulness when non-compliance with their international obligations was due to severe financial difficulties and turmoil. Until recently, and especially in the context of the most rapidly-growing field of international adjudication, namely investment treaty arbitration, the impact of financial crises on host States' performance of their obligations under international investment law was mainly, if not exclusively, scrutinised under non-precluded measures (NPM) treaty clauses[5] and the customary state of necessity defence,[6] following the saga of investment claims against Argentina. In contrast, the invocation of *force majeure* in international adjudication as a circumstance precluding international wrongfulness by States in financial straits and its contemporary relevance would seem to have declined after the Second World War.[7]

Recent events in Europe, and their relationship to the negative effects of the enduring financial crisis, may suggest that invocations of *force*

Primary/Secondary Rules: Unitary Terminology of a Fragmented System' (2011) 22 EJIL 993, 1016–20.

[5] On the interpretation and application of NPM clauses in investment agreements, see, e.g., William W Burke-White and Andreas von Staden, 'Investment Protection in Extraordinary Times: the Interpretation and Application of Non-Precluded Measures Provisions in Bilateral Investment Treaties' (2008) 48 Va JIL 307; Diane A Desierto, 'Necessity and "Supplementary Means of Interpretation" for Non-Precluded Measures in Bilateral Investment Treaties' (2010) 31 U Penn J Intl L 827; Antoine Martin, 'Investment Disputes After Argentina's Economic Crisis: Interpreting BIT Non-Precluded Measures and the Doctrine of Necessity Under Customary International Law' (2012) 29 J Intl Arb 49; Youngjin Jung and Sangwook Daniel Han, 'What to Do With the Dilemma Facing the State of Necessity Defense Under the Investment Treaties and How to Interpret the NPM Clause?' (2011) 12 JWIT 397.

[6] Regarding the necessity defence, see, e.g., Andrew D Mitchell and Caroline Henckels, 'Variations on a Theme: Comparing the Concept of Necessity in International Investment Law and WTO Law' (2013) 14 Chi J Intl L 93; Giorgio Sacerdoti, 'BIT Protections and Economic Crisis: Limits to Their Coverage, the Impact of Multilateral Financial Regulation and the Defence of Necessity' (2013) 28 ICSID Rev 351; August Reinisch and Christina Binder, 'Debts and State of Necessity' in Juan Pablo Bohoslavsky and Jernej Letnar Cernic (eds) *Making Sovereign Financing and Human Rights Work* (Hart 2014) 115–28.

[7] Andrea K Bjorklund, 'Emergency Exceptions: State of Necessity and Force Majeure' in Peter Muchlinski, Federico Ortino and Christoph Schreuer (eds), *Oxford Handbook of International Investment Law* (OUP 2008) 498–9; Alexis Martinez, 'Invoking State Defenses in Investment Treaty Arbitration' in Michael Waibel and others (eds), *The Backlash Against Investment Arbitration* (Kluwer 2010) 315–17.

majeure by affected sovereigns have re-emerged. For instance, in response to a question by the Economic and Monetary Affairs Committee of the European Parliament on the role of the 'Troika' in the Eurozone crisis and the 'leeway' granted to EU Members States under fiscal adjustment programmes 'to decide upon the design of the necessary measures (consolidation or structural reforms)',[8] the Cypriot Ministry of Finance answered that 'the Cyprus government was forced to accept' the application of the bail-in instrument on bank deposits in March 2013 'under duress',[9] arguably referring to a *force majeure* situation[10] resulting from pressure by the Troika.[11] Importantly, Iceland was the first sovereign, perhaps in decades, to extensively and explicitly plead *force majeure* before an international court. In the *Icesave* case, Iceland claimed in front of the Court of Justice of the European Free Trade Association (the EFTA Court) that the economic crisis amounted to *force majeure*, excusing any non-compliance with its international obligations (under EU law in particular).[12]

---

[8] In the context of the European Parliament's probe that led to the adoption of the European Parliament resolution of 13 March 2014 on the enquiry on the role and operations of the Troika (ECB, Commission and IMF) with regard to the euro area programme countries (2013/2277(INI), the Economic and Monetary Affairs Committee sent a questionnaire to the Member States concerned (Greece, Cyprus and Portugal) and the EU institutions involved (the European Council, the European Commission, the European Central Bank and the Eurogroup).

[9] Ministry of Finance of Cyprus, Answer to the questionnaire supporting the own initiative report evaluating the structure, the role and operations of the 'troika' (Commission, ECB and the IMF) actions in euro area programme countries <www.europarl.europa.eu/document/activities/cont/201401/20140114ATT77319/20140114ATT77319EN.pdf> accessed 7 December 2016.

[10] Under international law, situations of duress are generally considered to be covered by *force majeure* as a circumstance precluding wrongfulness, and this is why they are not treated separately for the purposes of State responsibility: see, e.g., James Crawford, *State Responsibility: The General Part* (OUP 2013) 278, n 27.

[11] On whether and how coercion by the EU institutions could lead to a *force majeure* defence by EU Member States under fiscal adjustment programmes, see Anastasios Gourgourinis, 'The Shared Responsibility of the EU for Member States' Financial Crisis Measures as a Defence in International Investment Claims' in Christina Binder, August Reinisch and Mary Footer (eds), *Select Proceedings of the European Society of International Law 2014* (Bloomsbury 2016) 195–215.

[12] Case E-16/11, *EFTA Surveillance Authority v Iceland (Icesave)* [2013] EFTA Ct Rep 4.

With the above in mind, the aim of the present chapter is to examine anew the availability of *force majeure* as a justification for measures taken in systemic financial crises. The focus is on its potential as a defence *à la européenne* (i.e., drawing not only from general international law, but also from EU law) for EU Member States in investment arbitrations under intra-EU bilateral investment treaties (BITs) implicating of crisis measures. This question has now acquired practical importance, since EU Member States affected by the financial crisis, such as Greece, Spain, Italy, the Czech Republic and Cyprus, face, or are reportedly threatened to face, claims by investors under BITs in force with other EU Member States.

Accordingly, the chapter will start from an analysis of the *Icesave* case and the invocation of *force majeure* therein as the most recent example of how the defence may be put forward by States in economic distress (II); it will then proceed to an examination of the contours of *force majeure* under both general international law (III) and EU law (IV), engaging in a comparative exercise yet to be undertaken in academic scholarship.[13] The analysis will operate as a necessary prelude for addressing whether and how a *force majeure* defence may be put forward for financial crisis measures in intra-EU investment arbitration (V), before concluding with some brief remarks (VI).

II. THE *ICESAVE* CASE AND ICELAND'S INVOCATION OF *FORCE MAJEURE*

In 2011, the Surveillance Authority of the EFTA[14] launched an application before the EFTA Court[15] against Iceland in the aftermath of the

[13] Perhaps the sole exception being the early (and fairly inconclusive, at least in comparative terms) attempt in Bruno Loyant, *Recherches sur la notion de force majeure en droit communautaire et en droit international: contribution á l'étude des faits justificatifs de non-exécution des obligations internationales*, Mémoire pour le Diplôme d'E´tudes Approfondies de Droit européen (Université de Rennes, UER de sciences juridiques 1978).

[14] The EFTA is an intergovernmental organisation for free trade and economic integration founded in 1960 by Austria, Denmark, Norway, Portugal, Sweden, Switzerland and the UK, later joined by Finland, Iceland and Liechtenstein. Following the accession of certain of EFTA Members in the EU, the EFTA Member States today are Iceland, Liechtenstein, Norway and Switzerland.

[15] On the working and structure of the EFTA Court, as well as its relationship with the CJEU, see, among many, Carl Baudenbacher, *The EFTA*

collapse of the latter's domestic banking sector in 2008. The Authority alleged that Iceland's failure to ensure payment of the minimum amount of compensation to depositors in the UK and Netherlands branches of its *Landsbanki* Bank was not in conformity with Directive 94/19/EC,[16] referred to at point 19a of Annex IX to the Agreement on the European Economic Area (EEA Agreement),[17] and/or Article 4 of the latter.[18] In what has been a milestone judgment regarding the liability of States for national deposit insurance schemes in Europe, the EFTA Court on 28 January 2013 dismissed all claims. The Court found, first, that Directive 94/19/EC did not impose an obligation of result on EEA States to use, if necessary, their own financial resources to guarantee compensation, should their national deposit guarantee scheme be unable to fulfil their

---

Court in Action: Five Lectures (German Law Publishers 2010); Carl Baudenbacher and Michael-James Clifton, 'Courts of Regional Economic and Political Integration Agreements' in Cesare Romano, Karen J Alter and Chrisanti Avgerou (eds), *Oxford Handbook of International Adjudication* (OUP 2014) 256–60; Vassilios Skouris, 'The Role of the Court of Justice of the European Union in the Development of the EEA Single Market: Advancement through Collaboration between the EFTA Court and the CJEU' in EFTA Court (ed.), *The EEA and the EFTA Court: Decentred Integration* (Hart 2014) 3–12.

[16] Directive 94/19/EC of the European Parliament and of the Council of 30 May 1994 on deposit-guarantee schemes, [1994] OJ L135/5, as then applicable under the EEA Agreement. Cf. for its recent revision, Directive 2014/49/EU of the European Parliament and of the Council of 16 April 2014 on deposit guarantee schemes Text with EEA relevance, [2014] OJ L173/149.

[17] The EEA Agreement is an international agreement, entered into force in 1994, and concluded between the European Communities (now EU), the Member States of the EU and three EFTA States. The EEA agreement has established a two-track legal regime, applicable in the trade relations between one or more EFTA States and one or more EU Member States, as well as the trade relations of the EFTA States *inter se*. It aims to extend the EU's internal market to these three EFTA States, with the exception of common policies in the fields of agriculture, fisheries, taxation, foreign trade and currency. For more detail, see Elvira M Méndez-Pinedo, *EC and EEA Law: A Comparative Study of the Effectiveness of European Law* (Europa Law Publishing 2009).

[18] See further background on the *Icesave* case and its implications in Michael Waibel, 'Iceland's Financial Crisis – *Quo Vadis* International Law' (14 *ASIL Insights*, 1 March 2010) <www.asil.org/insights/volume/14/issue/5/icelands-financial-crisis-%E2%80%93-quo-vadis-international-law> accessed 24 April 2015; Michael Waibel, 'Iceland Not Responsible for the Liabilities of its Deposit Insurance Scheme' (*EJIL:Talk!*, 28 January 2013) <www.ejiltalk.org/iceland-not-responsible-for-the-liabilities-of-its-deposit-insurance-scheme/> accessed 24 April 2015.

obligations;[19] and, second, that Iceland did not illegally discriminate between domestic and foreign depositors under the Directive or Article 4 EEA.[20] Hence, Iceland was found not to have violated its obligations under the Directive and the EEA Agreement.[21]

However, the EFTA Court emphasised the exceptional circumstances surrounding the case and found, in the context of its analysis of the existence of an alleged obligation of result for Iceland to guarantee the minimum coverage of deposits, that:

> the Directive does not envisage that the defendant itself must ensure payments to depositors in the *Icesave* branches in the Netherlands and the United Kingdom, in accordance with Articles 7 and 10 of the Directive, in *a systemic crisis of the magnitude experienced in Iceland.*[22]

Moreover, after having dismissed the nationality-based discrimination claims against Iceland, and only for the 'sake of completeness', the EFTA Court added that:

> [O]ne would have to bear in mind that the EEA States enjoy *a wide margin of discretion in making fundamental choices of economic policy in the specific event of a systemic crisis* provided that certain circumstances are duly proven. This would have to be taken into consideration as a possible ground for justification.[23]

Interestingly, the EFTA Court also pointed out[24] that this proposition had been admitted by the Authority itself in the earlier case of *Sigmarsson* before the EFTA Court: in that case, measures preventing inbound capital transfers into Iceland in the wake of the financial crisis were eventually found to meet the conditions for the application of Article 43(2) and (4)

---

[19] *Icesave* (n 12) paras 117–185.

[20] Ibid., paras 203–228.

[21] For more detail on the findings of the EFTA Court in *Icesave* and its future repercussions, see, e.g., Mathias Hanten and Marion Plaschke, 'EU Law Impact on Deposit Protection in the Financial Crisis: *Icesave*' (2014) 51 Common Market L Rev 295, 300–308; Damien Chalmers, '*Icesave* – Limited Homogeneity and Unlimited Judicial Interpretation' in EFTA Court (n 15) 407–16; Niall J Lenihan, 'How Has the EU Protected Depositors in the Financial Crisis?' (2013–2014) 16 Cambridge YB Eur Legal Stud 289, 295–8.

[22] *Icesave* (n 12) para. 178 (emphasis added).

[23] Ibid., para. 227 (emphasis added).

[24] Ibid.

EEA, allowing EEA States to take protective measures.[25] Therefore, even if the reference by the EFTA Court in *Icesave* to its previous *Sigmarsson* judgment does not apply to the facts of the case,[26] one could still argue that, albeit indirectly and implicitly, it touched upon the *force majeure* defence vigorously raised by Iceland in the proceedings. For, in essence, and although the EFTA Court in *Icesave* did not need to explicitly address the *force majeure* defence under EU law, since no breach was found at the outset, the passage cited above very much took up Iceland's argument.

More specifically, Iceland argued before the EFTA Court that, even if Directive 94/19/EC were to impose an obligation of result to fund the guarantee scheme in the event of collapse, any alleged non-compliance would still be justified by *force majeure* under EU law. In fact, the EFTA Surveillance Authority in its Letter of Formal Notice of 26 May 2010 to Iceland[27] responded to the Icelandic Government's letter of 23 March 2010 (where it was asserted that deposit guarantee schemes are not designed to deal with anything that goes beyond a mid-size banking failure, 'let alone a meltdown of the whole financial system'), with the following:

> The terms of the Directive itself cannot support such an argument. According to the case law of the Court of Justice, a Member State cannot plead exceptional circumstances to justify non-compliance with a directive in the absence of a specific legislative provision in the directive to that effect.[28]

In other words, the Authority rejected from the very beginning any defence based on exceptional circumstances 'such as a serious and general financial crisis', to the extent that the Directive (or EEA law or EU law more generally) did not explicitly provide for one.[29] Moreover, in

---

25 Case E-3/11, *Pálmi Sigmarsson v The Central Bank of Iceland* [2011] EFTA Ct Rep 432, paras 42, 50.

26 Hanten and Plaschke (n 21) 306–7: 'In the case at issue, the foreign depositors did not move capital, but held capital in their home countries, i.e. on their accounts with the relevant branches in the Netherlands and the UK only, so Article 40 EEA does not apply'.

27 EFTA Surveillance Authority, Letter of formal notice to Iceland for failure to comply with its obligations under the Act referred to at point 19a of Annex IX to the EEA Agreement and Article 4 of the EEA Agreement of 26 May 2010 <www.eftasurv.int/media/internal-market/lfn-icesave.pdf> accessed 19 May 2016.

28 Ibid., 10.

29 Ibid., 10–12.

its later Application, the Authority, inter alia, added (perhaps adopting a more flexible stance) that, only if there had been a 'total physical impossibility', and for reasons beyond its control, would Iceland be justified in not complying with its obligations under the Directive – which was not made out on the facts.[30] Unsurprisingly, the European Commission, the UK and the Netherlands sided with the Authority.

In its defence, formulated with the assistance of, inter alia, Professor Miguel Poiares Maduro, former Advocate General at the European Court of Justice (now Court of Justice of the European Union – the CJEU or the Court), Iceland invoked the *force majeure* defence under EU law (assuming *arguendo* it was in breach of its obligations under the Directive and EEA law).[31] Particularly, it challenged the Authority's understanding of *force majeure* as follows:

> [*F*]*orce majeure* does not require 'physical impossibility', but rather 'abnormal and unforeseeable' events, which could not have been avoided if all due care had been taken. Nor does it require that the State ought to have acted as if with perfect hindsight. 'All due care' is not equivalent to 'strict liability': it means 'appropriate steps' that can be taken 'without making unreasonable sacrifices'.[32]

It was on the above basis that Iceland asserted that the 2008 global financial crisis and the wholesale collapse of the Icelandic banking system readily qualified as 'abnormal and unforeseeable' events,[33] and, furthermore, that no 'appropriate steps' could have been taken 'without making unreasonable sacrifices' as regards either the inability of its deposit guarantee scheme, or any deposit guarantee scheme, to withstand systemic crisis, or Iceland's own inability to pay depositors.[34]

The EFTA Court did not need to decide on the availability and/or the merits of Iceland's *force majeure* defence under EU law (since no breach was found). Still, it cannot be ignored that the *Icesave case* saw the first

---

[30] EFTA Surveillance Authority, Application submitted pursuant to the second paragraph of Article 31 of the Agreement between the EFTA States on the Establishment of a Surveillance Authority and a Court of Justice by the EFTA Surveillance Authority against Iceland of 14 December 2011 <www.eftasurv.int/media/public-documents/618446_Icesave-application.pdf> accessed 24 April 2015, paras 149, 155.

[31] *Icesave* (n 12) Defence by the Government of Iceland of 8 March 2012 <www.eftasurv.int/media/public-documents/628325.pdf> accessed 24 April 2015, paras 246–263.

[32] Ibid., para. 250 (internal references to case-law omitted).

[33] Ibid., para. 251.

[34] Ibid., paras 252–256.

elaborate invocation of *force majeure* (rather than state of necessity) in international adjudication by a State for measures taken in response to systemic financial turmoil, perhaps for as long as since the early cases of the previous century.[35] And taking into consideration the rather limited success of recent invocations of financial necessity in the context of NPM clauses in BITs and/or in the general international law on state responsibility,[36] one would be further tempted to wonder whether, in principle, *force majeure* is another available alternative for justifying financial crisis measures. To this end, and before examining *force majeure* under EU law (i.e., as invoked by Iceland in the *Icesave* case), it is worth revisiting the contours of the concept under general international law as a circumstance precluding international wrongfulness.

III. *FORCE MAJEURE* IN GENERAL INTERNATIONAL LAW

Distinctly apart from the instances where primary rules themselves include an exception of non-performance on the basis of *force majeure*, Article 23 of the International Law Commission's Articles on the Responsibility of States for Internationally Wrongful Acts,[37] provides for the *force majeure* defence as a circumstance precluding wrongfulness under general international law:

1. The wrongfulness of an act of a State not in conformity with an international obligation of that State is precluded if the act is due to *force majeure*, that is the occurrence of an irresistible force or of an unforeseen event, beyond the control of the State, making it materially impossible in the circumstances to perform the obligation.
2. Paragraph 1 does not apply if: (a) the situation of *force majeure* is due, either alone or in combination with other factors, to the conduct of the State invoking it; or (b) the State has assumed the risk of that situation occurring.

---

[35] Bjorklund (n 7) 498–9.

[36] For rare examples to the contrary see *LG&E Energy Corp, LG&E Capital Corp and LG&E International v Argentine Republic*, ICSID Case No ARB 02/1, Decision on Liability (3 October 2006) paras 226–261; *Continental Casualty Company v The Argentine Republic*, ICSID Case No ARB/03/9, Award (5 September 2008) paras 170–230.

[37] ILC, 'Responsibility of States for Internationally Wrongful Acts, with Commentaries' (2001) YBILC Vol. II Part Two.

For a successful invocation of the defence, the act to be justified must be 'due' to *force majeure*, namely 'the occurrence of an irresistible force or an unforeseen event',[38] 'beyond the control' of the State invoking it, rendering performance of the international obligation at issue 'materially impossible'. In fact, Article 23 of the ILC Articles refers to two types of events: 'uncontrollable, to the extent that either in view of their strength (irresistible events) or in view of their unexpected occurrence (unforeseen events) they leave no room for the state to react against them'.[39] It appears that Article 23 of the ILC Articles covers *force majeure* defined *largo sensu*,[40] i.e., both unforeseen events, as well as occurrences of irresistible forces which are not necessarily unforeseen or unforeseeable (*force majeure* defined *stricto sensu*).[41] In other words, two cases of 'material impossibility' are provided.

'Material impossibility', a key constituent element of *force majeure*, has traditionally been surrounded by controversy, being 'but an indication of the profound effects of the tension between stability and flexibility in the context of circumstances precluding wrongfulness' more generally.[42] More specifically, in situations of *force majeure*, the will of the State in

---

[38] Ibid., Commentary to art. 23, 76, para. 2: 'The adjective "irresistible" qualifying the word "force" emphasizes that there must be a constraint which the State was unable to avoid or oppose by its own means. To have been "unforeseen" the event must have been neither foreseen nor of an easily foreseeable kind.'

[39] Federica Paddeu, 'A Genealogy of *Force Majeure* in International Law' (2011) 82 BYBIL 381, 394.

[40] ILC, '"Force Majeure" and "Fortuitous Event" as Circumstances Precluding Wrongfulness: Survey of State Practice, International Judicial Decisions and Doctrine' (1978) YBILC Vol. II Part Two 69, para. 13: '"*Force majeure*" has been defined, *lato sensu*, as an unforeseen or foreseen but inevitable or irresistible event external to the obligor which makes it impossible for him to perform the obligation concerned.' [footnote omitted]

[41] On the distinction between *force majeure* and fortuitous events, see ibid., 70–71, paras 17–19. Note that art. 31 of the provisionally adopted 1980 Draft Articles on State Responsibility, which became what is now art. 23 ILC with only limited adjustments/additions, was entitled '*Force majeure* and fortuitous event' and reflected the decision of the ILC not to devote two separate articles, but to deal with 'both these closely related situations together'. See ILC (1979) YBILC, Vol. II Part One 123, paras 4–6.

[42] Sotirios-Ioannis Lekkas and Antonios Tzanakopoulos, '*Pacta Sunt Servanda* versus Flexibility in the Suspension and Termination of Treaties' in Christian J Tams, Antonios Tzanakopoulos and Andreas Zimmermann (eds), *Research Handbook on the Law of Treaties* (Edward Elgar 2014) 330.

question is constrained by external factors beyond its power or control.[43] These external factors must also be causally linked to the material impossibility of performance of the obligation at issue.[44] Examples of *force majeure* would include natural or physical events (e.g., earthquakes, floods or drought, natural disasters), as well as human action (e.g., insurrections, military operations or duress/coercion by another State),[45] taken alone or in combination.[46]

The commentary to Article 23 of the ILC Articles further states that the situation of *force majeure*

> must be irresistible, so that the State concerned has no real possibility of escaping its effects. *Force majeure* does not include circumstances in which performance of an obligation has become *more difficult*, for example due to some political or economic crisis.[47]

Interestingly, the above passage appears to have been amended from the ILC's Commentary to the provisionally adopted Article 31 ('*Force majeure* and fortuitous event') of the 1980 Draft Articles:[48]

> The adverb 'materially' preceding the word 'impossible' is intended to show that, for the purposes of the article, it would not suffice for the 'irresistible force' or the 'unforeseen external event' to have made it *very difficult* for the State to act in conformity with the obligation or to know that its conduct was in breach of the obligation. In other words, the Commission has sought to emphasize that the State must not have had any option in that regard.[49]

So, while the ILC in 1980 distinguished between *force majeure* and fortuitous event (both under the provisionally adopted Article 31), on the one hand, and distress, on the other, emphasising that the former involved involuntary or unintentional conduct, and that the latter included cases of

---

[43] ILC (n 37) 76, para. 1.

[44] Ibid., para. 2.

[45] Ibid., para. 3; Crawford (n 10) 296–8.

[46] Cf. Sandra Szurek, 'Circumstances Precluding Wrongfulness in the ILC Articles on State Responsibility: *Force Majeure*' in Crawford and others (n 4) 475, 477: 'One can think of a case where a State would be unable to help foreigners in a region devastated by a natural catastrophe, because it is occupied by rebel forces which the State is not capable of removing.'

[47] ILC (n 37) 76, para. 3 (emphasis added).

[48] ILC (1980) YBKILC, Vol. II Part Two 30–34.

[49] ILC (n 41) 133, para. 40 (emphasis in the original).

lack of a 'real choice' or 'free choice',[50] in the 2001 Commentary to Article 23 ILC reference is made to conduct which is 'involuntary or at least involves no element of free choice'.[51] These differences in the formulation over time and the ILC's changing approach to the element of material impossibility in the *force majeure* defence are perhaps important, particularly if one considers the explicit reliance by the *Rainbow Warrior* Tribunal on the ILC's Commentary to the 1980 Draft Articles, just before the oft-cited *obiter* that the test of the applicability of *force majeure* as a circumstance precluding wrongfulness 'is of absolute and material impossibility'.[52]

Writing after the adoption of the ILC's 2001 text, James Crawford criticised the *Rainbow Warrior* Tribunal for 'equating … material impossibility with "absolute" impossibility', which he considered to be 'perhaps misleading',[53] and rightly so. Indeed, the judgment of International Court of Justice (ICJ) in the *Gabčíkovo-Nagymaros* case,[54] and the ILC's Commentary to Article 23,[55] confirm that the *force majeure* defence under Article 23 is not limited to absolute impossibility. The same result is reached under a systematic view of the relationship between *force majeure*, distress and state of necessity as circumstances precluding wrongfulness set out in Articles 23–25 of the ILC's Articles: cases where conduct is 'involuntary or at least involves no element of

---

[50] Ibid., 123, para. 4, and particularly 133, para. 2, explaining that in cases of distress:

> [T]here is theoretically a choice, so that the conduct adopted is not entirely involuntary. However, this choice is not a 'real choice' or 'free choice' as to the decision to be taken, since the person acting on behalf of the State knows that if he adopts the conduct required by the international obligation he, and the persons entrusted to his care, will almost inevitably perish.

[51] ILC (n 37) 76, para. 1.

[52] *Case concerning the difference between New Zealand and France concerning the interpretation or application of two agreements, concluded on 9 July 1986 between the two States and which related to the problems arising from the Rainbow Warrior Affair*, Decision of 30 April 1990, 20 RIAA 215, 253.

[53] Crawford (n 10) 299. Cf. Szurek (n 46) 480, arguing that '[f]or reasons of legal security, only a narrow concept of *force majeure* is adopted in international law'.

[54] See *Gabčíkovo-Nagymaros Project (Hungary/Slovakia)*, Judgment, ICJ Rep (1997) para. 102.

[55] ILC (n 37) 77, para. 4: 'The degree of difficulty associated with *force majeure* as a circumstance precluding wrongfulness, though considerable, is less than is required by article 61 [VCLT] for termination of a treaty on grounds of supervening impossibility … .'

free choice'[56] are covered by *force majeure* rather than distress (which covers voluntary conduct or at least conduct involving no element of free choice in cases of peril to the author's life or the lives of persons entrusted to her care) or necessity (which covers voluntary conduct).[57] In other words, material impossibility in terms of *force majeure* analysis essentially corresponds to what Special Rapporteur Ago referred to as 'relative impossibility' concerning situations where performance would be at the cost of a 'sacrifice that could not reasonably be required';[58] hence, and for the purposes of the present chapter, reference hereinafter is to be made to 'material/relative impossibility' in the context of Article 23 of the ILC Articles, as opposed to 'absolute impossibility' under Article 61 ('Supervening impossibility of performance') of the Vienna Convention on the Law of Treaties (VCLT).

In particular, one may recall that in *Gabčíkovo-Nagymaros* the Court referred to the *travaux préparatoires* of the Diplomatic Conference which led to the adoption of the VCLT. Referring to a proposal made during the Diplomatic Conference to extend the scope of supervening impossibility of performance, under what is now Article 61 VCLT, to cases such as impossibility of payment due to serious financial difficulties, the Court noted that:

> although it was recognized [during the Diplomatic Conference] that such situations could lead to a preclusion of the wrongfulness of non-performance by a party of its treaty obligations, the participating States were not prepared to consider such situations to be a ground for terminating or suspending a treaty, and preferred to limit themselves to a narrower concept.[59]

---

[56] Describing such instances of *force majeure,* Special Rapporteur Ago noted that 'the will of the organ exists in theory but in practice is nullified by a perilous situation'; Roberto Ago, 'Eighth Report on State Responsibility – the Internationally Wrongful Act of the State, Source of International Responsibility' in ILC (n 41) 48–49, paras 103, 106.

[57] ILC (n 37) 76, para. 1; 78, para. 1; and ibid., 80, para. 2.

[58] Ago (n 56) 49, para. 106. Admittedly, Ago drew a thin line between *force majeure* and distress: see further the criticisms and analysis in Paddeu (n 39) 451–4. It appears, though, that the reference in ILCs Commentary to art. 23 to conduct 'involuntary' or at least involving 'no element of free choice' (n 37) also supports the coverage of material/relative impossibility scenarios under *force majeure*.

[59] *Gabčíkovo-Nagymaros Project* (n 54) para. 102. Cf. Mark Villiger, *Commentary on the 1969 Vienna Convention on the Law of Treaties* (Nijhoff 2009) 761, noting that art. 61 VCLT does not address cases where a treaty cannot be performed by reason of *force majeure*, this being an issue of State responsibility proper; Joe Verhoeven, 'The Law of Responsibility and the Law of

In essence, absolute impossibility as required under Article 61 VCLT can be seen as '-1', while merely enhanced difficulty of performance would be '1'. Material/relative impossibility in the sense of Article 23 of the ILC Articles would then be situated in between, as 'zero', covering cases of involuntary conduct or at least involving no element of real or free choice, where performance of the obligation in question would be an unreasonable sacrifice: for instance, if compliance would jeopardise the very existence of the State or the fulfilment of its essential governmental functions, any 'real' or 'free' choice would be effectively nullified. Proving 'zero' should, thus, suffice for a *force majeure* invocation as a circumstance precluding international wrongfulness as per Article 23 of the ILC Articles.

Still, as Article 23(2) of the ILC Articles prescribes, the situation of *force majeure* must not be 'due', either alone or in combination with other factors, to the conduct of the State invoking it, nor should the State have renounced its right to rely on *force majeure*, by agreement or otherwise. While the second caveat provides for the possibility of expressly renouncing the capacity to invoke *force majeure*,[60] the first one sets a threshold of impermissible contribution of the State to the *force majeure* situation. This threshold is not negligible, but it is lower than the similar provision precluding States from invoking the state of necessity defence under Article 25 of the ILC Articles. Article 23(2)(a) ILC requires that the State 'has caused or induced' the situation of material/relative impossibility, hence not barring the invocation of *force majeure:*

> in situations in which a State may have unwittingly contributed to the occurrence of material impossibility by something which, in hindsight, might

---

Treaties' in Crawford and others (n 4) 108: 'Article 23 ARSIWA relating to *force majeure*, … embraces, but is not restricted to, impossibility of performance'; Oliver Dörr and Kirsten Schmalenbach (eds), *Vienna Convention on the Law of Treaties: A Commentary* (Springer 2012), 1057:

> If, however, in an exceptional case, the fulfillment of a treaty obligation would jeopardize the very existence of the State or render impossible the performance of essential governmental functions, the States Parties cannot invoke impossibility in the sense of Art 61 [VCLT] but *force majeure* to preclude the wrongfulness of its non-performance,

citing Alfred Verdross and Bruno Simma, *Universelles Völkerrecht: Theorie und Praxis* (3rd edn, Duncker & Humblot 1984) 522. Cf. Crawford (n 10) 299: 'Although … the same facts might amount to both *force majeure* and a supervening impossibility of performing a treaty … that will not necessarily be so'.

[60] ILC (n 37) 78, para. 10.

have been done differently but which was done in good faith and did not itself make the event any less unforeseen.[61]

Put differently, Article 23(2)(a) of the ILC Articles 'is not so broad as to encompass *any* contribution' of the State to the situation of *force majeure*; rather, the invoking State's role must be determinative for material/relative impossibility to be 'due' to it.[62] Conversely, Article 25(2)(b) of the ILC Articles dictates that necessity may not be relied upon if the State 'has contributed to the situation of necessity': it appears that the requirement of sufficiently substantial contribution, 'phrased in more categorical terms' than Article 23(2)(a),[63] requires less for barring the invocation of necessity, compared to 'causation or inducement' in the context of the plea of *force majeure*. And of course, the invocation of *force majeure* is always subject to the general caveat on circumstances precluding wrongfulness regarding their temporary effect ('if and to the extent that the circumstance precluding wrongfulness no longer exists') and questions of compensation for material loss under Article 27 ILC.

The *force majeure* defence was considered by the ILC as belonging to the corpus of general international law,[64] capable of qualifying both as general principle of (customary) international law, as well as a general principle of law.[65] Interestingly, the ILC has further noted that *force majeure* is also recognised as a general principle of law by the CJEU,[66] citing the *Denkavit België* and the *Commission v Italy* cases.[67] In the light of this reference, and before examining the potential for the invocation of *force majeure* in the context of investment proceedings under intra-EU BITs, the chapter will now explore the content of the concept in EU law.

---

[61] Ibid., para. 9.

[62] Szurek (n 46) 478; Crawford (n 10) 300–301.

[63] ILC (n 37) 84, para. 20, also noting that the contribution must be 'sufficiently substantial and not merely incidental or peripheral.'

[64] For the differentiation between general and particular international law, see Gourgourinis (n 4) 1004–16.

[65] ILC (n 37) 77, paras 6–7 and 78, para. 8; ILC (n 41) 53, para. 113. Cf. also Paddeu (n 39) 476–93; Crawford (n 10) 295; *Anaconda Iran, Inc v Islamic Republic of Iran*, Interlocutory Award (10 December 1986) 13 Iran-USCTR 199, para. 43; *Mobil Oil Iran Inc v Islamic Republic of Iran*, Award (14 July 1987) 16 Iran-USCTR 3, para. 117.

[66] ILC (n 37) 78, para. 8, n 357.

[67] Case 101/84, *Commission of the European Communities v Italian Republic* [1985] ECR 2629; Case 145/85, *Denkavit België NV v Belgian State* [1987] ECR 565.

IV. *FORCE MAJEURE* IN EU LAW

As is the case in international law, *force majeure* appears in EU law either as an in-built exception to the primary rules of EU law, or as a defence justifying non-compliance. More specifically, the ECJ (now CJEU) first examined, in its 1968 *Schwarzwaldmilch* judgment, the *force majeure* exception in Article 6 of Regulation No 136/64/EEC related to agriculture. Under Article 6(2) of the Regulation, deposits lodged by the importer would not be forfeited if he had been unable to effect the obligation of importation 'for reasons of *force majeure*'. The Court, although hinting that *force majeure* situations were not restricted to absolute impossibility,[68] eventually limited itself to declare that:

> [I]n order to rely on *force majeure* within the meaning of this regulation, the importer must show that he was unable to effect the importation within the period laid down as a result of unusual circumstances outside his control, the consequences of which, in spite of the exercise of all due care on his part, he could not have avoided except at the cost of excessive sacrifice ...[69]

The opportunity to build upon the above definition of *force majeure* as 'not limited to absolute impossibility' was soon presented in the *Handelsgesellschaft* case, where the Court had to interpret *force majeure* in Article 9 of Regulation No 473/67/EEC (also related to agriculture).[70] Indeed, explicit references to *force majeure* have been included in various

---

[68] Case 4-68, *Firma Schwarzwaldmilch GmbH v Einfuhr- und Vorratsstelle für Fette* [1968] ECR 377, 386.

[69] Ibid., 388.

[70] See Case 11-70, *Internationale Handelsgesellschaft mbH v Einfuhr- und Vorratsstelle für Getreide und Futtermittel* [1970] ECR 1125, para. 23:

> The concept of *force majeure* adopted by the agricultural regulations takes into account the particular nature of the relationships in public law between traders and the national administration, as well as the objectives of those regulations. It follows from those objectives as well as from the positive provisions of the regulations in question that the concept of *force majeure* is not limited to absolute impossibility but must be understood in the sense of unusual circumstances, outside the control of the importer or exporter, the consequences of which, in spite of the exercise of all due care, could not have been avoided except at the cost of excessive sacrifice. This concept implies a sufficient flexibility regarding not only the nature of the occurrence relied upon but also the care which the exporter should have exercised in order to meet it and the extent of the sacrifices which he should have accepted to that end.

instruments of EU secondary legislation, relating, inter alia, to agriculture,[71] and customs. Thus, and ever since *Schwarzwaldmilch*, the Court has dealt with *force majeure* invocations by individuals or corporations, consistently holding that *force majeure* situations are not limited to absolute impossibility, but rather cases where performance would be possible only by making unreasonable sacrifices.[72] Moreover, the Court also consistently held that the meaning of *force majeure* must be determined by reference to the legal context of the various fields of EU law in which it is to operate.[73]

The case law of the Court may appear to have added a foreseeability criterion, when referring to *force majeure* situations as 'abnormal and unforeseeable circumstances'.[74] Ergo, one could be quick to observe an important difference between this definition of *force majeure* under EU

---

[71] For more details on the early case law on *force majeure* in the context of agriculture, see Bruno Loyant, 'La force majeure et l'organisation commune des marchés agricoles: étude d'un concept autonome de droit communautaire' (1980) 16 Revue trimestrelle du droit européen 256.

[72] See, e.g., Case 25/70, *Einfuhr- und Vorratsstelle für Getreide und Futtermittel v Köster and Berodt & Co* [1970] ECR 1161, para. 38; Case 284/82, *Acciaierie e Ferriere Busseni SpA v Commission of the European Communities* [1984] ECR 557, para. 11; Case 20/84, *NV De Jong Verenigde and Coöperatieve Melkprodukten Bedrijven 'Domo-Bedum' GA v Voedselvoorzienings in-en verkoopbureau (VIB)* [1985] ECR 2061, para. 16; Case C-325/96, *Fábrica de Queijo Eru Portuguesa Ld^a v Subdirector-Geral das Alfândegas, and Ministério Público* [1997] ECR 7249, para. 24. For an analysis of case law on *force majeure* pleas by traders, see, e.g., Michael Parker, '*Force Majeure* in EU Law' in Ewan McKendrick (ed.), *Force Majeure and Frustration of Contract* (Routledge 2014) 341–8.

[73] See, e.g., Case C-124/92, *An Bord Bainne Co-operative Ltd and Compagnie Interagra SA v Intervention Board for Agricultural Produce* [1993] ECR 5061, para. 10; Case C-263/97, *The Queen v Intervention Board for Agricultural Produce, ex parte First City Trading Ltd and Others* [1998] ECR 5537, para. 41.

[74] See, e.g., Case 145/85 (n 67) paras 10–11; Case 109/86 *Ioannis Theodorakis Biomichania Elaiou AE v The Greek State* [1987] ECR 4319, para. 11; Case 296/86, *Anthony McNicholl Ltd and others v Minister for Agriculture* [1988] ECR 1491, para. 11; Case C-347/93, *Belgian State v Boterlux SPRL* [1994] ECR 3933, para. 34; Case C-208/01, *Isabel Parras Medina and Adelina Parras Medina v Consejería de Agricultura y Medio Ambiente de la Junta de Comunidades de Castilla-La Mancha* [2002] ECR 8955, para. 19; Joined cases C-478/11 P to C-482/11 P, *Laurent Gbagbo (C-478/11 P), Katinan Justin Koné (C-479/11 P), Akissi Danièle Boni-Claverie (C-480/11 P), Alcide Djédjé (C-481/11 P) and Affi Pascal N'Guessan (C-482/11 P) v Council of the European Union*, Judgment of the Court (Grand Chamber) of 23 April 2013, [2013] ECR 258, para. 72.

law and *force majeure* under general international law reflected in Article 23 of the ILC Articles: namely, that, while the former may appear to require conjunctively 'abnormal' *and* 'unforeseeable' extraneous circumstances, under the latter *force majeure* is the occurrence of an 'irresistible force' *or* of an 'unforeseen event'.[75] But, still, there indeed exist instances where the Court has clearly distinguished between the concepts of unforeseeable circumstances and *force majeure*, at least in the context of procedural time-limits.[76]

Overall, it would then appear that *force majeure* under EU law, as is the case under Article 23 of the ILC Articles, is not limited to absolute impossibility, but rather denotes material/relative impossibility, generally including abnormal circumstances of *force majeure* defined *lato sensu* (i.e., both unforeseeable circumstances as well as occurrences of irresistible forces), not necessarily unforeseen or unforeseeable (*force majeure* defined *stricto sensu*). These abnormal circumstances must be extraneous

---

[75] Cf. in this regard Case C-314/06, *Société Pipeline Méditerranée et Rhône (SPMR) v Administration des douanes et droits indirects and Direction nationale du renseignement et des enquêtes douanières (DNRED)* [2007] ECR 12273, para. 34, first making reference to *force majeure* as abnormal and unforeseeable circumstances, and then proceeded further to analyse the concept of *force majeure* as containing both an objective element (relating to abnormal circumstances extraneous to the trader) and a subjective element (involving the trader's obligation to take appropriate steps without making unreasonable sacrifices). But in defining 'abnormality', perhaps what the Court had in mind is the wording of art. 45(2) of the Statute of the CJEU which prescribes that '[n]o right shall be prejudiced in consequence of the expiry of a time limit if the party concerned proves the existence of unforeseeable circumstances or of *force majeure*', i.e., distinguishing between *force majeure* and unforeseeable circumstances.

[76] See Case T-201/04, *Microsoft Corp v Commission of the European Communities* [2005] ECR 1491, para. 50; Case C-290/10 P, *Franssons Verkstäder AB v Office for Harmonisation in the Internal Market (Trade Marks and Designs) (OHIM)* [2010] ECR 109, para. 13; Case C-426/10 P, *Bell & Ross BV v Office for Harmonisation in the Internal Market (Trade Marks and Designs) (OHIM)* [2011] ECR 8849, para. 43; Case T-488/13, *GEA Group AG v Office for Harmonisation in the Internal Market (Trade Marks and Designs)*, Order of the General Court (Second Chamber) of 22 January 2015 [2015] ECR 64, para. 27:

> The Court of Justice has held that the concepts of unforeseeable circumstances and *force majeure* contain both an objective element, relating to abnormal circumstances unconnected to the applicant, and a subjective element involving the obligation, on the part of the applicant, to guard against the consequences of the abnormal event by taking appropriate steps, without making unreasonable sacrifices.

and outside the control of the party invoking *force majeure*,[77] and their consequences must be of such gravity so that, despite due care and all efforts employed, they could not have been avoided by taking appropriate steps without making unreasonable sacrifices.

It is under the general understanding of the concept as sketched above, that, even when the applicable EU legislation lacked an explicit reference to *force majeure*, private operators have been still permitted to raise the defence.[78] Furthermore, EU Member States themselves have been permitted to invoke *force majeure*, not only on the basis of explicit legislative provisions providing for the exception,[79] but even when such a provision was lacking, i.e., as a general defence. Essentially, the question that arises here is whether *force majeure* has become a general principle of

[77] Cf. Case C-314/06, *Société Pipeline Méditerranée et Rhône* (n 75), para. 40: 'The requirement that the circumstances must be extraneous … is not limited to those circumstances which are outside his control in a material or physical sense, but refers also to circumstances which are objectively outside the [operator's] control or situated outside his sphere of responsibility.'

[78] See Case 64-74, *Adolf Reich v Hauptzollamt Landau* [1975] ECR 261, paras 3–5; Case 6/78, *Union française de Céréales v Hauptzollamt Hamburg-Jonas* [1978] ECR 1675, para. 4; Joined cases 154, 205, 206, 226 to 228, 263 and 264/78, 39, 31, 83 and 85/79, *SpA Ferriera Valsabbia and others v Commission of the European Communities* [1980] ECR 907, paras 139–141; Case C-12/92, *Criminal proceedings against Edmond Huygen and others* [1993] ECR 6381, para. 31. For instance, in Case 149/78, *Metallurgica Luciano Rumi SpA v Commission of the European Communities* [1979] ECR 2523, paras 14–15, the Court read a *force majeure* exception into art. 60(2) of the Treaty constituting the European Coal and Steel Community (ECSC Treaty – 261 UNTS 140), establishing the general rule of compulsory publication of by operators of price lists and conditions of sale within the Common Market. The applicant argued that the situation on the reinforcement bars was such so that it could claim exemption in view of the existence of circumstances of *force majeure*: though the Court did not entertain this plea, it still found *obiter* that *force majeure*, adjusted to the specific legal context *in casu*, could be invoked by a diligent and prudent undertaking which was unable to comply without undue sacrifice with the obligation concerning publication under art. 60(2) of the ECSC Treaty

[79] See, e.g., Case C-105/02, *Commission of the European Communities v Federal Republic of Germany* [2006] ECR 9659, para. 89; Case C-377/03, *Commission of the European Communities v Kingdom of Belgium* [2006] ECR 9733, para. 95; Case C-334/08, *European Commission v Italian Republic* [2010] ECR 6869, para. 46.

EU law,[80] capable of invocation as a default defence (to the extent it is not specifically excluded), as is the case with the default application of general international law reflected in Article 23 of the ILC Articles.

The CJEU, drawing from domestic law principles existing in the majority of EU Member States, has used general principles of EU law in filling gaps to aid interpretation, similarly to general principles of law recognised by civilised nations in Article 38(1)(c) of the Statute of the ICJ.[81] So if, indeed, *force majeure* qualifies as a general principle of EU law, this would serve as a persuasive explanation for the Court's readiness to consider *force majeure* invocations, even when not explicitly provided by EU legislation. But, although, as mentioned before, the ILC readily considered that the CJEU has recognised *force majeure* as a general principle of law,[82] it appears that this issue in particular has not been free of ambiguity in EU law-related case law and literature.

While the concept of *force majeure* finds a place in most domestic legal systems (EU Member States included),[83] some commentators and Advocate Generals of the Court have concluded in the past that *force majeure* had yet to be expressly recognised as a general principle of EU law,[84]

---

[80] On general principles of EU law, see eg Rébecca-Emmanue′la Papadopoulou, *Principes généraux du droit et droit communautaire: origines et concrétisation* (Sakkoulas/Bruylant 1996); Xavier Groussot, *General Principles of Community Law* (Europa Law Publishing 2006); Takis Tridimas, *The General Principles of EU Law* (3rd edn, OUP 2013); Michael Wimmer, 'The Dinghy's Rudder: General Principles of European Union Law through the Lens of Proportionality' (2014) 20 Eur Pub L 331.

[81] See Anna Bredimas, *Methods of Interpretation and Community Law* (North-Holland 1978) 123–4; Michael Akehurst, 'The Application of General Principles of Law by the Court of Justice of the European Communities' (1981) 52 BYBIL 29, 31–40; Matthias Herdegen, 'The Origins and Development of the General Principles of Community Law' in Ulf Bernitz and Joakim Nergelius (eds) *General Principles of European Community Law* (Kluwer 2000), 3–23; Trevor C Hartley, *The Foundations of European Community Law* (6th edn, OUP 2007) 131–3; Joxerramon Bengoetxea, 'General Legal Principles Navigating Space and Time' in Ulf Bernitz, Xavier Groussot and Felix Shulyok (eds), *General Principles of EU Law and European Private Law* (Kluwer 2013), 46–51.

[82] See nn 64–65 and accompanying text.

[83] See n 1.

[84] See, e.g., Peter Gilsdorf, 'La *force majeure* dans le droit de la CEE á la lumière de la jurisprudence de la Cour de Justice' (1982) 18 Cahiers du Droit Européen 137, 141; James E Thompson, '*Force Majeure*: The Contextual Approach of the Court of Justice' (1987) 24 Common Market L Rev 259, 267–71; Konstantin D Magliveras, '*Force Majeure* in Community Law' (1990)

while others have taken an opposite stance.[85] The Court early in *IFG v Commission* admitted respectively that:

> it is true that the legal systems of the Member States provide, in certain contexts and legal relationships, for the possibility of derogation from the strict requirements of the law, especially from the legal consequences resulting from the non-fulfilment of an obligation, on account of *force majeure*.[86]

In that case the Court found that *force majeure* as invoked *in casu* was untenable, since 'a general legal principle to the effect alleged is not to be discerned in the national legal systems'.[87] Therefore, and as noted by a commentator, the Court's rejection of *force majeure* in *IFG v Commission* was in fact limited to the specific version pleaded, and it did not affect the general status of *force majeure* as a general principle of EU

---

15 Eur L Rev 460, 471; Robert Lombardi, '*Force Majeure* in European Union Law' (1997) 3 Intl Trade & Bus L Ann 81, 106; Opinion of Advocate General Capotorti in Case 38/79, *Butter- und Eier-Zentrale Nordmark eG v Hauptzollamt Hamburg-Jonas* [1980] ECR 643, para. 3; Opinion of Advocate General Jacobs in Case C-236/99, *Commission of the European Communities v Kingdom of Belgium* [2000] ECR 5659, para. 16.

[85] Opinion of Advocate General Mayras in Case 32-72, *Wasaknäcke Knäckebrotfabrik GmbH v Einfuhr- und Vorratsstelle für Getreide und Futtermittel* [1972] ECR 1189, para. 1197; James Flynn, '*Force Majeure* Pleas in Proceedings before the European Court' (1981) 6 Eur L Rev 102, 114; Papadopoulou (n 80) 272–5; Henry G Schermers and Denis F Waelbroeck, *Judicial Protection in the European Union* (6th edn, Kluwer 2001), 126–7; Opinion of Advocate General Trstenjak in Case C-101/08, *Audiolux SA ea v Groupe Bruxelles Lambert SA (GBL) and Others and Bertelsmann AG and Others* [2009] ECR 9823, para. 71. Cf. Commission notice C(88) 1696 concerning *force majeure* in European agricultural law, [1988] OJ C259/10-13, paras 1(d)–2, where the Commission stated that 'it is expedient not to take the view that the *force majeure* clause constitutes one of the general principles of Community law which apply even in the absence of an express provision', still noting that 'the *force majeure* clause simply gives expression, in a practical form, to the principle of proportionality which is undeniably one of the general principles of Community law'. Nevertheless, Magliveras (n 84), 463 is right to wonder what the Commission 'had in mind' when later including in art. 6(1) of its Proposal for a Council Directive on Civil Liability for Damage Caused by Waste ([1989] OJ C251/3) a reference that 'the producer shall not be liable under the Directive if he shows that the damage or injury to the environment results from *force majeure as defined in Community law*'. [emphasis added]

[86] Case 68/77, *Interkontinentale Fleischhandelsgesellschaft mbH & Co KG v Commission of the European Communities* [1978] ECR 353, para. 11.

[87] Ibid.

law, derived from the domestic legal systems of the Member States.[88] Indeed, in later cases, the CJEU never excluded, but rather appears to have implicitly recognised the existence of a general principle of *force majeure* in EU law.[89]

Moreover, in 2010, the CJEU reiterated that, while, as a matter of principle, Italy could invoke *force majeure* to justify its non-compliance with Directive 2006/12/EC on waste, and although the plea is not limited to absolute impossibility, it still required the previous exercise of 'all due diligence'.[90] Accordingly, it rejected Italy's plea that the non-performance of contractual obligations by private undertakings entrusted with the construction of certain waste disposal infrastructures constituted a *force majeure* situation, since Italy could have taken necessary precautions.[91]

More recently, in the *ÖBB* case, it was explicitly claimed that *force majeure* constitutes a general principle recognised in EU law. Advocate General Jääskinen admitted that *force majeure*, as a general principle, could be invoked even in the absence of an explicit legislative provision;[92] nevertheless, he noted that 'there is nothing unusual in the divergence in EU legislation with regard to the consequences of *force majeure*', (i.e., as a general principle providing a default defence) and that was exactly what Regulation (EC) No 1371/2007 on rail passengers' rights and obligations, purported to do.[93] Indeed, the CJEU in the *ÖBB* case did not accept the applicability of the 'general principle of EU law relating to *force majeure*' in the case at hand;[94] it agreed with the Advocate General that the interpretation of Article 17 of the Regulation, aimed at achieving a high level of consumer protection in the field of

---

[88] Papadopoulou (n 80) 273–4.

[89] See Case C-325/96 (n 72) para. 24; Case C-263/97 (n 72) para. 68: 'none of the general principles of Community law, and in particular the principles of *force majeure*, the protection of legitimate expectations, proportionality and equity, required exporters, in the circumstances described by the national court, to be authorised to retain all or part of any export refunds paid in advance'. Cf. Joined cases T-61/00 and T-62/00, *Associazione Produttori Olivicoli Laziali (APOL) and Associazione Italiana Produttori Olivicoli (AIPO) v Commission of the European Communities* [2003] ECR 635, para. 72.

[90] Case C-297/08, *European Commission v Italian Republic* [2010] ECR 1749, para. 85.

[91] Ibid., para. 86.

[92] Opinion of Advocate General Jääskinen delivered on 14 March 2013 in Case C-509/11, *ÖBB-Personenverkehr AG* [2013] ECR 167, paras 31–32.

[93] Ibid., paras 33–37.

[94] Case C-509/11 (n 92) Judgment of the Court (First Chamber) of 26 September 2013 [2013] ECR 613, para. 49.

transport, excluded the possibility of invocation of the *force majeure*, since this would undermine 'the essential purpose of protecting the rights of railway passengers pursued by that regulation'.[95] In fact, what the CJEU confirmed, at least implicitly, is that *force majeure* is a general principle of EU law and, as such, may be invoked as a defence, but that it is also always subject to the legal context in which it is to operate, especially if the purpose of the EU legislation in question is inherently incompatible with its invocation.

It can be deduced from the above that the Court never excluded the possibility of raising a *force majeure* defence (i.e., even when there was no exception in the applicable EU legislation). Rather, it considered the merits of the defence and thus, in principle, accepted its availability. This is not in itself revolutionary: one can recall that *force majeure* in general international law, as reflected in Article 23 of the ILC Articles, does not excuse performance when the State invoking it has assumed that risk (in the context of the *ÖBB case*, higher consumer protection in the field of rail transport even in the face of *force majeure* events). In other words, if the primary rule (of international law or EU law) excludes reliance on it. This is but one of the commonalities between *force majeure* in general international law and EU law, both constituting extraordinary defences justifying non-compliance.

To illustrate, in the 1985 *Commission v Italy* case, the Court indirectly acknowledged that a bomb attack, which destroyed statistical data of the Italian Ministry for Transport, 'may have constituted a case of *force majeure*' preventing Italy from compiling the statistical returns in respect of carriage of goods by road, in accordance with the rules laid down in Council Directive 78/546/EEC, albeit justifying non-compliance for a limited time period.[96] In the 1997 *Commission v Greece* case, the Court was reluctant to 'consider the question whether or not, in the event of *force majeure*, the Member States are obliged to pay interest pursuant to Article 11 of Regulation No 2891/77', since it had already found that the strike relied on by the Hellenic Republic could not have been regarded as a case of *force majeure* proper.[97] Again implicitly, the Court acknowledged in 2000 that Member States could, in principle, raise a *force majeure* defence, even though, in the circumstances of the case, it rejected Belgium's reliance on circumstances of a purely domestic

[95] Ibid., para. 51.

[96] Case 101/84 (n 67) paras 15–16.

[97] Case 70/86, *Commission of the European Communities v Hellenic Republic* [1987] ECR 3545, paras 7–9.

character pertaining to its political and administrative organisation.[98] However, shortly thereafter, the Court had the opportunity to note that, while Member States may not turn to domestic law justifications to excuse their non-compliance with EU law (as is the case with international law obligations as well), '[a] Member State which encounters temporarily insuperable difficulties preventing it from complying with its obligations under Community law may plead *force majeure* only for the period necessary in order to resolve those difficulties.'[99]

This latter, temporal, limitation mirrors the position regarding *force majeure* (and any other circumstance precluding wrongfulness) under general international law, as reflected in Article 27(a) of the ILC Articles. However, a notable difference appears to exist between the treatment of *force majeure* under international law and EU law: one may note that CJEU's case-law on *force majeure* fails to mention the possibility of compensating material loss if *force majeure* is successfully invoked, as potentially provided for in Article 27(b) ILC.

Ergo, and in light of the analysis in the preceding section, Iceland's assertion in the *Icesave* case – that the 2008 global financial crisis and the wholesale collapse of its banking system qualified as *force majeure* – would appear, at least *prima facie*, tenable. Moreover, important commonalities exist between *force majeure* under international law and EU law. How these may be combined in the context of investment claims against EU member states under intra-EU BITs for measures taken in the midst of financial crisis, as is developed in the following Section.

---

98 Case C-236/99, *Commission of the European Communities v Kingdom of Belgium* [2000] ECR 5657, paras 21–22.

99 Case C-1/00, *Commission of the European Communities v French Republic* [2001] ECR 9989, paras 131–132. France eventually failed to establish specific difficulties preventing it from compliance. cf. though, Case C-217/88, *Commission of the European Communities v Federal Republic of Germany* [1990] ECR 2879, para. 33:

> when a Member State in implementing a Commission regulation encounters unforeseeable difficulties which make it absolutely impossible to carry out the obligations imposed by that regulation, it must submit those problems to the Commission and suggest to it appropriate solutions. In such a case, the Commission and the Member State are obliged, by virtue of the reciprocal duties of genuine cooperation imposed on them in particular by Article 5 of the EEC Treaty, to work together in good faith in order to overcome those difficulties while complying in full with the provisions of the Treaty.

V. INVOKING *FORCE MAJEURE* IN INVESTMENT CLAIMS UNDER INTRA-EU BITS FOR FINANCIAL CRISIS MEASURES

Investor-State arbitration under intra-EU BITs has become one of the most debated issues in academic literature, entailing challenging questions regarding the interaction and overlap between international investment law and EU law.[100] As if these systemic challenges were not enough, investment claims under intra-EU BITs and the Energy Charter Treaty (ECT)[101] have been brought (or are reportedly forthcoming) against EU Member States affected by the recent financial crisis, regarding a variety of crisis measures,[102] including: the 2012 restructuring of the Greek government

---

[100] For the various facets of the *problématique*, see, inter alia, Rumiana Yotova, 'The New EU Competence in Foreign Direct Investment and Intra-EU Investment Treaties: Does the Emperor have New Clothes?' in Freya Baetens (ed.), *Investment Law Within International Law: Integrationist Perspectives* (CUP 2013) 387–414; Steffen Hindelang, 'Circumventing Primacy of EU Law and the CJEUs Judicial Monopoly by Resorting to Dispute Resolution Mechanisms Provided for in Inter-se Treaties? The Case of Intra-EU Investment Arbitration', (2012) 39 *Legal Issues of Economic Integration* 179; Christian Tietje and Clemens Wackernagel, 'Outlawing Compliance? The Enforcement of intra-EU Investment Awards and EU State Aid Law' (2014) Policy Papers on Transnational Economic Law No 41 <http://telc.jura.uni-halle.de/de/node/24> accessed 26 April 2015; August Reinisch, 'The EU on the Investment Path: *Quo Vadis* Europe? The Future of EU BITs and Other Investment Agreements' (2014) 12 Santa Clara J Intl L 111.

[101] 2080 UNTS 95; 34 ILM 360 (1995).

[102] For more detail see the contributions in this volume by De Luca, Mendelson and Paparinskis, Müller, Li and Kupelyants. See further United Nations Conference on Trade and Development (UNCTAD), *Recent Developments in Investor-State Dispute Settlement: Updated for the Multilateral Dialogue on Investment*, UNCTAD IIA Issues Note No (UN 2013) <http://unctad.org/en/PublicationsLibrary/webdiaepcb2013d3_en.pdf> accessed 26 April 2015, 23-24; Cecilia Olivet and Pia Eberhardt, *Profiting from Crisis: How Corporations and Lawyers Are Scavenging Profits from Europe's Crisis Countries* (Transnational Institute and Corporate Europe Observatory 2014) <http://corporateeurope.org/sites/default/files/profiting-from-crisis_0.pdf> accessed 26 April 2015. One could also mention, outside the intra-EU BIT context, the unsuccessful investment claim against Belgium regarding nationalisation and sell-off of the *Fortis* Bank in the aftermath of the 2008 global financial turmoil under the Belgium-China BIT; see *Ping An Life Insurance Company of China, Limited and Ping An Insurance (Group) Company of China, Limited v Kingdom of Belgium*, ICSID Case No ARB/12/29.

bonds[103] and the exclusion of a Cypriot bank's subsidiary in the bank bail-out programme implemented by Greece;[104] cuts in subsidies for renewable energy in Spain, Italy and the Czech Republic;[105] and the 2013 bank bail-in in Cyprus.[106] It is not yet known whether and how the EU Member States concerned will seek to rely on the financial crisis to defend these measures. Still, one cannot but notice an obvious tension between compliance with international investment law obligations and regulatory responses to the 2008 global financial crisis and its regional spill-over effects. Such was also the case of Iceland in the *Icesave* dispute before the EFTA Court. Accordingly, it is worth exploring whether, as a matter of principle, a *force majeure* invocation *à la européenne* (i.e., drawing from EU as well as international law) is available in investment arbitration under intra-EU BITs for financial crisis measures, as an alternative to state of necessity defences.

Until today, *force majeure* has been rarely invoked by host States and considered by investment arbitral tribunals. In a number of investment claims where *force majeure* was discussed, it was raised rather a matter of domestic law regarding breach of contract,[107] and, as such, the

---

[103] Such an investment claim was recently dismissed for lack of jurisdiction *ratione materiae*: see *Poštová banka, as and ISTROKAPITAL SE v Hellenic Republic*, ICSID No ARB/13/8, Award (9 April 2015) para. 379.

[104] See the pending claim *Cyprus Popular Bank Public Co Ltd v Hellenic Republic*, ICSID Case No ARB/14/16, and note also that, reportedly, the now defunct Cyprus Popular Bank held Greek sovereign debt as well and hence challenges the Greek PSI, in addition to the refusal of Greece's Central Bank to grant emergency liquidity assistance to its Greek branch.

[105] For the list of the known investment claims launched regarding the 'bubble' of renewable energy projects, see Energy Charter Treaty Secretariat, Investor-State Dispute Settlement Cases, <www.encharter.org/index.php?id=213&L=0#Blusun> accessed 26 April 2015.

[106] See Maurice Mendelson and Martins Paparinskis, 'Bail-Ins and International Investment Law: In and Beyond Cyprus' (in this volume) 193, Kyriaki Karadelis, 'Cyprus Threatened with Bailout Claim' (2014) Global Arbitration Review <http://globalarbitrationreview.com/news/article/32810/cyprus-threatened-bailout-claim/> accessed 26 April 2015, as well as the pending claim *Theodoros Adamakopoulos and others v Republic of Cyprus*, ICSID Case No ARB/15/49.

[107] See, e.g., *CMS Gas Transmission Company v Argentina*, ICSID Case No ARB/01/8, Award (12 May 2005) paras 227, 356; *Enron Corporation and Ponderosa Assets, LP v Argentine Republic*, ICSID Case No ARB/01/3, Award (22 May 2007) paras 214–218; *Sempra Energy International v Argentina*, ICSID Case No ARB/02/16, Award (28 September 2007) paras 243–246; *Duke Energy Electroquil Partners & Electroquil SA v Republic of Ecuador*, ICSID Case No

significance of the tribunals' reasoning and findings appears limited for our purposes. Nevertheless, in *LAFICO v Burundi*, the Tribunal rejected a *force majeure* defence, since the situation invoked squarely fell within the control of the State invoking it, being a unilateral decision of Burundi.[108] One could also refer to *Autopista v Venezuela*, concerning the respondent State's failure to increase toll rates in contravention of the Concession Agreement. In the circumstances of the case, Venezuela unsuccessfully argued that its failure to increase toll rates was excused by *force majeure* events (civil unrest, protests and threatened violence). Under the applicable law of Venezuela, *force majeure* was only available if external factors had rendered the performance of obligations impossible, and if the external factors were unforeseeable and unattributable. While the Tribunal found that the events were not unforeseeable when the Concession Agreement was negotiated,[109] it held, *obiter*, that the impossibility prerequisite under both Venezuelan law and international law did not mean 'absolute impossibility'.[110] More recently, in *Micula v Romania*, the Tribunal agreed with a suggestion, admittedly made *in passim* by claimants, that 'in theory, EU law could also possibly come into play as a circumstance precluding wrongfulness under ILC Articles 23, 24 or 25' (though Romania did not actually raise such a defence).[111]

Early international cases better illustrate that *force majeure* may be invoked as defence by a State facing severe financial difficulties. In the *Serbian* and *Brazilian Loans cases* before the Permanent Court of International Justice (PCIJ), litigants (albeit in a conspicuously complicated fashion) relied on *force majeure* as a general principle of law to justify their failure to make loan payments *in specie*. Although not successful on the facts, the availability of the defence was accepted in

---

ARB/04/19, Award (18 August 2008) para. 237; *RSM Production Corporation v République centrafricaine*, ICSID Case No ARB/07/02, Décision sur la compétence et la responabilité (7 December 2010) paras 176–185. On armed conflict and *force majeure* situations in investment treaty arbitration cases, see Christoph Schreuer, 'The Protection of Investments in Armed Conflicts' in Baetens (n 100) 18–19.

[108] *Libyan Arab Foreign Investment Company (LAFICO) v The Republic of Burundi*, Award (4 March 1991) 96 ILR 279, para. 55.

[109] *Autopista Concesionada de Venezuela, CA ('Aucoven') v Bolivarian Republic of Venezuela*, ICSID Case No ARB/00/5, Award (23 September 2003) paras 107–119.

[110] Ibid., paras 121–124.

[111] *Ioan Micula, Viorel Micula, SC European Food SA, SC Starmill SRL and SC Multipack SRL v Romania*, ICSID Case No ARB/05/20, Final Award (11 December 2013) paras 299, 329.

principle.[112] Similarly, in the 1905 *French Company of Venezuela Railroads case,* the Umpire stated that Venezuela was compelled by *force majeure* to desist from repaying debts to the claimant company, finding 'no purpose or intent' by the State to damage the company's interests, since, '[Venezuela's] first duty was to itself. Its own preservation was paramount. Its revenues were properly devoted to that end. The appeal of the company for funds came to an empty treasury, or to one only adequate to the demands of the war budget.'[113]

Shortly thereafter, in the *Russian Indemnity case*, an Arbitral Tribunal convened by the Permanent Court of Arbitration held that, if the performance of international obligations would 'imperil' the very existence of the State or 'seriously compromise its internal or external situation', the exception of *force majeure* would, in principle, apply (though the comparatively modest monetary sum owed to Russia by Turkey led to the rejection of the plea).[114] In the *Société Commerciale de Belgique* case, the PCIJ implicitly acknowledged that the serious financial situation of Greece before the Second World War could be invoked as *force majeure*, excusing Greece's failure to pay its debts.[115]

One could observe at this point that, according to the ILC's Articles and Commentary, the above instances are to be categorised as cases of state of necessity proper, rather than *force majeure*. Still, the view expressed in the ILC's Commentary to the provisionally adopted Article 31 of the 1980 Draft Articles was far less absolute, even regarding the case of default on sovereign debt:

> Failure to pay a debt has led to many international disputes in which *force majeure* has been expressly invoked by the debtor State as a circumstance justifying its conduct. Yet a detailed analysis of these cases [i.e. the *Russian Indeminity case* and *Société Commerciale de Belgique*] demonstrates that, in a

---

[112] *Case Concerning the Payment of Various Serbian Loans Issued in France (France v Serbia)*, Judgment, PCIJ, Series A, No 20 (1929) 39-40; *Payment in Gold of the Brazilian Federal Loans Contracted in France (France v Brazil)*, Judgment, PCIJ, Series A, No 21 (1929) 120. For analysis on the judgments, see Michael Waibel, *Sovereign Defaults Before International Courts and Tribunals* (CUP 2011) 60–68; Paddeu (n 39) 428–30.

[113] *French Company of Venezuela Railroads Case (France v Venezuela)*, French-Venezuelan Mixed Claims Commission, Opinion of the Umpire (31 July 1905) 10 RIAA 285, 353.

[114] *Russian Claim for Interest on Indemnities (Russia v Turkey)*, Award (11 November 1912), Permanent Court of Arbitration, 11 RIAA 421, 443.

[115] *Société Commerciale De Belgique (Belgium v Greece)*, Judgment, PCIJ, Series A/B, No 78 (1939) 177–8.

> number of instances, the situations concerned are ascribable to the notion of 'necessity' rather than to that of material impossibility of performance. *Nevertheless, situations of material impossibility of performing an obligation owing to external factors beyond the control of the State having the obligation can occur as regards payment of debts.*[116]

In other words, the ILC never considered that *force majeure* invocations by virtue of financial crisis are untenable.[117]

The view that *force majeure* is not available for situations of severe economic difficulties is often supported by a reference to the ILC's Commentary to Article 23 of the 2001 Articles, according to which reliance on *force majeure* 'does not include circumstances in which performance of an obligation has become *more difficult*, for example due to some political or economic crisis'.[118] This is bolstered by the erroneous assumption that *force majeure* under Article 23 of the ILC Articles is limited to cases of absolute impossibility.[119] Yet that view is incorrect. As discussed extensively in this chapter, the relevant test of material/relative impossibility under Article 23 of the ILC Articles covers cases of involuntary conduct and of instances in which the external events in question leave the State with no real or free choice, where performance of the obligation in question would be an unreasonable sacrifice (risking the very existence of the State or fulfilment of its essential governmental functions).[120] As has also been shown, the same

---

[116] ILC (1979) YBILC Vol. II Part Two 128, para. 22 (footnote omitted, emphasis added).

[117] See also Paddeu (n 39) 446, where it is emphasised that:

> [earlier] case-law did not, thus, concern *force majeure or* state of necessity as modern scholarship, with the benefit of hindsight, claims: in reality, it concerned both defences at a stage when they were being developed in international law. Indeed, this case-law was instrumental in shaping the notion of *force majeure* and in limiting it to situations of material impossibility of performance; but it was also instrumental in the subsequent development of a specific defence of state of necessity in international law, which is now codified in article 25 of the ILC Articles.

[118] ILC (n 37) 76, para. 3.

[119] See, e.g., ILA Committee on International Monetary Law, 'Report of the Committee in the Warsaw Conference' (1988) 63 Intl L Ass Rep Conf 418, 430 (n 13) 454–5; Sarah Heathcote, 'Circumstances Precluding Wrongfulness in the ILC Articles on State Responsibility: Necessity' in Crawford (n 4) 495; Robert D Sloane, 'On the Use and Abuse of Necessity in the Law of State Responsibility' (2012) 106 AJIL 447, 460, 463 and 489. Similarly, *Enron v Argentina* (n 107) para. 217.

[120] See supra nn 53–59 and accompanying text.

holds true for the *force majeure* defence under EU law.[121] Against the background of these approaches, and the early case law referred to, there seems to be no reason generally to exclude reliance on *force majeure* as a circumstance precluding the wrongfulness of measures taken during systemic financial crises.[122]

Indeed, the availability of a *force majeure* defence for measures taken in the midst of severe economic crisis is rather a matter of facts and construction of argument: what matters is whether, in light of the evidence, dramatic financial difficulties can be characterised as an irresistible force or an unforeseen event. If this is the case, then a State seeking to respond to a crisis will often violate its international obligations, both by regulatory acts and by omissions, as exemplified in the *Icesave* case. This, in fact, had been anticipated by the ILC, for, as Ago noted, examples of *force majeure*, 'may have the effect of rendering the performance of the international obligation definitively impossible, just as it may render it only temporarily impossible; it may prevent the State from honouring an obligation to act, or an obligation not to act'.[123]

Invoking an exception of *force majeure* serves to preserve 'a position already established (*de damno evitando*)', rather than 'enhance its [the State's] position and to promote its national interests (*de lucro captando*)' as necessity does.[124] *Force majeure* is about reactions to an actual occurrence of an irresistible force or of an unforeseen event, while necessity relates to safeguarding an essential interest *threatened* by a grave and imminent peril, i.e., displaying 'a certain preventive aspect which is lacking in cases of *force majeure*'.[125] To recall again Iceland's example, the aftermath of the 2008 financial crisis and the meltdown of

---

[121] See supra nn 69, 70, 72, 75, 76, 78 and accompanying text.

[122] Cf. Crawford (n 10) 299:

> In emphasizing the negligible amount of Turkey's debt, the *Russian Indemnity* tribunal seemed to leave open whether, say, Greece could claim that the financial crisis triggered in 2010 by its high sovereign debt renders the performance of international obligations materially impossible (provided, of course, that it could establish the other elements of *force majeure*).

[123] Ago (n 56) 49–50, para. 107. Cf. Aikaterini Titi, *The Right to Regulate in International Investment Law* (Nomos/Hart 2014) 257: 'However, in presuming involuntary state conduct, *force majeure* has no bearing on preventing regulatory chill. The defence a posteriori releases the state from its responsibility for non-observance of its obligation, but has no impact on the state's will to regulate.'

[124] ILC (n 40) 73–4, para. 29 (footnotes omitted).

[125] Ibid.

its banking system arguably left only little under threat and to prevent, and much more to preserve, so that indeed Iceland's defence regarding the non-payment of foreign deposits in the *Icesave* case appears to have been properly categorised as *force majeure*. The same would also generally be the case of anti-crisis regulatory measures of a non-discriminatory character and general application (such as debt restructuring processes, bank bail-outs excluding branches foreign banks, revocation of subsidies etc.), to the extent that 'social and economic forces beyond the power of the state to control through the exercise of due diligence'[126] make it materially/relatively impossible for the State to comply with its obligations or would impose/lead to disproportionate sacrifices.[127]

This is not to say of course that Iceland, for instance, could not (also) have invoked the state of necessity defence under Article 25 ILC, or even under EU law.[128] Equally, EU Member States operating as respondents in investment arbitration under intra-EU BITs for financial crisis measures, could potentially opt for a state of necessity defence (following Argentina's example), or an invocation of *force majeure* instead (like Iceland). But importantly, there may be instances in which reliance on *force*

---

[126] *Gould Marketing, Inc v Ministry of National Defence of Iran*, Interlocutory Award (27 July 1983) 3 Iran-USCTR 147, 153. See also the 'Consensus of Cartagena', i.e., the Communiqué of 11 Latin American countries on foreign debt and economic development issued in Cartagena de Las Indias in June 1984 (signed 22 June 1984) (1984) 23 ILM 1169, para. 7.

[127] See, e.g., Mauro Megliani, *Sovereign Debt: Genesis – Restructuring – Litigation* (Springer 2015) 438, making this argument regarding debt restructurings.

[128] Under EU law, and while practical or administrative difficulties, even on economic grounds, cannot justify, in principle, non-compliance with EU law (see, e.g., Case 288/83, *Commission of the European Communities v Ireland* [1985] ECR 1761, para. 28; Case C-42/89, *Commission of the European Communities v Kingdom of Belgium,* [1990] ECR 02821, para. 24); some limited leeway for contravention of EU law on the basis of legitimate self-protection and necessity is indeed provided according to the case law of the European Court of Justice (see, e.g., Case 16-61, *Acciaierie Ferriere e Fonderie di Modena v High Authority of the European Coal and Steel Community* [1962] ECR 289, para. 4; Case 1252/79, *SpA Acciaierie e Ferriere Lucchini v Commission of the European Communities* [1980] ECR 3753, para. 12; Case 263/82, *Klöckner-Werke AG v Commission of the European Communities* [1983] ECR 4143, paras 20–22; Joined cases 100 to 103/80, SA *Musique Diffusion française and others v Commission of the European Communities* [1983] ECR 1825, paras 89–90).

majeure may be preferable: as noted above, necessity is already precluded when a State has substantially contributed to the state of necessity.[129] By contrast, *force majeure* becomes unavailable only when the State has 'caused or induced' the situation.[130] More specifically, *force majeure* may be invoked, even if the party invoking it 'helped, by act or omission to bring it about',[131] as long as the irresistible force or unforeseen event was not 'due [to it], either alone or in combination with other factors'.[132] This difference, even taken on its own, may dictate the choice when deciding whether to invoke necessity or *force majeure* as circumstances precluding wrongfulness, especially given the willingness of arbitral tribunals, which, in their majority, have found Argentina to have substantially contributed to the 2001 financial crisis, and thus could not invoke the necessity defence.[133] But, in the case of *force majeure* defence, under both general international law and EU law,[134] material/relative impossibility is the key element, dynamically determined by factors such as unnecessary sacrifices, all due care and lack of causation or inducement of the irresistible force or unforeseen event by the invoking party: although the evidentiary threshold remains high, other parameters may also come into play in the context of *force majeure* defences for measures taken due to acute economic crisis, such as relevant policy recommendations by international financial institutions or supranational organisations, such as the EU, followed by the State concerned; or the practical inability of any, even well functioning, system to cope with fully fledged economic turbulences and, for instance, bail

---

[129] ILC (n 37) 84, para. 20.

[130] Ibid., 78, para. 9.

[131] *Gabčíkovo-Nagymaros Project* (n 54) para. 57: 'Hungary would not have been permitted to rely upon that state of necessity in order to justify its failure to comply with its treaty obligations, as it had helped, by act or omission to bring it about.'

[132] Article 23(2)(a) ILC.

[133] See, e.g., from the more recent arbitral caselaw, *Suez Sociedad General de Aguas de Barcelona SA and InterAguas Servicios Integrales del Agua SA v Argentine Republic*, ICSID Case No ARB/03/17, Decision on Liability (30 July 2010 para. 264; *Impregilo SpA v Argentine Republic*, ICSID Case No ARB/07/17, Final Award (21 June 2011) para. 358; *El Paso Energy International Company v Argentina*, ICSID Case No ARB/03/15, Award (27 October 2011) paras 649–665; *EDF International SA, SAUR International SA and León Participaciones Argentinas SA v Argentine Republic*, ICSID Case No ARB/03/23, Award (11 June 2012) paras 1172–1176. *Contra*, see *LG&E v Argentina* (n 36), para. 257; *Continental Casualty Co v Argentina* (n 36) paras 234–236.

[134] See supra nn 53–59, 69, 70, 72, 75, 76, 78 and accompanying text.

out each and every banking institution or maintain subsidisation schemes *ad infinitum*.

In view of the above, it can be expected that, in intra-EU BIT claims against Member States in financial dire straits, *force majeure* could provide a potential alternative defence, most certainly as a circumstance precluding wrongfulness under general international law. Moreover, investment tribunals can and should draw also from EU law as well as international investment law. This could serve to support the ILC's understanding, and also to supplement it, insofar as EU law emphasises the element of 'unnecessary sacrifices' in determining whether compliance with obligations has become materially/relatively impossible. Moreover, reliance on EU law could even lead tribunals to question whether, contrary to the *lex generalis* of Article 27(b) of the ILC Articles, States could avoid a duty to compensate investors affected by measures taken under *force majeure*.[135] Such forms of 'borrowing' from EU law could certainly be part of the exercise of a cross-regime comparison regarding *force majeure* as a general principle under the law on State responsibility and EU law.[136] Alternatively, one could also adhere to the view that customary international law rules, such *as force majeure* reflected in Article 23 of the ILC Articles, can also be an object of interpretation based on the principle of systemic integration,[137] thus allowing for the interpretative use of the general principle of EU law on *force majeure* (even so as to dispense with the possibility of compensation for material loss under Article 27(b)).[138]

---

[135] See, e.g., analysing the possibility of compensation for material loss, even if a defence is entertained, *CMS v Argentina* (n 107) para. 390; *LG&E v Argentina* (n 36) paras 260–261, 264; *Mr Patrick Mitchell v Democratic Republic of the Congo*, ICSID Case No ARB/99/7, Decision on the Application for Annulment of the Award (1 November 2006) para. 57, n 30; *EDF v Argentina* (n 133) paras 1171, 1178.

[136] See in this respect the methodology suggested in Stephan W Schill, 'General Principles of Law and International Investment Law' in Tarcisio Gazzini and Eric De Brabandere (eds), *International Investment Law: The Sources of Rights and Obligations* (Nijhoff 2012) 133, 145–54.

[137] Panos Merkouris, *Article 31(3)(c) VCLT and the Principle of Systemic Integration: Normative Shadows in Plato's Cave* (Nijhoff 2015) 269–300.

[138] For such an extensive use of interpretative tools, see, e.g., *Ambiente Ufficio SpA and others v Argentina,* ICSID Case No ARB/08/9, Decision on Jurisdiction and Admissibility (8 February 2013) paras 597–607, where the Tribunal inserted a 'futility exception' (drawing from customary diplomatic protection law) into art. 8 of the Argentina-Italy BIT in the context of systemic

Equally, and under a loose application of the *lex specialis* principle,[139] one might even argue in favour of directly invoking the *force majeure* exception as applied under EU law, *à l'européenne,* in cases involving intra-EU BITs and the Energy Charter Treaty. Subject to Article 55 of the ILC Articles ('*Lex specialis*'),[140] *force* majeure under Article 23 applies residually as *lex generalis* to the extent that the parties have not agreed on a more specific international norm dealing with the same subject matter.[141] Therefore, even though *force majeure* defences under international law and EU law deal with similar, but not identical subject matters, one could advocate a broad understanding of the applicable law in intra-EU BIT arbitration,[142] one that includes and prioritises the more specific EU law rule, rather than the *lex generalis* of Article 23 of the ILC Articles. This could be somehow in line with the finding of the *Eureko v Slovak Republic* Tribunal (applying an intra-EU BIT) that 'EU law may have a bearing upon the scope of rights and obligations under the BIT in the present case, by virtue of its role as part of the applicable law under BIT Article 8(6) and German law as the *lex loci arbitri*',[143] or with the conclusion of the *Electrabel* Tribunal (applying the ECT) that 'EU law (not limited to EU Treaties) forms part of the rules and principles of international law applicable to the Parties' dispute under Article 26(6) ECT'.[144]

Either way, and notwithstanding which normative construction is argued by parties and eventually chosen by arbitral tribunals, it would

---

interpretation, so as to dispense with an otherwise clear-cut and unqualified 18-month domestic litigation jurisdictional requirement.

[139] I have argued elsewhere in favour of such a strict application of the *lex specialis* principle. See for more detail, Anastasios Gourgourinis, '*Lex Specialis* in WTO and Investment Protection Law' (2010) 53 German YBIL 579, 604–18.

[140] 'These articles do not apply where and to the extent that the conditions for the existence of an internationally wrongful act or the content or implementation of the international responsibility of a State are governed by special rules of international law'.

[141] ILC (n 37), 140, para. 4.

[142] On the applicable law in investment treaty arbitration more generally, see, e.g., Hege Elisabeth Kjos, *Applicable Law in Investor-State Arbitration: The Interplay Between National and International Law* (OUP 2013); Christoph Schreuer, 'Jurisdiction and Applicable Law in Investment Treaty Arbitration' (2014) McGill J Disp Res 1.

[143] *Achmea BV v The Slovak Republic*, UNCITRAL, PCA Case No 2008-13, Award on Jurisdiction, Arbitrability and Suspension (26 October 2010) para. 279.

[144] *Electrabel SA v Republic of Hungary*, ICSID Case No ARB/07/19, Decision on Jurisdiction, Applicable Law and Liability (30 November 2012) para. 4.195.

indeed make sense to inform the understanding on *force majeure* prevailing in international law with insights from EU law, at least in the context of intra-EU BIT arbitration proceedings for crisis measures.

VI. CONCLUDING REMARKS

Using the recent invocation of the defence by Iceland in the *Icesave* case before the EFTA Court as the starting point, the present chapter has revisited the availability of *force majeure* in situations of severe financial crisis, as a matter of both general international law (as reflected in Article 23 of the ILC Articles) and EU law. The analysis has identified the many points of convergence between the two regimes and the potential for *force majeure* invocation, *à la européenne*, by EU Member States in investment arbitrations under intra-EU BITs. Given the substantial similarities between *force majeure* under general international law and EU law, there is certainly much to gain from the process of cross-fertilisation between the two regimes on available defences for non-performance of obligations in abnormal situations. This is not to say that *force majeure*, as any other circumstance precluding wrongfulness, is a panacea. Still, its possible pertinence as a defence for measures taken in the midst of severe financial crisis cannot be ignored, as the *Icesave* case manifestly proves.

13. International financial institutions in investment law and arbitration

Michael Wolfgang Müller

I. THE ROLE OF INTERNATIONAL AND SUPRANATIONAL INSTITUTIONS IN THE (NEW) GLOBAL FINANCIAL ARCHITECTURE

In response to the global financial crisis, the global financial architecture is being reassessed: proposals at both international and European level show a trend towards fortifying supra- and international institutions.[1] Internationally, already the statement of political leaders at the G20 London Summit 2009 called for 'a substantial strengthening of the international financial institutions, particularly the International Monetary Fund (IMF)'.[2] In the European Union (EU), mutual financial assistance has, in succession, been brought under the institutional framework of the European Financial Stabilisation Mechanism (EFSM), the European Financial Stability Facility (EFSF) and the European Stability Mechanism (ESM).[3] Financial assistance, both by the IMF and at the EU level is subject to lending conditionality, which has been used to impose far-reaching emergency measures, including capital controls, sovereign

[1] This chapter focuses on the role of the IMF, the European Commission and the ECB in the ESM, and of the SRB in the European Banking Union's SRM. The trend towards a strengthening of international institutions is, however, broader: see, e.g., Steve Charnovitz, 'Addressing Government Failure Through International Financial Law (2010) 13 JIEL 743, 753 on the role of the World Trade Organisation (WTO) and the International Labour Organisation (ILO) in international financial regulation.

[2] London Summit, Leaders' Statement <www.imf.org/external/np/sec/pr/2009/pdf/g20_040209.pdf> accessed 31 December 2015, paras 3, 17.

[3] Andrew Yianni and Nikita Aggarwal, 'Eurozone Financial Rescue and Stabilization Measures, and Their Legal Foundations' in Rosa M Lastra and Lee Buchheit (eds), *Sovereign Debt Management* (OUP 2014) 417, 425.

debt restructuring and bank resolutions.[4] Moreover, in the newly established (European) Banking Union, supervisory and regulatory powers have been conferred on supranational institutions. Most notably, the decision on the resolution of systemically important financial institutes will be taken at the European level by the specifically created Single Resolution Board (SRB).

In many cases, a fundamental goal of transferring decision powers to international institutions[5] is to coordinate regulatory strategies and thus ensure the stability of the global financial system.[6] Decisions taken at international level, however, can have serious implications: not only could they be questioned from the perspective of monetary sovereignty,[7] they may also be in conflict with individual rights.[8] In that latter case, it is the task of international law to attribute responsibilities: while the liability of organisations for internationally wrongful acts is still underdeveloped,[9] States might argue that they should not be held responsible

---

[4] For an overview, see Jean Pisani-Ferry, André Sapir and Guntram B Wolff, *EU-IMF Assistance to Euro Area Countries: An Early Assessment* (Bruegel 2013).

[5] In this context, the notion of 'international institutions' is used to refer to international organisations as well as organs and agencies thereof that fulfil certain functions in an inter- or supranational financial architecture; it is not meant to refer to banks and other financial institutes that operate transnationally (on their role in international arbitration see Dan Sarooshi, 'When International Financial Institutions Arbitrate: What Law Governs International Investment Arbitration' [2012] Butterworths J Intl Banking and Financial L 612). The differences stemming from the variety of institutional frameworks and competences will be addressed in the legal analysis where relevant.

[6] See, e.g., Emilios Avgouleas, *Governance of Global Financial Markets* (CUP 2012) 435 ff.

[7] See Claus D Zimmermann, 'The Concept of Monetary Sovereignty Revisited' (2013) 24 EJIL 797, 818, who, however, argues that measures aiming at financial and monetary stability rather respond to than infringe monetary sovereignty; Catherine H Lee, 'To Thine Ownself Be True: IMF Conditionality and Erosion of Economic Sovereignty in the Asian Financial Crisis' (2003) 24 U Pa J Intl Econ L 875, 904.

[8] See Matthias Goldmann, 'The Diverging Rationalities of Public Finance and International Law: A Plea for a Deliberative Approach' (ESIL Reflections, 16 November 2012) <www.esil-sedi.eu/node/237> accessed 31 December 2015.

[9] See, e.g., James Crawford, 'Holding International Organisations and Their Members To Account' (Fifth Steinkraus-Cohen International Law Lecture, 15 March 2007) <www.unawestminster.org.uk/pdf/crawford_lecture.pdf> accessed 31 December 2015; Daniel D Bradlow, 'International Law and the Operations of the International Financial Institutions' in Daniel D Bradlow and D Hunter (eds), *International Financial Institutions and International Law* (Kluwer 2010) 1, 16.

as they were forced to implement measures decided upon by international institutions.[10]

To what extent States can be held responsible for measures implemented upon decisions by international financial institutions is of particular importance in international investment law. Unless international organisations are bound by international investment law[11] investors are restricted to claims against the host State. Section II provides an overview of three areas where measures implemented due to loan conditionality or decisions by the SRB can lead to international investment disputes: capital controls, sovereign debt restructuring and bank resolution. Section III analyses these measures with regard to the law of State responsibility and specifically asks whether the measures can be attributed to the nation States and whether States can raise the defence of *force majeure* with reference to the exogenous pressure applied by financial institutions. Section IV discusses to what extent the role of international institutions can be considered in drafting and interpreting international investment agreements. Finally, Section V assesses the possibility for international financial institutions to participate in investment proceedings.

II. POTENTIAL CONFLICTS WITH INTERNATIONAL INVESTMENT LAW

International investment law plays an increasingly important role in financial disputes. Particularly, emergency measures taken in times of

---

The normative framework of the 2011 ILC Draft Articles on the Responsibility of International Organizations (YBILC 2011, Vol. II Pt Two) will be discussed below Section III.A.i).

[10] Maurice Mendelson and Martins Paparinskis, 'Bail-Ins and the International Investment Law of Expropriation: In and beyond Cyprus' [2013] Butterworths J Intl Banking and Financial L 475, 477.

[11] The recent EU approach towards investment law allows for the possibility of the EU to be a defendant in investment arbitration; cf. Regulation (EU) No 912/2014 (23 July 2014), OJ L 257/121; and, as regards EU-third state agreements, e.g., art. X.20 of the signed but not yet ratified Comprehensive Economic and Trade Agreement between the EU and Canada (Consolidated CETA Text) and sect. 3 art. 5 of the EU Commission's draft chapter on investment protection in a Transatlantic Trade and Investment Partnership between the European Union and the United States of America (Commission Draft TTIP); for a discussion of these developments see below III.1c) and V.2.

economic financial crises have been challenged before investment tribunals.[12] Prospective disputes in the areas of capital controls (A), sovereign debt restructuring (B), and bank resolution (C) may especially involve international financial institutions.

A. Capital Controls

In the course of the financial crisis, capital controls, such as the restriction and taxation of international transactions, have been suggested as a possible regulatory mechanism to prevent contagious effects in the global financial system.[13] The IMF, in an 'ideational change',[14] accepted

---

[12] See, in detail, Giorgio Sacerdoti, 'BIT Protections and Economic Crises: Limits to Their Coverage, the Impact of Multilateral Financial Regulation and the Defence of Necessity' (2013) 28(2) ICSID Rev 351.

[13] Most prominently Jonathan D Ostry and others, 'Capital Inflows: The Role of Controls' (2010) IMF Staff Position Note, 19 February 2010 <www.imf.org/external/pubs/ft/spn/2010/spn1004.pdf> accessed 31 December 2015; Jonathan D Ostry and others, 'Managing Capital Inflows: What Tools to Use?' (2011) IMF Staff Discussion, Note, 5 April 2011 <www.imf.org/external/pubs/ft/sdn/2011/sdn1106.pdf> accessed 31 December 2015; Ricardo Hausmann and others, 'Letter to Secretary of State Clinton, Secretary of Treasury Geithner and Ambassador Kirk' 31 January 2011 <www.ase.tufts.edu/gdae/policy_research/CapCtrlsLetter.pdf> accessed 31 December 2015; this view is in line with the EU's approach to the free movement of capital, see arts 64, 66 and 75 of the Treaty for the Functioning of the European Union which allow for restrictions of capital movements in exceptional circumstances; Jan Kleinheisterkamp, 'European Policy Space in International Investment Law' (2012) 27 ICSID Rev 416, 421. See also G20 Seoul Summit, Leaders' Declaration <www.g20.utoronto.ca/summits/2010seoul.html> accessed 31 December 2015: '[W]e called on the FSB, IMF and BIS to do further work on macroprudential frameworks, including tools to mitigate the impact of excessive capital flows'.

[14] Manuela Moschella, 'The Institutional Roots of Incremental Ideational Change: The IMF and Capital Controls After the Global Financial Crisis' [2014] BJ Pol Intl Rel 1; see International Monetary Fund, 'The Liberalization And Management Of Capital Flows: An Institutional View' (2012) <www.imf.org/external/np/pp/eng/2012/111412.pdf> accessed 31 December 2015; for an evaluation of the IMF policy on capital controls during the financial crisis, see Barry Eichengreen and Andrew K Rose, 'Capital Controls in the 21st Century' (2014) Center for Economic Policy Research Policy Insight No 72 <www.cepr.org/sites/default/files/policy_insights/PolicyInsight72.pdf> accessed 31 December 2015; Kevin P Gallagher and Yuan Tian, 'Regulating Capital Flows in Emerging Markets: the IMF and the Global Financial Crisis' (2014) Global Economic Governance Initiative Working Paper 5 <www.bu.edu/pardee/files/2014/05/Regulating-Capital-Flows-Working-Paper1.pdf> accessed 31 December 2015.

the introduction of capital controls in Ukraine, Latvia, and Cyprus and even recommended their use in Brazil and Colombia.[15]

Therefore, it seems possible that the IMF might even make capital controls a condition for financial assistance.[16] Under its Articles of Agreement, the IMF is entitled to do so.[17] Capital controls could, however, be challenged under free transfer of capital guarantees in some investment agreements as well as under the standards of indirect expropriation and fair and equitable treatment (FET).[18] In investment disputes brought under these standards, arbitral tribunals would need to assess how the pressure resulting from lending conditions imposed upon States might affect the assessment of the measures taken.

B. Sovereign Debt Restructuring

A similar question could be raised with regard to sovereign debt restructuring, such as the Greek 2012 sovereign debt 'haircut'. The payment of a second bailout package by the IMF and the EFSF was preceded by an agreement that private investors would be involved in the debt restructuring.[19] The envisaged restructuring consisted of an exchange of existing instruments against new bonds issued by Greece (€31.5 per

---

[15] Annamaria Viterbo, *International Economic Law and Monetary Measures* (Edward Elgar Publishing 2012) 198; Guntram B Wolff, 'Capital Controls Will Put the Euro at Risk' *Financial Times* (London, 25 March 2013).

[16] On prospective IMF approaches towards capital controls, see Kevin P Gallagher and Yuan Tian, 'Practicing What They Preach: The IMF and Capital Controls' (*Triple Crisis: Global Perspectives on Finance, Development and Environment*, 13 June 2014) <http://triplecrisis.com/practicing-what-they-preach-the-imf-and-capital-controls/> accessed 31 December 2015.

[17] Articles of Agreement of the International Monetary Fund, 60 Stat 1401; 2 UNTS 39, arts V(3)(a) and VI(3); see Viterbo (n 15) 183.

[18] For an assessment see Prabash Ranjan, 'Capital-Flow Management Measures and International Investment Law: Never the Twain Shall Meet?' (in this volume) 257, as well as Viterbo (n 15) 151; Abba Kolo and Thomas Wälde, 'Economic Crises, Capital Transfer Restrictions and Investor Protection under Modern Investment Treaties' (2008) 3 Capital Markets LJ 154; Matthias Ruffert 'Free Flow of Capital' in Rüdiger Wolfrum (ed.), *Max Planck Encyclopedia of Public International Law* (OUP 2014) <http://opil.ouplaw.com/view/10.1093/law:epil/9780199231690/law-9780199231690-e1506?rskey=bLsyvs&result=1&prd=EPIL> accessed 31 December 2015.

[19] Euro Summit Statement, 26 October 2011 <www.consilium.europa.eu/uedocs/cms_data/docs/pressdata/en/ec/125644.pdf> accessed 31 December 2015. For comment see Christoph Ohler, 'Restructuring Sovereign Debt on the Bases of Collective Action Clauses' (in this volume) 129, Yanying Li, 'Sovereign Bond

€100), bonds issued by the EFSF (€15 per €100) and securities linked to the Greek gross domestic product.[20] Fearing too many holdout creditors, Greece retroactively inserted Collective Action Clauses (CACs) into the existing sovereign bonds, according to which the decision of a qualified majority became binding on all private creditors.[21] It has been argued that this measure could amount to an indirect expropriation of creditors who were deprived of substantial parts of their initial investment as well as to a violation of the standard of non-discrimination, as official creditors were not involved in the debt restructuring.[22]

For some time, it seemed as if three awards by tribunals established under the International Centre for the Settlement of Investment Disputes (ICSID) on claims brought subsequent to Argentina's 2005 default had opened the door to investment arbitration for disputes on sovereign debt restructuring.[23] In the meantime, however, this door (or 'Pandora's box', as it was argued)[24] seems to have been closed again: in the case concerning the Greek sovereign debt restructuring, jurisdiction was denied as the

Disputes Before Investment Treaty Tribunals: Safeguarding the Exercise of Collective Action Clauses with a Single-Limb Voting Mechanism' (in this volume) 135, and Hayk Kuypelyants, 'Police Powers of the State in Sovereign Debt Restructurings' (in this volume), as well as Philip R Lane, 'The European Sovereign Debt Crisis' (2012) 26 J of Econ Perspect 49, 59; Andreas Witte, 'The Greek Bond Haircut: Public and Private International Law and European Law Limits to Unilateral Sovereign Debt Restructuring' (2012) 9 Manchester J Intl Econ L 307, 329.

[20] See Hellenic Republic Ministry of Finance, 'Invitation Memorandum' (24 February 2012); unfortunately, the document is no longer available online; an extensive discussion is provided by Otto Sandrock, 'The Case for More Arbitration When Sovereign Debt Is to Be Restructured: Greece as an Example' (2012) 23 Am Rev Intl Arb 507, 513.

[21] Greek Bondholders Act 4050/2012 <www.isda.org/uploadfiles/_docs/Act_of_the_Bank_of_Greece_9_March_2012.pdf> accessed 31 December 2015; Jeromin Zettelmeyer, Christoph Trebesch and Mitu Gulati, 'The Greek Debt Restructuring: An Autopsy' (2013) 28 Economic Policy 513, 517, 525; Sandrock (n 20) 514.

[22] See James Wilson and Gerrit Wiesmann, 'Germans Seek Lawsuit Over Greek Debt Swap', *Financial Times* (London, 12 March 2012).

[23] *Abaclat and others v The Argentine Republic*, ICSID Case No ARB/07/5, Decision on Jurisdiction and Admissibility (4 August 2011); *Ambiente Ufficio SpA and others v The Argentine Republic*, ICSID Case No ARB/08/9, Decision on Jurisdiction and Admissibility (8 February 2013); *Giovanni Alemanni and others v Argentina*, ICSID Case No ARB/07/8, Decision on Jurisdiction and Admissibility (17 November 2014).

[24] Michael Waibel, 'Opening Pandora's Box: Sovereign Bonds in International Arbitration' (2007) 101 AJIL 711.

sovereign bonds in question were not regarded as investment under the applicable BITs and Article 25 of the ICSID Convention.[25]

Of course, this does not need to be the last word. If future disputes on sovereign debt restructuring are brought before investment tribunals, it is not unlikely that they have to address questions on the involvement of international institutions: the restructuring of private claims is a common and important feature of IMF conditionality.[26] This is due to the fact that IMF lending only aims at coping with liquidity problems and is subject to a debt sustainability analysis.[27] By means of lending conditions, the IMF aims at restoring sustainability, inter alia, by lowering the level of sovereign debt. Since the IMF in a recent review came to the conclusion that past sovereign debt restructurings have been 'too little and too late',[28] it is likely that new conflicts regarding creditors' rights will arise.

C. Bank Resolution

Lastly, future disputes could arise also out of attempts to prevent sovereign defaults by restructuring systemically important financial institutions without resort to public money. In Cyprus, the auditors from the European Commission, the ECB and the IMF (the 'Troika') required private creditor participation in the restructuring of two failing banks. A so-called 'bail-in' scheme had to be implemented which provided for the cancellation of shares and the conversion of debt to equity.[29] In the end, 37.5 per cent of deposits exceeding €100,000 were converted to equity.[30]

---

25 *Poštová banka, A.S. and ISTROKAPITAL SE v Hellenic Republic*, ICSID Case No ARB/13/8, Award (9 April 2015) paras 350, 371.

26 Rosa M Lastra, 'The Role of the International Monetary Fund' in Lastra and Buchheit (n 3) 49, 68.

27 Ibid., 60.

28 IMF, 'Sovereign Debt Restructuring – Recent Development and Implications for the Fund's Legal and Policy Framework' (2013) <www.imf.org/external/np/pp/eng/2013/042613.pdf> accessed 31 December 2015, 15.

29 European Commission Directorate-General for Economic and Financial Affairs, 'The Economic Adjustment Programme for Cyprus 2013' (2013) Occasional Papers 149 <http://ec.europa.eu/economy_finance/publications/occasional_paper/2013/pdf/ocp149_en.pdf> accessed 31 December 2015. For comment see Maurice Mendelson and Martins Paparinskis, 'Bail-Ins and International Investment Law: In and Beyond Cyprus' (in this volume) 193, as well as Jenny Giotaki, 'The Cypriot "Bail-in Litigation": A First Assessment of the Ruling of the Supreme Court of Cyprus' [2013] Butterworths J Intl Banking and Financial L 485.

30 Ian Jack and Tom Cassels, 'Cyprus: An Analysis of the Impact of the Resolution Methodology on Stakeholders' Claims Including the Emergency

In the EU, the strategy to avoid public bailouts was subsequently placed on a broader footing: the Bank Recovery and Resolution Directive (BRRD)[31] and the Regulation establishing a Single Resolution Mechanism (SRM)[32] built a new framework for bank resolution.[33] The most remarkable example of such institutionalisation is the approach taken by the newly established 'Banking Union': here, resolution decisions are taken at the European level by the SRB, subject to objection by the Council and the Commission, and have to be implemented by the Member States.[34]

Creditors who suffered a loss under the Cypriot bail-in have brought an investment claim[35] which is expected to be based mainly on expropriation and violation of the FET standard in the applicable treaty.[36] In the

---

Liquidity Assistance' (2013) 8(4) Capital Markets LJ 450, 451. On the Cyprus case, see also the recent decision of the Court of Justice of the European Union (Grand Chamber), Joined Cases C-8/15 P to C-10/15 P, *Ledra Advertising Ltd et al v European Commission and European Central Bank*, ECLI:EU:C:2016:701, Judgment of 20 September 2016. The Court held that while the Commission's decision to sign a Memorandum of Understanding can, in general, be challenged under arts 268, 340 TFEU, the measures taken in Cyprus did not violate the creditors' right to property guaranteed by art. 17(1) of the Charter of Fundamental Rights of the European Union.

[31] Directive 2014/59/EU of the European Parliament and of the Council of 15 May 2014 establishing a framework for the recovery and resolution of credit institutions and investment firms and amending Council Directive 82/891/EEC, and Directives 2001/24/EC, 2002/47/EC, 2004/25/EC, 2005/56/EC, 2007/36/EC, 2011/35/EU, 2012/30/EU and 2013/36/EU, and Regulations (EU) No 1093/2010 and (EU) No 648/2012, of the European Parliament and of the Council, [2014] OJ L173/190.

[32] Regulation (EU) No 806/2014 of the European Parliament and of the Council of 15 July 2014 establishing uniform rules and a uniform procedure for the resolution of credit institutions and certain investment firms in the framework of a Single Resolution Mechanism and a Single Resolution Fund and amending Regulation (EU) No 1093/2010, [2014] OJ L225/1 (SRM).

[33] For an overview see Michael Schillig, 'Bank Resolution Regimes in Europe – Part II: Resolution Tools and Powers' (2014) 25 Eur Bus L Rev 65, 88; Peter King and Alexander Wood, 'The EU Recovery and Resolution Directive: Preventing Another Financial Crisis' [2013] Butterworths J Intl Banking and Financial L 641, 642.

[34] Art. 18 (1), (9) SRM (n 32); see Nicolas Véron and Guntram B Wolff, *From Supervision to Resolution: Next Steps on the Road to European Banking Union* (Bruegel 2013).

[35] *Marfin Investment Group Holdings S.A., Alexandros Bakatselos and others v Republic of Cyprus*, ICSID Case No. ARB/13/27.

[36] Mendelson and Paparinskis (n 10) 477.

future, the new European framework might also give rise to investment proceedings against bail-ins, in the course of which the role of the SRB could be subject to debate.[37]

III. INTERNATIONAL INSTITUTIONS AND THE LAW OF STATE RESPONSIBILITY

The responses in the scenarios just summarised (capital controls, sovereign debt restructuring, and bank bail-ins) point to two important mechanisms by which international institutions are able to induce measures that can potentially conflict with investor rights: lending conditionality and decision-making by supranational bodies. Whether States can be held liable for these measures, is, in the first place, determined by the international law of State responsibility. The International Law Commission's Draft Articles on the Responsibility of States for Internationally Wrongful Acts (ILC Articles),[38] which codify secondary rules of State responsibility,[39] play an important role in international investment law as international investment agreements normally do not provide special rules on attribution and circumstances precluding wrongfulness (with the exception of non-precluded measure clauses).[40] The participation of international institutions in the decision-making process raises two important questions for the law of State responsibility. First, can the measure still be attributed to the respective nation State? (A). Second, if the measure is still attributable, can the State raise the defence of *force majeure* on grounds of having acted under external pressure? (B).

---

[37] Cf. Michael Wolfgang Müller, 'Creditor Protection in Bank Resolution: a Case for International Investment Arbitration?' (2015) 10(3) Capital Markets LJ 276.

[38] ILC, 'Articles on the Responsibility of States for Internationally Wrongful Acts' YBILC (2001) Vol. II Part Two 26.

[39] James Crawford, *State Responsibility: The General Part* (OUP 2013) 114; Luigi Condorelli and Claus Kress, 'The Rules of Attribution: General Considerations' in James Crawford, Alain Pellet and Simon Olleson (eds), *The Law of International Responsibility* (OUP 2010) 221.

[40] Pavel Šturma, 'International Investment Law and State Responsibility' in Rainer Hofmann and Christian J Tams (eds), *International Investment Law and General International Law* (Nomos 2011) 111, 114; Martins Paparinskis, 'Investment Treaty Arbitration and the (New) Law of State Responsibility' (2013) 24 EJIL 617, 627. On non-precluded measure clauses see below Section IV.A.

A. Attribution

The main rules on the attribution of acts to a State are codified in Articles 4, 5 and 8 of the ILC Articles, which have already been relied on in investment decisions.[41] They provide that an act is attributable to a State when the person acting was either a State organ under domestic law (structural approach), exercised governmental authority in the particular instance (functional approach) or acted 'on the instructions of, or under the direction or control of' the State (control approach).[42] Taking the three standards together, 'all activities of the State, in whatever form it chooses to act, are attributable to the State'.[43]

In general, this rule is independent of the circumstances of the act, including the involvement of international organisations.[44] The ILC Draft Articles on the Responsibility of International Organizations normally only 'provide a second layer of responsibility for the organisation. State responsibility remains intact'.[45] A different assessment might, however, be based on the ECtHR's decision in *Behrami and Saramati v France*, according to which a State can be exonerated from international liability

---

[41] See, e.g., *Salini Construttori SpA and Italstrade SpA others v The Hashemite Kingdom of Jordan*, ICSID Case No ARB/02/13, Decision on Jurisdiction (29 November 2004) para. 84; *Emilio Maffezini v Kingdom of Spain*, ICSID Case No ARB/97/7, Award (13 November 2000) para. 76; *Tokios Tokelès v Ukraine*, ICSID Case No ARB/02/18, Decision on Jurisdiction (29 April 2004) para. 45; and, in detail, Kaj Hobér, 'State Responsibility and Investment Arbitration' (2008) 25 J Intl Arb 545.

[42] Christina Knahr, 'International Investment Law and State Responsibility: Conditions of Responsibility' in Hofmann and Tams (n 40) 95, 96.

[43] Hobér (n 41) 568.

[44] Under the ILC Draft Articles, attribution is an 'essentially normative' concept (Crawford (n 39) 133); the factual circumstances of an act are considered in the context of circumstances precluding wrongfulness.

[45] Emily Sipiorski, Christian Tietje and Grit Töpfer, 'Responsibility in Investor-State-Arbitration in the EU – Managing Financial Responsibility Linked to Investor-State Dispute Settlement Tribunals Established by EU's International Investment Agreements' (2013) 10 Transnational Disp Management 5, 14. This secondary responsibility of international organisations is without relevance unless international organisations join international investment agreements. In that case, the conduct of the international institution could be attributed according to Art. 5 DARIO; see Angelos Dimopoulos, *EU Foreign Investment Law* (OUP 2011) 259. However, as the example of the EU shows, it is likely that special arrangements on the distribution of liability will be made.

when it acted under Security Council orders.[46] However, not only is the ECtHR's approach of denying simultaneous attribution to both international organisations and Member States highly disputed,[47] it is also regarded as restricted to actions authorised by the United Nations.[48] In any case, and most importantly, the approach is, according to the ECtHR's own reasoning, limited to situations where an international institution retains 'ultimate authority and control' over the measure in question.[49]

Against this background, this section will discuss questions of attribution with regard to lending conditionality (i) and decisions taken by the SRB (ii). Thereafter, the implications of the proposed EU investment framework on the question of attribution will be assessed (iii).

i. Lending conditionality

As the above examples have shown, lending conditionality is an important method of the IMF's and Troika's policy-making.[50] While the frameworks for both IMF and ESM conditionality provide for 'national

---

46 *Behrami v France and Saramati v France, Germany and Norway* [2007] EHRR SE10.

47 Andrew Clapham, 'The Subject of Subjects and the Attribution of Attribution' in Lawrence Boisson de Chazournes and Marcelo Kohen (eds), *International Law and the Quest for Its Implementation* (Martinus Nijhoff 2010) 45, 57; the ECtHR's reasoning has further been criticised, e.g., by Marko Milanović and Tatjana Papić, 'As Bad as It Gets: The European Court of Human Rights's Behrami and Saramati Decision and General International Law' (2009) ICLQ 267, 275; Bernhard Knoll, 'Rights Without Remedies: The European Court's Failure to Close the Human Rights Gap in Kosovo' (2008) 68 Zeitschrift für ausländisches öffentliches Recht und Völkerrecht 431, 437.

48 Heike Krieger, 'A Credibility Gap: The Behrami and Saramati Decision of the European Court of Human Rights' (2009) 13 Journal of International Peacekeeping 159, 179.

49 *Behrami v France* (n 46) para. 133; see the detailed discussion of this standard provided by Luis I Gordillo, *Interlocking Constitutions* (Hart 2012) 268 ff.

50 Scott L Greer, 'Structural Adjustment Comes to Europe: Lessons for the Eurozone from the Conditionality Debates' (2014) 14 Global Social Policy 51, 53. The legal basis of lending conditionality is art. V(3)(a) IMF Articles ('The Fund shall adopt policies on the use of its general resources') and art. 12(1) ESM Treaty ('the ESM may provide stability support to an ESM Member subject to strict conditionality'). For the ESFS, lending conditionality was stipulated in art. 2(1)(a) ESFS Framework Agreement.

ownership'[51] of the adjustment programmes which are the condition for obtaining international credit, in practice things may 'have worked a bit differently':[52] it has been reported that borrowing countries saw themselves with hardly any choice but to implement measures drafted by the IMF.[53] Technically, however, all programmes have to be implemented in the respective borrowing State before they have external effects on investors.[54] Even though governments may politically see no choice but to accept the terms, legally the State is by no means legally forced to do so.[55] Measures introduced by the government or the parliament in the context of lending conditionality thus remain fully attributable to the borrowing State.[56]

---

51 See IMF Guidelines on Conditionality <www.imf.org/External/np/pdr/cond/2002/eng/guid/092302.htm> accessed 31 December 2015; IMF, Factsheet on Conditionality <www.imf.org/external/np/exr/facts/conditio.htm> accessed 31 December 2015; Mohsin S Khan and Sunil Sharma, 'IMF Conditionality and Country Ownership of Programs' (2003) 18(2) World Bank Research Observer 227, 240. Similarly, art. 13(3) ESM Treaty requires that the memorandum of understanding 'detailing the conditionality attached to the financial assistance facility' is negotiated 'with the ESM Member concerned'. On the substantive differences between IMF and ESM conditionality, see Pisani-Ferry and others (n 4) 22.

52 Rosa M Lastra, 'IMF Conditionality' (2002) 4 J Intl Bank Reg 166, 169.

53 Pisani-Ferry and others (n 4) 22. The role of international lenders in the Greek and Cypriot restructurings can be inferred from Euro Summit Statement, 26 November 2011 <www.consilium.europa.eu/uedocs/cms_data/docs/pressdata/en/ec/125644.pdf> accessed 31 December 2015; European Commission, 'The Economic Adjustment Programme for Cyprus 2013' (2013) Occasional Papers 149 <http://ec.europa.eu/economy_finance/publications/occasional_paper/2013/pdf/ocp149_en.pdf> accessed 31 December 2015, 39; European Stability Mechanism, 'Cyprus – ESM Financial Assistance for Cyprus' <http://esm.europa.eu/assistance/cyprus/index.htm> accessed 31 December 2015.

54 The measures in Greece and Cyprus were implemented by the Greek Bondholders Act 4050/2012 and the Cypriot Comprehensive Law on the Resolution of Credit and Other Financial Institutions respectively. See Zettelmeyer and others (n 21) 517, 525; Giotaki (n 29) 485; Pisani-Ferry and others (n 4) 40.

55 Celine Tan, 'Regulation and Resource Dependency: The Legal and Political Aspects of Structural Adjustment Programmes' in Bradlow and Hunter (n 9) 167, 180; Axel Dreher, 'IMF Conditionality: Theory and Evidence' (2009) 141 Public Choice 233, 235.

56 See also Erik Denters and Annamaria Viterbo, *International Monetary Fund (IMF)* (Wolters Kluwer 2013) 70.

ii. Resolution decisions

Within the Banking Union, the competence to take resolution decisions has formally been transferred to European level.[57] Although the decisions are addressed to the national resolution authority which then takes measures with legal effects,[58] one might argue that in this constellation it is no longer the State organ's act, but the 'decision addressed to the Member State [which] indirectly'[59] inflicts damage on the investor. However, from the perspective of international law rules on State responsibility[60] the internal obligation of Member States to comply with the decision is not determinative: despite this obligation the implementation remains an act that is attributable to the State.[61] The ECtHR has expressly distinguished its approach of shifting attribution to the international organisation in cases of 'ultimate authority and control' from situations where the impugned act is 'carried out by the respondent State authorities, on its territory and following a decision by one of its own Ministers'.[62] Carrying out the decision of an international organisation thus can make the State liable under international law.[63]

The distinction, however, points to potential conflicts arising out of further integration. If a supra- or international institution were to take measures with immediate, direct legal effects on investors, it could no longer be argued that the respective measure was, at least formally, carried out by a State organ. In this situation, the current framework of investor-State arbitration, without the possibility of holding international organisations liable, might come to its limits. An indirect way of 'piercing the institutional veil'[64] might be possible in some cases – if the

---

[57] Art. 18(1) and (9) SRM.

[58] Art. 18(9) SRM.

[59] Richard Happ, 'The Legal Status of the Investor vis-à-vis the European Communities: Some Salient Thoughts' (2007) 10 Intl Arb L Rev 74, 77.

[60] Thomas Eilmansberger, 'Bilateral Investment Treaties and EU Law' (2009) 46 Common Market L Rev 383, 424.

[61] Dimopoulos (n 45) 260.

[62] *Behrami v France* (n 46) para. 151, with reference to the ECtHR's earlier decision in *Bosphorus v Ireland* [2005] 41 EHRR 1. For a more detailed analysis of the decisions' complex interplay, see Cedric Ryngaert, 'The European Court of Human Rights' Approach to the Responsibility of Member States In Connection With Acts of International Organizations' (2011) 60 ICLQ 997.

[63] Cf. Crawford (n 9) 7.

[64] Cf. (with regard to the EU) Ramses A Wessel, 'The EU as a Party to International Agreements: Shared Competences, Mixed Responsibilities' in Alan Dashwood and Marc Maresceau (eds), *Law and Practice of EU External Relations* (CUP 2008) 152, 185. Frank Hoffmeister, 'Litigating Against the

host State alters the legal framework and precludes legal redress, this might be seen as a violation of the FET standard.[65] This approach, however, is limited to cases where the investment was made before a transfer of competences takes place. In the long run, a more general solution allowing for international organisations to be held responsible for the violation of investor rights is necessary. The next paragraph discusses whether the recent EU approach can serve as a model for such a solution.

iii. The prospective EU framework

The prospective EU investment framework acknowledges the problem of divided competences and in consequence provides for the possibility of EU responsibility in investment law.[66] The EU will be party to the envisaged EU investment agreements.[67] The allocation of responsibility

---

European Union and Its Member States – Who Responds Under the ILC's Draft Articles on International Responsibility of International Organizations' (2010) 21 EJIL 723, 731.

65 Legal stability has been seen as an element of the FET standard. However, it has also been held that the State under some circumstances is entitled to change the legal framework; see, particularly, *CMS GAS Transmission Company v The Argentine Republic,* ICSID Case No ARB/01/8, Award (12 May 2005) para. 277; *Saluka Investments BV v The Czech Republic*, UNCITRAL, Partial Award (17 March 2006) para. 305; *Parkerings-Compagniet AS v Republic of Lithuania,* ICSID Case No ARB/05/8, Award (11 September 2007) para. 332; Rudolf Dolzer and Christoph Schreuer, *Principles of International Investment Law* (2nd edn, OUP 2012) 145; Jeswald W Salacuse, *The Law of Investment Treaties* (OUP 2010) 232.

66 Thus, it builds on a debate about divided competences between EU and Member States that can be found in various areas, including, most prominently WTO law and the Law of the Sea; cf. Wessel (n 64) 185; Romualdo Bermejo Garcia and Rosana Garciandía Garmendia, 'The EU as an Actor at the WTO: Its Strengths and Weaknesses Throughout History' (2012) 3 Eastern J European Studies 49, 57. The financial implications of investment arbitration, however, might restrain the Union's eagerness 'to take up responsibility' for violations of investment law, which makes a comparative assessment difficult; cf. Freya Baetens, Gerard Kreijen and Andrea Varga, 'Determining International Responsibility Under the New Extra-EU Investment Agreements: What Foreign Investors in the EU Should Know' (2014) 5 Vanderbilt JTL 1203, 1243.

67 The competence in the area of investment has been transferred to the EU under art. 207 TFEU; the EU is currently negotiating IIAs with several third States. See August Reinisch, 'The Future Shape of EU Investment Agreements' (2013) 28 ICSID Rev 179; Marc Bungenberg and August Reinisch, 'Special Issue: The Anatomy of the (Invisible) EU Model BIT' (2014) 15 JWIT 375.

between Union and Member States is addressed in an EU regulation[68] which distinguishes between internal and external responsibility.[69] The provisions on internal responsibility are quite straightforward: while the Union bears the financial consequences of treatment that was afforded or required by the EU, in all other cases the Member States remain liable.[70] 'Put differently, financial responsibility should fall internally on the entity responsible for defining the content of the treatment afforded to the foreign investor'.[71] In the case of decisions by the SRB this would mean that although the treatment of the investor finally was 'afforded' by the Member State, the financial liability would lie with the Union.[72]

The regulation's rules on external responsibility are more complicated: the regulation does not contain explicit rules on the attribution of conduct but merely addresses the question who should 'act as defendant'. The Union shall act as defendant when the treatment in question was afforded by the EU, or, in the case of treatment afforded by a Member State, when the Commission chooses for the Union to act as defendant.[73] In order for this provision to be workable, the envisaged EU International Investment Agreements (IIAs) have to allow for joint attribution as only in that case a decision between two potential defendants can be made.[74]

B. *Force Majeure*

In light of the preceding discussion, most of the measures taken in response to the financial crises will remain attributable to the host State. However, the exogenous pressure that is exercised by international institutions might give rise to the customary international law defence of

---

[68] Regulation (EU) No 912/2014 (n 11).

[69] Sipiorski and others (n 45) 9.

[70] Art. 3 Regulation (EU) No 912/2014 (n 11).

[71] Jan Kleinheisterkamp, 'Financial Responsibility in European International Investment Policy' (2014) 63 ICLQ 449, 459.

[72] In the context of the SRM, a similar provision is made in art. 87(4) SRM for domestic court proceedings.

[73] Arts 4, 9(2) Regulation (EU) No 912/2014 (n 11); on the procedural consequences, see below Section V.2.

[74] Art. 8(1) Regulation (EU) No 912/2014 (n 11) explicitly makes reference to such agreements. Art. X.20 Consolidated CETA Text and sect. 3 art. 5 Commission Draft TTIP contain provisions catering for a potential defendant status of both Member States and the European Union.

force majeure. Article 23 of the ILC Articles, which is regarded as reflecting a general principle of international law,[75] provides:

1. The wrongfulness of an act of a State not in conformity with an international obligation of that State is precluded if the act is due to force majeure, that is the occurrence of an irresistible force or of an unforeseen event, beyond the control of the State, making it materially impossible in the circumstances to perform the obligation.
2. Paragraph 1 does not apply if:
   (a) the situation of force majeure is due, either alone or in combination with other factors, to the conduct of the State invoking it; or
   (b) the State has assumed the risk of that situation occurring.

The strict interpretation of the defence in general international law stipulates a high threshold for its success.[76] In the first alternative, the notion of 'irresistible force' requires that States have been unable to oppose or overcome the constraint by any means.[77] In the case described above, States, however, had some degree of influence on the decision or could at least refuse to implement the measures. Irresistible force could only be established if the external pressure placed upon the State by the international institution left it with no choice but to violate its obligation

[75] Cf. *Autopista Concesionada de Venezuela v Venezuela*, ICSID Case No ARB/00/5, Award (23 September 2003); *Mobil Oil Iran, Inc et al v Iran*, Iran-US Claims Tribunal, 16 Iran-USCTR 3, 39.

[76] The defence was discussed and rejected in *Autopista Concesionada*, ibid., para. 107; *Sempra Energy International v The Argentine Republic*, ICSID Case No ARB/02/16, Award (28 September 2007) para. 217 and, recently, in *Niko Resources (Bangladesh), Ltd v Bangladesh Petroleum Exploration & Production Co Ltd and Bangladesh Oil Gas and Mineral Corporation*, ICSID Case No ARB/10/11 and ARB/10/18, Decision on the Payment Claim (11 September 2014) para. 191. For a detailed analysis see Anastasios Gourgourinis, 'Financial Crisis as *Force Majeure* Under International Law and EU Law: Defending Emergency Measures, *à l'Européenne*, in Investment Arbitration Under Intra-EU BITs' (in this volume) 281, and further Alexis Martinez, 'Invoking State Defenses in Investment Treaty Arbitration' in Michael Waibel and others (eds), *The Backlash against Investment Arbitration* (Wolters Kluwer 2010) 315. In private international law contracts, *force majeure* clauses often have weaker requirements; see Mark Augenblick and Alison B Rousseau, 'Force Majeure in Tumultuous Times: Impracticability as the New Impossibility' (2012) 13 JWIT 59.

[77] Andrea K Bjorklund, 'Emergency Exceptions: State of Necessity and Force Majeure' in Peter Muchlinski, Federico Ortino and Christoph Schreuer (eds), *Oxford Handbook of International Investment Law* (OUP 2008) 459, 520.

towards the investor.[78] The second alternative might, therefore, be the more promising avenue. However, the notion of an 'unforeseen event' – the event 'must have been neither foreseen nor of an easily foreseeable kind'[79] – is likely to pose an ever more demanding threshold: with an intensifying institutionalisation of the global financial architecture chances will decrease that States can claim pressure by an international institution as unforeseeable.

Moreover, in both alternatives, preventing a violation must be 'materially impossible'; circumstances that render compliance more burdensome due to economic or socio-political consequences are not sufficient.[80] They could only be considered under the defence of necessity.[81] In addition, even if the exogenous pressure was seen as rendering compliance materially impossible, another barrier is set by the requirement that the State must not have 'contributed to the situation': here, unsustainable governmental policies which made crisis measures and external funding necessary[82] as well as the voluntary transfer of powers to supranational organisations would have to be considered.

C. Conclusions

The analysis of the international law on attribution and circumstances precluding wrongfulness leads to a first result: only in very limited cases can the involvement of an international institution exonerate States from international liability tout court.

---

78 James Crawford, *The International Law Commission's Articles on State Responsibility: Introduction, Text and Commentaries* (CUP 2002) 170; Bjorklund (n 77) 499.

79 ILC Articles (n 38), Commentary to art. 23 para. 2; Crawford (n 39) 296.

80 *Rainbow Warrior (New Zealand v France)* [1990] 20 RIAA 217, 253.

81 This defence, which is not based on the external factors as such but on the overall circumstances, will be dealt with below in Section IV.B. For a detailed discussion of the differences between the concepts of necessity and *force majeure* see Anastasios Gourgourinis, 'Financial Crisis as *Force Majeure* Under International Law and EU Law: Defending Emergency Measures, *à l'Européenne*, in Investment Arbitration Under Intra-EU BITs' (in this volume) 281; Bjorklund (n 77) 462; Šturma (n 40) 116.

82 See *Sempra v Argentina* (n 76) para. 217.

IV. INTERNATIONAL INSTITUTIONS AND INVESTMENT TREATY STANDARDS

The result of the previous section makes it necessary to explore whether the participation of international institutions in the decision-making process can be taken into consideration within the substantive law of investment agreements – i.e., it might change the analysis of whether a measure breaches standards of investment protection if it was not taken in the sole discretion of the State but influenced by international or European institutions. It is submitted that the role of international institutions can be catered for in both treaty drafting (A) and treaty interpretation (B).

A. Drafting of Investment Agreements

IIAs can refer to constraints set by international institutions in a number of ways. As discussed above, they could alter the secondary rules of State responsibility and with that, particularly in the case of the EU, provide for an international organisation's liability in investment law.[83] Moreover, they can take account of special circumstances of international institutions' involvement in financial regulation and provide for a 'normative shortcut'[84] to harmonise investment protection and the global financial architecture. An example of this method can be found in balance of payment clauses allowing States to temporarily introduce exchange restrictions.[85] These may be linked to the framework of the World Trade Organization (WTO)[86] or the IMF. For example, art. 6 of the France-Uganda BIT contains the following provision:

> In case of a serious balance of payments difficulties and external financial difficulties or the threat thereof, each contracting party may temporarily restrict transfers, provided that this restriction: i) shall be promptly notified to

---

[83] See above Section III.A.iii.

[84] Jörg Kammerhofer, 'The Theory of Norm Conflict Solutions in International Investment Law' in Marie Claire Cordonier Segger, Markus W Gehring and Andrew Newcombe (eds), *Sustainable Development in World Investment Law* (Wolters Kluwer 2010) 83, 97.

[85] In more detail, see Prabash Ranjan, 'Capital-Flow Management Measures and International Investment Law: Never the Twain Shall Meet?' (in this volume) 257 and Viterbo (n 15) 249.

[86] See, e.g., Agreement between Japan and the Republic of Singapore for a New-age Economic Partnership <www.mofa.go.jp/region/asia-paci/singapore/jsepa.html> accessed 31 December 2015.

> the other party; ii) shall be consistent with the articles of agreement with the International Monetary Fund; iii) shall not exceed in any case six months; iv) would be imposed in an equitable, non discriminatory and in good faith basis.

Under provisions like this, capital controls that are even suggested by the IMF and fully comply with the IMF's Articles of Agreement are likely to be exempted from constituting a violation of investment standards.

Furthermore, a growing number of IIAs comprise non-precluded measure clauses, disapplying investment standards in extraordinary circumstances,[87] and prudential carve-out clauses allowing for State action aimed at preserving the stability of the financial system.[88] Similarly to balance of payment clauses, these provisions could be linked to the institutional framework of global financial regulation. As these clauses would only allow for measures that are in compliance with the framework agreed on an international or supranational level, they could potentially help achieve a balance between legitimate financial regulation and the protection of investors. Even though few such provisions have been agreed to date, balance of payment clauses recognising the permissibility of measures compatible with the IMF framework (which can be found in existing IIAs) could serve as models.

B. Interpretation of Investment Standards

However, even where IIAs do not explicitly cater for these situations, the decisions and recommendations of international financial institutions can be taken into consideration in the interpretation of a number of investment standards. The standards of expropriation and FET as well as the defence of necessity allow for an evaluation of the circumstances of individual measures. The evaluation of the public purpose of an act and of its proportionality (i) could allow for a reference to the involvement of financial institutions (ii).

---

[87] William W Burke-White and Andreas von Staden, 'Investment Protection in Extraordinary Times: The Interpretation and Application of Non-Precluded Measures Provisions in Bilateral Investment Treaties' (2008) 48 Va JIL 307, 311; Antoine Martin, 'Investment Disputes after Argentina's Economic Crisis: Interpreting BIT Non-Precluded Measures and the Doctrine of Necessity Under Customary International Law' (2012) 29 J Intl Arb 49, 51.

[88] Anne van Aaken and Jürgen Kurtz, 'Prudence or Discrimination? Emergency Measures, the Global Financial Crisis and the International Economic Law' (2009) 12 JIEL 859, 891; Viterbo (n 15) 250.

i. Standards referring to public purpose and proportionality

Under most IIAs, expropriations are only lawful when they serve a public purpose and are carried out non-discriminatorily and against compensation. Beyond this classic formula, tribunals have often considered 'regulatory takings' to be lawful without compensation provided they are carried out in pursuance of a 'legitimate public purpose'.[89] Under the broad standard of investment law, which includes direct and indirect takings,[90] the introduction of capital controls, the restructuring of sovereign debt and the conversion of bank debt to equity could be regarded as indirect expropriations.[91] In order to decide on the lawfulness of such measures, tribunals would have to discuss the public purpose of the measure, and might, as some tribunals have done in the context of regulatory takings, also perform a proportionality analysis.[92]

Moreover, the same measures are also likely to be discussed under the FET standard. Understood as an 'embodiment of the rule of law',[93] the FET standard has been held to require, inter alia,[94] compliance with

---

[89] See, e.g., *SD Myers, Inc v Government of Canada*, UNCITRAL, Partial Award (13 November 2000) para. 281; *Methanex Corp v USA*, Final Award (03 August 2005) para. IV.D.7; *Saluka v Czech Republic* (n 65) para. 255; Michael Waibel, 'Creditor Protection in International Law', in Pieter HF Bekker, Rudolf Dolzer and Michael Waibel (eds), *Making Transnational Law Work in the Global Economy: Essays in Honor of Detlev Vagts* (CUP 2010) 452.

[90] See Ursula Kriebaum, 'Expropriation' in Marc Bungenberg and others (eds), *International Investment Law* (CH Beck, Hart and Nomos 2014) 959; Salacuse (n 65) 292.

[91] See above Section II.

[92] *SD Myers v Canada* (n 89) para. 281; *Marvin Roy Feldman Karpa v United Mexican States*, ICSID Case No ARB(AF)/99/1, Award (16 December 2002) paras 103–105; *Técnicas Medioambientales Tecmed, SA v United Mexican States*, ICSID Case No ARB (AF)/00/2, 96, Award (29 May 2003) para. 122; see Caroline Henckels, 'Indirect Expropriation and the Right to Regulate: Revisiting Proportionality Analysis and the Standard of Review in Investor-State Arbitration' (2012) 15 JIEL 223.

[93] Stephan W Schill, 'Fair and Equitable Treatment' in Stephan W Schill (ed.), *International Investment Law and Comparative Public Law* (OUP 2010) 151, 158.

[94] For further elements of the FET standard, see Dolzer and Schreuer (n 65) 145; Alexandra Diehl, *The Core Standard of International Investment Protection* (Wolters Kluwer 2010).

the legitimate expectations of investors,[95] due process[96] and good faith.[97] In the analysis under these standards, again, questions of proportionality may be addressed.[98] The four-step proportionality analysis requires that a measure serve a legitimate purpose as well as being both suitable and necessary to achieve that aim without being excessive.[99] It therefore requires a 'weighing of the Claimant's legitimate and reasonable expectations on the one hand and the Respondent's regulatory interest on the other'.[100]

Measures taken in times of economic and financial crisis may give rise to the customary international law defence of necessity.[101] In order to comply with Article 25 of the ILC Articles, capital controls, sovereign debt restructurings or bank recapitalisations would have to be the 'only way for the State to safeguard an essential interest against a grave and imminent peril'.[102] While some tribunals denied the application of the defence whenever another measure would have been available,[103] the

---

[95] *Tecmed v Mexico* (n 92) para. 154; *LG&E Energy Corp, LG&E Capital Corp, and LG&E International, Inc v Argentine Republic*, ICSID Case No ARB/02/1, Decision on Liability (03 October 2006) para. 127; critical: Kenneth Vandevelde, 'A Unified Theory of Fair and Equitable Treatment' (2010) 43 NYU JILP 43, 67.

[96] *Waste Management, Inc v United Mexican States*, ICSID Case No ARB(AF)/98/2, Award (2 June 2000) para. 98; Diehl (n 94) 445.

[97] *Tecmed v Mexico* (n 92) para. 133.

[98] See, e.g., *SD Myers v Canada* (n 89) para. 255; *Saluka v Czech Republic* (n 65) para. 304; *Total SA v The Argentine Republic*, ICSID Case No ARB/04/01, Decision on Liability (27 December 2010) para. 164.

[99] Benedict Kingsbury and Stephan W Schill, 'Public Law Concepts to Balance Investors' Rights with State Regulatory Actions in the Public Interest – the Concept of Proportionality' in Schill (n 93) 75, 87; on the genealogy of the concept of proportionality in domestic and international law, see Alec Stone Sweet and Jud Mathews, 'Proportionality Balancing and Global Constitutionalism' (2008–2009) 47 Col J Transnatl L 72.

[100] *Saluka v Czech Republic* (n 65) 306.

[101] On the relationship between the necessity defence and non-precluded measures clauses see *Sempra Energy International v The Argentine Republic*, ICSID Case No ARB/02/16, Annulment Decision (29 June 2010) paras 165, 169; José E Alvarez and Kathryn Khamsi, 'The Argentine Crisis and Foreign Investors: A Glimpse into the Heart of the Investment Regime' (2009) YB Intl Inv L & Pol 379, 466.

[102] In more detail on the necessity defence, see Bjorklund (n 77); Martinez (n 76).

[103] *CMS v Argentina* (n 65) para. 323; *Enron Corporation and Ponderosa Assets, LP v Argentine Republic*, ICSID Case No ARB/01/3, Award (22 May 2007) para. 309.

Enron annulment decision took the wording as the starting point for another proportionality analysis, examining whether other measures would have been less severe and similarly effective.[104]

ii. Interpretation and deference

The preceding discussion suggests that, in interpreting and applying the standards governing expropriation and FET, as well as the necessity defence, arbitral tribunals have frequently assessed whether State measures pursued legitimate policy objectives and sought to safeguard essential interests. If the test of proportionality is applied, the underlying State interests need to be balanced against investor interests.[105] In this regard, tribunals need to take into account a broad range of considerations, including conflicting obligations of the host State under international law. A normative starting point for this might be the doctrine of systemic integration based on Article 31(3)(c) of the Vienna Convention on the Law of Treaties (VCLT).[106] According to this provision, the interpretation of treaty standards must take into account the entirety of international obligations 'applicable in the relations between the parties'. It has been argued that the notion 'applicable' (instead of 'in force' or 'binding') leads to some flexibility of interpretation,[107] whereby it may be sufficient that the obligation arises out of a legal framework to which both the home and host State of the investor are parties.

Applying a broader focus in balancing interests, tribunals could take into account obligations under EU law (as the obligation to implement decisions by the SRB) in cases arising out of Intra-EU IIAs. Moreover, requirements set by lending conditions might be understood as *de facto* legal obligations.[108] If an approach under Article 31(3)(c) VCLT is taken,

---

104 *Enron v Argentina* (n 103), Annulment Decision (30 July 2010) para. 370.

105 *Saluka v Czech Republic* (n 65) para. 306; *Total v Argentina* (n 98) para. 121; Mara Valenti, 'The Protection of General Interests of Host States in the Application of the Fair and Equitable Treatment Standard' in Giorgio Sacerdoti and others (eds), *General Interests of Host States in International Investment Law* (OUP 2014) 26, 55.

106 See Vid Prislan, 'Non-Investment Obligations in Investment Treaty Arbitration: Towards a Greater Role for States?' in Freya Baetens (ed.), *Investment Law Within International Law. Integrationist Perspectives* (CUP 2013) 450, 466; Bruno Simma and Theodore Kill, 'Harmonizing Investment Protection and International Human Rights: First Steps Towards a Methodology' in Christina Binder and others (eds), *International Investment Law for the 21st Century: Essays in Honour of Christoph Schreuer* (OUP 2009) 678, 694.

107 Simma and Kill (n 106), 697.

108 Goldmann (n 8).

the obligations could be regarded as 'applicable' in the relations between the borrowing countries and other States Members of the IMF. But even pressure exerted upon the State which does not amount to a legal requirement could play a decisive role in the balancing exercise: in *Tecmed*, the Tribunal explicitly referred to local communities demanding action to be taken against a landfill.[109] A similar argument could be made with regard to the pressure exerted by international financial institutions.

However, the more elegant approach might be to point not to the exogenous forces as such but to their rationale.[110] In the cases referred to above, it could be pointed to the policy goals of financial stability, crisis management and sustainability of public debt. The fact that these goals are agreed upon at international level might strengthen their relevance.[111] Moreover, the independent analysis of the circumstances by the international institution might be understood as an indication of the measure's proportionality.[112] In interpreting investment standards with regard to the decisions and recommendations of international financial institutions, tribunals could contribute to the harmonisation of international investment law and the global financial architecture.

V. INTERNATIONAL INSTITUTIONS IN INVESTMENT ARBITRATION

For decisions and recommendations by international institutions to play a role in the interpretation and application of IIA standards, they need to be brought to the attention of investment tribunals. This may of course happen indirectly, namely if a defending State claims to have acted under international influence. However, such an indirect involvement may not do justice to the importance of international institutions. Against this background, this section discusses two ways of giving a direct role to international institutions in arbitral proceedings: their participation as *amici curiae* (A) and the new EU proposal according to which the EU can choose to 'act as defendant' (B).

---

[109] *Tecmed v Mexico* (n 92) para. 122.

[110] Henckels (n 92) 232.

[111] Mendelson and Paparinskis (n 10) 477.

[112] Pia Acconci, 'The Integration of Non-Investment Concerns as an Opportunity for the Modernisation of International Investment Law: Is a Multilateral Approach Desirable?' in Sacerdoti and others (n 105) 166.

A. *Amicus Curiae* Participation

Following increased calls for public involvement and transparency in investment arbitration[113] and the trend in arbitral practice to accept third-party submissions with the consent of the disputing parties,[114] *amicus curiae* participation has been introduced in various arbitration frameworks: the ICSID Arbitration Rules[115] and the United Nations Commission on International Trade Law (UNCITRAL) Rules on Transparency[116] now contain provisions on the participation of non-disputing parties in arbitration proceedings.[117] Focussing on the ICSID Arbitration Rules, this section will describe the legal framework for *amicus curiae* participation (i); discuss the extent to which the concept can be applied with regard to international financial institutions (ii); and discuss limitations and potential developments of the concept (iii).

---

[113] Lucas Bastin, 'Amici Curiae in Investor-State Arbitration: Eight Recent Trends' (2014) 30 Arb Intl 125, 137; Suzanne A Spears, 'Making Way for the Public Interest in International Investment Agreements' in Chester Brown and Kate Miles (eds), *Evolution in Investment Treaty Law and Arbitration* (CUP 2011) 271, 272; Eugenia Levine, 'Amicus Curiae in International Investment Arbitration: The Implications of an Increase in Third-Party Participation' (2011) 29 Berk J Intl L 200, 208; generally Nigel Blackaby and Caroline Richard, 'Amicus Curiae: A Panacea for Legitimacy in Investment Arbitration' in Waibel and others (n 76) 253.

[114] On the instances of *amici* participation before the amendment of the frameworks see Tomoko Ishikawa, 'Third Party Participation in Investment Treaty Arbitration' (2010) 59 ICLQ 373, 378.

[115] ICSID, Rules of Procedure for Arbitration Proceedings (Arbitration Rules) (2006) <https://icsid.worldbank.org/apps/ICSIDWEB/icsiddocs/Pages/ICSID-Convention-Arbitration-Rules.aspx> accessed 31 December 2015.

[116] UNCITRAL, *Rules on Transparency in Treaty-Based Investor-State Arbitration* (United Nations 2014) <www.uncitral.org/pdf/english/texts/arbitration/rules-on-transparency/Rules-on-Transparency-E.pdf> accessed 31 December 2015.

[117] Moreover, in 2003 the NAFTA Free Trade Commission issued a Statement on Non-Disputing Party Participation; see <www.state.gov/documents/organization/38791.pdf> accessed 31 December 2015. For a comparison between the NAFTA and ICSID frameworks with regard to third-party participation, see Sarah Schadendorf, 'Human Rights Arguments in Amicus Curiae Submissions: Analysis of ICSID and NAFTA Investor-State Arbitrations' (2013) 10 Transnational Dispute Management 1, 5.

i. The framework for *amicus curiae* participation

In the ICSID Arbitration Rules, Rule 37(2) allows for submissions by non-disputing parties.

> After consulting both parties, the Tribunal may allow a person or entity that is not a party to the dispute (in this Rule called the 'nondisputing party') to file a written submission with the Tribunal regarding a matter within the scope of the dispute. In determining whether to allow such a filing, the Tribunal shall consider, among other things, the extent to which:
>
> (a) the non-disputing party submission would assist the Tribunal in the determination of a factual or legal issue related to the proceeding by bringing a perspective, particular knowledge or insight that is different from that of the disputing parties;
> (b) the non-disputing party submission would address a matter within the scope of the dispute;
> (c) the non-disputing party has a significant interest in the proceeding.
>
> The Tribunal shall ensure that the non-disputing party submission does not disrupt the proceeding or unduly burden or unfairly prejudice either party, and that both parties are given an opportunity to present their observations on the non-disputing party submission.

Moreover, according to Rule 32, third parties can be allowed 'to attend or observe all or part of the hearings'. Similar provisions can be found in the UNCITRAL Rules on Transparency.[118]

The purpose of *amicus curiae* participation is to allow for a more comprehensive assessment of the circumstances of the measure in question.[119] It has been argued that third parties could clarify non-investment considerations that might be the basis of regulatory actions.[120] While the introduction of these public perspectives might initially appear more favourable to the defendant State, it has been argued that the pendulum could easily swing to the other side.[121] This could particularly be the case when alleged regulatory concerns are not acknowledged by the third party. In the past, most non-disputing parties submitting *amicus*

---

[118] For submissions by third parties see arts 4, 5 UNCITRAL Rules on Transparency (n 116). Additionally, according to art. 6 of the Rules hearings shall be public anyway.

[119] Ishikawa (n 114) 402.

[120] Spears (n 113) 272.

[121] See, in the context of the question, whether subnational governments could be *amici curiae* Andrea K Bjorklund, 'The Participation of Sub-National Government Units as Amici Curiae in International Investment Disputes' in Brown and Miles (n 113) 298, 308.

curiae briefs were non-governmental organisations (mainly concerned with environmental questions)[122] and business corporations.[123]

ii. International financial institutions as *amici curiae*

Having been called a 'speculative topic'[124] in 2002, the recent participation of public bodies in international (investment) arbitration constitutes a 'significant development'.[125] The change is due particularly to the European Commission's interest in participating in investment proceedings in which EU Member States are defendants.[126] The European Commission 'has recently readopted an active and ambitious role in

---

[122] See, e.g., *Glamis Gold Ltd v United States*, UNCITRAL, Award (8 June 2009) para. 8; *Aguas del Tunari, SA v Republic of Bolivia*, ICSID Case No ARB/02/3, Decision on Respondent's Objections to Jurisdiction (21 October 2005); *Suez, Sociedad General de Aguas de Barcelona SA, and InterAguas Servicios Integrales del Agua SA v Argentina*, ICSID Case No ARB/03/17, Order in Response to a Petition for Participation as Amicus Curiae (17 March 2006); for an overview of the investment case law concerning third parties see Ishikawa (n 114); Lucas Baskin, 'The Amicus Curiae in Investor–State Arbitration' (2012) 1 Cam J Intl & Comp L 208, 214; Amokura Kawharu, 'Participation of Non-Governmental Organizations in Investment Arbitration as Amici Curiae' in Waibel and others (n 76) 275.

[123] See, e.g., *Glamis Gold v US* (n 122) para. 286 on a submission of the US National Mining Association:

> On February 15, 2007, the Tribunal issued its decisions on the non-disputing party applications to file submissions in separate letters to each of the National Mining Association, the Quechan Indian Nation, Sierra Club and Earthworks, and Friends of the Earth. The Tribunal decided to accept each submission and consider it, as appropriate, in accordance with the principles stated in the FTC Statement and the particular criterion mentioned by Respondent that each submission bring 'a perspective, particular knowledge or insight that is different from that of the disputing parties'.

[124] Christine Chinkin and Ruth Mackenzie, 'Intergovernmental Organizations as "Friends of the Court"' in Laurence Boisson de Chazournes, Cesare Romano and Ruth MacKenzie (eds), *International Organizations and International Dispute Settlement: Trends and Prospects* (Brill 2002) 155.

[125] Bastin (n 113) 130.

[126] See Regulation (EU) No 1219/2012 of the European Parliament and of the Council of 12 December 2012 Establishing Transitional Arrangements for Bilateral Investment Agreements Between Member States and Third Countries [2012] OJ L351/40, art. 13(c): 'The Member State and the Commission shall fully cooperate in the conduct of procedures within the relevant mechanisms, which may include, where appropriate, the participation in the relevant procedures by the Commission'; Bjorklund (n 121) 313.

investment arbitration, analyzing the relationship between intra-EU investment agreements and EU law'.[127]

In order for an international institution's request to appear as *amicus curiae* to be successful, the requirements set out in Rule 37(2) ICSID Arbitration Rules must be met. First, the international institution must be a 'non-disputing party'. If taken literally, this criterion is met as long as the respective measures can be attributed to the defendant State, since international organisations generally cannot appear as defendants before investment tribunals.[128] Even if the notion of 'non-disputing party' was understood more strictly as a requirement of full independence from either of the parties,[129] it can be argued that international financial institutions play a neutral role in providing for the stability of the international financial architecture and are thus independent of the Member States.[130]

Secondly, it might be questionable whether international financial institutions can add a different and valuable perspective to the investment proceedings and consequently comply with Rule 37(2)(a) of the ICSID Rules of Arbitration. It has especially been argued that the participation of important political actors in investment proceedings hardly contributes to the proceedings and merely leads to the politicisation of investment

---

[127] Carlos González-Bueno and Laura Lozano, 'More Than a Friend of the Court: The Evolving Role of the European Commission in Investor-State Arbitration' (*Kluwer Arbitration Blog*, 26 January 2015) <http://kluwerarbitrationblog.com/2015/01/26/more-than-a-friend-of-the-court-the-evolving-role-of-the-european-commission-in-investor-state-arbitration/> accessed 31 December 2015; for some awards mentioning the European Commission as *amicus curiae AES Summit Generation Ltd & Another v Republic of Hungary*, ICSID Case No ARB/07/22, Award (23 September 2010) para. 8.2; *Electrabel SA v Republic of Hungary*, ICSID Case No ARB/07/19, Decision on Jurisdiction, Applicable Law and Liability (30 November 2011) para. 1.18; *Eureko BV* [in later stages *Achmea BV*] *v The Slovak Republic*, PCA Case No 2008-13, Award on Jurisdiction, Arbitrability and Suspension (26 October 2010) para. 154; *Ioan Micula & Others v Romania*, ICSID Case No ARB/05/20, Award (11 December 2013) para. 27.

[128] See above Section III.

[129] *Bernhard von Pezold & Others v Zimbabwe* ICSID Case No ARB/10/15 and *Border Timbers Ltd & Others v Zimbabwe*, ICSID Case No ARB/10/25 (joined), Procedural Order No 2 (26 June 2012) para. 49; see Bastin (n 113) 138.

[130] Cf. Boris Kasolowsky and Caroline Harvey, 'The Participation of the European Commission as a Non-Party in Investment Treaty Disputes: An Appraisal of the Procedural Framework in Light of the Draft Regulation on Transitional Arrangements' (2013) 10 Transnatl Disp Managmnt 8.

arbitration.[131] However, in cases where international institutions were involved in the decision-making process, their participation in the proceedings seems to be important in clarifying the circumstances of the measures in question.[132] This might even help to detect situations where the implementation of a measure was unnecessarily harmful to the investor and thus prevent States from hiding behind an international recommendation or decision.[133] A problem might, however, arise, if the European Commission has already prepared the defence for the defendant Member State under Article 13 of Regulation 1219/2012 and, in consequence, cannot contribute new information in the *amicus curiae* submission.[134]

Thirdly, the non-disputing party must establish a significant interest in the proceedings (Rule 37(2)(c)). In previous cases, it has been deemed sufficient that an organisation had a special opinion regarding the case at hand and an actual legal interest was not required.[135] Although international lenders are not immediately affected by an award against the borrowing country, they might argue that their international reputation can be harmed if measures taken in the context of Structured Adjustment Programmes were found in violation of international law. Furthermore, they can establish an interest in the legal assessment of certain measures with regard to future programmes.[136] Where international organisations are obliged to compensate Member States for damages incurred in implementing their decisions,[137] the significant interest is more obvious.

iii. Limitations and potential developments of the concept

Under the current framework, the participation of *amici curiae* is limited in two directions: on the one hand, third parties have no right to participate in the proceedings.[138] Whether they can make submissions to such proceedings is decided upon by the Tribunal at its own discretion. In order to strengthen the regard for international institutional concerns, it

[131] On the debate see Christina Knahr, 'The New Rules on Participation of Non-Disputing Parties in ICSID Arbitration: Blessing or Curse?' in Brown and Miles (n 113) 319, 335; Blackaby and Richard (n 113) 272.

[132] See above Section IV.B.ii.

[133] Therefore, the submission also addresses a matter within the scope of the dispute; see Rule 37(2)(b) ICSID Arbitration Rules (n 115).

[134] Kasolowsky and Harvey (n 130) 9.

[135] See Levine (n 113) 215.

[136] Ibid.

[137] See above Section III.A.iii.

[138] Ishikawa (n 114) 404.

could be suggested that international (governmental) institutions be granted a right to submit statements on measures which grew out of international decisions or recommendations. Admittedly, it would be most important to see to it that the proceedings are not unduly delayed by these submissions.

On the other hand, the framework does not provide for the Tribunal or for one of the parties to request a submission by a third party. The concept of 'necessary third party'[139] might be desirable in order to obtain a statement on the circumstances of the measure, be it to exculpate or to blame the State. While individuals can be called as witnesses or experts, the concept of 'necessary third party' could refer to the institutional context and require a formal statement of the respective international institution. In *Eureko*, the Tribunal, acting with the consent of the parties, requested the European Commission to submit a statement which was consequently delivered.[140] As with *amicus curiae* participation in general, arbitral practice might be the trigger for institutional reform, this time introducing a provision allowing tribunals to request third-party statements.

B. International Institutions as Defendants in Investment Arbitration

The EU Regulation on Financial Responsibility Linked to Investor-to-State Dispute Settlement Tribunals[141] provides for the possibility for the EU to act as defendant in investment arbitration proceedings.[142] This shall be the case whenever the treatment in question was afforded by the Union,[143] or, in the case of treatment afforded by a Member State, upon decision by the Commission pursuant to Article 9(2) of the Regulation. This paragraph reads:

> The Commission may decide by means of implementing acts, based on a full and balanced factual analysis and legal reasoning provided to the Member States, in accordance with the advisory procedure referred to in Article 22(2), that the Union is to act as the respondent where one or more of the following circumstances arise:

139 Mendelson and Paparinskis (n 10) 477.
140 *Eureko v Slovak Republic* (n 127) para. 145; see Bastin (n 113) 130.
141 Regulation (EU) No 912/2014 (n 11).
142 See above Section III.A.i.
143 Art. 4 Regulation (EU) No 912/2014 (n 11).

(a) the Union would bear all or at least part of the potential financial responsibility arising from the dispute in accordance with the criteria laid down in Article 3; or
(b) the dispute also concerns treatment afforded by the institutions, bodies, offices or agencies of the Union.

The first criterion refers to situations where the Union bears financial responsibility and thus has an interest to ensure the best defence against the claim. Under this provision, it is likely that for proceedings arising out of resolution decisions by the SRB, the Commission would opt for the Union to act as defendant. Also the second criterion refers to the attribution of competences and liabilities under the EU framework and caters for situations where the treatment has been afforded jointly ('also', Art. 9(2)(b)) by EU and Member State organs.

Moreover, Article 9(3) allows for the Commission to decide that the Union shall act as defendant 'where similar treatment is being challenged in a related claim against the Union in the WTO, where a panel has been established and the claim concerns the same specific legal issue, and where it is necessary to ensure a consistent argumentation in the WTO case'.

This provision is an attenuated version of two further criteria of the 2012 Proposal for the Regulation.[144] While Article 8(2)(a) and (b) of the 2012 Proposal are similar to what is now Article 9(2) of the Regulation, Article 8(2)(c) and (d) contained two further criteria allowing for the Commission to decide that the Union should act as defendant, where:

(c) it is likely that similar claims will be brought under the same agreement against treatment afforded by other Member States and the Commission is best placed to ensure an effective and consistent defence; or,
(d) the dispute raises unsettled issues of law which may recur in other disputes under the same or other Union agreements concerning treatment afforded by the Union or other Member States.

These criteria were criticised for leaving an almost unfettered discretion to the Commission as it is usual for investment claims to raise unsettled issues of law.[145] While the discretion of the Commission certainly has been limited in the adopted version of the Regulation, its main characteristic remains: the EU framework on foreign direct investment contains

[144] COM(2012) 335 final; on the new provision as well as on the category of cases 'in which the Member State declines to act as respondent' cf. Baetens and others (n 66) 1226.

[145] Sipiorski and others (n 45) 24.

rules on financial liability and defendant status and it does not provide for a new system regarding the attribution of international responsibility between an international organisation and its Member States.

While a more definite attribution of responsibility might be desirable as regards legal clarity, from the perspective of the investor the solution set up by the Regulation seems favourable: for investors it is sufficient to notify the Commission of the envisaged investment claim,[146] they are kept out of assessing the complex division of competences between the EU and the Member States and do not risk having their claim declared inadmissible for suing the wrong defendant.[147] In order to have legal effects against the investor, the framework has to be implemented by a provision in the EU investment agreements.[148] This provision could be similar to the requirement suggested by a Commission Statement concerning the Energy Charter Treaty.[149] According to this statement, in the case of an alleged violation of an investment standard, the investor should be under an obligation to inform the Union which will then determine the proper defendant within 30 days.[150] Failure to inform might lead to the inadmissibility of the claim.[151]

VI. CONCLUSIONS

The current legal framework of investment protection is based on investor-State relations. International organisations are not bound by investment obligations. Under the law of State responsibility, acts are attributed to the State even when carried out in consequence of a recommendation or decision by international financial institutions. The interpretation of investment protection standards, however, allows for

---

146 See art. 7 Regulation (EU) No 912/2014 (n 11).

147 Baetens and others (n 66) 1259 call this the 'investor-friendliness' of the Regulation; cf. also Stephan W Schill, 'Luxemburg Limits: Conditions for Investor-State Dispute Settlement Under Future EU Investment Agreements' in Marc Bungenberg, August Reinisch and Christian Tietje (eds), *EU and Investment Agreements* (Nomos/Hart 2013) 37, 49.

148 See art. 7(1) Regulation (EU) No 912/2014 (n 11).

149 Reinisch (n 67) 193.

150 Statement submitted by the European Communities to the Secretariat of the Energy Charter pursuant to art. 26(3)(b)(ii) of the Energy Charter Treaty, [1998] OJ L69/115. Similar provisions can be found in art. X.20 Consolidated CETA Text; sect. 3 art. 5(1) Commission Draft TTIP.

151 Hoffmeister (n 64) 736.

international institutions' rationale for action to be taken into consideration. Tribunals can be informed of these by *amici curiae* submissions.

The EU approach to foreign direct investment points into a new direction. The EU is supposed to be a party to IIAs. The most important questions arising from this matter will concern the allocation of internal and external responsibility and the determination of the proper respondent in investment proceedings. Reliable frameworks of international financial institutions' responsibility under international investment law could help towards maintaining a high level of investment protection while simultaneously taking the changing structures of the global financial architecture into account.

Index